Painting Borges

SUNY series in Latin American and Iberian Thought and Culture

———————

Jorge J. E. Gracia and Rosemary Geisdorfer Feal, editors

Painting Borges

Philosophy Interpreting Art Interpreting Literature

Jorge J. E. Gracia

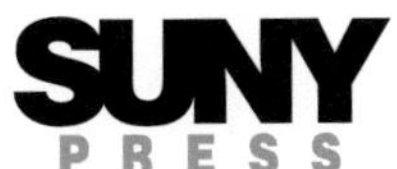

SUNY PRESS

Cover art: León Ferrari, *El inmortal* (The Immortal), 2003, 59" × 19.7" × 19.7", acrylic, ink, wire, and plastic flowers, vines, and cockroaches

Published by State University of New York Press, Albany

For information, contact State University of New York Press, Albany, NY
www.sunypress.edu

Production by Eileen Meehan
Marketing by Anne M. Valentine

Gracia, Jorge J. E.
    Painting Borges : philosophy interpreting art interpreting literature / Jorge J.E. Gracia.
        p. cm. — (SUNY series in Latin American and Iberian thought and culture)
    Includes bibliographical references ( ) and index.
    ISBN 978-1-4384-4178-8 (pbk. : alk. paper)
    ISBN 978-1-4384-4177-1 (hardcover : alk. paper)
    1. Art and literature.   2. Art—Philosophy.   3. Borges, Jorge Luis, 1899–1986—Themes, motives.
4. Borges, Jorge Luis, 1899–1986—Illustrations.   I. Title.

P53.G64 2012
700.1—dc23   2011025286

10 9 8 7 6 5 4 3 2 1

. . . good readers are poets as singular, and as awesome, as great authors themselves.

Jorge Luis Borges, Preface to the First Edition,
A Universal History of Iniquity, 193

Contents

I
Painted Stories

IDENTITY AND MEMORY

FREEDOM AND DESTINY

II
Identity and Interpretation

Stories

The list below contains thirteen stories, twelve are objects of interpretation in Chapters 2 through 13, and one is the object of an interpretation by Arthur Danto that I discuss in Chapter 14. Throughout this book, I refer to the stories by their English titles for the sake of English readers and in order to distinguish them from the works of art, some of which have the same titles as the stories. The titles of the stories are placed within double quotation marks.

"El otro" ("The Other") 1975
"Funes, el memorioso" ("Funes, the Memorious") 1944
"El sur" ("The South") 1944
"La intrusa ("The Interloper") 1970
"El jardín de senderos que se bifurcan" ("The Garden of Forking Paths") 1941
"Las ruinas circulares" ("The Circular Ruins") 1941
"La casa de Asterión" ("The House of Asterion") 1949
"El inmoral" ("The Immortal") 1949
"La rosa de Paracelso" ("The Rose of Paracelsus") 1983
"La escritura del dios" ("The Writing of the God") 1949
"El milagro secreto" ("The Secret Miracle") 1944
"El evangelio según Marcos" ("The Gospel According to Mark") 1970
"Pierre Menard, autor del *Quijote*" ("Pierre Menard, Author of the *Quixote*") 1944

Plates

In the text I refer to the works of art by their original titles. They appear first, regardless of the language, followed by their translation in parentheses. The titles of all works of art have been placed in italics to distinguish them from the stories by Borges with the same titles, which have been placed within quotation marks. After each title follows the year of creation, dimensions (height, width—and depth in one case), and medium.

Preface

This book grew out of a life-long love of literature, art, and philosophy. My love of literature goes back to the time I had the mumps when I was ten years old. Before then my reading had been consigned to comic books, particularly those that had to do with horror. But I got sick and had to stay in my room for two weeks. During my illness, my sister, who was twelve years older than I, read classic stories to me. I particularly remember "The Beauty and the Beast" and some pieces from "The Arabian Nights." After I recovered, I began to read fiction myself, and in a year had become a voracious consumer of literature. I delved deeply into my father's library, especially fascinated with nineteenth-century French and English novels. I read things that I can't imagine reading now, tedious narratives by Alexandre Dumas in *The Countess de Charny,* never skipping a line for fear I would miss something important. I am sure such drudgery successfully atoned for all of my past and future sins.

My love of art began in the fourth year of high school, while attending St. Thomas Military Academy. One of my classmates liked to paint and he introduced me to it. This led not only to dabbling with brushes, oils, and charcoal, but eventually with a decision to try to combine science and art by choosing architecture as a career after graduation.

To philosophy, I was first introduced in the last year of high school with a course on logic and one on the history of philosophy. I found both fascinating, but did not seriously consider a career in this field. Coming from a science-oriented family, the idea of becoming a philosopher was too bohemian. Philosophy, like literature and art, was something one was expected to know but did on the side. Instead, I followed my interests in art and science by enrolling in architecture at the Universidad de La Habana, with added classes at the Escuela Nacional de Bellas Artes San Alejandro. Philosophy had to wait a few more years until I came to the United States and attended college.

Although my fascination with literature goes back to my childhood, it was only in college that it became an object of serious reflection due to an unexpected personal crisis. I had come to the United States without any significant knowledge of English and had been thrown into college without appropriate linguistic preparation. The experience was both traumatic and exhilarating. The environment was exclusively English, and I was only able to understand, speak, and write Spanish. I had to learn to communicate in English in a very short period of time and in the process I became enthralled by language. How is it that it works? Where did words get their power, causing fascination, empathy, anger, sorrow, delight, and tears? And how could they evoke visual images and convey abstract ideas? At the time, it seemed obvious that the way to find answers to these questions was to turn to English literature, which I did in earnest. This was the most challenging thing I could do, whereas mathematics, which I had declared as a major when entering college, was easy in comparison; so I lost interest in it and became an English major.

Unfortunately, the many literature and writing courses I took in college did not help me achieve the understanding I craved: to know the secret of language. The instructors tended to talk about the history of the works we studied, their influence on others, the motifs they used, and mostly the ideas they expressed. I found none of these very helpful in grasping what made them work as literature, how language functioned in them, or the value they had as works of art. And if, as happened very often, the instructors talked almost exclusively about the ideas of the works we studied, why not just turn to philosophy instead? What could literary critics have to add to what philosophers said, if all they talked about was the thoughts conveyed through texts? Why not go into the discipline that traditionally had dealt with these? So I did, becoming a student of philosophy, although I never gave up my love of literature and I never forgot the questions that had bothered me so much in college.

The combination of literature, art, and philosophy remained on the back burner for a long time. I made a first attempt to bring it back to life with a National Endowment for the Humanities Seminar I directed in 2006 which explored their intersections in the context of Cuban-American culture. But it is only recently that I have been trying to bring them together conceptually, by raising some of the questions they pose more systematically, in the context of the artistic and philosophical interpretation of literature and the philosophical interpretation of art. That works of literature, art, and philosophy may become objects of interpretation, as well as interpretations of each other, provides an extraordinary opportunity to explore their differences, similarities, and the challenges they pose. Yet, in the vast literature on aesthetics, I found no single source entirely devoted to the exploration of the artistic interpretation of literature in particular.

I dealt with the philosophical interpretation of art in *Images of Thought: Philosophical Interpretations of Carlos Estévez's Art* (2009). Here I turn to the artistic interpretation of literature from a philosophical perspective, thus the subtitle of this book: "Philosophy Interpreting Art Interpreting Literature." This interpretation is carried out in the context of twelve stories by Jorge Luis Borges and their interpretations by twelve Argentinean and five Cuban artists. Some of the artists reside in their countries of origin and others outside of them, bringing to bear different perspectives and interests to their art. Their works and the relation of these to the stories constitute in turn the bases of my philosophical analyses and interpretations. The topic of this book has received no significant attention among those interested in philosophy, Borges, or Argentinean and Cuban art, in spite of its centrality and the vast number of publications devoted to those specific topics.

This book is intended primarily as an exploration of what I consider to be the central philosophical problem raised by interpretation, but secondarily also as an investigation of the relations between philosophy, literature, and art as well as of Borges's stories and recent Argentinean and Cuban figurative art. It is part of a larger overall project devoted to this investigation. Another part of the project was an art exhibition and symposium, entitled "Painting Borges: A Pictorial Interpretation of His Fictions/Pintando a Borges: Una interpretación pictórica de sus ficciones," that took place in the Pabellón de las Bellas Artes, in the Puerto Madero campus of the Universidad Católica Argentina, in Buenos Aires. The symposium took place between June 23 and 25, 2010, and the art exhibition between June 23 and July 31, 2010. The papers from the symposium were published in an issue of the journal *CR: The New Centennial Review* and most of the works of art exhibited in Buenos Aires will be traveling to the United States for intinerant exhibitions in 2012 and 2013 at venues such as the American University Museum in Washington, DC; Stark Gallery of Texas A & M University, at College Station; Cantor Gallery of The College of the Holy Cross, Worcester, MA; The Abud Family Foundation for the Arts in Lawrenceville, NJ; Latino Arts Center in Milwaukee, WI; and the Anderson Gallery of the University at Buffalo, in Buffalo, NY. The list of works exhibited and of the hosting venues is given at the end of this book.

The chapter of the book devoted to literature, art, and philosophy is indebted to "Borges's *Pierre Menard:* Philosophy or Literature?" (2002), the chapter on interpretation borrows some of the ideas developed in *A Theory of Textuality: The Logic and Epistemology* (1995), the discussion of the works by Héctor Destéfanis and Ricardo Celma incorporates some materials from "The Presence of the Absent in Interpretation: Foucault on Velásquez, and Destéfanis and Celma on Borges" (2011), and the Preface and Introduction are indebted to the exhibition catalogue *Pintando a Borges: Una interpretación pictórica de sus ficciones/Painting Borges: A Pictorial Interpretation of His Fictions* (2010). My gratitude goes to the publishers and editors of these venues. I also need to thanks friends and colleagues with whom I had conversations at various times or whose work I have used. Among these I should mention Lynette Bosch, Charles Burroughs, John Carvalho, Mireya Camurati, Rosemary Feal, William Irwin, David Johnson, Carolyn Korsmeyer, Eduardo Mendieta, and Robert Stecker. I am particularly grateful to the scholars who participated in the symposium that took place in Buenos Aires in June of 2010 and with whom I engaged in conversations and from whose presentations I profited greatly: Lisa Block de Behar, Samuel Cabanchick, Magdalena Cámpora, Norma Carricaburo, Andrés Claro, Pablo Oyarzún, Diana Pérez, Marcelo Sabatés, and Saul Sosnowski. I am also most grateful to the artists who agreed to participate in this project and allowed me to use their work in the book. I profited from and enjoyed the vigorous discussions with students in a graduate seminar I offered in the fall of 2009. Most of the students were philosophers, but some came from Comparative Literature, English, Romance Languages, and Visual Art. Among these I would like to single out for especial mention Joel Potter, Mark Spencer, Geoffrey Krawczyk, Stephanie Rivera-Berruz, Brock Decker, and Deacon Newhouse, who were always willing to challenge my views and interpretations. Above all, I am grateful to the artists who participated in this project for their interest, patience, and permission to reproduce images of their art. Without their enthusiastic support and the time they devoted to working with me, this book would have been impossible. Finally, I am grateful to the College of Arts and Sciences of the University at Buffalo for helping to defray the cost of the reproduction of the art images included in this book, to Eileen Meehan for marshaling the manuscript through the production process, and to Ciahnan Darrell for preparing the index.

Introduction

The artistic interpretation of literature is nothing new. A great part of the history of Western art has been concerned with rendering stories, myths, and adventures first recorded in literary genres into the media of art. The subjects of much Greek and Roman art were the myths of the gods that had first been cast in oral or written texts. In late antiquity and in the Middle Ages, many of these stories were replaced by the Judeo-Christian stories found in the Bible. In the Renaissance, as many works of art dealt with Christian stories as with classical subject matter. Michelangelo's rendition of the story of Genesis on the ceiling of the Sistine chapel is perhaps the most dramatic and well known of these. The images of God giving life to Adam, of his creation of Eve, their temptation by the serpent, and their subsequent expulsion from Paradise, among others, are all effectively retold by Michelangelo's frescoes. Interpretations of literature are so common that it is hard to walk into an art museum and not be confronted with works whose subject matter is literary. How many artistic depictions of Dante's *Divine Comedy*, Cervantes's *Don Quixote*, and Shakespeare's *Romeo and Juliet* have been produced?

In spite of this abundance, the general investigation of the artistic interpretation of literature is relatively infrequent. Most commentators are content with discussing particular artistic interpretations of literary works, ignoring the more general questions that such interpretations raise, questions such as: How are artistic interpretations of literature different from other kinds of interpretations? What makes them interpretations as opposed to something else? And what are their legitimate limits?

The Problem and the Task

The task of this book is not to investigate, let alone adequately answer, these and the many other related questions that surface in the context of the artistic interpretation of literature. Such a task is well beyond the boundaries of this enterprise, but I hope to formulate some questions and suggest some ways of considering them that should help us understand the general phenomenon and to explore some of the problems that it raises.

The problems posed by the artistic interpretation of literature spring from the differences between literature and art, although not every aspect of literature is different from every aspect of visual art. Indeed, literature is art, visual art often integrates literary texts into itself, and literary texts often evoke visual images similar to the ones that are used in visual art. Still, there are important contrasts.

One of these is that literary works are always composed of language, and language is in turn composed of a vocabulary and the rules whereby that vocabulary is arranged into units that convey more or less complex meanings. Particular words and rules are essential to particular languages and give them the character they have, thus distinguishing them from other languages. Literature depends on language and feeds on it. Visual works of art, by contrast, are composed of images and, although there may be some rules of composition that visual art obeys at some times, these rules are much more open and their adoption is up to individual artists—the latitude of the artists in how they use or abuse them is much broader than that of writers with respect to the rules of language. True, some art uses texts, but it is not essential for art to do so, or to follow the rules of the language to which they belong. Often artists use letters and words for their value as images, rather than for the meanings they have in particular languages and this is something that literature does not do systematically.

The dependance of literature on language, and the fact that language always begins with sounds, carries with it a burden that is not present in visual art. The literary is usually related to sound. Most obviously this is so in poetry, but it is also true in prose. Indeed, we often talk about characteristics of prose that are sound related. Literary critics have no qualms about referring to works in prose in terms of a certain cadence or even rhythm. Visual art, by contrast, does not carry this burden—sound is not something that characterizes its medium. The medium of visual art is images, and the burden of images is not oral; it has to do with color and shape, among other things.

Apart from this source of contrast and difficulty there are matters of extension that separate literature and visual art. A novel may have one thousand pages, but a painting is very limited in scope by comparison. Most paintings can be seen whole from a visual standpoint, and thus be completely present to the observer at once. But this is not possible with most works of literature in that they have to be read over a period of time. Indeed, even those that are short, have a kind of discursive dimension, either oral or visual, that does not characterize visual art, except in the case of film. But even film, which shares some properties with literature, illustrates some other differences between literature and art. In a novel we can get into the minds of the characters through the narratives of their psychological states, but in film we can only glance at a mood or feeling revealed through images. Visual art is more circumscribed than literature in what it can express and how it can express it.

The differences between literature and art point to the difficulties involved in the interpretation of literature in visual art. The difficulties do not have to do with whether artists can create interpretations of literary works, but whether their interpretation can be legitimate. The challenge for artists is to create visual interpretations of works that are not visual. And how can something visual be an interpretation of something in which the visual is secondary to sound? Pictorial interpretations of literature abound, and some are regarded as great masterpieces both of art and of interpretation. So, we are entitled to ask: What is the secret of their success? How do the artists achieve this feat? What techniques and procedures do they use to present us with interpretations of literature that successfully bridge the gap between literature and visual art?

The Plan

I propose to approach these questions by, first, examining some examples of artistic interpretations of literature and, second, reflecting on what they tell us about the issues that they raise. I also add brief interpretations of the literary texts we will consider in order to compare them with artistic interpretations and thus get a better understanding of how visual art interprets literature.

I could have chosen some of the many famous examples of the phenomenon found in the history of art. Why not go to Michelangelo, Leonardo, or Goya? One reason is that the variety of literary works they and others have interpreted is too great, creating unnecessary distractions. Another is that the religious stories and myths so frequently used by them add further difficulties that complicate matters to no end; it is one thing to interpret a literary text that has no religious overtones, and another to interpret one that believers consider a divine revelation. Then there is the exhausting, and often irrelevant for our purposes, discussions of these works by critics and historians of art. To pick a work such as Michelangelo's pictorial interpretations of Genesis in the Sistine Chapel would have forced me to deal with many issues that are only marginally related to the core topic of present interest. The weight of the past is sometimes too heavy and counterproductive. In short, I needed to simplify matters in order to maintain a focus, and I chose two ways of doing it. First, I selected only one literary author, and second, I picked contemporary artists whose work is not burdened with a long history of criticism.

Considering the philosophical bent of this book, it was also essential to have a literary author whose work has philosophical depth, and artists who are sensitive to conceptual content. The choice of author was not difficult. Jorge Luis Borges is one of the most prominent literary figures whose work is also profoundly philosophical and thus lends itself easily to this inquiry. Indeed, some have gone so far as to argue that he is a philosopher, and that his work, apart from its literary merits, should be considered part of philosophy. Moreover, he has been the source of discussion and interest among some of the greatest philosophers of the twentieth century. Two of the most important philosophy books published in the last fifty years have found in Borges's work a good point of departure for their analyses. Michel Foucault's *The Order of Things* finds in the Chinese encyclopedia mentioned in Borges's "The Analytic Language of John Wilkins" the foundation for a theory of categories. And Arthur Danto's *The Transfiguration of the Commonplace* uses Borges's "Pierre Menard, the Author of the *Quixote*," as the basis of his discussion of the identity of works of art. The philosophical fascination with Borges should not be surprising insofar as his stories are filled with conceptual puzzles that prompt the reader to think about the most fundamental issues related to human existence. Indeed, one of the great advantages of choosing Borges is that his fictions abound not just with conceptual puzzles, but also with factual incongruities and historical inaccuracies presented as fact that cry for resolution but also impede it, opening endless avenues of interpretation and speculation. The lines between reality and fiction merge in unexpected ways, forcing audiences to play an active role in the construction of the world they reveal.

Once the choice of author was made, the field of artists narrowed. It made sense to choose artists who had already produced interpretations of Borges's stories, thought that their art had been influenced by Borges, or were fascinated by some aspects of Borges's work. Borges is perhaps the most important literary figure Argentina has produced and so it is understandable that among Argentinean artists his work has had a most evident impact. This is particularly true of artists who are *porteños*, born and raised in Buenos Aires, for Borges is quintessentially a *porteño* even though he was not born in the city. So it was not difficult to find the artists I needed. However, because interpretation is a matter of perspective, it was also necessary to use artists whose work manifests different points of view. I thought it would be useful to have substantial variety in the artists so that their artistic creations would illustrate the many avenues that interpreters follow when confronted with literature. I searched for artists at different career stages, women and men, belonging to different social classes, with different ideologies and interests, and even having different ethnic origins, some who live exclusively from their art and some who have to do other things to survive, artists who began to create when they were children and artists who started their careers at a mature age, painters, engravers, and multifaceted and mono-faceted artists.

Some of the artists work exclusively in one medium, some use one primary medium but also work in others, and some have no favorite medium. Some have a definite style and a range of topics they explore, whereas others have not limited themselves to one style or a limited range of topics, but continue experimenting with a variety of approaches and subjects. In terms of generations in particular, seven of the seventeen artists are in their fifties—an age in which artists are often at the height of their artistic maturity and already have a substantial body of work—with five over sixty and five under fifty. Of those over fifty, two are in their sixties, and one each in their seventies, eighties, and nineties. And for those under fifty, three are in their forties and two in their thirties. The oldest artist is over ninety years old, and the youngest is in her early thirties. In short, I looked for variety as far as possible, although the nature of our topic, and its philosophical perspective, favored those whose work is figurative and sensitive to conceptual content.

Apart from this variety, I also thought important to include some artists who were neither Argentineans nor from Buenos Aires. This city in particular, like New York, has a culture that is unique, and I felt that to expand the value of this investigation I needed to consider art from another cultural matrix. But what to choose? I found the lead for this in José Franco, a Cuban artist who resides in Buenos Aires and had produced works based on Borges's stories. The idea of including him made sense in that it would reveal how an adopted Argentinean would look at Borges. In time this led me to think of other Cubans living outside Argentina, and particularly of those who reside in the United States. This would help to compare interpretations from artists from three nationalities, insofar as Cuban-American artists are as American as they are Cuban. My familiarity with Cuban-American art made the task easier. At the same time, with all this variety of origin and perspective, it became important to maintain a certain unity and focus, which I achieved by restricting, with one exception, the artworks to paintings, drawings, etchings, and mixed media, all on a flat format.

In consultation with the artists, their current interests, and the work that they had done before, I selected twelve stories by Borges, which I gathered under three topics: identity and memory, freedom and destiny, and faith and divinity. These are favorite topics for Borges, who likes to explore them in various contexts, including three particular ones: tales about Argentinean culture and society, such as "The South," "The Interloper," "Funes, the Memorious," and "The Gospel According to Mark"; stories about mythical figures and civilizations, such as "The House of Asterion," "The Writing of the God," "The Immortal," and "The Circular Ruins"; and stories about intellectuals, including himself, such as "The Garden of Forking Paths," "The Secret Miracle," "The Other," and "The Rose of Paracelsus." Two artistic interpretations by different artists are given of each story, adding up to twenty four works of art by seventeen different artists.

The works of art fall into two categories: works produced before this project was undertaken and works produced for this project. And the artists fall into three categories. Some had created works dealing with Borges before but did not create any works for this project (León Ferrari, Etienne Gontard, Mirta Kupferminc, Nicolás Menza, Estela Pereda), some had produced works before but also produced some for this project (Alejandro Boim, Ricardo Celma, Claudio D'Leo, Héctor Destéfanis, Carlos Estévez, José Franco), and some created works for this project but had not done so before (Luis Cruz Azaceta, Laura Delgado, Mauricio Nizzero, Alberto Rey, Paul Sierra).

The book is divided into two parts. Part I consists of twelve essays on the stories and the art. Their titles are taken from Borges's stories and each is divided into three sections. The first presents an interpretive summary of the plot of the story together with a brief analysis of its significance; the other two are devoted to the discussion of the artworks that interpret it. Images of the works are included in the appropriate places.

The essays are gathered into the three sections mentioned that reflect some of the central themes explored in the stories. The first concerns identity and memory. The identity central to Borges's thought is personal: Who am I? Am I the same person today that I was long ago? How does my identity incorporate my experiences and surroundings, and the social and national contexts? Memory is essential to identity because it is through memory that we can think about ourselves and our experiences. But what is memory? What are the boundaries between fiction and reality in it? And how does memory affect identity?

The second section is devoted to freedom and destiny. Again, the freedom explored by Borges is personal. Am I free? Is freedom real or apparent? How free am I? And how do the people and events that are part of my world curtail my freedom? Freedom is tied to destiny. Is there a predetermined end that I will reach regardless of what I think or even do? Or is the end open to change by what I, or others, do? And what is the role of chance in the fulfillment of my destiny?

The third section explores faith and divinity. Borges is particularly interested in the relation of religious faith to doubt and evidence. Must faith be blind, or does it require evidence? Does doubt disqualify faith or is it integral to it? Can faith change the course of events? These questions and their answers lead us to divinity. Has God revealed himself to us, and does he answer our prayers? Or is God a mere creation of humans, derived from their ignorance and fear?

The breakdown of the discussion of the stories and their interpretations uncovers various avenues that the artists follow, what they emphasize, what they ignore, and the various strategies they use to convey certain ideas or views. This is particularly important when the stories under interpretation have, as in most cases, strong philosophical content.

The interpretations of Borges's fictions raise many interesting hermeneutical questions. The variety of media, approaches, and strategies the artists use lead to the core of the philosophy of interpretation. All the works, with the exception of one, are pictorial when this is taken broadly, although some are paintings and others are drawings and etchings. The range of media employed varies widely, going from oil, acrylic, markers, ink, coffee, and digital images on canvas, plaster, or paper. Styles also differ, for although all works are figurative, they range from cubism to abstract expressionism, surrealism, and super-realism. Color goes from muted to brilliant, and monotone to multitone. And although some of the works are traditional in many ways, others move in novel directions.

The discussion of the hermeneutical issues raised earlier is taken up in Part II of the book, which is devoted to the philosophical analysis of the artistic interpretation of literature. A first and necessary step in the understanding of the complex relation between an object of interpretation and its interpretation is to establish some parameters about the identity of the relata, which here are the works by Borges, the works of art that interpret it, and my philosophical discussions of both the stories and the works of art. In the first chapter of Part II, then, I explore the identities of works of literature, art, and philosophy and propose a theory about how to distinguish them.

This is followed by a chapter whose task is to lay out the structure, kinds, and aims of interpretation. It begins with a discussion of the structure of interpretation, both internal and contextual, considering such things as the author, audience, and context of the work under interpretation and of the interpretation, among others. Then it briefly discusses various phenomena often confused with interpretation, before turning to its aims and kinds.

The next chapter takes up the topic of how the artists who have interpreted the stories by Borges discussed in this book approached their task and the strategies they used to bridge the gap between art and literature. What is their focus, what have they neglected, what have they emphasized, how far away from the work do they move, and how have they transformed a text into a picture? It provides a classification of the strategies used and the way they are illustrated by the works of the artists.

Last, I include a chapter on the limits of interpretation that tries to determine the boundaries that must be respected in the artistic interpretation of literature in order for the interpretations to be legitimate. Because interpretations can be either understandings or instruments to cause understanding, the question of whether there are limits to interpretations takes two forms: whether there are limits to the understanding of works under interpretation, and whether there are limits to the instruments used to cause their understanding. The answer to the second question is parasitic on the answer to the first, and it is clear: there are limits to the instruments used to cause the understanding of interpretanda insofar as not everything can be used to cause such understanding. The important question for us, then, is the first. And the key to the answer is the degree to which interpretations satisfy the aims for which they are undertaken, which in turns gives rise to different kinds of criteria.

The Artists and Their Work

The role that the artists play in the process I have outlined cannot be overestimated. So I begin by saying something about them, their background, their interests, styles, careers, and work. This should help us understand what they have done. Seventeen artists participated in this project, and in the following paragraphs I shall say something about each of them. I have arranged my comments alphabetically to avoid any impression of preferential treatment. The information my comments contain has been gleaned from publications, interviews I filmed with each of the artists personally, and information posted on their Web sites. What I say, however, is entirely the product of my own impressions, judgments, and inferences.

Luis Cruz Azaceta was born in 1942, in Marianao, which is a suburb of Havana, Cuba. He came to the United States in the early sixties, in the first exodus resulting from Castro's Revolution. He settled in New York City, where he attended The School of Visual Arts, and currently resides in New Orleans. His work has received wide recognition; it is present in important museum collections in North and South America and in Europe, and it has been exhibited in Australia, the Dominican Republic, Ecuador, England, France, Germany, Mexico, Panama, Puerto Rico, El Salvador, Spain, the United States, and Venezuela. Among the many honors Azaceta has received are Fellowships from the Guggenheim Foundation, the National

Endowment for the Arts, and the New York Foundation for the Arts. The renown he has achieved has allowed him to devote himself completely to his art. The work has a strong character that occasionally borders on the shocking. A cartoon-like quality often reveals ties to popular culture and the long tradition of drawing and satire characteristic of much Cuban art, but Azaceta adds an element of suffering and pain that deepens the impact of the art, making it transcend particular cultures and circumstances. A good portion of the work explores the phenomenon of exile, emigration, and cultural dislocation, effectively employing the context of the rafts (*balsas*) used by the Cubans who, in desperation, have risked their lives to cross the channel that separates the island from the United States. More recently, Azaceta has been exploring labyrinths and journeys by concentrating on venues of travel such as airports and terminals, using them as symbols of the human existential predicament. The interpretation of Borges's story he created for the present project fits within this framework, both in that it deals with the Minotaur, a monster who is trapped in the labyrinth in which he resides, and continues a stylistic journey that has led Azaceta to greater simplicity and sharp drawing techniques in which solid colors are juxtaposed to create an engaging image. This is the first work of Azaceta on a Borges story, although he has always felt the challenge of Borges's fictions. He found in "The House of Asterion" a venue of interpretation to express some of his most cherished ideas about human solitude and despair.

Alejandro Boim was born in Buenos Aires in 1964. His interest in art began when he was eight years old in response to an incipient love for a teacher, Leticia. He began to draw for her after she called him Alejandro instead of Boim. At fourteen he did a workshop in art, and after graduating from high school he entered the Escuela Nacional de Bellas Artes Prilidiano Pueyrredón in Buenos Aires. Then he left for France, where he studied art at the Université Paris VIII, Saint Denis. After returning to Buenos Aires, he continued painting and teaching art. His work is always motivated by a curiosity which has led him to incorporate into it elements from the work of other artists he likes. The pieces tend to have dark tones, following his interest in Caravaggio and Rembrandt. Among other artists from whose work he has profited are Klimt, Alonso, and the members of the naturalist movement in France. The medium is primarily painting and the work figurative and realist—he regards it as avant garde in that it is a reaction against the overwhelming dominance of abstraction in the twentieth century. Boim has never been interested in the movement of "art for art's sake"—his art always responds to a personal interest. Unlike many other artists, he does not create series; each piece is unique and a reaction to what has gone on before—it is, as he puts it, "a way to fight boredom." If he produces a red piece, the next piece will contrast with it by being, for example, blue. After several years in Buenos Aires, Boim moved to Montreal, where he works and offers private lessons to advanced students and artists. He paints between three and six hours every day, and has already created a substantial body of work that has received considerable recognition through various prizes and expositions in Argentina, Canada, France, and Spain. He is a recipient of the Gran Premio Nacional de Dibujo de Argentina (2008). Boim is not a devotee of Borges, although he has maintained an interest in his poems and conferences in particular. In general he is somewhat reticent about Borges's prose, because he finds that this author tends to stretch words excessively. But he likes some of his stories, such as "The South," the object of his interpretation here.

Miguel Cámpora was born in 1961, in San Nicolás, province of Buenos Aires. He studied art in the Escuela de Bellas Artes. His work has been exhibited in Argentina, Austria, Colombia, and the United States, and was recently selected for an exhibition by the World Bank. Cámpora is particularly interested in topics that have to do with Argentinean society and its proverbial origin, the countryside, what Argentineans call "*el campo*." Issues of fairness, exploitation, poverty, and displacement can be found in most of his pieces, joined to questions of social and national identity. What does it mean to be Argentinean? Where does he fit in this complicated society? Depictions of the countryside south of Buenos Aires take a good portion of the work. We see people and animals in vast expanses of land, migrating, moving, finding new places to survive and make their own. The human figures are rough, weathered, ravaged by the enormity of the land and its merciless oppression and beauty. The faces are grim, sad, resigned. Some colors are vivid, like the yellows of the pampa, but the greys and greens are subdued and mixed, adding a mood of sadness and struggle. Cámpora had not worked on particular works of Borges before he undertook to contribute to this project, although he had always had an interest in him, particularly in the stories that, like "The South," have to do with the Argentinean countryside.

Ricardo Celma is one of the most accomplished young artists in Argentina today. His work consists primarily in painting, but also sculpture and drawing. He was born in 1975 in Buenos Aires. He sees himself as a careful observer, and his art reflects this attitude. At first one's reaction is to classify the work as a kind of super-realism, but upon closer scrutiny there is a major difference between this movement and Celma's work. Celma does not see his art as competing with photography and his topics are not the standard ones in super-realism. He prefers a characterization that brings his work closer to the literary revolution that swept through Latin American letters in the twentieth century known as magical realism, and thus as a reaction against the excesses of contemporary art. For him, the kind of art common today is forced upon artists by curators and gallery directors who have displaced artists as arbiters of good art. They have taken the place of God and the Church in art, becoming the authorities who determine value and destiny. This imposes limitations on the artists who are forced to comply with their whims in order to survive. Already as a child, Celma wanted to be a painter. He grew up surrounded by books on painting, and after he produced a portrait of his grandmother in profile, the family understood his vocation. His siblings are engineers and scientists, so in high school he had to face the question of survival. How could he earn a decent living? Design was a possibility, but then he got some students to study art with him and this solved his problem. From the beginning he felt a special attraction for late Gothic and Flemish painting and for the ornamental Baroque in the works of Ribera and Rembrandt, and later for the descriptions of pain that flourished in the nineteenth century and the Baroque. He tried abstraction for a while, but eventually rejected it, because he needs to tell stories that have a rational denouement. He feels himself to be a kind of writer in that his work consists of narratives of moments he considers sacred. In these narratives woman has a special place and is almost always included in his work. He is fascinated by the psychology of women, the mystery of what they think, of their motives and intentions. This leads to portraits that are engaging, but thoughtful and mysterious, simultaneously revealing and concealing. Celma is a graduate of the Instituto Universitario Nacional de Arte, and the Escuela Nacional de Bellas Artes Prilidiano Pueyrredón. He visited Mexico and resides in Buenos Aires. His work has drawn attention in Argentina, Canada, China, France, Holland, Japan, Mexico, Panama, Peru, Spain, Switzerland, Thailand, and the United States, and has been recognized with a variety of prizes, including the Primer Premio, Salón de Pintura, Sociedad Argentina de Letras, Artes y Ciencias (SALAC). Borges has always been a writer of interest to Celma for obvious reasons: the complexity and depth of Borges's work has attracted and challenged him. "The Gospel According to Mark" is not the first of Borges's works that has given rise to a pictorial interpretation by Celma, but it is the one used here.

Laura Delgado is the youngest artist participating in this project. She was born in 1978 in Buenos Aires. Like most other children, she enjoyed painting and drawing, but there was no space for art in a family of accountants like her own. So when the time came, she turned toward psychology, in which she received a degree from the Universidad de Buenos Aires. But she was not certain that psychology was for her. This feeling was solidified when she participated in a painting workshop that awakened her vocation in art. She enrolled in Escuela Nacional de Bellas Artes, without objection from her family and she then went on to Escuela de Bellas Artes Ernesto de la Cárcova and the Instituto Universitario Nacional de Arte. For a while she practiced both psychology and art. Her initial work in art was academic, and was greatly influenced by mannerism, but eventually she turned toward a realist expressionism, in which she uses color as a symbol, and works with a loose stroke of the brush. She looks back to the Renaissance, and then to the work of El Greco, Goya, Alonso, and Nicolás. She does not see art as fundamentally demonstrative, but rather as suggestive. Some subjects that attract her in particular are children, animals, and everyday objects, which she organizes so that they speak to us of identity, memory, and the self. In 2001, economic catastrophe hit Argentina hard and this yielded an explosion of new spaces for people who wanted to sublimate their financial difficulties. In their desperation they turned to art, literature, and other cultural forms, and this created a demand for art workshops, making it possible for Delgado to leave psychology altogether and turn exclusively to art. Delgado is a prolific artist whose work has already caught the attention of the art-loving public in Argentina, Costa Rica, and Peru, and has been recognized with various prizes, including the Segundo Premio, 14 Salón Mercosur Internacional "Diógenes Taborda," Museo ITIMuseum. Unlike many of the artists represented here, her initial reaction upon reading Borges when she was younger was rejection; she felt horrified by what she perceived as his pedantry and artificiality. Indeed, one of the stories that she found most objectionable is "The Other" (of which she has produced three different interpretations), because she thought the story had nothing to do with "the other," but was exclusively about Borges. After some years away from Borges, she came back to him and developed a new appreciation for his work, a fact that paved the way for her participation in this project. Indeed, apart from three interpretations of "The Other," she created two of "Funes, the Memorious." Two of these pieces are used here.

Héctor Destéfanis is a mature artist with an established career, born in Buenos Aires in 1960. He is Profesor Titular in the Instituto Universitario Nacional de Artes and he is in charge of the Extensión Cultural of the Museo de Artes Plásticas Eduardo Sívori. His work has traveled to various countries—Argentina, Italy, the United States, and Uruguay—and has been recognized with various prizes, including the Segundo Premio de Dibujo, Salón Manuel Belgrano awarded by the Government of the City of Buenos Aires. Destéfanis describes himself as a painter and drawer rather than as an artist. A look at his creations shows a strong influence of drawing, even in paintings. He began drawing when he was four years old in a middle class family from which the father was absent. He studied publicity in the Universidad El Salvador in Buenos Aires, but he hated his work in this field, and kept drawing on the side. When he turned twenty he enrolled in the Escuela Nacional de Bellas Artes Prilidiano Pueyrredón. His art is motivated by a sense that Argentinean artists have forgotten about themselves qua Argentineans, when in fact the key to the creation of universal art is precisely to begin with the particular. He begins to work, then, with what impresses and surprises him first in his surroundings, and generally ends where he began. The result is an abstraction from what he sees, and the creation of a new reality that is the product of emotion, the stuff out of which art is made, according to him. He creates surrealist spaces in which figures, colors, tones, and values enter in dialogue and carry a psychological burden, such as the loneliness of death. He begins a painting by applying color, because this is most obvious to the senses, and then gradually generates a figure. This leaves the work with large areas where certain colors predominate, breaking up the surface into separate spaces that interact in various ways. In this context, shadows play important roles, suggesting more than they tell, and creating ambiguities and possible avenues of interpretation. The brushstrokes and drawing lines can be separate or merge, and figures can be truncated or presented in full. His work has been compared to that of Hopper, because of its metaphysical spaces. The artists who have influenced him the most were his teacher, Roberto Duarte, and classics such as Goya. Given Destéfanis's surrealist leanings and metaphysical preoccupations, it is not surprising that he has taken an interest in Borges, interpreting his work pictorially on a number of occasions. For this project he produced an interpretation of "The Gospel According to Mark," which is included here, and two renditions of "The Circular Ruins."

Claudio D'Leo is a *nom de plume* that Claudio Barrera uses as an artist. D'Leo is a mature artist, born in 1959 in Buenos Aires. He is an architect by training, but architecture did not satisfy his artistic needs, so he enrolled in the Escuela Nacional de Bellas Artes Prilidiano Pueyrredón and devoted himself to art. At present, he teaches art in the Universidad del Museo Social Argentino and is Dean of the Faculty of Arts in the same university. His work has been exhibited in various venues in Argentina, Colombia, the United States, and Uruguay, and has received recognition through various prizes, such as the Premio Alianza Francesa, Centro Alfredo Fortabat. D'Leo's paintings have a strong social dimension, in which art is used to expose abuse and violence and the evils of an unconcerned society. For example, he created a series of oils on homeless people in Buenos Aires, and has often used his art to criticize structures of power in Argentina. Apart from his work at the university, he also offers workshops at a center closely oriented to the community. Some of his art has a sense of coming from the underground and being in opposition to anything associated with the establishment. Although he abandoned architecture for art, his art has not abandoned architecture. There is a strong structural aspect to it that is clearly visible. This is one of the reasons why his creations also appear to have been strongly influenced by cubism and other currents in art that take a more scientific approach. The main explicit influence on his work is that of the Ecuadorian artist Oswaldo Guayasamin, whose style, technique, and motifs are clearly echoed in the work of D'Leo. Indeed, after spending some time in Ecuador working with this artist, D'Leo broke away from a series of elements that were present in his art prior to this time, one of which is a white background. Contrary to prior practice, he begins with painted canvases, often starting with dark colors, on top of which he adds light that merges into darkness. The influence of Caravaggio and his frames of penumbras are clearly visible in it. This stage supercedes the early period, in which he used a Cubist style that explored multidimensionality and geometric structures to visualize an object from different points of view. Like several of the artists represented here, D'Leo has worked on Borges a number of times. One of his pieces, from the early part of his career, is on "The Aleph," but more recently his interests have shifted to subjects that deal with the human condition, such as the work represented here, which concerns "The Immortal."

Carlos Estévez is a Cuban artist, born in Havana in 1969. He presently resides in the United States. He is a graduate of the Instituto Superior de Arte in Havana. Although still relatively young, he has already achieved considerable recognition. His work has been exhibited in many countries, including Argentina, Austria, Belgium, Brazil, Canada, Chile, China, Costa Rica, Cuba, Cyprus, the Dominican Republic, Ecuador, England, France, Israel, Italy, Japan, Lebanon, Martinica, Mexico, Norway, Panama, Puerto Rico, Portugal, Russia, Spain, Sweden, Switzerland, the United States, and Venezuela. Among his many prizes is the Gran Premio, Primer Salón de Arte Cubano Contemporáneo in Havana. He has been very prolific, having produced hundreds of works. His art has attracted substantial attention in Europe, the United States, and Latin America, where it is found in major public and private collections. The range of the art extends from sculptures and installations to oil and acrylic paintings on canvas and paper, drawings on paper, assemblages, collages, and combinations of these. Estévez works with traditional materials, but has also incorporated nontraditional elements in the art. He regularly collects objects of various kinds, particularly artifacts such as bottles and gadgets he finds in rummage sales and flea markets, which he later integrates into his works. Estévez's art is unique and its style easily recognizable. Its originality is a most prominent characteristic. One author who comes to mind as a background influence is Leonardo da Vinci. We find the same interest in machines, wheels, and contraptions. Estévez has also a fascination with anatomy, although for him this tends to concentrate on bugs, birds, fish, butterflies, lizards, and other animals. His humans are frequently puppets, mechanical devices with minds and emotions. Other common images found in the work are buildings and balloons. The mind behind the art seems to be as fascinated with new discoveries and the mechanics of the world as that of Renaissance and Enlightenment scientists and explorers. This quality is evident in his use of balloons and early models of machines. Much of this art alludes to the age of exploration, when Europeans were engaged in the expansion of their world. It aims at pushing the boundaries of the imagination, while using wheels, pulleys, and levers to explore the nature of the world that surrounds us, and in particular the world of the mind and our emotions. Estévez's art is a laboratory of sorts, an observation platform. Given his metaphysical interests, it is not surprising that he has been interested in Borges. The two works included here were created for this project as interpretations of "The Rose of Paracelsus" and "The Garden of Forking Paths," a third dates from an earlier time, and a fourth was painted in 2011.

León Ferrari was born in Buenos Aires in 1920. He works with many materials, such as plaster, cement, wood, wires, plastic, metals, and pottery, and has used many techniques, including sculpture, photography, heliography, video, text, and so on. He is probably the most internationally celebrated artist from Argentina today, having been chosen as the best artist on the Venice Biennial in 2007, and having received many significant international prizes and accolades. His work has been exhibited in many important venues throughout the wold, including the MoMA. But this success did not come easily. Until recently, he had to live by doing other things in addition to art, and in 1976 he had to leave his native land for political reasons. Part of his difficulties arose from his acerbic criticism of the structures of power in Argentina, and particularly of the alliance between military governments and the Catholic Church, as well as various religious beliefs and values common in Argentinean society. He was trained as an engineer and most of his life earned a living by working in related jobs. A trip to Europe, the result of an attempt to find a cure for his three-year old daughter whose prognosis had been hopeless, took him to Florence, and then to Rome, where he began studying pottery. In 1955, when he was 35 years old, he tentatively started an enterprise that produced cellulose. Five years later, in 1960, he had his first exhibition in the bookstore Galatea, where he first presented his work with wires. This initial breakthrough informs many of his subsequent works, even some pieces that do not use wires. One can grasp the expression of this initial insight in the multiple interlocking lines of some works and even in the kind of cursive writing that has become so distinctive of some of his creations. It was not until 1976, during the military dictatorship in Argentina, that his criticism of religion began, and also the integration of the Braille script in his art. For years his work was harshly criticized by members of the art establishment, and galleries, museums, and universities ignored it. It achieved considerable notoriety when in an exhibition in 2004, in the Centro Cultural Recoleta in Buenos Aires, a group of thugs, led by a Catholic priest, attacked the exhibition, breaking, among other pieces, the very one presented here on Borges's "The Immortal." Ferrari has been interested in Borges for quite some time. In particular, he has worked on various of his poems, integrating Braille and photographs of nudes.

José Franco was born in Havana, Cuba, in 1958. He now resides in Buenos Aires. With a substantial body of work and a long list of accomplishments, he is a very well-known artist.

His work is represented in the collections of important museums in Europe, and North and South America, and has been exhibited in many countries, including Argelia, Argentina, Bolivia, China, Cyprus, Cuba, the Dominican Republic, Ecuador, England, France, Germany, Hungary, Italy, Mexico, Panama, Spain, Sweden, the United States, Uruguay, and Venezuela. Among the many recognitions he has received is a Guggenheim Fellowship. His taste for art goes back to his childhood. His family was neighbors and friends of the Cuban painter Eduardo Abela, and in his secondary school days he became a friend of Abela's son and visited his home frequently. He was fascinated by the artist's workshop, next door to which resided the caricaturist Juan David. He entered the Escuela Nacional de Artes Plásticas San Alejandro in the early seventies, where he worked primarily in sculpture. After graduating from San Alejandro, he enrolled in the Instituto Superior de Arte, where he took classes with five members of the Russian Academy of Moscow, and through them became acquainted with Russian Realism. At the time he concentrated on colonial themes and emulated the work of Amelia Peláez and other Cuban artists. After the Russians left, the art world in Havana became open to new currents, and in a biennial he was first introduced to conceptualism. His school thesis was entitled "Abstraction and Reality," giving a sense of his interests at the time. His work incorporated nature, particularly animals, and eventually abstraction. Magritte, Duchamp, and Warhol have had a great influence on Cuban artists, and Franco is no exception. Indeed, in an important venue, the Salón de Mayo, Franco saw a work by Magritte that made a lasting impression on him. The piece depicted a man, dressed as a leopard, holding a weight that was a head. After this experience, Franco's art took the turn that he has followed ever since: the interest in animals and nature, using the black line of the draftsman typical of much Cuban art. The work has a surrealist sense mixed with an emphasis on vegetation that reminds one of Rousseau. Franco's interest in Borges goes back to Cuba, where the writer was popular in spite of his politics. In an art exhibition in Panama, seeing some of Franco's work on animal skins, someone mentioned Borges's story "The Writing of the God" and this prompted him to read more. He realized that Borges had been fascinated with tigers from childhood—indeed, one of the few surviving childhood drawings from Borges is of a tiger. When Franco arrived in Argentina, he began to paint on literary subjects and organized an exhibition in 1996, with a slightly modified title of Borges's story, whose lead work had the same title. For this project he has produced a painting with the same title as the first and inspired by it.

Etienne Gontard was born in 1934, in Buenos Aires, from a French Huguenot family of German origin. He wanted to paint from childhood, but instead of following this inclination, he studied business and practiced that profession until 1986, after which time he devoted himself entirely to art. All along, however, he had explored his original interest in art and had his first solo exhibition in 1976, when it became clear that he had become serious about what until then had been a hobby. He explored the various currents of contemporary art, cubism, expressionism, conceptualism, and dabbled in photography, but he never incorporated in his work the insights of Magritte's surrealism, which was popular at the time. His work may be described as having an expressionist root with a post-conceptual character. He has kept an interest in nature, particularly the Argentinean landscape and animals, but the work is not that of a naturalist; he always alters what is presented to him into an image of what he sees. He studied oil painting in the sixties with Ignacio Colombres, acrylic painting in the seventies with Kenneth Kemble, and etching with Eduardo Levy. He has frequently visited countries in South America in connection with his art, has also traveled to Mexico, the United States, and Europe, and has had exhibitions in Ecuador and Uruguay. In 1983 he joined the Grupo Intercambio, and he set up his studio, where he also taught, in Palermo, and later in Olivos. He has participated in numerous group exhibitions and has had many solo exhibitions. Most important in the last ten years, he participated in the Retrospective of the Group Intercambio in the Foundation of the Banco Mercantil Argentino (1998), the Outlet de las Artes in Puerto Madero (2002), Artistas Argentinos in the Palais de Glace (2008), and France est Magnifique in the Hotel Sofitel Arroyo (2009). His pictorial interest in Borges goes back to 1991, when he participated in an exhibition devoted to the writer, for which Gontard created two works, "La intrusa" (included here) and a pencil portrait of Borges that was stolen. The part of Borges's work that interests Gontard has to do with the description of human beings and their complex emotional interrelations.

Mirta Kupferminc was born in Buenos Aires in 1955. Educated in the Escuelas Nacionales de Bellas Artes Manuel Belgrano, Prilidiano Pueyrredón and Ernesto de la Cárcova, she is one of the most versatile of Argentinean artists today. She was trained in engraving, but has done extensive work in sculpture, painting, drawing, photography, videos, and installations. Among the many expressions of her work is the creation of a handmade book, of limited edition, in which she cooperated with Saul Sosnowski. Kupferminc is very active worldwide, and her art is known in many countries, including Argentina, England, France, Germany, Hungary, Israel, Japan, Poland, South Africa, Spain, Taiwan, and the United States. Among her prizes is the Primer Premio Salón Nacional Argentina. She has not developed a particular style, but rather uses a variety of approaches to reach ends that are aesthetically informed but have a contextual focus. Most of her work integrates different media and techniques, making it difficult to classify, since it does not easily fit into any single one of the established categories. Nonetheless, there are clear recurring motifs in it, and some of her pieces remind us of aspects of surrealism.

Two of the most commonly used motifs are a chair and the figure of the poet. Both appear tri-dimensionally and on flat art. The first has evolved in many different ways, developing wings, optical illusions, and various colors, and appearing in different contexts. Its symbolism varies from context to context, sometimes referring to waiting, but other times to learning and meditating, among others. In all cases the device is used to bring the audience into the work. The image of the poet also is used in various ways to recall learning, patience, and creativity. It was originally done in clay, a reference to the story of Genesis, but later it began to appear painted in other contexts. Both, the chair and the poet, are motifs connected to an important element that informs a great part of Kuperminc's art, the exploration of her Jewish background. This is carried out through allusions to Jewish culture and roots, and it is one of the points of contact of her work with Borges, who was fascinated by Jewish history and the Jewish experience. She is one of the living Argentinean artists who has frequently, intently, and consistently related her work to Borges's stories. Indeed, she recently had an entire exhibition devoted to work on Borges and the Kabbalah at the University of Maryland.

Nicolás Menza is one of the most prolific and visible artists in Argentina today. He has had a very large number of exhibitions in many countries, including Argentina, Bolivia, Brazil, Chile, Cuba, France, Germany, Italy, Israel, Peru, Spain, Sweden, the United States, and Uruguay. Among his many awards is the Primer Premio de Dibujo, Salón Municipal Manuel Belgrano (Buenos Aires Government), Museo Eduardo Sívori. He was born in Buenos Aires in 1960, into a family in which he was the only male child and was surrounded by sisters. He began to draw and paint at a very early age and took the activity so seriously that before going to play, he always spent some time drawing. During adolescence he engaged in many creative activities—painting, music, theater, literature, and philosophy, among others—but at eighteen he decided to devote himself to art and enrolled in Escuela Nacional de Bellas Artes Prilidiano Pueyrredón, and later in Escuela de Bellas Artes Ernesto de la Cárcova. His work displays extraordinary variety: boxes, sculpture, installations, painting, and drawing. Although he is probably best known for his oils, temperas, and pastels, he finds in drawing the advantage that it is a more narrative medium in which color is suppressed in order to decrease psychological sensuality. His use of color is one of the most obvious and impressive features of his art—his creations are filled with brilliant, almost electric colors, big splashes of them, with areas of impasto, arranged in architectural designs that remind us of the Italian metaphysics of De Chirico and Morandi, artists to whom Menza acknowledges a debt. The style is recognizable, but it is not easy to describe or characterize. In part this is because Menza's work is a very personal expression that seeks to be unique. Some of his art borders on the grotesque, the metaphysical, the latent—an implicit expression of what is hidden—and is complex and challenging. But there is also the context of Buenos Aires, the city that formed him and continues to be present in his creations. One can see a surrealist quality, as well as elements of expressionism and symbolism in the work, but none of them owns it; the work transcends schools and fads. Among recurrent themes are women, clowns, children, still lifes, the painter and his materials, toys, scenes from Buenos Aires such as the typical cafes, and of course Borges's work. The last one has been a constant source of inspiration for Menza. He began to read him early on and has continued exploring his labyrinths ever since. He has created many works related to Borges, including portraits of the writer, but more important for us here, many interpretations of his works, both the stories and the poems. The key to this fascination is the structure of the thought. Menza finds an affinity between Borges's modus operandi and his own, the way they approach the world, a certain metaphysical pattern of understanding that is common and bridges the gap between literature and art. Here I include his interpretations of three stories: "The Circular Ruins," "The Garden of Forking Paths," and "The Secret Miracle."

Mauricio Nizzero was born in Buenos Aires in 1958. He graduated from Escuela de Bellas Artes, and currently teaches metal design in the Escuelas Técnicas Raggio, where he is one of the directors. He is prolific and has produced many public works. His art has been exhibited in Argentina and Uruguay and has received various awards, including the Premio Bienal de Pintura de Quilmes. His work consists to a great extent in drawings, although he also paints, but even his paintings have a strong drawing flavor. He began drawing when he was a child. He had an aunt who was an artist in Chile. When she visited at Christmastime when he was six, he had gifts for everybody but for her, so he made a drawing of a package and gave it to her and this event marked an important moment in his life. He always felt the need to say something through the metaphors of drawings. He went to a technical secondary school where he spent many hours drawing with an emphasis on the ornamental, and working with metals. In the Escuela de Bellas Artes, he began sculpting and then followed with color and tri-dimensional space. He has often painted street murals. For him teaching is important because it gives him the possibility of an encounter with the visual arts and literature. He has a loose style that avoids what he considers unnecessary details in order to concentrate on an important element he wishes to express. He focuses on first impressions—the sensation of the moment and the before and after—in order to capture the human comedy and human conduct, that is, the crucial instant viewed through the filter he, as artist, imposes on the occasion. His interest in Borges goes back some years, and although he had not produced interpretations of his works before, they have now surfaced in various creations. In the process of interpretation he applies the filter he uses in his art, looking at the work of literature through a funnel that enhances what impresses him as the key aspect. One reason he likes Borges is because of the emphasis on memory, which he considers essential in the creative process and inspiration. Memory is convenient in that it is selective and glides over unessential details. In connection with this project, Nizzero produced a number of works, two of which are included here. They deal with the stories "The Other" and "Funes, the Memorious."

Estela Pereda is the second most senior artist whose work is included here. She was born in 1931, in Buenos Aires and has had a long and distinguished career. Her art has been exhibited in many countries, including Argentina, Canada, Ecuador, France, Mexico, Puerto Rico, the United States, Uruguay, and Venezuela, and has received many awards, such as the Medalla de Oro de la Asociación de Críticos and the selection for the mural and prize "Nunca Más," for the Faculty of Engineering of the University of Buenos Aires. Pereda grew up in a family with a strong artistic presence. Both her mother and grandmother were artists, and now her daughter also has followed suit. Her mother was a well-known writer and her grandmother created tapestries that she integrated into other works as well. The grandmother's family had an Italian origin with a strong tradition of creating objects; they were artisans and artists and Pereda's mother frequently took her to workshops, when she was thirteen or fourteen. When the time came to choose a career, although she wanted to go to the Escuela Nacional de Bellas Artes, she did not have the courage to do it and chose instead something practical that could help her earn a living. She enrolled in the career of public translation, in the Faculty of Law, but never finished. She married young and moved to the country, and only slowly got back into art, in 1962. Her training took place in the workshops of Mariette Lydis, Bernard Bouts, Vicente Puig, Héctor Basaldúa and Araceli Vásquez Málaga, and she was part of the Grupo Intercambio. She studied the masters from the Renaissance, whose influence is still evident in her work, as is the case with Mantegna on the piece included here, which is an interpretation of Borges's "The Interloper." The move to the country awakened in her an appreciation for *mestizo* art. She had the opportunity of visiting the Christian chapels of northern Argentina and Chile, where the native peoples had left a record of their reading of the Christian stories and created an idiosyncratic art. Pereda was inspired by this and began to re-read these works, incorporating in her art elements from the land and its fruits. Yet, in her own words, she tried "to avoid becoming a folklorist," turning instead into what she calls "an Americanist" whose aim is to uncover and rediscover the riches of America. *Mestizo* art, with its musical angels and armed archangels, prompted her to introduce many changes in her work, but she never developed a set style. She has always liked to experiment and change. Her art varies in the use of media, which goes from oil and acrylic to drawing, sculpture, carving, weaving and sawing, the use of paper and collage, tempera, and the incorporation of various ready-made objects she finds. Among the topics that have particularly interested her is the place of women in society in general, and especially in Argentina. This is where the work I use here fits, and the explanation for her interest in Borges. Another of her pieces on Borges, a portrait, juxtaposes part of the image of the writer and a labyrinth.

Alberto Rey was born in Havana, Cuba, in 1960. His family emigrated to the United States when he was three years old. He is currently State University of New York Distinguished Professor at the State College at Fredonia. He holds a BFA from Indiana University of Pennsylvania and a MFA from State University of New York at Buffalo with additional postgraduate work at Harvard University. He has received many awards, including the State University of New York Chancellor's Award for Excellence in Research and Creative Activities. His art is in the permanent collections of several important museums in the United States, and has been exhibited in Mexico, Spain, the United States, and the Vatican. Originally an abstract painter, Rey eventually turned to realism as he began to explore his Cuban identity. During the 1990s he focused on depicting Cuban landscapes recovered from old black-and-white photographs, exploring Cuban and American locales, representing Cuban cultural objects, such as bars of guava and bottles of rum, painting portraits of Cubans and Cuban Americans, and integrating religious images in his art. All of these pieces combine to raise issues having to do with identity, which are affected by religion, places, pop culture, and people. By this time, Rey had developed a painting technique over plaster in turn placed over canvas with a wood backing. This was an attempt to recover a feel for the work of old masters. The return to the history of art has always been important to him, as we see in his interpretation of Borges's "The Rose of Paracelsus" for which he uses as point of departure a detail of a work by Caravaggio. This piece also points to his continuing interest in questions concerned with religious faith. The exploration of places and his interest in fishing led Rey to look into his natural surroundings in a series of works dealing with New York State fish and flora, particularly around the place where he currently resides, as well as in Cuba. These are large canvasses of live and dead fish, underwater videos, and combinations of some of these in a large installation.

Paul Sierra was born in Havana, in 1944, and emigrated to the United States in 1961. He resides in Chicago, and studied art in the School of the Art Institute in that city. He is a senior artist with a large number of exhibitions and a substantial body of work, and has lived from his art for many years. His creations have been exhibited in France, Mexico, Puerto Rico, the United States, and Uruguay, and are included in important collections in the United

States and Europe. Among the many awards he has received are two Cintas Fellowships. Sierra started drawing and doing watercolors when he was a small child. He had an uncle who was a Sunday painter, and let him use his paints. He fell in love with painting then and eventually enrolled in The School of the Art Institute in Chicago. At about twenty-two or twenty-three he had his first solo show and did not sell anything. He quit school and went into advertising to subsidize his painting, which he did after hours and on weekends. Eventually he was making more money from painting than from the advertizing business, so he quit advertizing and has been exclusively devoted to painting ever since. He is one of those artists who early on are able to support themselves with their art, even though he did not compromise his art and did not paint to suit clients. His work is strong and vigorous, the colors vivid, the brushstroke powerful, and the topics often disturbing: a man falling from a burning skyscraper, a lonely figure in a landscape, swimmers going against the current, crashed automobiles, and a dead Minotaur. But much of it can be strangely beautiful, lush landscapes, birds, and butterflies in starry nights, and golden fish swimming in creeks in the forest. In the landscapes he often places an animal or a statue that stands alone, and he never uses more than one figure. Loneliness and uniqueness are recurrent themes, but also the idea of paradise. Obviously there are influences, one can detect those of Rousseau, Gauguin, Goya, and De Kooning. In contrast with many Cuban painters living outside Cuba who work on Cuban themes, Sierra has never done so. His art is universal and finds inspiration in literature and the work of the masters. The Chicago Art Institute has been a great resource for him, and it is no surprise that he would be interested in Borges. Nor is it surprising that for his story he chose "The House of Asterion," a work about a monster who suffers loneliness and isolation, and ends up welcoming death.

I

Painted Stories

IDENTITY AND MEMORY

2

The Other

"The Other" is one of those stories in which Borges challenges the reader to solve a puzzle for which there seems to be no solution. The central difficulty posed by the story concerns personal identity and memory, appearance and reality. Are we the same persons throughout our lives? Is an old Borges the same person he was when he was young? Are they both real, is just one of them real, or are both of them unreal? The older and younger Borges are very different, but we would like to say they are one and the same. And how does memory play into this?

John Locke and David Hume claimed that memory is the key to personal identity. Borges's memories make him the person he is and provide continuity throughout his life. But memories are in a constant Heraclitean process of change and are notoriously unreliable, more so in old age, which is the situation with the narrator of the story. Memory selects and fails. Our memories today are different from our memories a year ago, let alone when long periods of time are involved. We can never be sure that we remember accurately. Sometimes what we remember vividly was not as we remember it and what we remember vaguely turns out to be right. Certainty is elusive because we lack an internal criterion to measure the legitimacy of our memories, particularly since remembering and forgetting are inextricably tied. How can an older Borges be the same as a younger one? And, given memory's unreliability, can we tell what is fact and what is fiction? Perhaps our memories are mere dreams.

"The Other" is a memory within a memory, a story within a story, as so many of Borges's fictions are. The action takes place in February 1969, in Cambridge, north of Boston. Borges is sitting on a bench by the Charles River when suddenly, under the impression that he had lived the experience before, he hears—for he is nearly blind—that someone has sat at the other end of the bench. The person in question turns out to be a much younger version of himself and Borges engages him in conversation. His former self thinks they are sitting in Geneva, on a bench by the Rhone, and not by the Charles River in Cambridge. Both cannot be right. Either Borges is right or his former self is right, in which case either Borges is dreaming his other self or his other self is dreaming Borges; one of the two is a dream of the other.

Neither thesis is easy to prove, although the older Borges tries hard to prove that he is the real one to the younger. The older Borges seems to have forgotten some things the younger knows, such as that once in his youth he had met an elderly gentleman who in 1918 told him he was Borges. And the younger seems to be very different in some ways from the older; he has ideals about the brotherhood of mankind, whereas the older Borges is rather cynical. The knowledge the older Borges has of certain facts known only to himself cannot prove that the younger is his dream, because it would be natural for the younger to know these facts if he were the dream of the older Borges.

The older Borges proposes a strategy to solve the puzzle. He asks the younger to give him a coin and he hands him a dollar bill. In looking at the dollar bill, the younger is shocked by its date, 1964, which presumably indicates that the older Borges is real and they are not sitting by the Rhone in 1918. But we are told that this does not work, because the older Borges, who is blind, was told months later that dollar bills do not have dates. (In fact, dollar bills do have dates.) Further confirmation eludes us in that the younger Borges destroys the dollar bill and the older Borges never keeps the coin he received from the younger.

One solution to the puzzle is that the older Borges is dreaming the younger dreaming himself. After all, the older Borges states at the outset of the encounter that he had a sense of having lived the moment before. However, this is disputed at the end of the story, when the older Borges tells us that the encounter was real and he was wide awake, having had a good night's sleep, when he spoke to the younger Borges. The younger, however, spoke to him in a dream, a reason why the older Borges could not remember his encounter with his older self when he was young. Still, his reality and wakefulness may also be mere dreams, or simply unreliable memories. It is not clear what is real and what is unreal.

The puzzle is never satisfactory resolved, since its solution depends on the emphasis placed by readers on the many and conflicting elements of the story. This brings us to another aspect of the tale that I have not mentioned. So far I have spoken of two persons, but actually there are three others. One is the writer of the story, who is not the same as the older Borges sitting on the bench in Cambridge, for the account of the meeting was not written at that time but rather months after the event that may, or may not, have taken place. Another is Borges, the reader of the story, who read it later still. And the third is the reader who is not Borges, you and/or me, who has read the story at various times after it was written. What do we make of these additional three persons? Do they play a role in the tale? Are they relevant for an understanding of it? Or do they merely add an unnecessary distraction? It is impossible to be sure, and that is part of the tale's charm and the reader's challenge. For the reader, as Borges says elsewhere, is part of a story, a character of it, and even perhaps an invention of its other characters.

Laura Delgado has painted three interpretations of "The Other," of which I use only *La otra* here. It carries as subtitle a line from Borges. The entire title reads: *La otra—éramos demasiado distintos y demasiado parecidos* (The Female Other—We Were Too Different and Too Alike). The line gives us the reason why Borges, the writer, thinks the older and younger Borges cannot find common ground: they could not deceive each other, which makes conversation difficult. This line points to three interrelated topics developed in the story: personal identity, memory, and communication, and Delgado interacts with all three in her painting.

La otra is mainly painted with acrylics, but it also incorporates the use of ink and pastels. We see a young girl sitting at a table, with pencil in hand, concentrating on the task of finishing a drawing on a sheet of paper. We cannot see her face, because she covers it with the hand she is not using to draw. The figure she has created on the paper is in many ways typical of what children draw: a girl with a big smile on her face, eyes with large eyelashes, prominent cheeks with pimples, and an elaborately decorated summer dress. Some facial features are exaggerated—very large eyes, eyelashes, and mouth. The expression is ambiguous, in spite of the original impression of mirth. The mouth is drawn as a circle and a line in the form of a half moon; the line suggests a smile and the circle the lips, but the two introduce an element of uncertainty: we do not know whether the girl is smiling or pouting—is she happy, sad, or both? The eyes confirm the impression; they do not clearly show a happy, light mood; they are serious, perhaps too intent, and even somewhat sad. A bow adorns her hair, similar to the one on the young artist. She is standing with extended hands on a landscape, the sun shining overhead, a flower by her side, and grass along the bottom of the picture. The drawing dominates the canvas, occupying two-thirds of it. It looks as if it were meant to be a portrait of the girl as she sees herself and is capable of drawing. Although the bow she wears is reproduced in the drawing, everything else is very different between the image and the artist. In reality there is no flower, sun, grass, elaborate summer dress or even a face we can see. The girl is in a rather dark room, painted against a dark background only lightly illuminated on one side, which explains the light shed on the picture under construction. And she is dressed in what appears to be a winter blouse.

Both the composition and the use of the glossed line from the story as a subtitle indicate that Delgado has focused her interpretation on the way we think of ourselves as both like and unlike what we are. Perhaps Borges's story is not so much about identity over time, as it appears at first glance, but rather about self-image. Can we see ourselves as we are? How is the image we have of ourselves similar and different from the way we are? The fact that Delgado has painted a child is significant in that children are at an age where their identity is being formed, when they are discovering who they are and developing a view of themselves. Delgado was trained in psychology and her insights in the field inform her work. That one of the hands of the girl is covering her eyes further suggests that she is shutting herself within, that the picture that she has drawn is not a picture of what she looks like, but a picture of what she sees herself as being, perhaps what she would like to be—herself in a new dress in a pleasant landscape where the sun is shining and she is surrounded by grass and flowers. Reality appears quite different. She is sitting in a closed room, without much light, and we gather it is winter from the clothes she wears, when flowers are missing from the fields, grass has wilted, and sunshine is sparse. A mirror would reveal her outward appearance, but a self-portrait reveals what is within, the inner experience, which we do not always welcome. The size of the disproportionate drawing in comparison with the girl in the painting indicates how our sense of self-identity is so much larger than we are. The expression on the drawing introduces an element of emotional uncertainty, perhaps a revelation of an unintended sadness. But the girl's feelings about what she wants are strong, for she has drawn an image with almost exaggerated features.

A significant fact about the work is that the gender of the main figure in the painting is different from that of the story's protagonist. Delgado has put herself in the work. She has focused on her own identity as a woman, leaving Borges out of the picture, both as a person and as male, along with the age of the protagonist and the setting. Her interpretation focuses on self-image and female identity. What we see is indisputably feminine and harks back to the artist. But the dialectic is similar to that of the story. There is Delgado the girl who draws the picture, and the girl drawn on the picture, Delgado the painter and viewer. So there are similar diachronic modalities involved insofar as Delgado the artist and viewer are of a different age from Delgado the drawer and the drawn. This is very much like what we have in the story with at least one sure exception and another possible one. The sure exception is that the painted Delgado, the drawer, is like her picture, young; whereas the Borges of Cambridge is older than the Borges of Geneva.

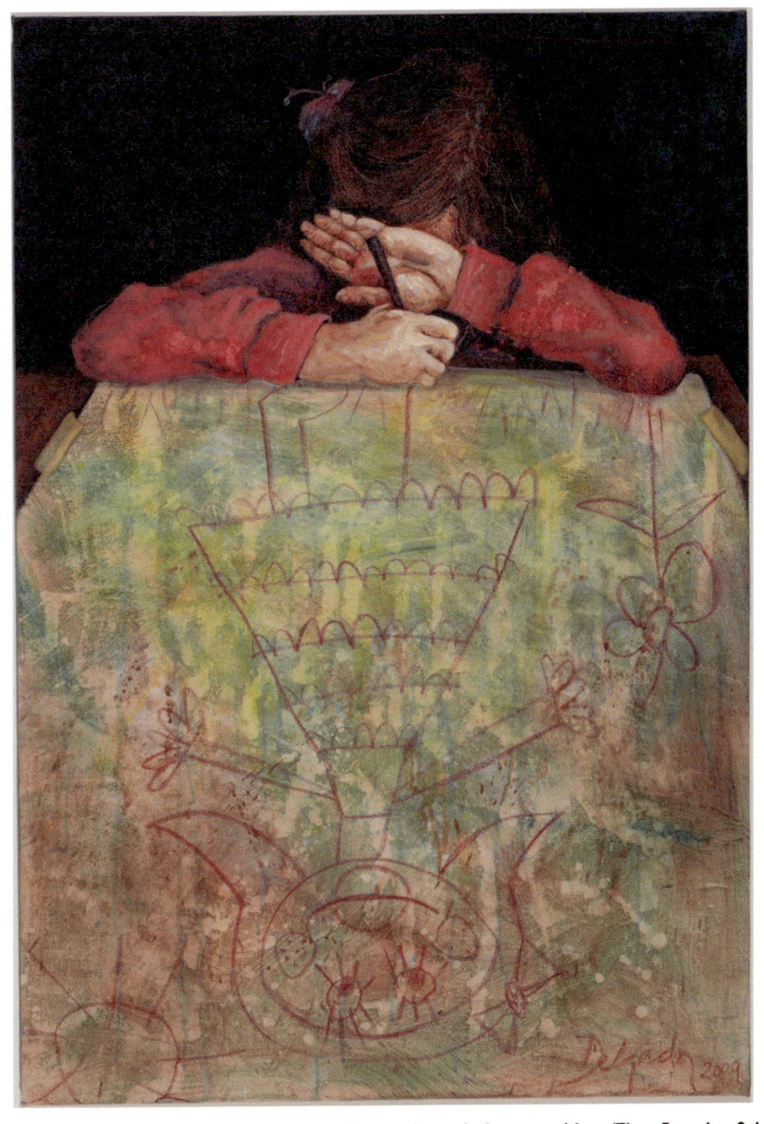

I. Laura Delgado, *La otra—éramos demasiado distintos y demasiado parecidos* (The Female Other—We Were Too Different and Too Alike), 2009, 39.5" × 27.5", mixed media on canvas.

The possible exception is that the younger Borges of Geneva is a dream of the older Borges of Cambridge, and the drawing by the girl is not a dream of herself. Still, one could argue that, if not a dream, the drawn girl is an idealization, a construction, just as the Borges of Geneva is a construction, or perhaps more accurately a reconstructed memory, of the Borges of Cambridge that time has idealized. And here is where memory can be brought in by Delgado, for the drawing may not be an entire product of the imagination; it is probably a reconstructed memory of what happened. When we draw ourselves, we have become objects to ourselves constructed on the bases of memories. In doing so we both remember and forget ourselves because we both take and lose hold of what we are, insofar as we cease to be what we are when we become the objects of our reflection.

So who is Borges and who is Delgado? Just as the story, the painting poses a question that it leaves unanswered. The girl's gesture of covering her eyes raises many questions about our encounter with ourselves. Is her gesture one of concentration, unhappiness, fear, refusal, or escape? Is she thinking hard about how to draw the next line? Because the picture is unfinished—the girl is still drawing it and many parts of it are still waiting to be drawn, such as the shoes. Is the girl unhappy with the drawing? Is she afraid of what she has drawn or could draw, and aims to shut the picture out, to escape, refusing to look at it? Perhaps she has revealed something she did not intend to reveal. Perhaps she does not want to see herself, just as the younger Borges shows no great interest in what will happen to him in the future. Or is the gesture merely an indication that she is tired or that she is playing a game of hide and seek with herself, replicating again an element of play present in Borges's narrative?

That the drawing is upside down may just mean that it is unfinished, still on the table where it is being created. But it could also mean that, like a mirror image, what we see of ourselves is the reverse of what we are, that our perspective on what we are is as distorted as anybody else's perception of us, distorted by our point of view, memories, feelings, needs, and desires, and by the objectification required to see and think ourselves. The unfinished picture indicates that our identities, what we are and what we think of ourselves, are not completed, but results of never-ending processes, always incomplete and in the works. Developing an identity takes effort, thus the concentration of the young artist, who covers her eyes to look at herself in her mind and avoid the distraction of the outside.

Like Borges's story, this work presents us with the interplay among different perspectives on the identity of a subject: the author, the author at a certain time, the author's view of herself, and the audience's view of each of these. The extraordinary thing about all this is that the perspectives find no firm common ground of communication in spite of their many elements in common, precisely because they are so alike and so different—their likeness is a subterfuge that leads both to understanding and misunderstanding.

Mauricio Nizzero's pictorial interpretation of Borges's story in *El otro* presents a very different perspective from the one Delgado's work displays. He has drawn two figures. One is sitting on a bench. As Borges describes him, he is older, with graying hair; his gaze is lost in thought, focusing on nothing in particular, meditating, somewhat sad, and perhaps recalling the past; he wears a suit and a bow tie, not mentioned in the story, but probably an accurate description of a professor at the time, which Borges was while in Cambridge; his legs are crossed and his arms go behind the bench, holding him in position; he is immobile, at rest, tired, maybe a prisoner manacled to his memories.

The other figure in the picture, by contrast, is all motion, energy, and vigor. He is in the act of running, apparently from the older Borges, although his location and position would make this physically impossible. In reality he could not be in a position to begin running, for there is not sufficient space between him and the sitting figure to achieve the motion he displays. This suggests that his motion is possible only because he is not part of the physical reality depicted in the work; he is a product of the sitting Borges, and as agile and faithful as his thoughts. One of his arms is simultaneously depicted in two positions. In one, it is stretched and the hand is pointing to the head of the sitting figure, supporting the conjecture that he is merely a thought of the other Borges. In the other position, just like the other arm, the arm is presented as it would be if the figure were in the act of running, balancing the body's inclination forward. His legs are intertwined with those of the sitting Borges, and his face is turned to his left, but not quite in the direction of the sitting Borges, and wears an expression of surprise, perhaps excitement, or even alarm, with his mouth open and the eyes alert, not due to physical exertion, but because he is excited and awed by something. Perhaps there is an element of fear and escape in the expression—he is horrified at a future in which he will be blind and old. Now he is young and full of life, unlike the sitting Borges, who appears melancholic and resigned. He would rather think of going places, looking forward to an unknown but exciting future, whereas the old Borges is passive and looking back, remembering a past that is no longer real; his own reality consists of mere remembrances because he is blind. There was a real young man who was sitting at the Rhone in 1918, even if he did not meet the older man at the time.

Nizzero's interpretation has taken sides in the solution to the question posed by Borges's story. The younger Borges is a product of the mind of the older Borges, insofar as he could not exist as he is portrayed. The encounter between the two Borgeses takes place in the mind of Borges. At first one would surmise that it would be the mind of the older Borges, given the

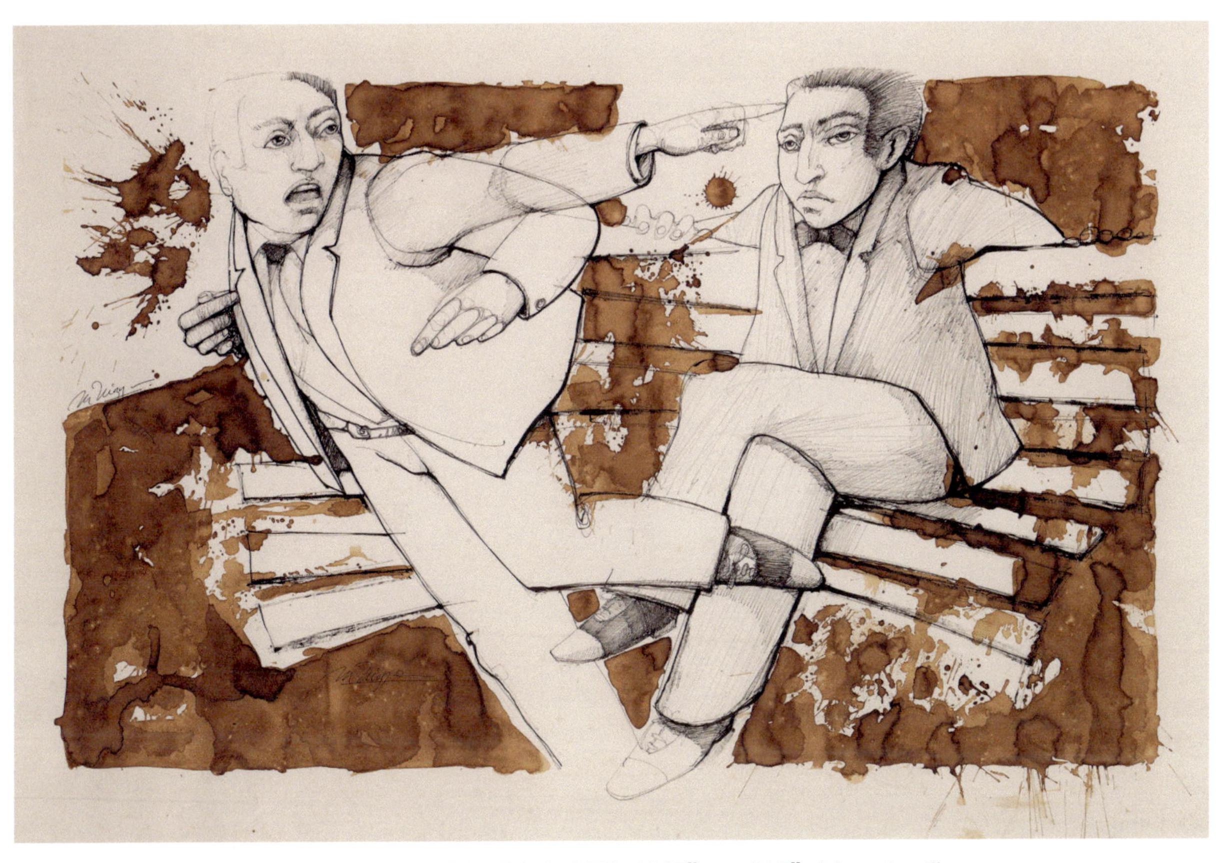

11. Mauricio Nizzero, *El otro* (The Other), 2009, 19.75" × 31.5", ink and coffee on paper.

direction of time—the younger Borges is a memory of the older one. One could also conjecture that it could be in the mind of the younger Borges, who can imagine the future, but the work of art indicates that it is indeed the older one. Following Borges's narrative, Nizzero's depiction makes clear that the younger Borges is not the product of a dream of the sitting figure, for the older Borges, as the story claims, is not sleeping, although the younger man is coming out of the sitting Borges's head. The implication is that he is a real memory from the past, brought to life in the thoughts of the older man, but nonetheless unreliable. After all, the Langsdorf tie he wears was not patented until 1924, long after the younger Borges was supposed to have been at the Rhone. And like memories, his depiction is unstable, fading in places. Indeed, the whole picture is rendered in blotches, representing the rough and spotty character of memories, where certain parts are strong and vivid, and others are weak and unclear. The monochromatic nature of the work also adds to its dreamlike quality and displays a surrealist tone typical of dreams— parts of the bench bend in an unnatural way, mirroring the impossibility of the situation. The yellow color evokes a line of the story in which the older Borges complains about his inability to see colors, and mentions yellow—the picture is drawn by Nizzero, not by Borges. The younger man's youth and expression of anticipation and surprise emphasize his differences with the older man. They are two people, separated not just by time, but also by their aspirations, experiences, and memories. The older Borges knows more and has lived longer than the younger, opening unexpected visions of the future for him; and he has forgotten much that is still fresh in the younger's memory.

In Nizzero's depiction, the actual encounter and its details, and the place and time of the event, seem immaterial. The emphasis is rather on the generational difference between the two figures, rather than on the problem of accounting for diachronic personal identity, that is, of the younger and the older men being in some sense one and the same Borges. There is one person, but the differences in age of the person at different times make it impossible for him at one time to understand himself at another. The younger wants to escape, he is running away from old age and a certain future that inevitably will bring him to it. Is the work of art about the question of identity or the recognition of identity? Does it have to do with who Borges is or with what he thinks he is? Or are these two questions one and the same? For Nizzero it seems that the questions merge, for the work of art, as Plato would have said, is a copy of a copy of a copy. Whatever happened is only real in the present as a memory, and as a memory it is unstable and unreliable.

But perhaps there is still another way of looking at this piece of art. In another work that Nizzero had done on this same story, he raised the question of a still third person who observes the other two. This could be another Borges, older and closer to the time of his death. He is observing the two Borgeses of the story, recounting a memory of a memory, going back to an earlier part of his life. This Borges completes the story, and is indeed the author of the written story. Indeed, he makes us realize that there are still two other persons involved in the event. One is Nizzero who has painted the story and the other is the audience of the story and the painting—that is we. For the sitting Borges "the other" is the younger Borges, for the younger Borges it is the sitting Borges who is "the other." For Borges the narrator, both of these Borgeses are "the other." In all these cases "the other" is part of Borges. But there is still another "other" that comes in as what Borges is for Nizzero and for the audience of both his painting and the story. Perhaps this is an important aspect of "The Other," namely, the appearance of the other as interpreter. If so, the significance of the story then changes from one concerned with time and identity, to one dealing with interpretation, insofar as the work leads to speculation as to the merging of five, or even perhaps as Borges would put it, "infinite" interpretive horizons.

3

Funes, the Memorious

"Funes, the Memorious" is one of Borges's most obviously philosophical stories. It is concerned with the nature of perception, memory, and thinking. The idea that our thinking is reducible to a great extent to the memory of our perceptions is old, but was perhaps most famously defended by John Locke, to whom Borges refers in the story. Our thoughts are nothing more than manipulated memories of perceptions, but the memories must not be exact, otherwise we cannot generalize and form the abstract ideas that serve us to make connections. To say that Hunter is a cat, I must have a general idea of Hunter—not of Hunter at this or that particular time—and a general idea of cat—not of this or that particular cat. Thinking requires that we forget the particularities of what we perceive in order to form both general concepts and concepts of individual things throughout time and change. In this story, Borges narrates the case of Ireneo Funes, who could do neither.

The story begins and ends with the recollection by the narrator, presumably Borges, of Funes, "his taciturn face, Indian features, and extraordinary *remoteness*," in the third and last time Borges met him. At first the recollection appears clear, but it is in fact vague if compared with what we are told later about Funes's own memory. Then the narrator goes back to an earlier time to describe Funes as an Uruguayan tough in contrast with the highbrow, dandy, city slicker Borges in Funes's eyes. A brief detour gives us to understand that Funes had become a glorified figure in Uruguay, "a precursor of the race of supermen," according to a well-known writer, and the author has been asked to write his recollection of him for a volume in his honor.

Considering Funes's tragedy, this reference to the Nietzschean superman appears ironic, for Funes is nothing if not a pathetic figure.

Borges the narrator encountered Funes first as a boy who could always tell the correct time and remember the names of everyone he met. Later he learned of an accidental fall from a horse that had crippled Funes and changed his life—he remained "hopelessly crippled" and never moved from his cot, where he laid with his eyes fixed on a fig tree or a spiderweb. Borges saw him twice through an iron-barred window, once with the eyes closed, and another time absorbed in the contemplation of an artemisia, both times immobile. Then he received a flowery letter, in perfect calligraphy, from Funes, requesting to borrow one of the books Borges was using to learn Latin, and a dictionary, for a short time. The presumption that one could quickly learn Latin just with a book and a dictionary sounded like a joke to Borges, but he did comply with the request in order to disabuse Funes.

Shortly after, Borges received bad news about his father's health and, while packing for the trip, realized he was missing the books he had lent Funes. He walked over to his house to recover the books, and when Funes's mother opened the door, Borges heard him reciting parts of the chapter on memory in Pliny's *Naturalis historia*. Funes welcomed him and told him his remarkable story.

When Funes woke up from the unconscious state caused by the accident, he discovered an extraordinarily rich world, very different from the one he had known. Before, he had been, as he thought the rest of mankind still was, "blind, deaf, befuddled, and virtually devoid of memory." After his accident, "perception and memory were perfect." The result was not only that he could memorize entire works in different languages of which he had no prior knowledge, but that he could recall every thing he had experienced. Indeed, he did not remember just a dog he had perceived, but every single perception of the dog he had at every instant: "the 'dog' of three-fourteen in the afternoon, seen in profile" and "the 'dog' of three-fifteen, seen frontally." This prompted Funes to try to develop a language of numbers that would identify each number with a proper name, and to catalogue every experience he had ever had. Realizing that the tasks would be interminable, and perhaps useless, he eventually gave up.

The dizzying world in which he lived made sleep difficult for Funes and, Borges suspects, also thinking, for "[t]o think is to ignore (or forget) differences, to generalize, to abstract." In Funes's world, nothing could be forgotten. He could not stop remembering and noticing, accumulating endlessly the infinite minutiae of perception. The human curiosity to know, praised by Aristotle at the beginning of the *Metaphysics* as the motivation for wisdom and science, became an addiction that prompted Funes indiscriminately to collect everything. But there was never enough time to gather all that he wanted. Sleep became impossible in this frenzied and endless search to know and keep everything. Borges closes the story with a description of Funes, lying on his cot, "monumental as bronze—older than Egypt, older than the prophesies and the pyramids," and with a fear that Borges's presence would add to Funes's predicament.

Laura Delgado's two paintings, entitled, *Funes, vaciadero de basura I* and *Funes, vaciadero de basura II,* take their titles from something Borges reports Funes told him in an attempt to describe his memory: "My memory, sir, is like a garbage heap." This comment encapsulates one of the main motifs of the story: A memory that does not discriminate is of no use; indeed, it is counterproductive. Like garbage, it collects what should be discarded.

In the first painting, Delgado has painted a carton full of discarded objects, arranged haphazardly, against the dark background of a wall: a sneaker, a pail containing the skull of a goat, pieces of newspaper, a briefcase inside of which we see a blanket and a yo-yo, among other things, and an old and partly discolored piece of cloth. The second painting presents us with a small enclosure, perhaps a utility room, in which objects of various kinds project shadows. There is a sink on the right, a faucet is facing us, and on the left we see a garbage bin partly covered with a throw or blanket, and containing a pail full of broken cardboard with parts of texts printed on them. Between the garbage bin and the sink, we see a bottle, an old pump, and a dustpan. On top of the sink a small, brown-colored, glass bottle has a funnel sticking out of it. The walls of the room are tiled with children's drawings on them, including images of children and of a sailboat of the sort young children draw, while the shadow of the pump is projected on one of the walls. The tiles look old and discolored in places.

Two things are notable in these two ensembles. One is the vivid colors of the objects painted—the reds, blues, greens, and yellows stand out as bright and living. Another is the details of the objects: most of them are painstakingly drawn and painted. We see every significant element of the sneaker in the first work—the holes for the strings, the state of the materials, the occasional stain. And in the second, the printed numbers on the cardboard and the design and folds of the blanket are carefully and clearly depicted. But this is not photorealism or ultra-realism. Rather, it is a kind of expressionist realism in which colors become symbols and the brushstroke can be loose. One is drawn to the garbage heap depicted in each painting even though neither it, nor the objects it contains, has any obvious value. The paintings make observers curious and raise their interest. Indeed, there is an attraction in the composition that is undeniable; we cannot help but become fascinated from the start by the brilliant complexity and engaging character of the images. The use of mixed media—acrylic, pastel, ink, and particularly collage—in both works adds to the variety and structure of the pieces.

Delgado's creations capture the fascination that the world of perception had for Funes. Having experienced the world in ways that are impossible for us to do, he could not bring himself to part with it. He found his accident fortuitous and spent the rest of his life in darkness, shutting out the growing number of images that assailed him in order to focus on those he had already encountered. A shoestring, or a piece of cloth, represents endless possibilities for exploration and enrichment. Even the temporary separation from the memories of past perceptions made sleep difficult for him.

The paintings exclude much of the context of Borges's story. They ignore Funes and the events that relate to him altogether. The only reference to the protagonist of the story is in the titles, and that seems more like references to the story than to Funes himself. Nothing in the works recalls him. And Borges, the ostensive narrator of the events, is also excluded. The paintings do not depict the characters of the story; they are just too obvious. The attention is turned instead to memory. This allows a focus on a single line of the story that can be effectively expressed pictorially and simply, revealing the principal thrust of the story for the artist: the nature of memory, good and bad.

Memory is frequently regarded as an asset, a wonderful and desirable tool to help us navigate our existence and to satisfy our cravings for continuity and emotional involvement with the past and self-identity. Before reading Borges, Delgado thought of it as sublime, but this story opened for her another dimension of it, one that is not only haphazard, but also terrible. Delgado explores both the good and bad dimensions of memory and their relation to identity through the objects depicted in the garbage heap. In a room that takes the place of the mind or its memory, we see an ensemble of objects, none of which is privileged but all of which have significant memory connotations: an old sneaker stands for the experiences of childhood and for the road we travel; cardboard pieces point to the learning aspects of our lives; colorful old blankets bring back memories of childhood, dreams, a love affair, and illness, and may symbolize, as textiles often do, the multifaceted and intricate weave of our lives; the children's drawings on the walls recall moments in which we tried to capture our identity or those of others; a sailboat can stand for a first encounter with the sea, or it may prompt us to think about our voyage in life, who we are, and where we are going; the suitcase in the first painting is a symbol of travel, and when not traveling, is a place where we store and collect things; the garbage pail may remind us of picking up the debris we leave behind and that often requires collecting for disposal; a pump can turn into a phallic symbol of sexuality and erotic love, and its shadow may be a harbinger of possible darkness in the future, the unaccounted consequences of an erotic encounter; an old glass bottle indicates the frailty of memory and the self; the old skull

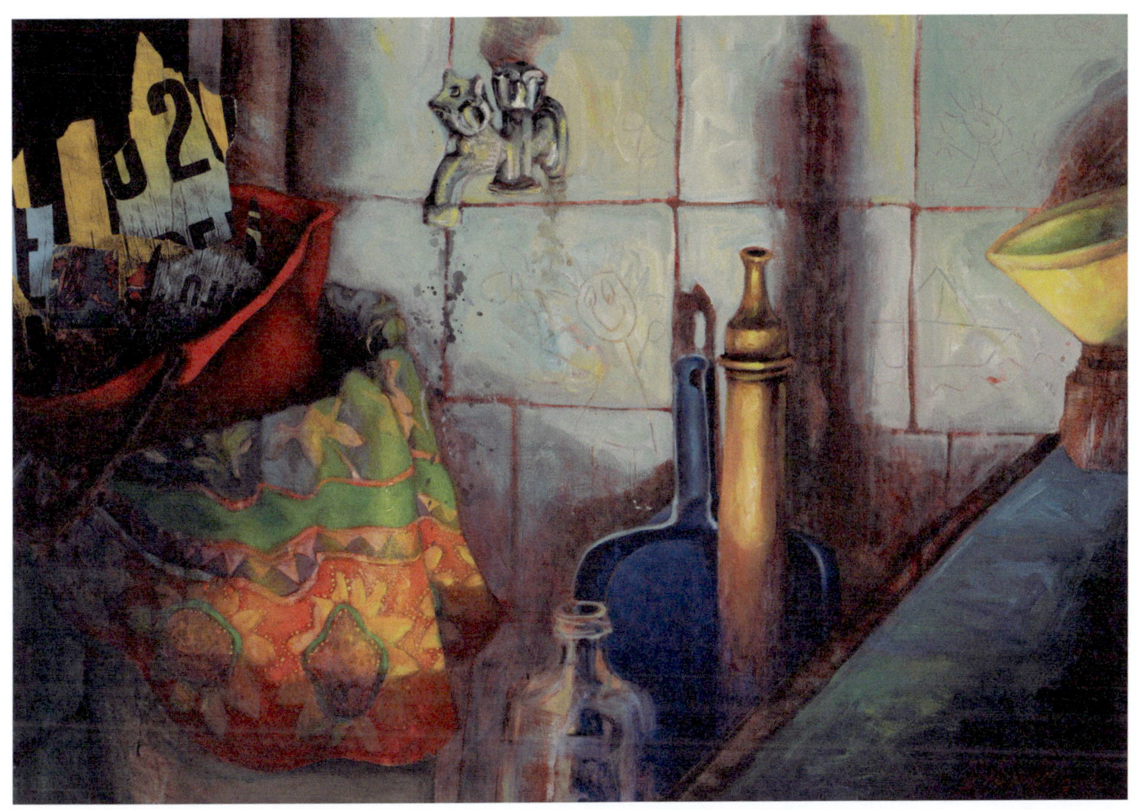

III. Laura Delgado, *Funes, vaciadero de basura II* (Funes, The Garbage Heap II), 2009, 27.5" × 39.5", mixed media on canvas.

reminds us of death; the water faucet is a symbol of the fluidity of our selves and our identities; the dustpan and the sink suggest cleaning; and the funnel indicates perhaps that all this needs to be filtered and accommodated, without loss, into what looks like an impossibly small jar, perhaps a symbol for our selves.

These memory remnants are pieces of ourselves that become symbols for various aspects of our identities. The room where they are can be a place for washing, utility, storage, or garbage, just as our minds or our memory are places where we clean, manipulate, keep, or discard our experiences. Its walls and shadows feel claustrophobic and limiting. The contents are lifeless objects, although they hark back to life—a still life that points to the reality in which they once played a role. We are conglomerates of our pasts, haphazard piles of elements that, as random accumulations, produce no understanding, but upon reflection and selection can lead to greater knowledge of ourselves and the world.

Through the use of a realistic technique and vivid colors that attract the observer's gaze, Delgado captures the fascination the senses exercise on us. Indeed, one might even conjecture that the message of the painting is as much about the nature of memory as about the captivating draw of sensation. And there is also the tie to identity and ourselves. In this sense these two paintings are closely related to the painting we examined earlier from Delgado, *La otra*.

Mauricio Nizzero's *Funes, el memorioso,* is a very different work from Delgado's *Funes, vaciadero de basura I* and *II*. It is more closely tied to the narrative, focusing on the description of Funes at the beginning and end of the story, through which it reveals the tale's core.

We are presented with the last scene of the narrative rendered in abstract spaces, a form that looks like a bed or a cot, and a stain that turns out to be a door. There are no horizons, no clear planes of orientation, and no definite boundaries. Images merge into each other in a fluid surface that stimulates the memory of the narrator. We have no sense of time or space. The painting resembles the reflection on an antique mirror, with blotches and splashes, giving us a biased and fuzzy image of what it reflects. Or perhaps it represents an image mediated by floaters in the eye of the perceiver that affect vision in unexpected ways.

Funes lies on his cot, covered with a sheet except for the feet that stick out from it. His hands are crossed over the chest, with fingers, large and coarse, that contrast with Borges's description of them as "slender, leather-braided." There is no evidence of any movement, suggesting the immobility of a bronze monument mentioned in the text. The blanket functions like a gird that contains and submits him, but also reminds one of a shroud, a cover for the dead. The blotches on the painting evoke a confused space, filled with too many details, but partly broken. And the inclined body appears like a dead body prepared for a wake, although the face, and particularly the eyes show no evidence of repose. One of them is almost closed, suggesting meditation or remembrance, but the other is fully open, almost impatiently looking, hungrily searching—the eyebrow raised, signaling that Funes is intently observing something, or that a noise has caught his attention. The concentration on the face evokes Borges's description at the beginning of the story: "his taciturn face, its Indian features, its extraordinary *remoteness.*"

Borges, as narrator, appears to be peaking behind a wall or curtain, almost trying to pass unnoticed. His presence is tentative. He looks tired and sleepy in contrast with Funes, almost in a stupor. We must remember that they had spent the whole night together in a dialogue that Borges recalls as exhausting and terrifying. The unclear location and details indicate that the very narrative by Borges is a matter of memory, which, unlike the precise memory of Funes, is unclear, anecdotal, unreliable, and loose, in part a result of his own imagination and perspective. Besides, most of what Borges narrates is secondhand; it is a rendition of what Funes tells him, and therefore mediated by his remembrance. How can we trust his account of the events that happen in the story, then?

Funes, by contrast, cannot sleep because of the vividness of his perceptions and memories. We must imagine that, while speaking with Borges, he is recalling an infinite number of things and perceiving even the minutest changes both in the external world and in his own body. The semi-closed eye signals his concentration on his memories and internal perceptions, the open eye suggests his perception of his surroundings at the moment of Borges's visit. He is prostrated on a bed, frustrated by the inability to grasp and keep everything that surrounds him. As Nizzero recalls, for Funes, "something that could be marvelous and unique has become a tragedy." His body is immobile, a prisoner of his mind, as he is a prisoner in his room, whereas Borges, by contrast, is aware of the dialogue and its implications, and only vaguely attentive to his surroundings, perhaps intent on minimizing the impact of his presence.

Nizzero's work does not focus primarily on the nature of memory or the details of perception. It revolves around Funes's tragedy, his loneliness, quiet desperation, obsession, and immobility. Funes does not move, trapped by the rich scene he cannot help but watch. We know who he is, and the exact nature of his tragedy, from the reference to Borges's story in the title, but not from anything in the work. The work reveals to us only the desperate misery of someone who is a prisoner of his mind, which may be another dimension of the story, and perhaps more significant than the obvious reference to memory and perception.

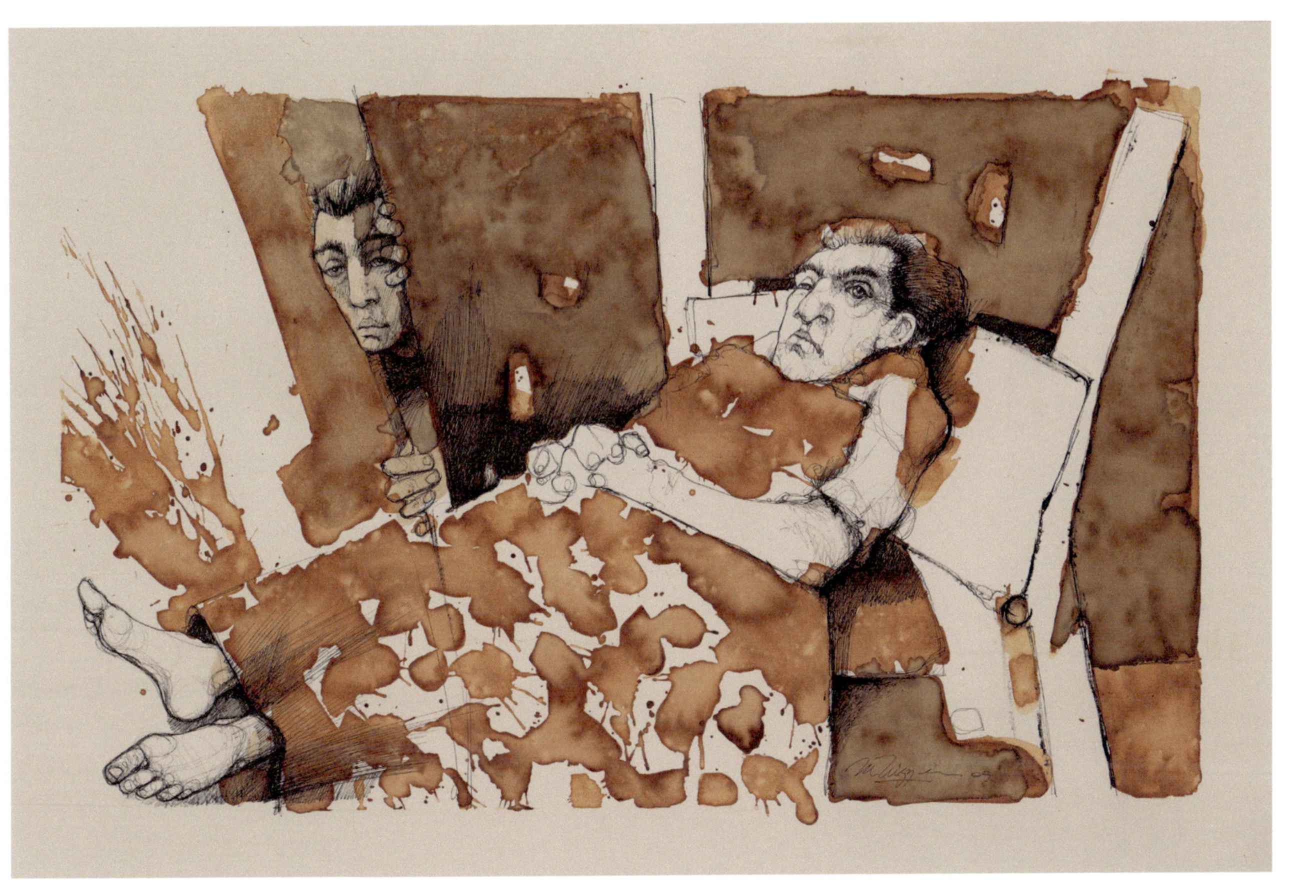

IV. Mauricio Nizzero, *Funes, el memorioso* (Funes, the Memorious), 2009, 19.75" × 31.5", ink and coffee on paper.

4

The South

"The South" is one of the most celebrated of Borges's stories. Indeed, some have thought, perhaps even Borges, that it is Borges's best story. Regardless of one's opinion on this matter, it is clear that it is a powerful treatment of identity. However, in contrast with the first two stories in this section, this one adds a different angle to the question of self-identity and memory, namely, the dimension of our social identity, who we are and want to be in the context of society. This topic is explored in terms of mixed ancestry and ethnic and national identification, but it could apply as well to race. As usual with Borges, he is a pioneer in that he explores topics that during his time had yet not become hot for literary authors and philosophers. The issues involved in hybrid identities have captured the attention of the public long after he first raised it in this story. How can we deal with a hybrid ancestry, racial origin, or ethnic self? How do our social roots affect the way we feel about ourselves and the world and influence our choices? Do we freely decide or are we bound by circumstances? And if we are free to decide, how do we go about making a decision and what factors affect it? These are questions that affected Borges directly, because he was, like the protagonist of the story, a product of hybrid ancestry, education, and social group. And he uses an accident he had as an excuse to explore it.

The story concerns Juan Dahlmann, who works as a librarian in a municipal library. His ancestry is mixed. One grandfather came from Germany and the other had died fighting against the Indians. In the pull between these lineages, Borges tells us that he "chooses the romantic ancestor, or that of a romantic death." His *criollismo* is supported with memories and heirlooms, and he dreams of returning to a large country house in the South of Buenos Aires that he had inherited and managed to keep over the years. Then he has an accident. He hits his head very badly and develops septicemia. After days of suffering, he is taken to a sanatorium where he undergoes a painful operation. He awakes sick, feeling as if at the bottom of a well, and hates himself, and his self-identity, weakness, and humiliation.

Ostensibly, he recovers and, after being discharged, undertakes his long-desired return to the house of his childhood memories. The trip to the train station mirrors the trip to the sanatorium, and in the station he encounters a large cat he remembers. Petting the magical cat feels illusory, an encounter between two senses of time. Once in the train he enjoys the passing landscape and the pleasure of the food served in the shining metal bowls he remembers from his childhood; the trip feels like one into the past. Indeed, he feels as if he were two men: one imprisoned in the sanatorium, and another gliding along through his native land. He dozes off, and when he awakens the car of the train where he travels appears different from the one he boarded in Buenos Aires.

Eventually he arrives at a station where the conductor informs him that he must get off, even though it is not the one Dahlmann intended. He walks to a country store to take a calash to his final destination, but decides to eat there before he leaves. Dahlmann thinks he recognizes the owner, but then realizes it is because he looks like one of the employees at the sanatorium. Three rough-looking young men are sitting at one of the tables, and a small, dark, dried up, old man, living in a sort of eternity, lays motionless on the floor. Dahlmann minds his own business, but clearly stands out as an incongruity in the rough countryside. He notices that someone has thrown a ball of bread at him, and pays no attention to it until another is thrown. The owner, who strangely addresses him by his name, tells him to ignore it, and this makes Dahlmann realize that the provocation now has been identified publicly as directed at him and he cannot let it go. He faces the young men and one insults him and pulls a knife. Dahlmann is not armed, but the old man throws him a knife, and "[i]t was as if the South itself had decided that Dahlmann should keep the challenge." He instinctively picks up the knife and understands that this commits him to a fight in which he will die. He thinks, "They'd never have allowed this sort of thing to happen in the sanatorium." As he goes out, without hope or fear, he feels that in contrast with dying in the sanatorium, his death here would be a liberation, a joy, and a fiesta.

There are at least two main ways to read this story. One is by accepting the narrative literally. The protagonist has an accident, recovers from septicemia, and dies in a fight on the trip to his country house. In the other, supported by many of the incongruities in Dahlmann's narrative, the second part of the story is a hallucination that occurs in the sanatorium while Dahlmann is on the operating table.

Alejandro Boim's *El sur* (The South) depicts a scene in the countryside. The painting is dominated by a figure, presumably Dahlmann, either coming down from the sky and perhaps about to land or rising up from the ground. His arms are folded upward, and dark streaks go up from the hands and the head. Roughly below him on the ground, there is something brightly illuminated, the details of which are not quite distinguishable. It could be some irregularity of the ground of the countryside, or perhaps more significant, a body lying down on an operating table. The dark streaks going from Dahlmann's hands and head to the top end of the painting suggest the fantastic character of the trip. He is well dressed, although conservatively, as a librarian would be: blue suit, white shirt, tie, black shoes and socks, and a hat. The suit has been well ironed, showing the creases of the pants, and the shoes are polished. Clearly we have a fashionable man, perhaps even a dandy, obviously a city man to the core. This fact strongly contrasts with the country scene. The suit has been painted carefully, in a way that gives it a shine. It used to be a common uniform of a certain class in Buenos Aires. The man wears glasses and he has a pleasant expression; he might be even smiling, and he resembles Borges.

In the background we see a hill and the outline of lush trees and vegetation, something that does not correspond to the flat pampas, adding to the unreality of the scene. To the left of the suspended man, an old and poorly maintained two-story masonry building, simple and unimpressive, echoes the architecture in the *pampas*, common enough in stores, eating places, and bars. The picture is generally dark, and many of the details are fuzzy. Apart from the lighted spot to which I referred before, the only light in the painting comes from the front wall of the building, some paths on the ground, and the hill behind. It looks like dusk, with the last light of the day brushing a few surfaces of the canvas, the last effort of the sun on its way toward the incoming darkness of night, perhaps an indication of the tragic end, in which Dahlmann finds his death.

One way to understand this painting is as an interpretation in which the second part of Borges's story is a description of a romantic hallucination. The floating figure is Dahlmann's hallucinatory creation of himself in the story where he would find a glorious death in a fight with rough laborers of the Argentinean countryside. Boim has used floating figures in his art before, but this does not mean that his use of this motif is always particularly significant, although it seems to be here. The building does look like the place where Dahlmann meets his fate, but it could also look like the kind of house he had inherited: two-stories, square, with few windows and doors. This is the place where he would like to be in his imaginary construction and where he is going. The figure could be interpreted as either rising or landing: rising insofar as it could be the mental creation of the man undergoing surgery; and landing in that it is returning to the romanticized place of Dahlmann's childhood. Dahlmann is imagining himself in the Argentinean countryside, in the house of his grandfather, close to the location where the fight occurs. He is happy because that has always been his goal, the romantic return to what he considers to be his roots. He is realizing the myth of the *gaucho*, the rough country *macho* who lives and dies by rules of challenge and honor. These rules are represented by the old man who throws him the knife, giving him the option to live by the standards he admires. On his deathbed, at the sanatorium, Dahlmann becomes the man he thinks he is, or at least would like to be, by dying in his idealized dream.

What looks like an illuminated figure somewhere below Dahlmann raises further questions. It could represent a dead Dahlmann or a Dahlmann about to die, and either lying on the ground outside the bar or on the operating table. Or he may be lying on the operating table at the same time that he is imagining himself on his way to the countryside, fighting a gaucho, and dying on the occasion. But why this light spot in a picture marked by darkness? Maybe it is just a matter of what is generally the case at operating tables. Or it could symbolize that this is in fact reality, in contrast with the imaginary self in the country created by Dahlmann's distraught mind. Or it could be that the anesthesia of the operation creates the wonderful hallucination, bringing life to what is otherwise a drab and uninspired existence. The overall darkness and shadows emphasize the hallucinatory character of the scene.

Instead of one painting, Miguel Cámpora's interpretation of Borges's story consists of a triptych: *El sur* (The South), *La duda* (The Doubt), and *El paso de Eros* (Eros's Passage). In the first we are presented with a family in a room in which we see a train through a window; they are at the point of beginning a trip. Four people—a young boy, a teenager, a woman, and a man—are in what appear to be a somber and desperate condition, pensive, and ravaged by uncertainty. The man wrings his hands, with eyes closed the woman adopts the posture of a thinker, the young boy clings to his dog with an expression of distrust and perhaps fear, and the teenager reclines on a bed in a fetal position with a hand holding his head in a posture of intense preoccupation. A cat sits intently watching the man, a symbol of eternity, and perhaps of death, mentioned in the story.

The second painting is even richer in symbolism. A boy in a corner holds a cat that looks intently at the nude figure of a man sitting with open legs on a straw stool. The man's head is injured, and he partly covers the wound and most of his face, perhaps in a gesture of pain or shame. On his shoulders are perched two ravens, one of which is picking at his ear, or perhaps whispering to him. Behind this ensemble, two other figures are visible. On the left is a naked boy riding a toy horse; he is hunched over it with his hands on his knees. On the right, another man, bare from the waist up, is looking over and walking toward a precipice. In the

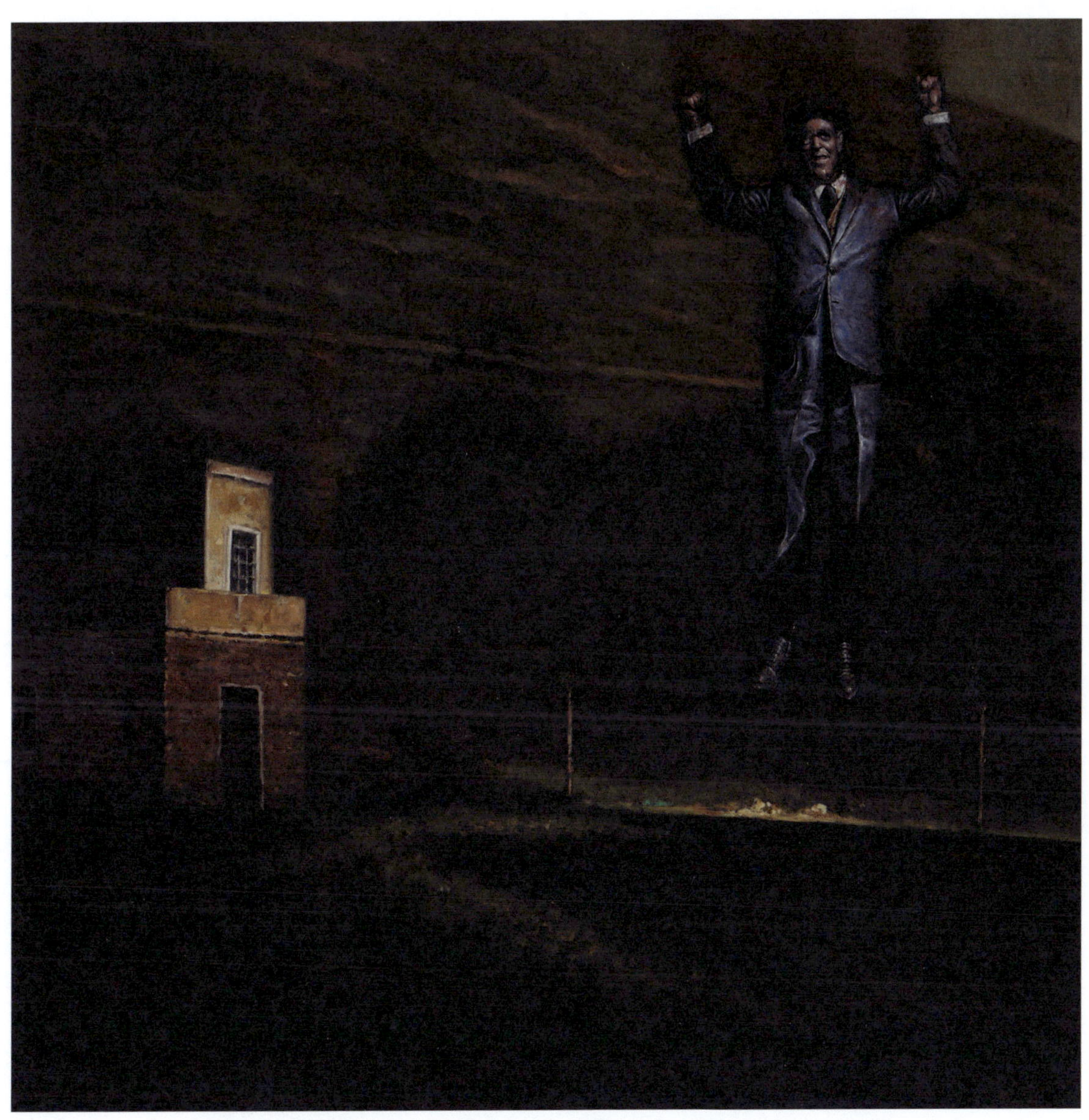

V. Alejandro Boim, *El sur* (The South), 2009, 24" × 24", oil on canvas.

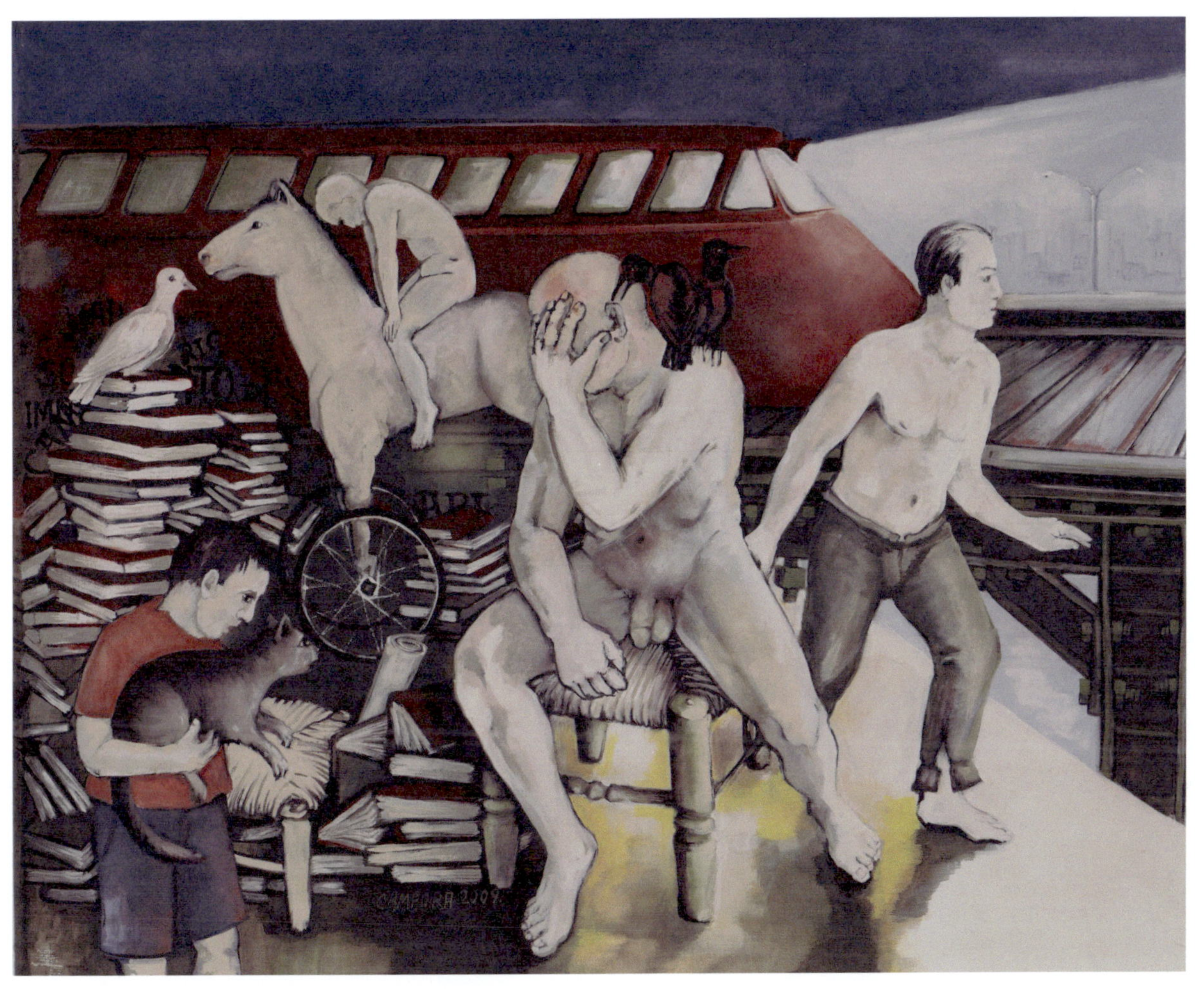

VI. Miguel Cámpora, *La duda* (The Doubt), 2009, 31.5" × 39.5", acrylic on canvas.

background we see piles of books, over some of which stands a white dove and a train about to cross over a bridge with a light that illuminates the rails.

The third panel returns to the original family. They have left the train and are walking away from it, but they do not appear to be the same people. Originally, the man was bald but now he is not; and his clothes are different, now he wears an open shirt, whereas before he wore a sweater, shirt, and tie. The woman looks much younger and thinner. The boy's face has become more chubby, and he is dressed differently. And the teenager appears younger.

The three paintings are unified by the metaphor of the trip represented by the train, but the core of the interpretation is found in the centerpiece. Here we enter a world of dreams in which what appears to be the same man, Dahlmann, is presented in four different ways: two as a child and two as a man. One child is playing with a cat, the other is riding a horse; one of the men is deep in thought, and the other is walking toward the abyss. A world of memories meets the present.

Cámpora's painting interprets Borges's story as a metaphor for life's journey in which doubts and decisions consume our energies and may have tragic consequences. Dahlmann's duel is not with the man who teases him in the store, but with himself. This is an internal, rather than an external struggle. It is an altercation of the self trying to find itself, and it occurs in the mind. The way in which the figures are presented, assembled in a kind of surrealist space that could not exist, evokes the hallucinatory character of the tale. The nude man holding his head, presumably because of the pain of the accident, or out of shame because he hates himself, his identity, and his weakness, can also indicate that everything in the picture is happening inside his mind: the train, the memories, the precipice, the books, and the animals. One part of him rejects what he is and desires, indicated subtly by the nude figure of the center painting, but the other is open to dreams, to be what he wants to be even if it leads to an abyss. He is vindicated because he overcomes the horror of his ordinary life and becomes free to dream of freedom, courage, and glory in death. The topic of the painting is doubt, choice, and identity, rather than Dahlmann's social identity. The concern has shifted, opening the painting to a more universal interpretation.

5

The Interloper

"The Interloper" is one of the most brutal stories that Borges ever wrote. Unlike many of his other stories that deal with philosophical problems and conceptual puzzles, this is a classic treatment of the human situation, and most of all of human love and passion, although it is also about identity and the condition of women in society. Also in contrast to his other work, in which women and sex play little or no role, this story raises questions that are intrinsic to both. This has initiated and fed a controversy as to how well it fits in the Borgesian corpus.

This is a story about two brothers who love each other and of a female interloper who comes between them, the conflict between brotherly love and the love men have for women. It is also a story of the land, the countryside, where men are rough and unsophisticated, where violence is the ultimate means of solving human conflict, and where women are objects to be bought and sold, used and discarded, loved and hated. It is a tale of human struggle and pain. The plot is simple and so is the narrative. No word is wasted, no flourishes adorn it; and this gives it an unusual power. But is the story fundamentally about a woman and her place in a male-dominated world, or is it about love between men and women or between men? And if it is about love between men, is the love filial or homosexual? Borges never admitted to any homosexual dimension to the story, but the reference to *II Kings* at the beginning is actually to a text of *II Samuel* that speaks of homosexual love.

Two brothers live together in harmony and peace in the outskirts of Buenos Aires in the 1890s. They are tall, redheaded, and rough, reflecting their mixed ancestry and culture. They stand out from the rest of the population and stick to each other in a very close relationship that perhaps goes beyond brotherly love. One day, the oldest, Cristián, brings home a not-bad-looking woman, Juliana Burgos. She becomes their servant and he displays her at local parties, "lavishing ghastly trinkets upon her." Eduardo, the youngest, lives with them, but then he takes a trip and when he returns he brings back with him a girl that he throws out shortly after. It is obvious that he is in love with Cristián's woman, although he does not want to acknowledge it. But Cristián realizes it and offers her to him: "I'm going off to that bust over at Farías place. There is Juliana—if you want her, use her."

This opens up a new modus vivendi in which the brothers share Juliana, but the arrangement does not last. They never mention her, but often find excuses to argue with each other because both want her. Eventually they talk about the situation among themselves—Juliana is not given a say, she is a mere object whose fate is to be decided by them. And so they choose to take her to a bordello where they sell her to the madam. Still, even out of the house, she comes between them; they are unable to get her out of their minds and reestablish their original way of life. They begin to visit the whorehouse separately to see her until one day, by chance, Cristián meets Eduardo there and they bring Juliana back to their place. However, this does not resolve the conflict, for Juliana has come between them, souring their original relationship. So Cristián kills Juliana, leaving her body on a field. When he gets back to the house he asks his brother to accompany him, to take some skins "over to the Nigger's place." On the way there, he throws out his cigar, saying to Eduardo "Let's go to work, brother. The buzzards'll come in to clean up after us. I killed 'er today. We'll leave 'er here, her and her fancy clothes. She won't cause any more hurt." Deeply moved, they embrace, closer than ever, having now another source of unity: the sacrificed woman and the obligation to forget her.

Estela Pereda's "*Si la querés, usála,*" picks up on the words that Cristián says to his brother when he offers Juliana to him: "If you want her, use her." The brutality of the expression is heightened in Argentinean Spanish, where the accents in the third and fourth words shift from the first to the second syllables. It conveys the way Cristián thinks about Juliana—she is a thing to be used, and object of pleasure to be shared at will—and underlines the rough, blunt talk of countryside toughs.

The painting has an inscription along the right-hand side, which corresponds to part of the floor depicted, where Pereda notes the colors she has used: shadow earth, black, red earth, emerald green, and chrome. Then she adds the title of the picture, dedicates it to Borges and Mantegna, specifies the collection to which it belongs, signs it, and repeats a phrase and the title: " *'ahí la tenés a la Juliana, si la querés usála' HOMENAJE a Jorge Luis Borges y a Andrea Mantegna LA INTRUSA del Informe de Brodie de Jorge Luis Borges, Estela Pereda, 1991. Se despidió de Eduardo . . . no de Juliana que era una cosa . . . ahí la tenés 'si la querés usála . . .' Jorge Luis Borges.*"

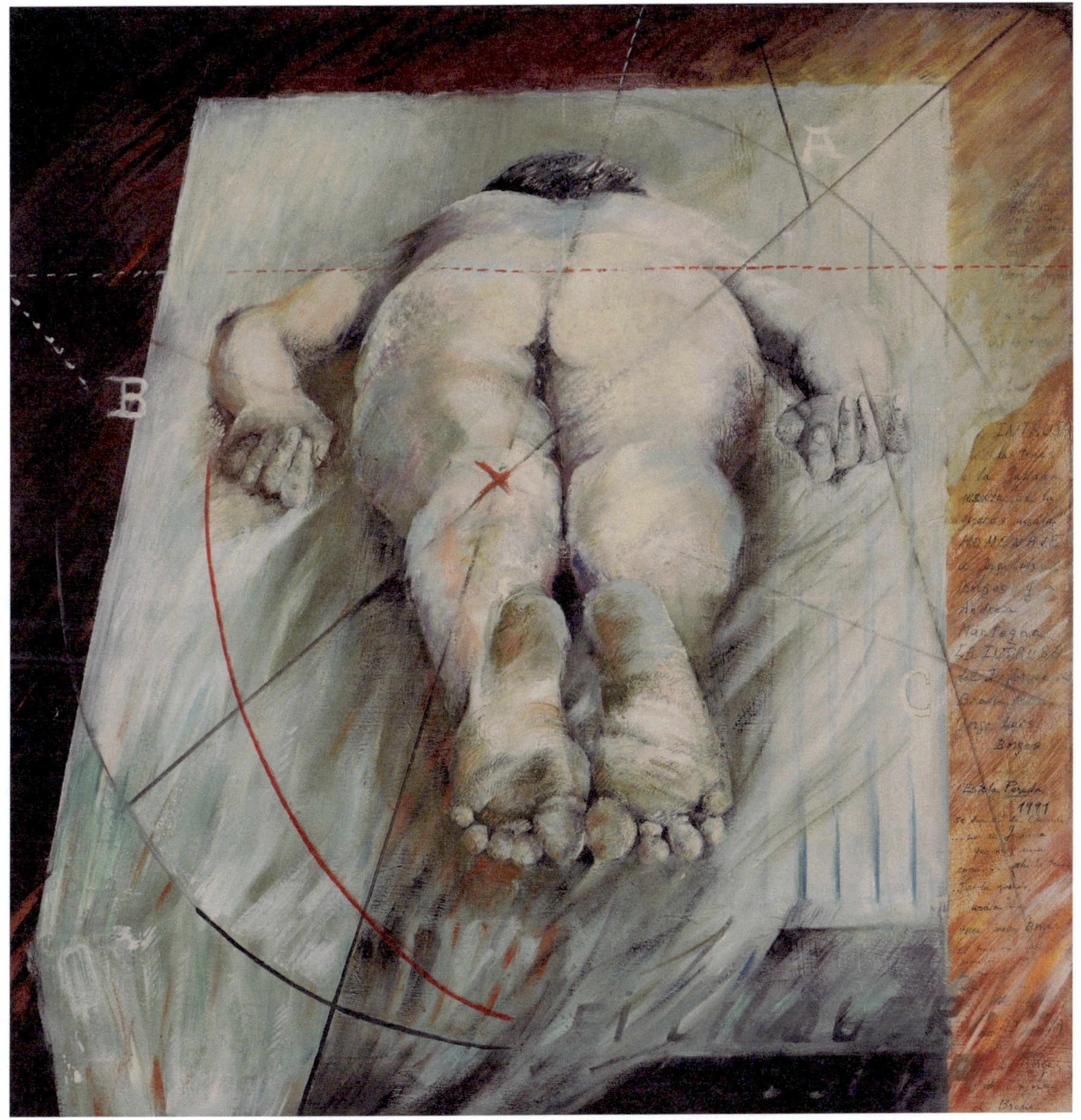

VII. Estela Pereda, *"Si la querés, usála"* (If You Want Her, Use Her), 1991, 39.5" × × 39.5", oil on canvas.

Some of the original writing has been partly erased, as if to emphasize the desire of the brothers to eliminate the memory of the woman who had come between them.

As a woman, Pereda is particularly sensitive to the view of women revealed in the story and picks Cristián's words, offering Juliana to Eduardo, as the focus of her interpretation. The painting is a powerful expression of the feelings and views in the story. The work is part of the series "Torsos and Measurements" that Pereda created between 1985 and 1997, where the signs and drawings that accompany the human figures in the works are intended to reveal and evaluate the interior feelings of men and women, that is, qualities that paradoxically are impossible to translate into traditional measurements and drawings. The aim is to rescue the sacred in humans and nature, a veiled reference to Pythagoras and his view that the universe is made up of numbers. As her dedication to Mantegna indicates, Pereda is strongly influenced by the Renaissance and its revival of Greek and Roman antiquity in the treatment of the human body.

Pereda's piece presents us with a woman lying down on a kind of mattress, bed, or table, which is mostly covered with a sheet. We see the woman from behind, her feet are close to us and her head farther away. She is nude. The only part of her head we see is her black hair. Her arms are loosely stretched on the sides of her body, with semi-opened hands. Apart from her feet, the most prominent part of the body to the viewer is the lower back. The wide hips and thighs are the sort traditionally coveted by men looking for pleasure particularly in the unsophisticated countryside, but we are not sure whether she is alive or dead. The immobility of the pose suggests unconsciousness, a living being that has ceased to exist. Traces of orange and red on the sheet might indicate that we are looking at Juliana's body after Cristián has killed her. But most likely the position of the body merely suggests submission—the acceptance of Cristián's offer to Eduardo, and her treatment as a mere thing, an object to be used and disposed off by men at their will and pleasure. There is no evidence of violence on the body. Maybe the figure indicates mental and spiritual, rather than physical, death.

Juliana has no say in any matter of interest to the brothers, even matters that pertain to her, her future, affection, or wishes. Here is a body to be used as a man wishes, a body without will or thought, an object of pleasure or abuse. The position suggests complete submission, perhaps even sodomy, a brutal penetration from behind, where her face and eyes are irrelevant to the satisfaction of the *macho's* fantasies. Superimposed on the body is a circle with lines that cross off-center. Three lines cross in one place highlighted in reddish orange that also informs the background and of which there are vestiges on the sheet. This goes back to the series of "Torsos and Measurements" of which the painting is a part. The lines that crisscross the body are meant to reveal something about the inner workings of the person whose body we see. The circle is a symbol of wholeness, but it has been fragmented and divided by lines, meaning that the wholeness has been destroyed. Juliana is a broken woman, broken by the treatment she has to suffer at the will of the brothers. The cross is a reference to pain, sacrifice, and atonement. Juliana suffers the pain and is sacrificed to atone for the brothers' guilt.

In Borges's story, Pereda reads the condition of women and the feelings it generates, certainly at the time the story takes place, but perhaps even at the time the painting was produced. It becomes a symbol of women's position in society, where they become instruments of men to satisfy their needs, emotional and sexual. Their inward feelings are submission and perhaps fear. Men want and take women without asking, and they dispose of them when they consider that they have become useless or a nuisance. And yet, matters are not so simple, for down deep men struggle to keep hidden strong feelings of attachment, the yearning for their love. These masculine feelings are plain in the story, but Pereda has omitted reference to them in order to focus on the brutal condition of women. She paints Juliana in a position that harks back to Mantegna's *Lamentation over the Dead Christ,* where Jesus lies, face up, on a kind of bed similar to that on which Juliana rests, while women mourn him. But Juliana has no one to mourn her, if she is dead. Although she may not be physically dead, she is emotionally dead insofar as she submits without struggle to the will of the brothers. When she is killed by Cristián, her body is left for the buzzards to eat. She no longer merits attention after her death, after she has ceased to be of use, except as a bitter memory.

The painting ignores the relations among the various characters in the narrative to focus on the single point of the status of women, how they are treated by men, and the feelings at play. There are no references to the actions, events, or any character other than Juliana. Indeed, the only reference to the story comes in the use of the line from Borges in the title, and the added part on the writing "there you have her." The lack of attention to particularity makes it clear that the work makes a universal statement unrelated to the idiosyncracies of the tale.

Etienne Gontard's *La intrusa* uses a very different approach to Borges's story from that employed by Pereda's interpretation. There is more narrative in it, and the artist depicts all major players in the tale. The point of view is not feminine or feminist; the painting focuses more on a key scene of the narrative that reveals the human and sexual relations at play in the story. It is the moment when the two brothers meet at the brothel and decide to bring Juliana back after the older brother had sold her to the madam.

The principal characters are presented in a room. There is no obviously central figure in the painting. On the upper left-hand side we see a barred window frequently used in bordellos

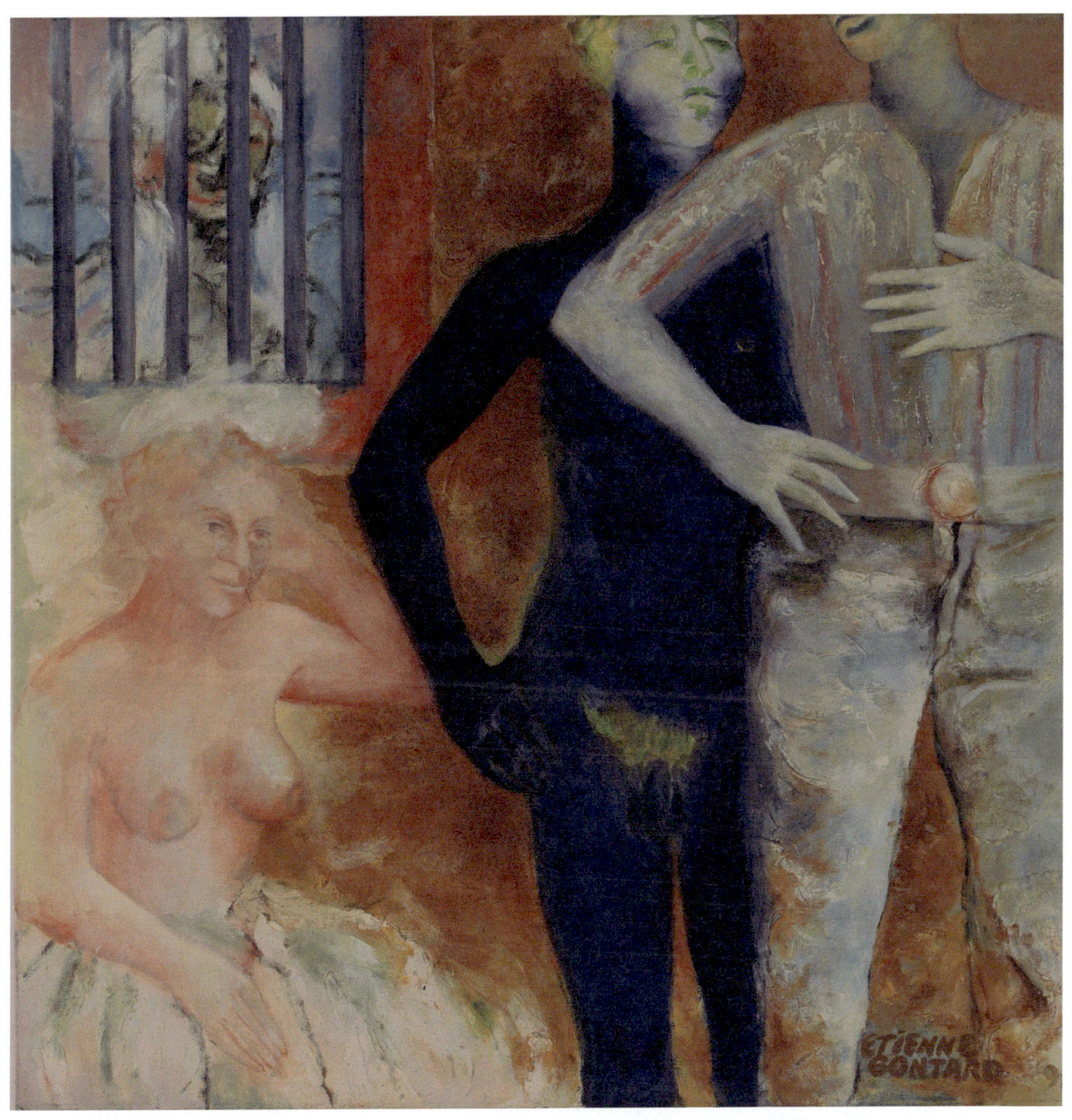

VIII. Etienne Gontard, *La intrusa* (The Interloper), 1991, 39.5" × × 39.5", acrylic on canvas.

at the time to protect the madam, the outlines of whose ghastly face are revealed through them. Below the window, another woman, Juliana, is sitting, and on the right of the picture two male figures, Cristián and Eduardo, stand. Juliana is nude from the waist up, while she arranges her hair with her left hand in a maybe coquettish fashion. She wants to appear pretty, and perhaps she is glad to go back to the brothers—to be shared by two young men who are in some fashion in love with her and shower her with ghastly trinkets and dresses is much better than to be the object of pleasure by many occasional seekers of sex. She has full breasts with generous nipples, and her countenance is appealing. The expression on her face is thoughtful and her eyes, echoing the description in the story, are slightly slanted, perhaps an indication of mixed blood, but she has blonde hair, perhaps another sign of mixing or just an artifice of attraction. The two brothers on the right are close together and appear to be engaged in conversation. The farthest to the right is slightly taller than the one to the left, and he is fully clothed. His right hand is resting on his hip in a kind of delicate pose and his left hand is set against his heart, a gesture that indicates his love for the male next to him, his brother. We see only his chin and part of his mouth, perhaps appropriately since it is he that we hear speak most frequently in the narrative—the rest of the head is outside the picture. Next to, and partly behind, him we see the other male. He is nude, with a body painted in dark blue, except for his face, which takes the same color as that of the other male figure, and the hair on the head and between his legs, which is blond with some tenuous references to red. The color suggests that he is a shadow, a negative of his brother, who is the more powerful presence in the story, and the one who takes initiatives and makes decisions about their lives and their relationship. The highlighting of his hair on the head and the pubic area indicates possible sources for the feelings he entertains for his brother—the face and genitals.

Juliana is prominently presented, and the only fully depicted character in the work, revealing that she is a key figure in the composition. The two brothers, by contrast, are only partly presented, one evident mostly in body, indicating that they are secondary to her. However, the fact that the two brothers occupy a place at the forefront of the painting vouches for their importance. But, we may ask, is one more important than the other? The one that occupies the forefront would appear to be so in virtue of this fact, although most of his face is hidden. The other is fully presented, but he is slightly behind. That one of the brothers is nude indicates he is Eduardo, the younger brother. His unexpected nudity suggests both that, in contrast with his fully dressed brother, he is more vulnerable and more conflicted about his strong physical attraction to Juliana. His actions are also more erratic and irrational—he leaves and returns, he finds a substitute for Juliana and throws her out—whereas the older brother's sensitivity leads him to share Juliana with Eduardo and then eventually kill her. He is more detached and rational even if more ruthless and cruel. Both perceive the problem her presence has created, the unspoken rift and rivalry between brothers who love each other. But the older brother's analysis of their predicament is more accurate and explicit, and his ultimate solution more permanent; Juliana's murder is despicable, but it is the only move Cristián can think of to deal with their situation in a world in which women are mere objects to men. The figure of the madam is shadowy, devoid of personal characterization, no more than a reference to the social context.

In contrast with Pereda's focus on one element of the story, Gontard's interpretation presents us with a more comprehensive approach, although he leaves various strands for the audience to follow. He omits reference to the details of the action, the brothers' trips and their discussions, the return of Juliana to the bordello, and Juliana's murder. Instead, he focuses on the closeness of the brothers, the love of the older for the younger, the passion of the younger for Juliana, the misconstrued rationality of the older, Juliana's condition as a mere and marginal object of desire, the horror of the madam, and the condition of women in society. But the location and depiction of the two brothers in the painting, their close proximity, the gesture and tilt of the head of the older toward the younger, and the nudity of the younger, who stands between the older brother and Juliana, may suggest the existence of more than brotherly love between them. Is there a homoerotic factor at play in the story, whether it does or not materialize in a relationship, or even becomes the subject of explicit awareness in either of them? And if this is the case, then what is the function of the woman? Is she an obstacle to the continuation, or fulfillment, of the desire of the brothers for each other and thus the reason she is eliminated, even though she may have served to obscure this forbidden attraction for a time? Or is Juliana's role to satisfy their forbidden love for each other as an intermediary?

A last point to note is that Juliana and the madam are tied by a kind of white effluence, a white fog that seems to unite them, and that they occupy a part of the picture separate from that occupied by the brothers. Do they share something that separates them from the males? Are they both victims, in their different roles, of men's passions, domination, and cruelty? And which of them is trapped by the bars on the window, bars that may symbolize society or the complex human relations that surround the women? Is the madam looking into a cell where Juliana is, or is she trapped in the bordello from which Juliana is being rescued by the brothers? Juliana may be happy for her liberation, but her only way out seems ultimately to lead to her death at the hand of the master that society has given her.

6

The Garden of Forking Paths

"The Garden of Forking Paths" is one of Borges's most frequently discussed stories. It raises a variety of questions that philosophers, literary critics, and artists have found fascinating. One, for example, concerns the status of the infinite possibilities that open up at every instant of time: Are they real or unreal? Do I drink a cup of coffee or a cup of tea? If I drink a cup of coffee, what is the status of the cup of tea that I did not drink? And if I drink a cup of tea, what is the status of the cup of coffee? What are the differences between them and how are they related to truth? The problem is immortalized in Chapter 9 of Aristotle's *On Interpretation*, where he raises the question of the truth value of a proposition about a sea battle that would happen the next day, such as, "The battle will be won by the Athenians."

Another related question has to do with freedom and destiny. How does the infinite number of possibilities that open up at every fork of the road in our lives affect our future choices and destinies? For some, it is clear that we are free to choose, but each choice opens and closes further avenues. If I have two choices, A and B, and I choose A, that opens up a seemingly endless number of further possibilities, but it excludes B, including another infinite number of possibilities. Are we, then, free because we can choose, even if the choices impose on us a framework of further choices?

The story, like many others from Borges is actually a tale within a tale, complicated even further by the facts that the main narrative on which it is based is missing the first two first pages and the tale is self-reported in the *History of the European War.* The war in question is supposed to be the First World War, and the history written by Liddel Hart. However, Hart never wrote a book with this title, the page references to the books he wrote do not coincide with Borges's references in the various editions of this story, and Borges's mention of *el Jefe* in it fits Hitler's profile. This and other incongruities suggest the war in question is the Second World War. One story functions as a fold for the other, and the weave of relations between the two opens unexpected avenues of meaning and interpretation. The narrative is signed by Dr. Yu Tsun, a former professor of English in the *Hochschule* at Tsingtao.

The events take place in England. Col. Richard Madden, a determined Irishman, has discovered that Tsun, a consular official and a spy for the Third Reich, and Runeberg, his associate, have uncovered the location of the new British artillery park on the Ancre and are looking for a way to convey this information to the Leader, so the German air force can bomb it. Tsun has found out that Runeberg has either been arrested or killed and he must finish the task by himself. But how is he to convey the name of the town to the Leader? His aim is not the glory of Germany, a nation he considers barbaric. He is merely trying to demonstrate to the Leader—a despicable man whom he hates because he thinks Tsun's race inferior—that a yellow man can save his armies.

The solution becomes clear to Tsun, although it is not revealed to the reader until the very end of the narrative. He must kill a man with the name of the town where the British artillery park is located, so that when this is published, the Germans will know where to attack. The name of the city is Albert, so Tsun looks up the address of a person with that name in the telephone book. After he finds it, he searches in his pockets for the gun with one bullet that he will need in order to accomplish his task. Albert lives in Ashgrove, so Tsun takes a train there, although he carefully buys a ticket to a different town to cover his tracks. As the train pulls out, he sees Madden at the end of the platform, but he has gained an advantage. He arrives at his destination and is given directions to Albert's house: "The house is far away, but you'll not get lost if you follow that road there to the left, and turn left at every corner." This is the way, Tsun recalls, to find the center of a certain kind of maze.

The connection with mazes brings him to the memory of his grandfather, Ts'ui Pen, governor of Yunan province, who gave up his temporal power in order to write a novel and construct a labyrinth. At this point begins the second tale within the tale. For Pen had spent thirteen years in his tasks and had died presumably without completing them, since no one has been able to find the labyrinth and the manuscript of the novel he left looks like a jumble of chaotic writings.

As Tsun approaches Albert's house, he is surprised to hear Chinese music coming from a gazebo. Albert opens the gate and greets him in Chinese. He asks Tsun if he wishes to see the garden of forking paths, which turns out to be Pen's garden. Tsun is intrigued and decides that he has some time before he kills Albert, who proceeds to tell him that he had solved the mystery surrounding Pen's labyrinth. No one had found the labyrinth because everyone thought that the novel he had retired to write and the labyrinth he intended to build were two different things. In fact, they are one and the same. The novel, just like a labyrinth, is full of contradictions. Albert found the key to the puzzle in a letter from Pen in which he had written: "I leave to several futures (not all) my garden of forking paths." Albert figured out that *The Garden of Forking Paths* is a huge riddle, a parable whose subject is time." This is why the term 'time' never appears in the novel, which is an image of Pen's conception of the universe. In it, all possibilities are revealed. "Time forks, perpetually, into countless futures." Unlike Newton and Schopenhauer, who thought of time as uniform and absolute, Pen thought there was an infinite series of times, "a growing, dizzying web of divergent, convergent, and parallel times." That is why in one chapter of the novel the protagonist dies, and in a subsequent one he is alive. The possibilities are infinite, forking into different paths that open up endlessly.

At this point Tsun sees Madden approaching, and so he acts. He asks Albert to show him again the letter where he had found the key to the puzzle, and when Albert turns to get it, he shoots him. Tsun is arrested and sentenced to hang, but he succeeds in the task he had set for himself. The Leader understands the clue and the city of Albert is bombarded. Both stories end with Tsun's expression of contrition and weariness.

Nicolás Menza has produced two works with the title of Borges's story, differentiated only in that the second adds "II" to the title. The works are of the same size and were created in the same year. I focus on the first, whose image is reproduced here, although I make a passing reference to the second.

The central figure of the painting is a nude woman in profile, walking. Her head is bowed in a thoughtful gesture, and her figure casts a shadow in front of her on a vividly red-colored circle whose missing part appears to include the observer. She has come down a set of concrete stairs, with seven steps, that lead to a platform. Beyond the circle is a forest of lush and beautifully colored trees, in greens and blues, with occasional reds and browns. On the floor of the forest, paths bifurcate into further paths again and again, until we lose sight of them in the distance. The paths stand out by their yellow color against the green grass sprinkled with hints of flowers.

Menza has used Borges's works extensively. Indeed, Borges has been a strong influence throughout his life. But he never retells a story already told by Borges. Rather than focusing on the literal narrative, he seeks a point of unification, which is temporal and symbolic, and reveals a metaphysical core of the sort Borges is so fond. Menza sometimes begins with an intuitive idea evoked by the text, but in most cases he completes a work first and only then does he make a connection to a specific text.

As is usual with him, Menza has not tried to tell the details of Borges's "The Garden of Forking Paths." In this case he has changed the protagonist into a woman, and he has left out everything in the story, with the exception of the garden, which has become a forest of trees and, contrary to Albert's hypothesis, not a text. Still, Menza's work captures and expresses some of the key elements of the story that perhaps are less obvious to those focused on the action. One is the very idea of the garden as being not just a garden, but a lush and beautiful forest that functions as a metaphor for an unclear and mysterious, but enticing, future. We do not know it; we see only part of what is ahead, and cannot tell what is beyond the turns we take when we encounter bifurcating choices. The future is in itself undetermined, but our decisions determine it. The shadow in front of the figure is cast by the woman who decided to walk in a certain direction. But it is a shadow, and it is not clear what it will bring with it, for there are other forks, and endless possibilities. The woman does not know what the entire future will be, only the choices open to her at a particular time.

The platform behind the woman from which she proceeds may refer to the fact that in order to find our way in the world, we need to come down from the position of observer; we need to enter the garden and act, walk, and choose. A platform such as the one depicted by Menza is usually reserved for immobile statues, whereas living beings move on the earth. The safety and solidity of the platform on which we stand must be abandoned to join the world of reality, where insecurity and uncertainty face us.

Who is the woman? One way to think of her is as a symbol for every one of us. All of us originate in a woman, so a woman can represent both humanity as a whole and each of us in particular. Individually we live in a world with a particular horizon—the red circle in which the woman in slowly walking—but we are surrounded by endless choices that lead in different directions and bifurcate into further directions indefinitely. More specifically, she can also be a symbol of Eve, the first woman and the one blamed for our Fall from Paradise.

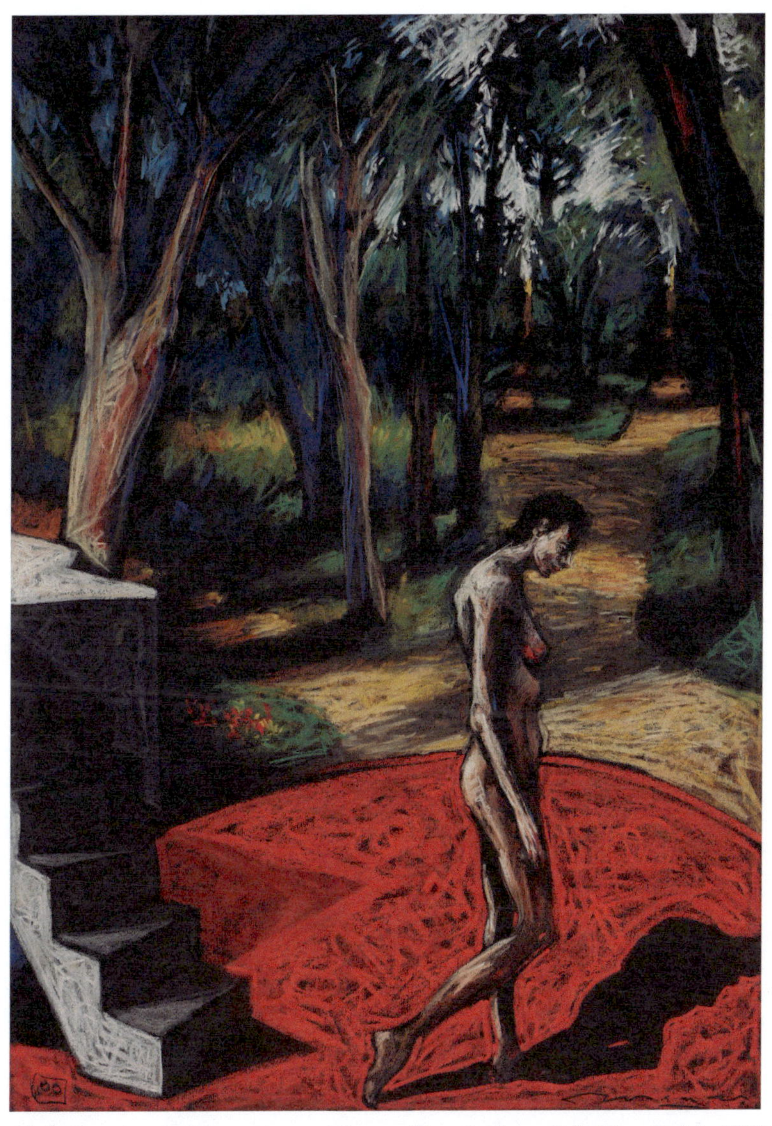

IX. Nicolás Menza, *El jardín de senderos que se bifurcan* (The Garden of Forking Paths), 2000, 39.5" × 27.5", pastel on paper.

Here she is placed in a forest, lush and beautiful, that evokes the Garden of Eden, but she is pensive, her head bowed in deep thought, and she is separated from the forest in that she is encircled, although she is walking, perhaps aiming to cross the circle and enter the forking labyrinths of the forest. Does this refer to the life of choices to which she is bound after the Fall? Has she already made the choice that will eventually lead her out of Paradise? If she is coming from the platform behind her, perhaps the main choice has already been made, with the platform standing for the state she was in before the choice to eat the apple was made. The whiteness and solidity of the platform hark back to a state of grace, in which life is simple and secure, of solid ground, and an ideal state created by God. Or is she pondering what to do, what forking path to take? Does she know the enormous implications of her choice, the imponderable consequences that it will bring about? The light in the picture provides no guidance, for the shadows projected by the figures conflict, sometimes going one way and at other times going other ways. There is no definite order, no indication of the rational and logical way to walk. And she is not looking at her surroundings, where perhaps she could find a clue to the direction she should follow. Rather, she is looking down, apparently not anywhere in particular, or perhaps she is observing her shadow projected on the ground, a premonition of the dark and painful future that awaits her. Possibly, the shadow may be a sign of the internal struggle she is undergoing.

Even though Borges's story is about men, no man is present in the painting. If the woman we see is Eve, then the man to accompany her would be Adam. But he is nowhere to be found, because the important choice is the woman's. Adam is a kind of clown in Genesis. He has the authority and what he decides counts because he was created by another masculine entity, God. He is *el macho,* but he is weak and stupid; he lacks interest. The intriguing figure is Eve, and the serpent knows it. The Devil chooses her because he knows that she will be attracted to the apple from the tree of knowledge. She wants to know good and evil, and she is the one who sins first. The rest of the story is merely the unfolding of the consequences of her decision and its translation into the masculine culture of the ancient Hebrews. So she convinces Adam to go along with her. Adam is absent from Menza's work, because he is irrelevant. The key to Genesis and to humankind is the female, and she is represented in Menza's painting with all the gravity that the situation requires.

If we take the woman in the picture to be Eve, then the garden of forking paths can be either the world in which she lives or the world outside Paradise that she will enter. The first interpretation is doubtful in that she appears to be walking so as to leave behind the world in which she had lived, symbolized by the platform from which she comes and the circle that encompasses her. It makes sense to think that, although she made a decision in Paradise, the everyday world of decision making is the one she will enter, one in which she will be asked to decide at every moment and to chart her future.

The static and grave solitude projected by the picture contrasts with its brilliant colors, the greens, almost phosphorescent blues, and the yellows and reds. This painting is without a doubt a landscape of sorts, but it is also clearly not a landscape. The trees are not trees. There seems to be no intention to paint trees or a landscape. The female figure appears in a space that extends well beyond her. She is not presented in front of a wall, as in other paintings by Menza, but placed in a dynamic location where we can see her from various angles and in front of various places. In other paintings he uses plazas or constructions of diverse sorts, but here he has depicted a forest that in some ways resembles the stage of a theater, a backdrop for the space where the action takes place and which integrates the spectator.

In *Los jardines que se bifurcan*, Carlos Estévez adopts in some ways a strategy similar to the one used by Menza. Estévez did not begin his interpretation of Borges's "The Garden of Forking Paths" by going first to the story and attempting a close illustration of it as a whole or in any of its parts. Rather, he began with the title and the memories he had of having read it. Only after he had finished his work did he go back to the story to see how his own original intuitions could be used to approach Borges's story and reveal important dimensions of it.

There are also similarities between the artists in the strong influence that Borges's work has exerted on both throughout the years, although it is only recently that Estévez has produced art dealing directly with particular works of Borges. His first work inspired by Borges, *El inmortal,* was produced in 1996. The attraction that Borges has exerted for Estévez has to do especially with Borgesian methodology. Like Borges, Estévez is a collector of bits of knowledge that are appropriated and then integrated into a vision of the human condition and the nature of the universe. And both, Borges and Estévez, seek to develop a kind of encyclopedia of human understanding that originates in the particular but aims at universality. Both are attracted to conceptual conundrums they effectively pose for their audiences but whose solution is ultimately left unresolved for the most part.

The title of Estévez's painting introduces an important change in the theme of the story. "Forking gardens" means something quite different from "the garden of forking paths." Indeed, in the first we have many gardens that fork in different directions, but in the second we have one garden that has many paths that fork in different directions. In the artist's work a plurality of domains contain many possibilities, whereas in Borges's story a single domain contains many possibilities.

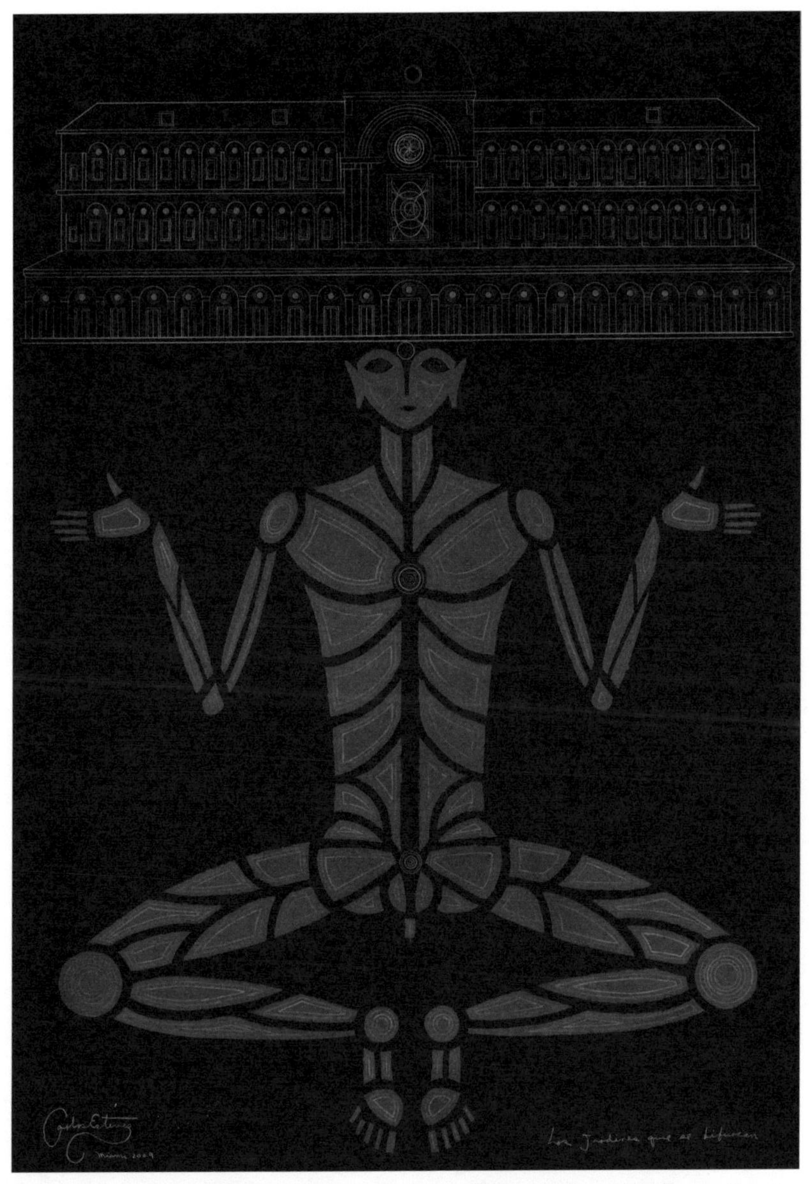

X. Carlos Estévez, *Los jardines que se bifurcan* (Forking Gardens), 2009, 39.5" × 27.5", pencil and gouache on paper.

Los jardines que se bifurcan presents us with one of the puppets that characterize a good number of Estévez's works. This time, unlike other art, there are no lines coming from above suggesting controlling forces other than the will of the figure. The body of the puppet looks like a collection of pieces, separated by spaces, but maintaining an overall form and harmony. The figure is colored in a brilliant green that immediately catches the attention of the observer and stands out from the black background. The separated parts of the body are crisscrossed with curved emerald-blue lines that, together with the spaces that separate the parts, lead in various directions.

Each of the parts suggests a different garden, rather than just a part of a single, larger garden, with paths that fork not only in different ways externally, but also within. The entire body of the puppet becomes a web of possibilities, of movements, decisions, and directions. One leads to others, which in turn lead to still others in a physical labyrinth that echoes the maze Albert discovered in Pen's novel, of which Estévez's work is a visual interpretation.

Decisions come from the mind and its inward deliberations, so the painting depicts the puppet in a meditating posture. His face—and the puppet is masculine since there is a penis hanging between his legs—is enigmatic. The pupils are drawn as large, concentric circles disproportionate to the space occupied by the eyes, and they are rendered in a lighter color that contrasts both with the intense emerald-blue of the body and the dark black of the background. They suggest a hypnotic trance or a mystical state. The eyes find echoes in three mandalas, one on the forehead, one on the heart, and the third on the groin. These are the centers of power: the mind involving rationality and knowledge, the heart embodying emotions and feelings, and the groin pointing to the appetites and particularly the libido. The mandala means wholeness, unity, and the subconscious, a place where the mystic finds integration with the universe.

At the top of the work, Estévez has put a building that takes the place of the puppet's brain. Its classical architectural style harks back to the origins of rational thinking associated with Greece. Each of the stories has rows of windows or doors, indicating sources of light, vantage points of observation, and seemingly endless possibilities of entering, leaving, and exploring. The building could also be a large library, another metaphor commonly used by Borges, that becomes an encyclopedia, a compendium of all knowledge. Or, perhaps, in closer relation to the story, it could symbolize Pen's novel, itself a metaphor for the universe, in which all possible outcomes and times are realized.

The composition of the work suggests that the puppet is deliberating because he believes he is free to choose. But the choice at every point opens and closes possibilities, both expanding and limiting his freedom and directing it toward a destiny unrecorded in the picture. Most importantly, the choices are internal, not external. The paths to follow are to be found in the very body and mind of the puppet as he meditates and channels his decisions through his body.

One last point is significant: although the puppet is in a meditative position, his arms and hands are open, in the eastern gesture we are used to seeing when a Catholic priest addresses an audience at mass and tells them *"Dominus vobiscum."* Perhaps the puppet does not wish God to be with those of us who see the picture, but rather intends to communicate a lesson learned from Borges's story, the universality and inexhaustible possibilities available in the universe.

7

The Circular Ruins

In "The Circular Ruins," Borges ostensibly discusses two of his favorite topics, the nature of time and the nature of reality, which in turn constitute venues to explore two other constants of his work, freedom and destiny. The imagery of the story and its title evoke the notion that time is cyclical and reality is appearance. The first was popular among pre-Socratic philosophers, some of whom thought that the past is endlessly repeated in the future, and it is echoed in Ecclesiastes, in the claim that nothing is new under the sun. The second view, that what we consider to be reality is appearance, was famously defended by Plato.

Neither view finds fertile ground in the West. Against the first, Augustine, inspired by the Judeo-Christian tradition, claimed that time is directional and there is an ultimate denouement in the universe. Likewise, philosophers like Aristotle and Descartes argued vigorously against the second view. Interwoven with the questions of time and reality are those concerned with freedom and destiny. If time is cyclical and we are mere simulacra, what do we make of our freedom and destiny? Perhaps the Stoics were right and we are free only to the extent that we understand our impotence to change the course of events. History is bound to repeat itself endlessly, and so are we, but unlike inanimate objects, we can arrive at that secret, and terrifying, understanding.

Borges's story takes its title from the location where the action occurs. A sorcerer, gray, taciturn, and ignorant of his name or of any details of his prior life, arrives by canoe at, and drags himself to, a "circular enclosure, crowned by the stone figure of a horse or a tiger, which had once been the color of fire and was now the color of ashes"—a former temple destroyed by fire. His immediate obligation is to sleep, but his supernatural goal is to dream a man.

He dreams that he is at the center of the circular amphitheater at the center of the ruined temple. He is surrounded by taciturn students from different centuries and locations, to whom he lectures on anatomy, cosmography, and magic, hoping to find one he can insert into reality. Some students are passive observers, but his expectations are encouraged by those who raise objections. From them, he chooses one who resembles himself, and makes amazing progress. However, disaster strikes and he is unable to continue dreaming in spite of his efforts. The lucidity of insomnia appalls him and he realizes the extraordinary difficulty of bringing order into the chaotic stuff of dreams.

Once the sorcerer gives up on his premeditated effort, he immediately begins to sleep again, although he is no longer focused on his dreams. During the full moon, he purifies himself, bows to the astral gods, and utters a powerful name. He falls asleep and almost immediately dreams a warm, active, and secret heart. Slowly, the dream progresses to the whole body, but the youth is still lifeless. Frustrated, the sorcerer prays to the god, who now appears to him simultaneously as horse, tiger, bull, rose, and tempest. The god reveals that his name is Fire and that he will bring to life the sorcerer's human creation in such a way that everyone but the god and the sorcerer will think the dreamed man is real. But, he orders the dreamer to send the youth away to the circular ruins down the river once he has been properly instructed, so that "a voice might glorify the god in that deserted place." The sorcerer obeys the god's instruction, although it pains him to think of his eventual separation from his creation. Once the son is ready, he erases his memory, so that he does not know that he is a mere simulacrum of the sorcerer's dreams, and then sends him away, thereby accomplishing the goal he had set out for himself.

After a few years, the sorcerer hears of a magical man, who can walk through fire without being burned, in a temple in the north. He knows it is his son, and fears that he might find out he is a projection of the sorcerer's dreams. His meditations end suddenly, when a Holocaust that had been predicted consumes the ruined temple. When the Fire does not burn him, he realizes, with relief, humiliation, and terror, that he, too, is another man's dream.

In the story, reality is the stuff of dreams. We are mere simulacra imagined by others, who are themselves simulacra, imaginings of others. The process of dreaming is repeated eternally, cyclically, bringing order out of chaos, not out of a conscious effort, but following the inexorable laws of the universe, in an endless Heraclitean flux. It is only the realization of this truth that can bring us relief.

In *Ruinas circulares*, Nicolás Menza paints a familiar figure of a nude woman. She is portrayed frontally, from the upper part of the chest up, with her head slightly turned so that we still see both of her closed eyes. Her red hair is short, her partly revealed breasts full, and

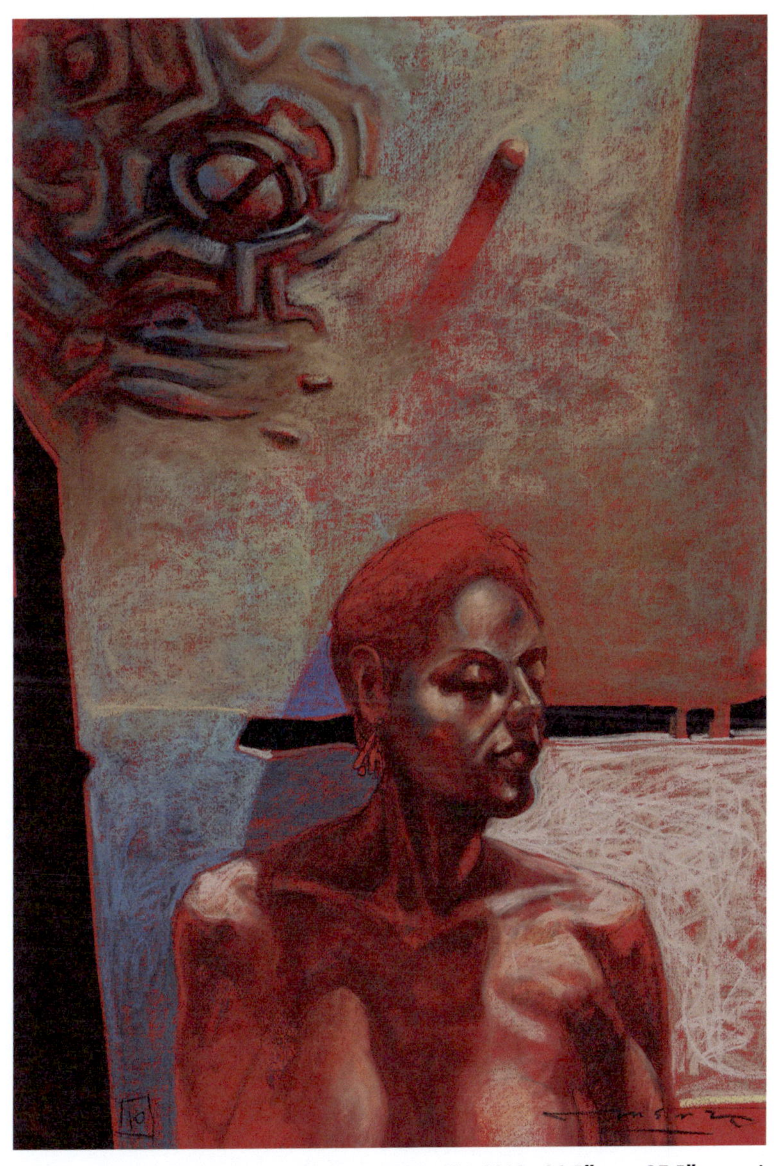

XI. Nicolás Menza, *Ruinas circulares II (Circular Ruins II)*, 2010, 39.5" × 27.5", pastel on paper.

her body strong. We see only one of her ears, from which hangs an elaborate earring of archaic design. Her features are forceful and lean; this is a woman who has lived and who has a firm character. Most importantly, she seems to be profoundly asleep, perhaps dreaming.

The female figure is set against a wall, as many others in Menza's paintings are. The wall breaks up into spaces dominated by one or two colors that merge into, and reveal, others. In the upper part, white and red predominate, merging into blues and oranges, and ending up in a blue block to the left. Toward the lower end of the picture, on the right, a tri-dimensional dark divider that extends across almost the full length of the picture suggests a horizon of sorts, which breaks up into three smaller parts—square, rectangular, of different sizes, perhaps evoking buildings—to make room below for a primarily white space, in turn divided at the bottom by a thick, yellow line from a red, square space that balances the painting and supports part of Menza's dark signature. At the far left a dark structure tapers up and introduces an element of finality. Near the top of the work, a dot, red and white, casts a shadow. The woman is located off center, slightly to the right, leaving room for the other most significant item depicted in the work: a geometrical composition of lines, figures, and circles resembling a labyrinth that appears to be a high relief of the ruins described in the story, placed on a wall and occupying the upper left-hand corner. It recalls a pre-Columbian ruin, rendered in blues, reds, and earth colors. The woman is partly covered by the light coming from the top left, with parts of her body in the shade.

This is not the only painting by Menza that uses the same theme. Four others, painted in 1999—*Ruinas circulares, Desideratum, Vigilia,* and *El eclipse*—also portray a woman in slightly different poses accompanied by similar geometrical artifacts in the left-hand corners of the works.

Obviously, Menza gives us a very free interpretation of Borges, but one that captures effectively one aspect of the Borgesian universe. Being an avid reader of Borges, he is not interested in the illustration of particular aspects of the story, although the painting plays with some elements of it. One cannot but think of fire when presented with the vivid reds that permeate the work, reflected like flames on the cheeks and part of the woman's body, and frequently appearing under variously colored crayon marks. Menza approaches his task by attempting to capture the structure of Borges's thought. His allusions have to do with the atemporal and recurrent themes of the Borgesian universe, the use of circularity to refer to recurrence, the fuzzy divide between dreaming and reality, and the ever-present notion of a labyrinth in which we are forever lost. Most salient are the dreamlike state of the woman and the artifact depicted in the corner. Perhaps the closed eyes indicate that the woman is dreaming the artifact that represents the ruins of the story, or perhaps the light that bathes her is a sign of an epiphany. Instead of a male sorcerer we have a female, but one who appears to have lived and weathered much. There is no attempt to portray her as a priestess; she is rather a preternatural figure who bridges the imaginary gap between fact and fiction. The rough circularity of the presumed ruins suggests the world, although its parts evoke the imperfections that characterize it. Perhaps Menza is giving us a glimpse of Borges's notion that the universe is our own creation, a point given further support by the absence of any other figure in the pastel.

The works inspired by Borges's "The Circular Ruins" mark an important development for Menza as an artist, because they explore the effect of light coming from outside the work and the resulting shadows that appear on it, almost as actors in the drama being enacted. The block of white paint on the right, with its heavy strokes, functions like a reflector that illuminates key elements of the female figure and leaves parts of her body in a penumbra. The shadows are balanced by the dark line that crosses the work behind the woman's head. What looks like a dowel inserted on the background wall, colored white and light red, also casts a shadow. The light shed on the picture further creates uncertainty in that it does not follow an expected pattern. It appears to be coming from the white patch on the right, but some shadows in the picture also suggest that it is coming from above. Is this a symbol of the revelation that finally dawns on the priest in the story? Part of the strength of this work rests on its simplicity. An intuition surfacing from the unconscious anchors the free associations of the audience.

Mirta Kupferminc's *Con el fuego* focuses on the fire and the structure of the ruins, rather than on the dreamer of Borges's story. The first thing the observer notices when approaching the work is fire, arranged in circles that evoke the circular ruins to which Borges refers. We see at least a half dozen circles, each inside another. The flames rise from them and reach higher at the far end of the picture. They are blue, although in some places they turn orange, purple, red, yellow, and green. The ground has the colors red and orange associated with fire and the black typical of coal and burned objects. The upper background of the work is taken up with what at first appear to be clouds of smoke in various shades and values of brown, although we also see some pinks, reds, and intense yellows and oranges suggestive of fire. On closer examination, however, these seeming clouds turn out to be partly burned pieces of paper at various stages of incineration. They form a kind of mandala, at the center of which we see, although not clearly, another, and perhaps many, progressively small, others—a reference to dreamers dreaming others who also dream others. Superimposed on them is what looks like a human female head and face with a body that resembles a bird. The hair is carefully gathered in an Eastern-style bun, which makes one think of the figure as a geisha wrapped in a kimono. But the image is not sufficiently clear so that one can tell for sure what we are looking at. Is it a female, or could it be

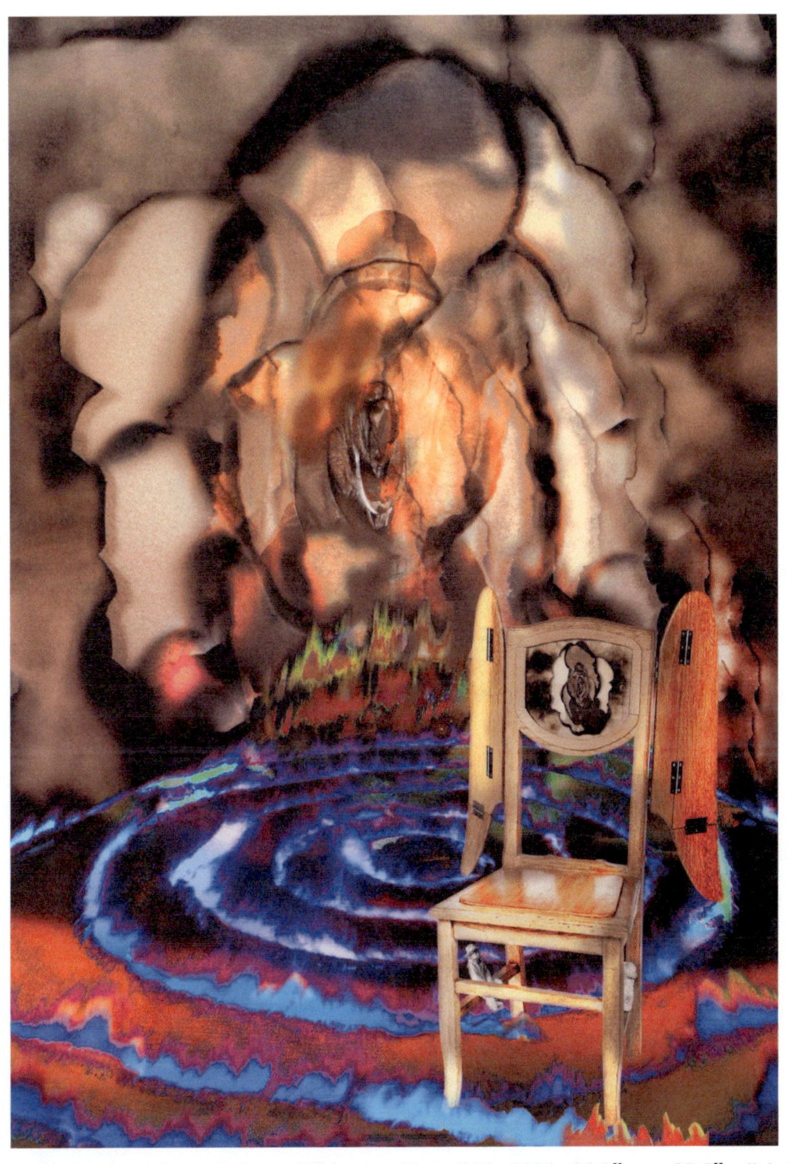

XII. Mirta Kupferminc, *Con el fuego* (With the Fire), 2/5, 2004, 39.5" × 27.5", digital print.

a male? One possibility is an endless line of sorcerers, each of whom is a simulacrum dreamed by another. Another is the god to which Borges refers, originally appearing to the sorcerer as a horse or tiger, and later as a horse, tiger, bull, rose, and tempest. And still another possibility is that these figures are representations of the poet also alluded to in other parts of the work.

An unusual element in this print, also frequently found in Kupferminc's art, is a chair, a motif that the artist began to use in 1994 and that informs much of her art since. Here it is located off center to the right. It is partly painted yellow and partly in the natural color of the wood, and has what look like open shutters in the shape of wings, hung on hinges. On the back of it we see a reproduction of the figure on the mandala above the circles of fire, surrounded by clouds. Two small men are sitting on the rungs that tie the front and back legs of the chair. The men look very much alike, dressed formally in white, wearing hats, and facing each other; they could be double images of the same man. The motif of the men also begins to appear in Kupferminc's work in 1994.

The painting has three intertwined foci. One is Fire, which is the god of the story, and cyclically creates, sustains, and destroys everything else. The basic substance of the work consists of the flames that burn the papers and in turn produce the second focus of the work, namely the simulacra we surmise on the background, vaguely suggested through the images on the burned paper. The third focus is the chair, which is inserted in the work and seems surprisingly unconnected to everything else happening in it. It is an implant, an object separate from both the fire and its effects, an extraneous element introduced to make a point. But what does it mean, and how is it related to the rest of the work?

A chair is a symbol of waiting, anticipation, rest, acceptance, observation, and study. It calls for someone to sit on it, cease action and observe, learn. Are we being invited to sit on it and get involved in the endless cycle of the universe? Are we being called to a peaceful rest in the midst of strife and destruction? Or does the chair signal the emptiness that follows our destruction in the process of nature? In Jewish culture, the locus of learning is a Yeshiva, a place to sit and learn. An empty chair also signals passing, leaving a vacancy where there had been life. There is also the possibility of interpreting it as the place of the redeemer, the Messiah that is expected. And what can we make of the wings? Wings symbolize escape, flight, and a search for freedom. The chair can be a symbol of meditation and study, but also of the flight that is possible through a free mind.

The two small male figures sitting on the rungs of the chair were originally three-dimensional, although made of clay and cement rather than wood. They are likenesses of the engraver Roberto Paez, a picture of whom impressed Kupferminc when she saw it in a magazine.

The figures symbolize the poet, the observer who sings of what he sees; but perhaps they also stand for the Jewish scholar, the learned man of the book. Another significant factor in the chair is that its back reproduces the image we see on the burned paper on the background. This brings up the question of the relation between the simulacra on the paper and the two little men. On one level of interpretation the men could be viewed as the simulacra to which Borges refers, the men made up of dreams, but appropriated by Kupferminc in her own system of symbols. Indeed, the two figures can themselves be regarded as copies of an original clay figure, itself a copy of the man who made them, and who is himself a simulacrum of clay made by God. The images on the burned paper and the back of the chair could be further simulacra, images created by the fire of life, which appear small and insignificant in contrast with the god Fire, indicating their minor role in the overall scheme of things.

But what if we see the background figures on the paper and the back of the chair as female? Then they become *personae* for the artist who takes the place of the sorcerer and is observed by the poet.

Kupferminc's work has taken Borges's story and placed it in the context of Jewish culture and mythology, giving it a meaning that speaks to a certain experience of the world. Although, as an artist, Kupferminc is primarily concerned with the formal structure of the work and its aesthetic qualities, she has sought to open Borges's story to an interpretation that at the outset would appear to be related to ideas and views that are far from what Borges may have had in mind. She has related the story not just to certain views of the human and the divine, but also to symbols that are common in a certain perspective on both. This approach shows how a story can be used to express and explore dimensions of an ethnos, adapting it to particular needs and wants.

8

The House of Asterion

"The House of Asterion" is one of Borges's shortest stories but, not for that reason, has it elicited less interest than many of the others. It fits well with Borges's fascination with labyrinths, because Asterion, whom Borges identifies with the Minotaur, lives in a labyrinth. This is a story of solitude and pain, the tragedy of a god who wants companionship, of man lost in a confusing universe from which he is unable to escape. It tells us of our own individual uniqueness and loneliness, of *angst* and death, and of the ignorance that pervades human existence. It also concerns destiny and the role we play in fulfilling it. The story places us on the pivot of freedom and determinism, which are perennial themes explored by writers, artists, and philosophers.

Are we really free when our destiny is already written on the stars, even if we appear to choose the very thing that is written? Does foreknowledge of the future necessarily determine it? Some argue that it does, insofar as what is correctly predicted necessarily happens, and necessity and freedom are incompatible. But others argue that foreknowledge does not impose necessity on what happens, insofar as it is not causally connected to the events in question. Borges does not take sides in the responses to these questions, but rather describes what happens to Asterion. It is for us to decide what this occurrence implies.

The story consists of a monologue by Asterion in which he disputes claims that he is arrogant, misanthropic, and mad. Although he never leaves his house, he is not a prisoner, for no doors are locked and anyone can enter. He does not leave it because of the terrible dread his presence inspires outside it. The house and he are unique, a reason why he cannot mix with ordinary people. He spends his time in multiple distractions and games, of which his favorite is imagining that "another" visits him. He shows the visitor the house, which is an interminable labyrinth, and laughs with him about the mistakes the Minotaur makes trying to find his way around it. The house is as big as the world, and is in fact the world. Indeed, it is possible that Asterion created it, along with the stars and the sun, and has forgotten about it.

Every nine years nine men come into the house to be freed from evil, and Asterion is overjoyed to meet them, but one by one they fall without him ever touching them. He leaves their bodies where they fall to help himself distinguish the interminable number of similar galleries and guide his wanderings. One of these men predicted the arrival of his redeemer, whom Asterion hopes will take him to a place with fewer galleries and doors. Will the redeemer be a man, a bull, or someone like Asterion? The story ends with a line from Theseus, the slayer of the Minotaur: "Would you believe it, Ariadne? The Minotaur scarcely defended himself."

From this we know that Asterion lets Theseus kill him, but is that his choice or is he bound by the prophecy? Is he voluntarily imprisoned or involuntarily trapped by his circumstances? And is his prison of his own creation or imposed on him? The story does not bend one way or the other. The situation is too complex and Asterion's predicament too terrifying to provide clear answers. But we do pity Asterion, more because he represents us than because of his own self.

And yet this might not be the most significant dimension of the story. Perhaps its point is rather that we are, like Asterion, composite monsters poorly adapted to the world, misfits residing in a place to which we do not belong. We crave something we cannot understand—love, communication, friendship, "another"—and end up killing it as Asterion appears to have done with his visitors. If this is so, we can understand why the only liberating exit is death.

In *La casa de Asterión*, Luis Cruz Azaceta has tried to express the feeling of pain in solitude that the Minotaur experiences, lost in his vast palace, which has become a trap for him. The work is done in black, grays, and white, symbolizing the melancholic mood of the story. The only exception is the set of nine red dots, presumably standing for the nine visitors who come to Asterion's house every nine years and perish during the visit. They symbolize companionship—a moment of communication to which Asterion looks forward with anxiety and happiness—that inexorably fails when the visitors drop dead one by one.

Azaceta has drawn the Minotaur as a human profile embedded on the house to indicate that he is both a part of, and trapped in, it. There is no sign of his nature as a bull, perhaps suggesting that this experience is all too human and applies to all of us: the Minotaur's predicament is the human predicament. He is either asleep or dead. His eyes are closed but the face has an expression of despair. Hard lines scar the forehead, the mouth, and the neck, indicating prolonged suffering. The mouth is frozen in a bitter rictus that could be the sign of reflective agony or postmortem rigidity. An incongruous mustache, almost comical, ironically graces the upper lip.

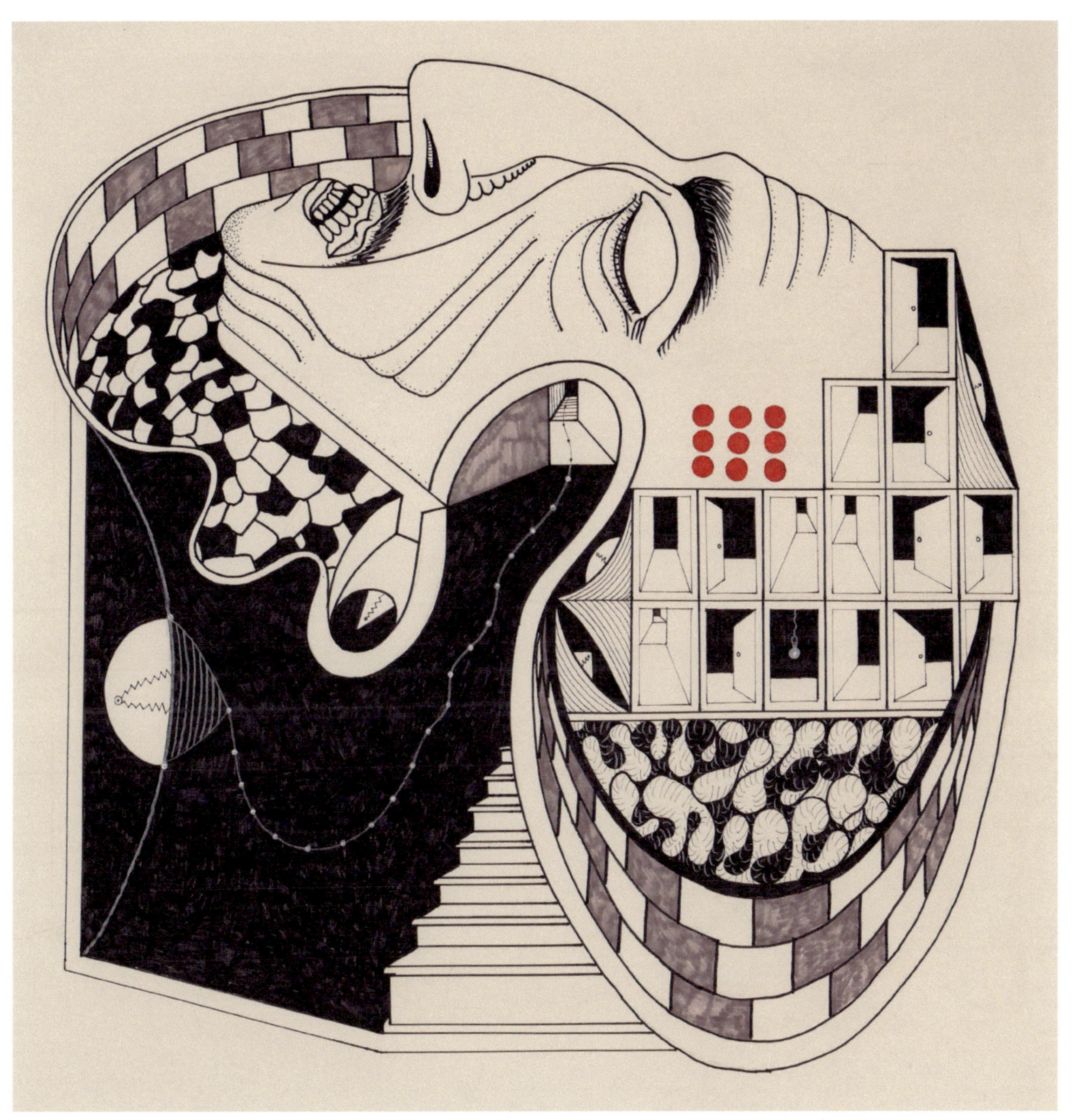

XIII. Luis Cruz Azaceta, *La casa de Asterión* (The House of Asterion), 2009, 29.5" × 29.5", markers on paper.

The rest of the work is devoted to the house, which is elaborately drawn. It has, as described by Asterion, exactly fourteen rooms and fourteen doors, signifying an infinite multitude. The rooms and doors vary in size, creating confusing messages as to their dimensions and relations. Some doors open to the right, some to the left, and some seem to open down. Some appear closer to the observer, and some appear far away. A wall encircles the house, creating spaces marked by floor tiles of various designs. Two stairs provide access at two different points, and a lamp, tied by a cord to a point to which one of the stairs leads, illuminates one side.

It is significant that the lines of demarcation between Asterion and the house are not clearly distinguishable. Is the house part of the head, is the head part of the house, are they symbolically integrated into one thing, or are they literally one thing? The encircling wall could be part of an elaborate dress. At least three interpretations suggest themselves. In one interpretation, this painting understands Borges's story to refer to our mental condition as human beings. The house is in our heads, our own creation. The labyrinth in which we live is of our own devising, it is a world of our making, and our solitude and despair are self inflicted. We are not prisoners of it because we have been forcibly locked up in it against our will, but because we construct it in recognition of our difference from everything else—we are monsters in comparison to what surrounds us. Only death can liberate us from the prison we have built by stamping out our consciousness.

In another interpretation, the world is not our creation but the reality that confronts us and of which we are a part. We are lost in it because it is an irrational labyrinth without escape in which we find ourselves alone and bewildered. Redemption is possible only through death; we can escape only by ceasing to exist.

In a third interpretation, it is not important whether the house is Asterion's creation or not. What is significant is that Asterion lives in the house, with all the consequences deriving from it. The point of the story is not about the origin of our prison, but about the outcome: to stay or to leave, when staying means imprisonment and solitude, and leaving means death and emptiness.

Like Borges, Azaceta does not tell us exactly which interpretation is correct. The story suggests that Asterion may have been the creator of his house and he may have forgotten it. And because of this, we cannot be sure. Azaceta's work leaves us with a similar doubt.

Paul Sierra's *Asterión* uses a very different interpretative strategy from Azaceta's work. The title of the piece does not refer to the house. Indeed, the painting ignores the house completely. Sierra focuses on Asterion and his fate at the hands of Theseus rather than on the labyrinth where he resides. Asterion is portrayed as a man with the head of a bull. The body is displayed from the waist up, immersed in a lush vegetation of thick green leaves with red, pointed ends. The head, covered with golden fleece and supported by a powerful, muscular neck, is tilted back. The mouth is open and the tongue sticks out. We see one eye, which is also open, but appears dead, without expression or shine. A few strings of red fleece encircle the body, which displays an open wound on the left side. The wound is bloodless and dry. Above the figure is the night sky, covered with shining stars, a reference to Asterion's creation.

The dry wound, the tilted head, the open mouth, and the expressionless eye indicate that Asterion is dead; we are presented with a corpse. This is a portrait of him after Theseus slew him with his sword. The red, sharp ends of the leaves of the vegetation that surround him make us think of the sword and the violence he suffered. And the bloodied strings of fleece that are loosely wrapped around his lifeless body bring back the memory of his self-imprisonment, even if they ostensibly refer to Theseus's trick to find his way back out of the labyrinth.

Asterion's ghost, not the living, suffering Minotaur, speaks to us in the story and he appears at peace in death. The stars connect us to his role as ruler of the heavens, and introduce a sense of relief and transcendent contentment. Asterion lives only as a voice in the story and in the magnificent sky he ruled and perhaps created. The vivid colors of the figure and the vegetation play up his tragic end in violence and pain. The bright reds, yellows, greens, and oranges give credibility to the tortured predicament of the Minotaur, but the dark sky, shining stars, and lifeless eye, introduce an element of resolution and serenity. Theseus succeeded because the Minotaur longed for a peace he did not have in the lonely labyrinth that was his house. He let himself be put to death, regarding his slayer as a redeemer. In the end, he was too human for his own good, helping to fulfill his destiny.

By leaving out of the painting any reference to the house, Sierra forces the viewer to focus on Asterion's death rather than on the motive for it. The contrast between the bloody vegetation on the lower part of the painting and the dark sky full of shining stars presents us with what may be thought of as two worlds from which we must choose. One is a world of violence and blood; the other is a world of peace and light. One is the realm of death and the other is the realm of life; these realms paradoxically stand for the opposites of our ordinary conceptions of death and life. For Asterion, the choice was clear, his tilted head faces the stars; he chooses life by choosing death.

Sierra's painting at first looks very different from his other creations. Missing are some marks that characterize them, such as the lush vegetation and the single figure in a landscape. But upon reflection there is much that fits his other work. The deceiving aspect is the complexity and the scale of the piece. The vegetation makes an appearance in the nasty looking plants that

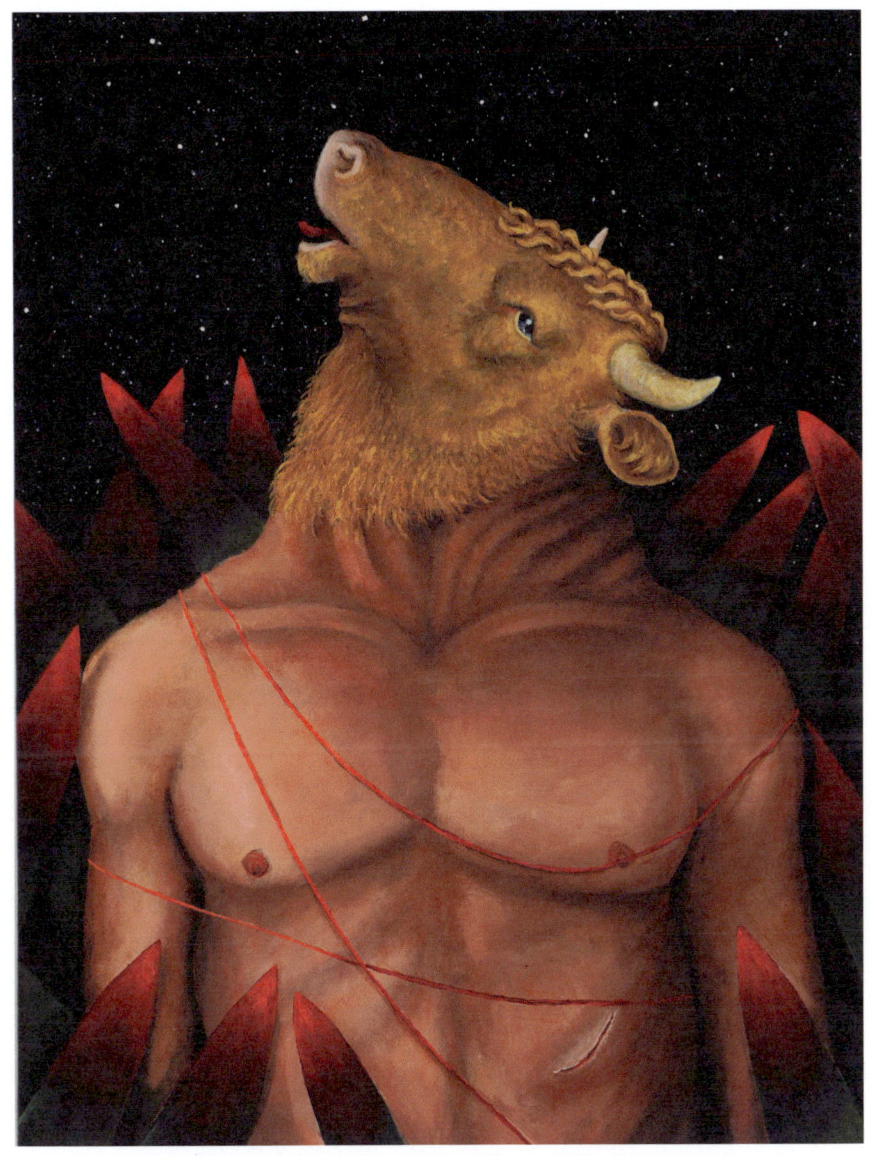

XIV. Paul Sierra, *Asterión*, 2009, 34" × 26", oil on canvas.

surround Asterion; however, it does not take over the canvas as it does in many of his other paintings. And the lonely figure is there, the dead Asterion, but his dimensions are large—he almost occupies the whole canvas, and is not located in a large space where his solitude is more evident.

9

The Immortal

"The Immortal" is one of Borges's longest stories. It opens with a substantial quotation of a text from Francis Bacon in which he refers to Solomon and Plato and draws an implication: there is no new thing under the sun and all knowledge is but remembrance, so all novelties are but oblivion. This is one of Borges's favorite themes. Just as in "The Circular Ruins," we are confronted in this story with the cyclical nature of time and the inevitability of destiny. The narrative is heavy with cryptic suggestions about immortality, the nature of the universe, human achievements, and the quest for understanding. But at the end we are left with more questions than answers. One of these is that, as in other of Borges's fictions, it is not clear whether most of the narrative refers to reality or to a dream, for at some point the protagonist falls asleep and then awakens and many fantastic events follow.

The story line is fairly clear. In London, a princess buys a copy of Pope's *Iliad* from Joseph Cartaphilus, an antique bookseller from Smyrna. In the last volume, she finds a manuscript divided into five chapters in which the Roman tribune, Marcus Flaminius Rufus, tells how he threw himself into the quest for the secret City of the Immortals. He first hears about the City from a rider who, bloody and exhausted, dies at his feet asking for the river that purifies all men of death, on the far shores of which the City is located. Ignoring the advice of philosophers who claim that immortality merely multiplies a man's deaths, Marcus throws himself into the pursuit of the City and its river to quench his thirst for immortality; he is accompanied by two hundred soldiers. After many disastrous adventures, the soldiers are about to mutiny and kill him, but he manages to escape. He is wounded by a Cretan arrow and finds himself alone, at which moment he sees pyramids and towers in the distance. This is the City of the Immortals, but exhausted, he falls asleep.

When he wakes, his hands are tied behind his back and he is lying on an oblong niche carved into the slope of a mountain. Around him he sees little gray men, belonging to the bestial lineage of the Troglodytes, emerging from similar niches. They do not speak. Marcus throws himself down the mountain toward a polluted stream and is eventually able to free himself. The Troglodytes pay no attention to him or his pleadings.

Consumed by the goal of his quest, Marcus can hardly sleep, and it appears as if the Troglodytes, divining his purpose, do not either. He crosses the stream on his way to the City and is followed by a few of the little men, although eventually only one remains. The City is built on an impregnable plateau, but Marcus finds a way in through a cave that leads to a maze through which Marcus eventually emerges onto a plaza. The City turns out to be an irrational jumble of buildings with no purpose. Its chaos horrifies him and he finds his way out. There he encounters the Troglodyte who had followed him, clumsily drawing symbols in the sand and erasing them. Suspecting some intellectual capacity in the man, Marcus tries to teach him but it is all in vain. He names him Argos, after the moribund old dog of the *Odyssey*. One day there is rain, and this seems to waken the village, and Argos speaks. He is Homer.

Marcus now achieves an epiphany, he understands. The Troglodytes are the Immortals. They had destroyed their City nine hundred years before and built a new one in its place "as a temple to the irrational gods that rule the world and to those gods about whom we know nothing save that they do not resemble man." At that point, thinking that all effort is vain, they decided to live in thought, devoting themselves to speculation. After centuries of living, they reached "a perfection of tolerance," for they realized that in the long run all things happen to everyone. We are all things, god, hero, philosopher, demon, and world. Nothing happens only once, and nothing is ever lost, and this presumably is immortality.

Homer and Marcus part in Tangier, and Marcus goes on his way to be many things in many places. The account appears fantastic because, Marcus explains, it is the story of two men while presumably there is only one. But now Marcus is close to his end, when he will be all men, and none. No images from memory are left, only words.

The story ends with a postscript that refers to a publication entitled, *A Coat of Many Colors,* in which the author claims that the tale of the rare-book dealer Joseph Cartaphilus is apocryphal because of the texts from other sources it integrates. But the narrator of Borges's story disagrees for, as he notes, "there are no longer any images from memory—there are only words." This, surely, is the consequence of the loss of individuality.

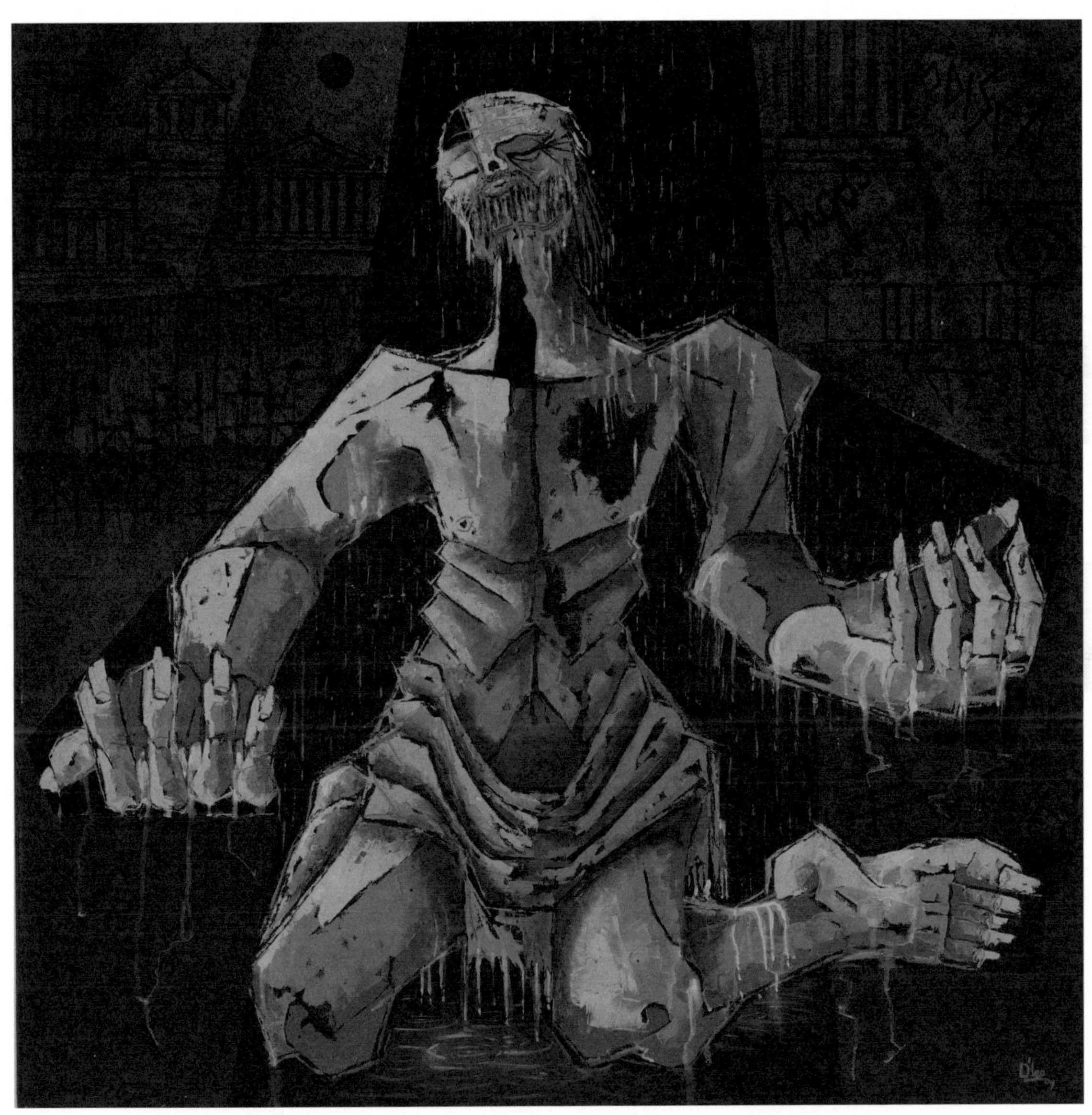

XV. Claudio D'Leo, *El inmortal* (The Immortal), 2009, 39.5" × 39.5", oil on canvas.

Claudio D'Leo's strategy in *El inmortal*, is to focus on the image of the Immortal, the man who is every man, at a dramatic point that signals the crucial event in Borges's story. This is the moment of communication between Marcus and the Troglodyte. The figure depicted in the painting is half kneeling, half seated on his legs. His arms are extended forward and the hands, of disproportionate size in comparison with the rest of the body, are opened. The face is slightly tilted to his right and back, and the eyes are closed. His expression reflects inner concentration, perhaps pleading, resignation, indifference, or even a moment of revelation where he realizes an enlightening truth. The body, worked in the typical style of the painter, is angular, full of geometrical overtones. Most prominent of all are the large hands, which emphasize the gesture of pleading, resignation, indifference, or enlightenment. The nails are grown, long and sharp. He is naked but for a piece of folded cloth that covers his lower torso.

The body appears decimated. The chest is thin and emaciated, as is the face. We see the prominent ribs of the chest. The position of the legs and feet allows us to see the top of one foot, where a band of some sort has an inscription on it. The body is spent, as if made out of paper or cardboard and pieces of it have been punctured and fallen off. It is located in a dark niche from whose top rain falls. The water drenches the figure and makes a pool on the floor. The unkempt beard, the arms, legs, and hands, and the piece of material that partly covers him are soaked. Outside the niche, we see juxtaposed images of Greek temples under a dark moon. We also see words, Greek letters, and mathematical symbols—metora, triglifo, Odisea, Ulises, α, β, the square root of 2, the parallel theorem, a right triangle that alludes to the Pythagorean theorem—and Argos, the name Marcus gave Homer. There is a strong architectural background where the images of various Greek temples and other structures are placed in no particular order, some columns and parts of the Greek orders appear on the right. An intriguing supporting structure of beams on the left suggests an ancient bridge or its remains. Above everything else, the mysterious moon watches silently over the improbable moment.

The painting does not refer to particular events of Borges's story. It is not a narrative of any sort. Rather, it captures a crucial moment of the tale, where memory and the present coalesce in a new awareness of the true nature of immortality. The central figure appears in the kind of unconcerned state of the Troglodytes just before the rain. But it also could be interpreted as revealing a beginning of the consciousness of the past. The water could be connected to the fountain that conveys immortality, the water of life eternal. The state of the body indicates the negligible importance given to it by the immortals, for whom it is a mere inconvenience, almost irrelevant in their sole dedication to thought. Is there a suggestion that what they have achieved is pernicious? That the physical side of humanity becomes decimated by neglect and a human being becomes more like a ghost of what he is when the body and its needs are forgotten? And is the expression on the Immortal's face one of pain, unconcern, pleading, resignation, or enlightenment? Are the immortals hoping to become human again, as Marcus eventually does? Or are they praying for death, perhaps obeying the advice of the philosophers that Marcus ignored?

In the story, the rain introduces the most dramatic moment of the plot, when the Troglodyte speaks for the first time, uttering the word 'Argos,' which unites him to Marcus. This is a moment of remembrance and universality, for communication first breaks the mute silence that had excluded Marcus. This is, after all, the meaning of immortality, the moment when a perishable human being can pass on a thought to someone else, making that thought imperishable, separate, and independent from the disintegrating body that we see so well represented in the picture. That moment of communication brings to life, through memory, everything the Troglodytes know: their science and architecture, their cultural successes and discoveries, their continuity to the past. No wonder the image of the Immortal is devastated, worn out, for it represents the knowledge and experience of humankind, the accumulation of human knowledge going back to the beginning. And all of it is prompted by the rain, a natural phenomenon that causes a supernatural one, for communication is a mystery, a divine revelation detonated by a word that goes well beyond the physical domain of nature.

Large hands are a frequent feature of D'Leo's work. He uses this image generally to evoke the notion of giving. But here it adds a dimension of communication, it is the reaching out and giving of the knowledge and science from the past. It is disinterested giving. And all this is contrasted to a nearly black background, which makes the image of the Immortal stand out bluntly in the encounter with the other. The city, with its labyrinths, and the bridge, which established the passage between the past and the present and made possible the survival of knowledge, stand behind. In that mysterious and divine moment in which Marcus and the Troglodyte communicate, they also become one: the human being that is all humankind. Here is where they achieve immortality, through the incorporation of history and the fusion of their horizons.

León Ferrari's *El inmortal* has a dramatic history that must be told, at least briefly, to understand the image of the work presented here. In 2004, at the opening of an art exhibition of Ferrari's work, a group of protesters, led by a Catholic priest, made their way into the gallery and proceeded to break some of the art. One of the most important pieces that was broken was *El inmortal*, the work that Ferrari had done as an interpretation of Borges's story with the same title. Ferrari has maintained the work in its broken condition as a reminder of the

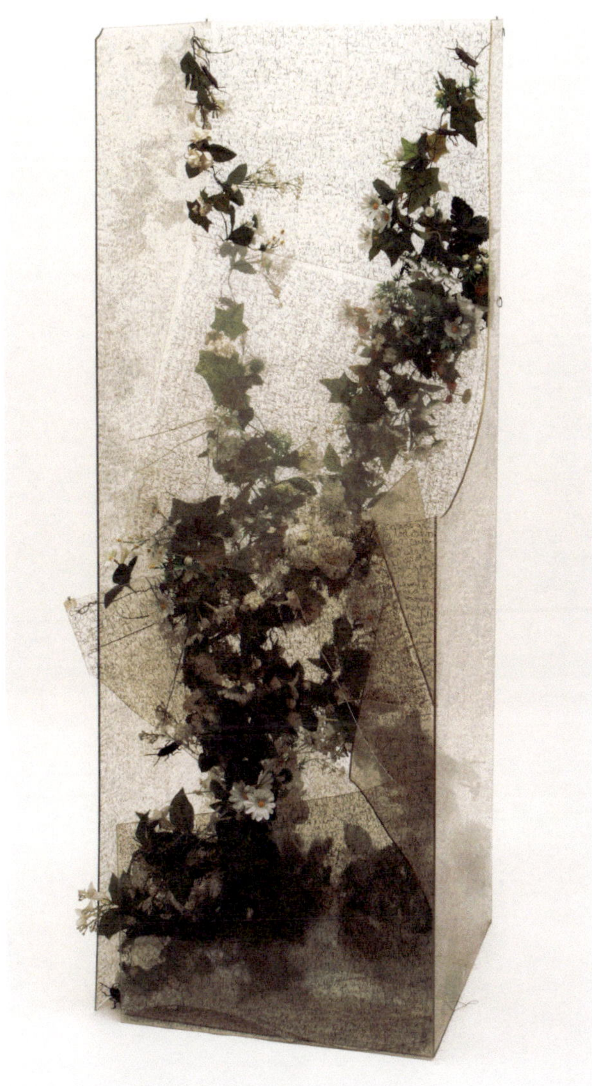

XVI. León Ferrari, *El inmortal* (The Immortal), 2003, 59" × 19.7" × 19.7", acrylic, plastic flowers and vines, ink, and wire.

event, which resulted in the closing of the exhibition, a lawsuit against the perpetrators who eventually lost in court, and the reopening of the exhibition at a later date. The objections of the Argentinean Catholic hierarchy were not against this particular work, but against others they deemed sacrilegious. Indeed, *El inmortal* has no evident relation to Catholic doctrine, although it certainly can be interpreted, like Borges's story, as espousing a view that is not concordant with Catholic dogma. The image reproduced here is of the work in its present broken form.

The piece consists of a fairly large prism made of transparent fiberglass sheets that are glued and held together in place by plastic cubes and screws. The prism encloses a space in which vines made of plastic are intertwined, giving us a luscious picture of nature. On the fiberglass walls, written on black ink, Ferrari has copied the entire text of the story in his usual cursive hand, with occasional curlicues and exaggerated lines and forms that give the text an aesthetic quality all its own. The lines are not straight or parallel, and the size of the text and the letters vary. The space is for the most part full, with little on the way of intervening blanks. The writing covers every space of the walls, including the ones at the top and bottom, and gives the plastic prism a visual texture that resembles a kind of cage made of wire. The fiberglass is transparent, but apart from the writing it has some irregularities in the form of horizontal lines that can be seen when light shines on the surfaces.

On the vine we also see plastic white flowers, roses and rose buds of various sizes, white orange blossoms, and some wild flowers. Three different kinds of vines climb all the way to the top of the prism, although English ivy stands out most prominently. Vines and flowers of different sorts are indiscriminately tied together in the same stems, as if they belonged to the same plant. The color of the leaves is generally of various shades of green, but some of the English ivy are turning pink in places and have pink and brown spots, signaling the coming of the fall. Most important is the presence of plastic cockroaches climbing throughout the vines, big, fat, repulsive creatures that appear well fed and thriving. All of this is tied together with wires and to the prism and its walls, beginning at the bottom and going all the way to the top.

The first impression one has of this piece is of a garden, overrun with vines and full of flowers and bugs, growing wildly and without arrangement, but surviving and even thriving. This is life untouched by humans; it is nature at its best. But what is the relation of the work to Borges's story? Obviously one is the writing of the text of Borges, which is a cage in which this ensemble is presented. The story encases and guards the inner contents of the prism, and this gives us a clue as to how to understand the thread that unites Ferrari's work to Borges's story. We could begin with the often repeated view that the only things that will survive the world as we know it are cockroaches. So they must be the immortals. But is Ferrari merely telling a joke or is he providing us with a more dramatic truth that we should grasp. He is certainly not beyond making a joke, and indeed, much of his art has humor, but the humor is usually biting and sharp; it does not produce a laugh, but a thought. Are we to take the survival of cockroaches as an indictment of humankind and a hopeless view of a future in which we will manage to destroy ourselves? In Borges's story humankind is not annihilated, but survives in a new form, as the Troglodytes, who at first appear to be a kind of lower version of ourselves, or of their former selves. Until we discover not only that they had a history marked by great achievements, but more importantly that they have somehow figured out what is fundamental for humanity. This is the truth that Marcus learns from Homer and that perhaps Ferrari is picturing for us. This means that there is more to the bugs than that they will have survived while humans will not. So what is that message? What are we to understand through Ferrari's visual interpretation of Borges's story?

Let's go back to the text of the tale, the cage that delimits the work of art, and let us remember that a text is a physical object, an object that can be seen, but whose content cannot be seen, and revealed only in the mind of those who understand it. So what is the meaning of the text? In order to answer this question we need to leave out, or bracket as the phenomenologists say, everything else but the world that the text has enclosed. This is our universe of discourse and understanding. Once we do this, what we see, leaving out all preconceptions and ideas, is the lush vegetation of the vines, the flowers blooming, and the cockroaches thriving. This is a story of rebirth, renewal, and survival, where life is present, and where the lowest and most despised bugs acquire beauty. This is not a pessimistic view of the universe; it is an optimistic view of growth and flourishing, but not tied to humanity. The universe will survive, and even if humanity ceases to exist, there is hope, because the cockroaches will live and evolve; there is a future, but it is a future based on nature, not on dogmas and religious beliefs. This is the truth of the piece. It is a hopeful message that at first comes through as sarcastic and pessimistic, but once we reflect on it, we see its hope and optimism. We may not be the immortals, but nature is in all its manifold ways, including the ones we tend to despise.

There may be, after all, an anti-religious dimension to Ferrari's interpretation that goes beyond what Borges seems to have had in mind. Borges was interested in the unity and survival of humankind and its knowledge, whereas Ferrari is interested in the unity and survival of the universe. So perhaps those who unwittingly broke this piece would find in this a basis to rationalize their anger, even though at the time they did not understand the piece's real significance, and simply attacked it because it was the first work they encountered in the exhibition. Indeed, the piece is eminently subversive, as much of Ferrari's art is, and that is, in fact, one of its most intriguing aspects.

10

The Rose of Paracelsus

The ostensive theme of "The Rose of Paracelsus" is faith. Does faith involve a leap as Søren Kierkegaard suggested? Is it a choice for the absurd, as Tertullian famously prescribed? Or does faith need to accord with facts and rationality, as Peter Abelard argued? At one level, the story seems to favor the first two alternatives, but at another it appears to contradict them, for it is also possible to read the story ironically. Blind acceptance on the part of a disciple appears to lower his value, as the sorcerer in "The Circular Ruins" implies.

Faith is not the only theme of the story. Other topics are explored, although they are less obvious, and many reveal themselves only to those who have a particular interest in them. One of these involves discipleship. Can there be true disciples, and if there can be, what is essential to their role? Borges refers to this topic in others stories as well. In "The Immortal," he mentions students who actively question a teacher, rather than passively accept his pronouncements. Another subtly suggested theme concerns communication. Can it happen and what are the requirements of it? Another is the ultimate nature of reality, a constant in Borges's works well represented in several of the stories discussed in this book. Still another concerns language and its power. Finally, there is the Faustian question concerning whether a goal is a result or the way. Is wisdom a state achieved at the end of a long process of reflection or is it the very process? The story poses these and other questions, but provides no definite answers. Readers have to fend for themselves.

In his laboratory, Paracelsus prays to his indeterminate God, any god, to send him a disciple. He forgets his prayer, but a stranger comes to see him who aspires to be his disciple, and offers him all his worldly goods in the form of a bag full of gold, if Paracelsus allows him to become his disciple. The famous alchemist and physician (1493–1541) was reputed to be able to produce the stone that turns all elements into gold, so Paracelsus has no use for gold and tells the student that if gold is what he is interested in, he can never become his disciple. The student replies that the gold is only a token of his good will. He wants Paracelsus to teach him the Art, the path that leads to the Stone. Paracelsus answers that the path is the Stone and so is the point of departure. "Every step you take is the goal you seek." Making sense of these words is the beginning of understanding, although Paracelsus's enemies say there is no Path.

Still, the student wants a proof before he begins the journey—which indicates that he has not understood what the teacher has said, thus confirming Paracelsus's first impression of him. When the student arrived, he held a rose in his left hand, a fact that troubled Paracelsus. The sage was famous for burning a rose and making it reappear again through his Art, so the student asks him for this proof. But Paracelsus accuses him of credulity, whereas he requires faith. The disciple disputes this conclusion: he demands proof precisely because he is not credulous. Nonetheless, Paracelsus points out that the student's credulity lies in his belief that Paracelsus can destroy the rose, for nothing can ever be annihilated. The rose can be burned only in appearance; in itself it is eternal, that is why it would take only a word from Paracelsus to make it appear again. The word in question is found in the science of the Kabbalah.

The student insists, but Paracelsus replies that if he were to do what the student wants, the student would not believe it. The miracle would not produce faith. After Paracelsus shows signs of impatience, the student forces the situation by throwing the rose into the flames, where it turns into ashes. An unmoved Paracelsus notes that many think he is a fraud; now the rose is destroyed and will be no more. The student feels ashamed for having revealed Paracelsus as a fake. He apologizes and promises to come back after he is ready. They part courteously, knowing that they will not see each other again. Once the student leaves, Paracelsus pours some ashes from one hand into the other, whispers a single word, and the rose appears.

In *Doubting of St. Thomas,* Alberto Rey goes back to a famous painting by Caravaggio, *The Incredulity of St. Thomas,* in which the master depicts the moment of doubt concerning Christ's resurrection in one of his apostles. Christ had died on the cross, his side pierced by a lance, which had penetrated into his heart, and he had been buried. But there were rumors of his appearance to some of his followers. For St. Thomas these reports are not enough. Indeed, it is not even enough that he sees Christ in front of him. He needs more than this to believe

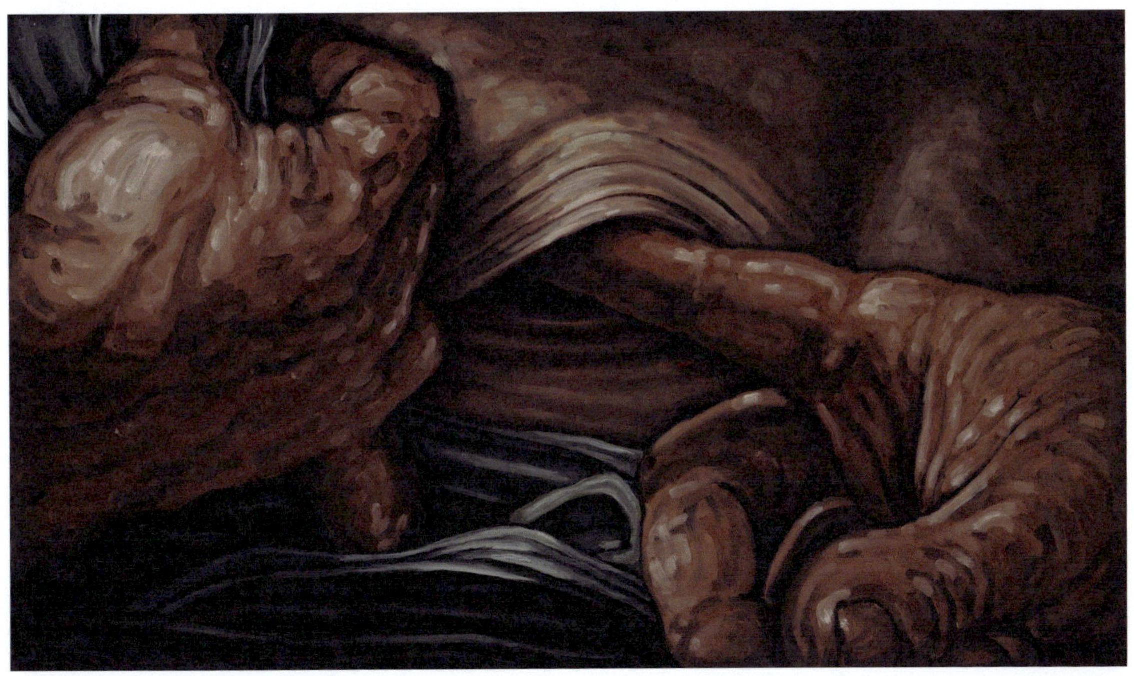

XVII. Alberto Rey, *Doubting of St. Thomas (La duda de sto. Tomás)*, 2009, 19" × 33", oils on plaster on canvas over wood.

what he rationally thinks makes no sense. To make certain, he puts his fingers inside Christ's wound to make sure that the person in front of him is the Christ who died on the cross and not an impostor.

Caravaggio's painting is a complicated composition with four figures. The figures on the forefront are Christ and St. Thomas. Behind St. Thomas are two other apostles. Christ has his head bowed in a sign of resignation, while St. Thomas puts his index finger inside Christ's chest wound and looks intently at it, with forehead wrinkled in amazement. Christ is holding St. Thomas's wrist, whether trying to take his hand away or leading it in is unclear. Among the figures on the background, St. Peter, looking patriarchal with a full beard, pays careful attention to what is happening. The garments of the Apostles are ragged, poor looking, and realistically depicted. These are rough fishermen facing a miracle.

Although Rey's work is based on the Caravaggio, his approach is different. His painting has been simplified to the core, and focuses on the key element that ties the Caravaggio to Borges's story, the question of faith. He has cropped Caravaggio's composition so that we see only Christ's hand pulling away his garment in order to uncover the chest wound being explored by St. Thomas's finger. In the Caravaggio, Christ's garment is white, but Rey has painted it blue, probably to highlight the contrast in the reduced depiction. The lean material allows Rey to develop in considerable detail the elements of the picture: the fingers, the folds of the wound, the chest, and the folds of the tunic. From seeing Rey's interpretation, we cannot guess what it is about, and indeed many observers see in it something quite different, even erotic, but its title and the cultural background most of us share in the West reveal a different significance.

By leaving out much detail and focusing on the action of St. Thomas, Rey has produced a painting that is both contemporary and conceptually powerful. Caravaggio was known for his radical innovations and his masterful technique. His work opens up the doors to the realism and pathos characteristic of the Baroque, which was later to be developed to new heights by Ribera and Zurbarán, among others. But Rey's rendition looks contemporary to us and enhances the conceptual power of the painting and its impact on the audience. In this, it is in line with the work of Borges. A strong image removes any distractions from its central theme, and uses only a gesture to convey its meaning. The scarcity of details helps the audience focus on the act of discovery.

The painting seems to emphasize the need for confirmation in faith. Faith is not a matter of blind belief or uncritical acceptance. No leap of faith is proposed; doubt and testing are part of faith. The question is, would putting his finger into Christ's wound be enough for St. Thomas? Would he not be like Paracelsus's presumptive disciple, who according to the master would not believe even if Paracelsus had restored the destroyed rose? Perhaps it is, but even if so, is Borges's story an endorsement of an unquestioned faith? Or is it rather a criticism of it?

Rey's strategy is in line with much of his work. He regularly incorporates appropriated images as a way of creating visual metaphors that establish connections to other artists, art history, cultural icons, and social conditions. These become avenues from which to expand the significance of a work in ways that allow viewers to personalize their understanding of his art.

One more comment in parting needs to be added. One interpretation of Caravaggio's work is that the biblical story is merely an ostensive excuse to convey a hidden, more radical theme related to sodomy. Obviously a finger penetrating a wound can be a metaphor for something erotic, and it is well to realize that artists at this time often used standard topics to make statements about more controversial ones. If this interpretation is taken seriously, what do we make of Rey's own rendition? The matter becomes complicated because most of those who look at the work by Rey do not think of male sodomy, but of female penetration. In my view, both of these interpretations of the Caravaggio and the Rey are rather forced. I prefer to think of the works as dealing with religious doubt.

Carlos Estévez's *La rosa de Paracelso* uses some of the common elements that characterize his work to present an unusual interpretation of Borges's story. Instead of exploring the most obvious central focus on the nature of faith, he has chosen two derivative topics of the story: discipleship and communication.

On the left we see a nearly empty glass vase with seven double stems that end in human heads. The stems, as should be expected of most vegetable matter, are painted green and the heads, which presumably stand for flowers, are painted bright yellow. The heads have different expressions and are addressing a figure on their left. Concentric circles, common in images of heads used by the artist, occupy the areas of the brains of the figures, and stand out in a red color. The figure is, like the heads in the vase, a kind of plant, with a flower, the rose of Paracelsus, at the top, painted in a geometrical style. The rose is imaginatively depicted with three levels: a red background in the form of a mandala on which are superimposed a double circle at the center surrounded by four oval drawings. Lines radiate from the center and reach the end of the red mandala, but transform themselves into a design of overlapping oval figures, one half of which falls within the red background of the mandala and the other half which extends beyond it over the black background of the artwork. The impression is of a red sphere with a core that radiates outward and is surrounded by a delicate mesh, almost like a fine lace enclosure that allows color and light to escape it.

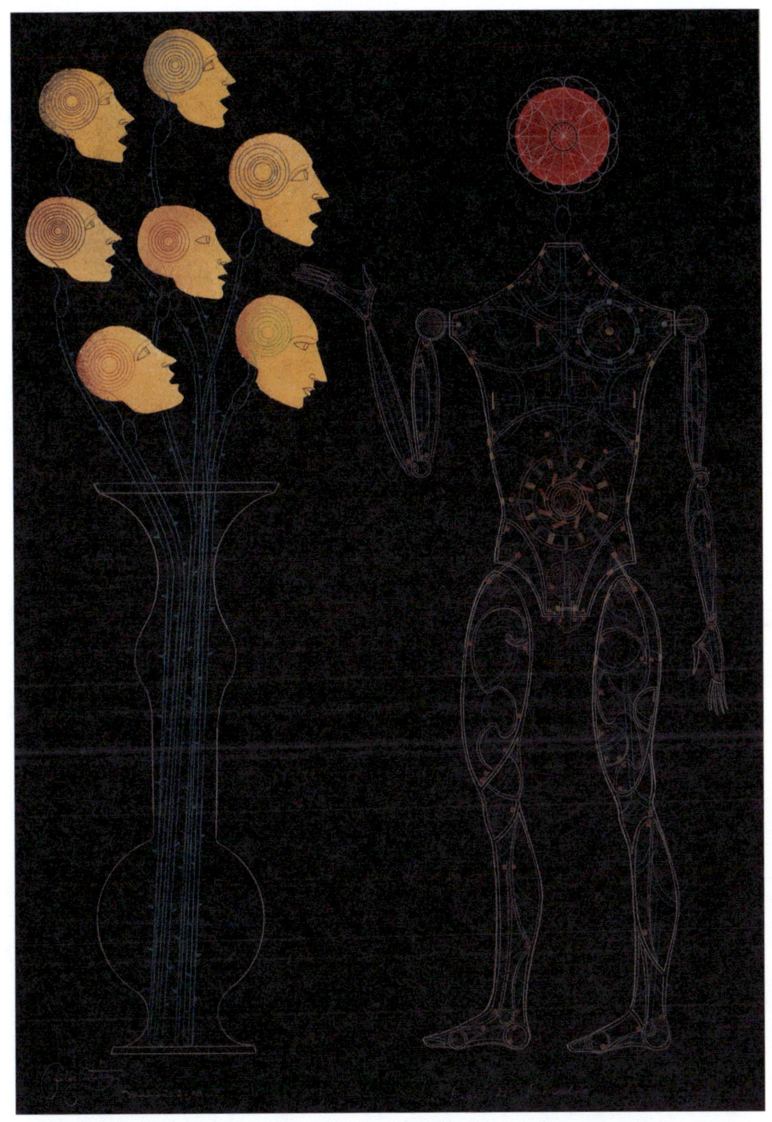

XVIII. Carlos Estévez's *La rosa de Paracelso* (The Rose of Paracelsus), 2009, 39.5" × 27.5", pencil and gouache on paper.

Below a thin stem that supports the rose, the plant transforms itself into a human body resembling a complex machine with tubes, levers, wheels, and other mechanical paraphernalia depicted in great detail and forming an attractive ensemble. Screw heads, looking like small squares, indicate the places where the inner parts of the figure convene and are tied together. The theme of the circle—the mandala of the head—is picked up in various parts of the figure. The largest and most complex of these is in the abdomen where we see a series of wheels, levers, and gears. A smaller mandala, simpler but emphasized by the color blue of the knots that tie its parts, is located in the area of the heart. Much simpler are concentric circles that indicate major joints between the body and the limbs and a larger one on the groin. Still smaller and simpler circles appear on the feet, and there are interlocking circles at the elbows.

The figure is standing, facing the observer, except for the feet, which are depicted sideways, directed toward the vase. One of the arms and hands is making a gesture toward the heads in the vase. The gesture is somewhat despondent, and the figure appears oblivious to the cacophony of voices coming from the flower heads. The stylized rose head, lacking eyes and other human features, appears to face the audience, rather than the heads, but as a sphere, it would not have a front, back, or sides. It is serene, absorbed in its brilliance and the workings within it, while shedding light around its surroundings, like a lighthouse in the night at sea.

The flower heads stand for potential disciples, students who clamor for the wisdom and knowledge of the teacher, but make noise rather than sense, missing the true significance of the rose. The nearly empty vase in which they are found indicates the poverty of the source of their knowledge, and its transparency makes clear that Paracelsus is aware of it. The rose is a symbol of Paracelsus's genius. It brightens the picture and creates a point of serenity and enlightenment. The figure is, in fact, Paracelsus, distant from the discordant voices of uncomprehending disciples who fail to grasp the truth. Communication is not occurring. Two incompatible dimensions, two levels of understanding, are depicted in the work, and the gap between them is never bridged. On the one hand are the yellow flowers, which symbolize the disciple in the story who fails to understand Paracelsus. And on the other is the figure with the rose head, which becomes a symbol of the misunderstood scientist, philosopher, or artist, who nonetheless goes on with his work. Estévez has used his interpretation of Borges's story to formulate a situation of which scientists, philosophers, artists, and other creative people are very much aware, but which is only hinted at in the story: the life and work of those who have something new to offer and the difficulty in communicating it to others and finding an audience that truly understands their insights.

11

The Writing of the God

"The Writing of the God" is one of Borges's most enigmatic stories. Its ostensive aim is to discover the secret of the universe. The answer is revealed, if at all, only indirectly. The idea that creators leave imprints on their creations is commonplace. Artists and writers have characteristic styles and interests that reveal their identity in their work. It is not surprising, then, that those who believe that a divinity created the world should try to find the creator's imprint on it. Indeed, this idea has been the basis of a famous argument for the existence of God, the so-called argument from design. According to it, the universe bears the marks of its creator, proving his existence. In Borges's story, the secret of the universe is supposed to be evident in the universe itself, having been put there by the god who created it, but we are not told clearly what it is.

The story is narrated by the protagonist, a Mayan or Aztec priest—interpreters disagree—who is incarcerated in a jail in the form of an almost perfect hemisphere. A wall divides it into two halves. On one side, Tzinacán, the priest of the Pyramid that the conquistador Pedro de Alvarado burned, is imprisoned. On the other side, the prisoner is a jaguar. A long barred window at the floor level makes possible for the priest to see the jaguar once a day, when a jailer lowers water and meat from an opening at the top of the ceiling. The priest spends his time waiting for the destiny that the gods have prescribed, and remembers the pains he suffered at the hands of his torturers. To pass the time, he tries to recall everything he knew, and once he stumbles upon the story that on the first day of creation, foreseeing many disasters and calamities, the god had written a magical phrase capable of warding off those evils, for the sake of his elect. Tzinacán, as the god's last priest, feels that he is destined to find the secret text. But where could it be written to be able to endure, be accessible, and yet remain hidden? After many hypotheses, he remembers that one of the god's names is jaguar, and this leads him to think that the god has entrusted his message to the skin of the animal. This seems to be confirmed by the jaguar's proximity to him in the prison.

The priest spends his time trying to decipher the many marks on the jaguar's skin: the black shapes, circles, stripes, rings, and red borders. But this is all in vain. "What sort of sentence," he asks himself, "would be constructed by an absolute mind?" The idea of a sentence makes no sense to him, and he speculates that it must be a word pregnant with "absolute plenitude," the word could not be less than the universe as a whole.

An infinity of grains of sand appears in his dreams and he feels confused and lost, until the hard fact of his circumstances hits him and brings him back to reality. He is a prisoner, and he accepts it. This is the moment of enlightenment: he experiences unity with the deity and the universe, which to him appear to be the same. He has a vision of a wheel of enormous height, made of water and fire, and infinite, although he could see its boundaries. It is composed of everything that has been, is, or shall be, containing all causes and effects. In it, the priest sees everything and understands everything, including the writing on the jaguar's skin.

The writing is a formula of fourteen random words—a number Borges often uses to refer to an infinity and was the sacred number of the jaguar divinity—and forty syllables, a number pregnant with symbolism. To speak it would make him omnipotent, but he will never speak it, as he has forgotten who he is. He is no one, because he has glimpsed the universe and its designs. Now he lies in darkness, allowing the days to forget him.

The title of José Franco's painting, *La escritura de Dios* is hermeneutically significant to the extent that it changes the title of the story. Borges's story is about *The Writing of the God*, but for Franco, it is the writing *of God*. In Franco's view this is not an essential difference, but nonetheless the change introduces a factor that should not be neglected. *The god* indicates my particular god, whereas *God* indicates everyone's one-and-only god. There is an element of universality in Franco's conception that is missing in Borges. In the end, it appears that both, Borges and Franco, are speaking about the God of the universe, but Borges, as usual, begins with the particular before he moves to the universal.

Franco's painting is a very large work with four key elements in it. Two versions of this work exist. The first was painted in 1996, but the one I am using is a version the artist created in 2010 for this book, based on the first, but differing from it in some respects. At its center is an outline of a humanoid, depicted from the shoulders up.

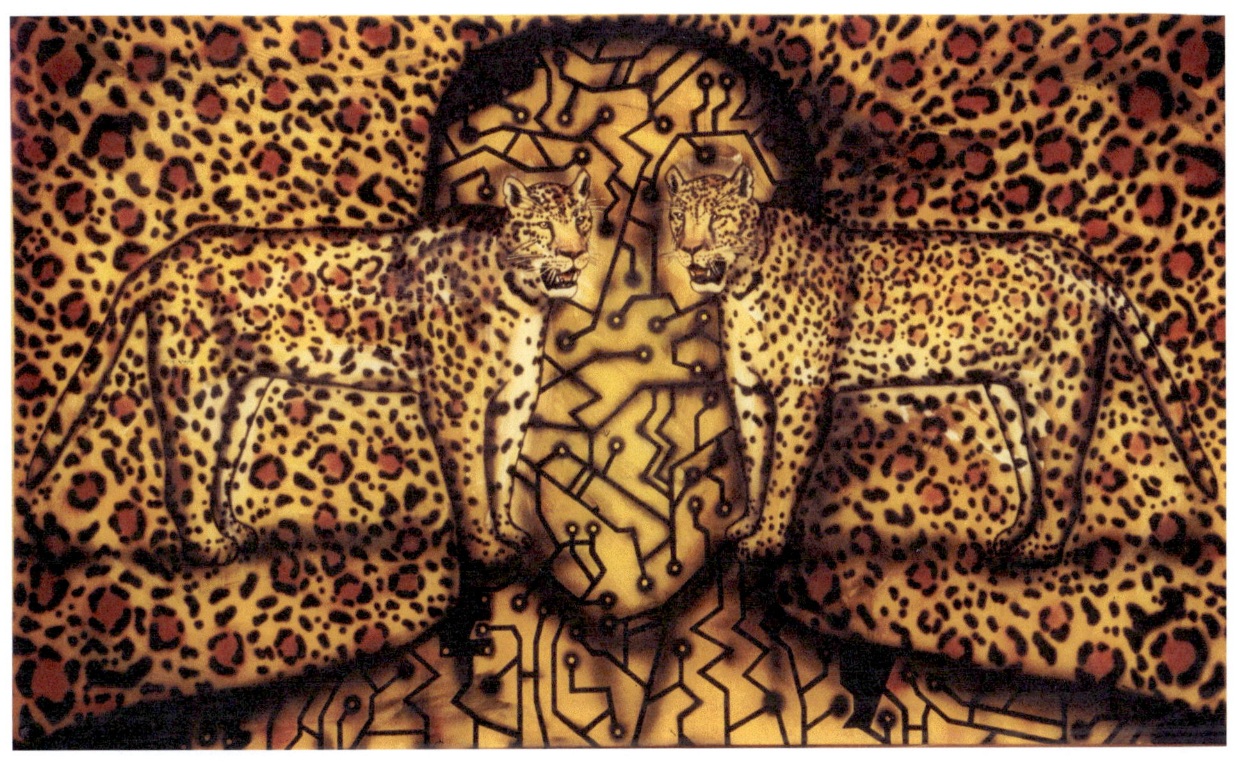

XIX. José Franco, *La escritura de Dios* (The Writing of God), 1995, 47.5" × 79", acrylic on canvas.

Most prominent in the painting is the head of the humanoid whose outline sets it apart from the background and the rest of the body. It has no facial features, being covered instead with multiple lines going in many directions and ending in small circles. Below it is the body, of which we see only the shoulders. The body is also covered with multiple lines and circles resembling electrical circuits and connections, but the color is more intense. We see the makings of a throat and four plates that seem to hold the body together, as if it were something mechanical, rather than organic.

Partly superimposed on the head and across its ears and cheeks are two jaguars whose heads are placed at about the location where one would expect the eyes of the face to be. The animals are standing, the front legs anchored on the shoulders of the human figure and merging with parts of the figure, but their back legs seem to stand on a kind of platform or shadow located above the shoulders of the man. The tigers are depicted in realistic detail, with open eyes and mouths. They are looking intently ahead, and their skins have the typical markings of jaguars: circles, dots, and elongated dots that could be lines. They contrast with the lines that mark the skin of the face and shoulders of the central figure.

The background of the painting is the skin of a jaguar, colored rather uniformly in varying shades of the yellow and orange characteristic of these animals. The markings are dark brown, and the insides of circles are often colored amber and shades of orange. The central figure and those of the jaguars are distinguished by darkening outlines.

In the story, we have a priest, a jaguar, a jail, a jailer, and an invisible god. There is also food and the recollections of the priest. But Franco has dispensed with most of these elements in the painting, limiting himself to a central human figure and two, rather than one, jaguars. The central image of the painting can be interpreted in at least three ways: as God, as the priest, or as both. The first interpretation can be supported if one adopts an Augustinian-Platonic view in which the universe is seen as an expression of God's nature, which is cashed out in mathematical and geometrical terms. The qualities of the universe, symbolized in the painting by the designs on both the jaguars' skin and the background, are an expression of the quantities that make up the ultimate nature of reality. This idea goes even farther back, to Pythagoras, for whom the universe was ultimately identified in mathematical terms. The notion of God the creator associated with geometrical designs and revealed in his creation fits this idea.

Although this interpretation is in principle possible, it is rather far-fetched. A more likely reading identifies the central figure with the priest, who in turn represents humankind. In this case the designs on the human figure are symbols of the denaturalization of humanity, its abandonment of nature, and its commitment to technology. The designs on the humanoid figure, then, are properly circuits and electrical connections that contrast with the natural markings on the skins of the jaguars and the painting's background, which stands, in turn, for the rest of the world. The role of the jaguars points to the way in which humanity can overcome its excessive emphasis on technology and recover a sense of nature by looking through the eyes of animals that, in contrast with humans, have not been estranged from nature and are still a part of it. It is most significant that the humanoid does not have eyes. Humanity is represented as blind; it cannot see or go beyond the world of technology it has developed. But if humanity puts itself in the place of animals, looking at the world through their eyes, it will see the writing of God in it: the secret of the universe, which is found in the divine wisdom that created it.

Finally, one could argue that it is not one or the other of these two interpretations that is most fruitful, but a combination of the two. The central figure stands for both God and humanity. After all, in the Judeo-Christian tradition, humanity is supposed to be a likeness of God. But in its self-centeredness, perhaps symbolized by the myth of Adam's story, it has abandoned its connection to the divine, becoming a casualty of its own creation. It is only through a return to nature by looking at the world through the eyes of an unspoiled animal kingdom that humanity can regain its connection to the divine, by reading God's message as it was intended. This is the secret of the universe, the truth that can save humankind and end all evils.

It is not surprising that Franco decided to paint a work inspired by this story. From the very beginning, his work has been concerned with the human struggle with nature, technology, and ecology. And one of the most prominent aspects of it has been the skins of animals, their designs and texture, particularly the skins of tigers, leopards, jaguars, and pumas. Indeed, *La escritura de Dios* is the centerpiece of a series of works he exhibited around Borges's idea that God writes on the skins of animals. His interpretation has used Borges to convey a message that is both consistent with Borges's story and also with his own perspective.

Mirta Kuperminc's *La escritura del dios* presents us with an interpretation of Borges's story different from that of Franco. The works themselves are very different. Franco's painting is static, symmetrical, and quite homogenous in color. Kuperminc's piece is dynamic, asymmetrical, and contains a variety of contrasting colors. Mystery and majesty may describe Franco's vision; after all, he may be depicting God. But Kuperminc has taken her inspiration from other aspects of the text, producing a work that is both whimsical and spiritual.

In her piece, the image of a Bengal tiger, rather than a jaguar, is dominant, occupying half of the total space. His eyes have an intent look, but we are not their object. They are yellowish green and unrevealing. The coat is lush but the marks on it appear at first to be disorderly. And his back supports a procession of figures that come down from the height of the head,

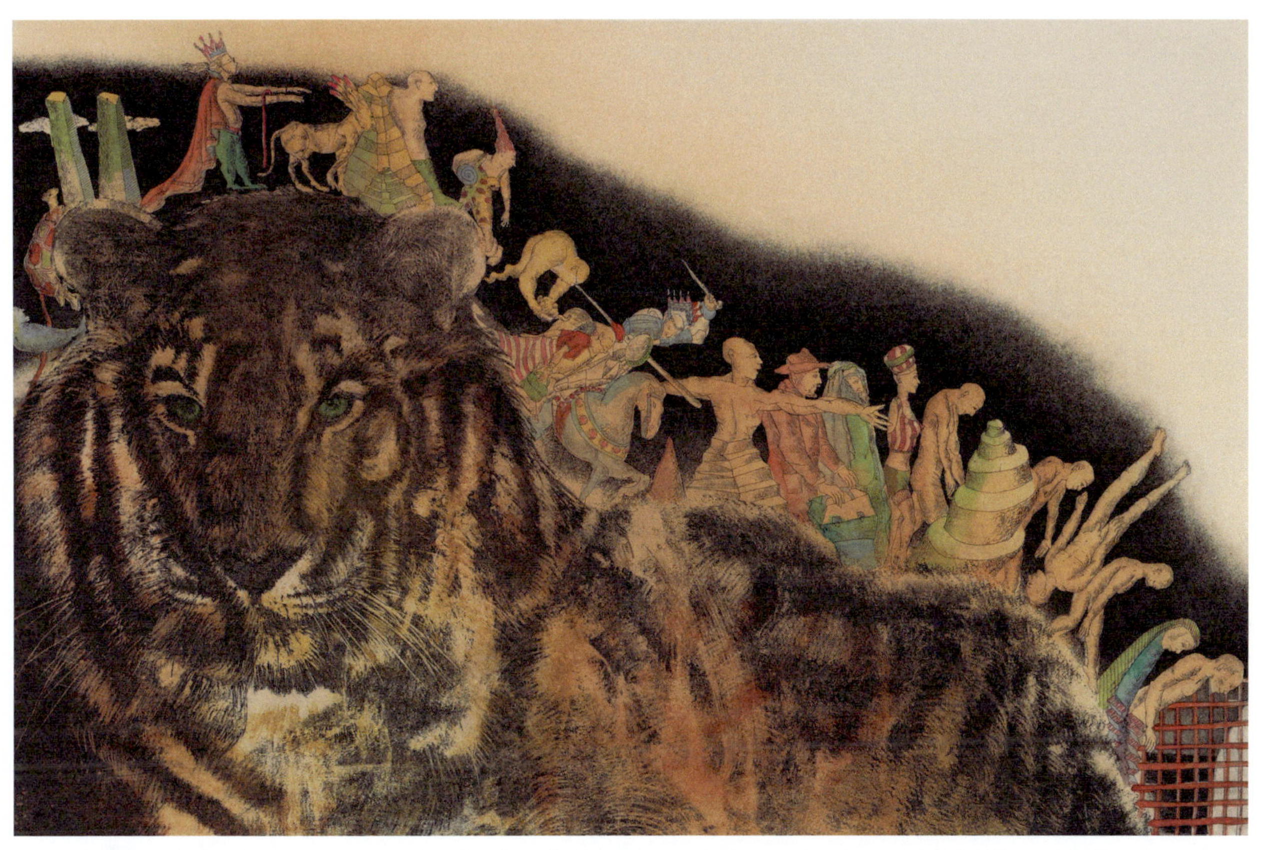

XX. Mirta Kupferminc, *La escritura del dios* (The Writing of the God), 2/5, 2 plates, 2004, 22.5" × 27.5", etching.

ending in a barred door or window at the bottom, on the other side of which is the prison where Tzinacán is held. The figures stand out on a dark background that follows the contours of the animal's back. The rest of the picture is only lightly colored in a very pale yellow, that constitutes a kind of background.

The tiger looks like a cutout collage, on whose top the figures have been etched. There are images of men, women, animals, and monuments. One can discern towers, one of which looks like the proverbial Tower of Babel, and pyramids of different sorts. The procession appears to depict biblical, pre-Columbian, and contemporary empires. One of the human figures is upside down, and another looks like a ghost or a genie. The garments vary widely. We see a medieval knight riding on a horse, and a man with a bag that may connote a diaspora or even the Holocaust. Some are naked, and one human figure has a ziggurat as a base. An Arab is next to a Jew. A woman stands tall and proud in colorful attire with uncovered legs and what seems to be a turban, almost oblivious to the action that surrounds her. A blind man, wearing glasses, elaborately dressed, and with his hands extended, brings up the rear, perhaps representing the stupidity of contemporary world leaders. After him come two towers, which stand out against the sky, and a cloud, suggesting the World Trade Center and the 9/11 disaster. The figures closer to the bottom of the hill and the prison bars of the story look despondent, exhausted by the effort; they are facing downward, their arms hanging limpid on their sides. Toward the middle we see more action: the medieval knight is in full charge; the man with a ziggurat for his lower half extends his arms in opposite directions; and the genie is intently looking at, and holding what may be a lamp.

What could be the significance of this ensemble in procession? One way of thinking of it is as representing the priest's quest as the human search for understanding of the universe, its calamities throughout the history of humankind, and the various cultures and empires that have dominated the ancient and modern worlds, the Middle Ages, the Jewish diaspora, the Middle East, Africa, pre-Columbian America, and others. But the procession goes in reverse order, beginning with towers that stand against the clouds and ending in a dungeon. Instead of an epiphany, we are presented with a figure of a blind man, groping in ignorance. Slowly, humankind moves along, but downhill, becoming exhausted by the effort, barred from the truth, and eventually ending in the dark prison shared by the priest and the tiger.

Another reading would be that the procession represents the history of the world and its kingdoms, cultures, and empires—history in march throughout the ages. After all, the priest recollects everything he knows, and at some point he becomes one with the universe and the god, losing his own self. This would be the moment of his epiphany and understanding. Or perhaps the procession refers to the images the priest considers in his search for the key to the revelation from the god. Can we give a Jewish twist to the work and see in the tiger the image of the Messiah, the chosen savior who tolerates and carries on its back the successes and failures of humankind?

And where is the divine text, the message from the god that the work reveals? It is supposed to be there on the god's creation; a message that is not hidden, although it is visible only to those who are ready to see it, to those who have been chosen to see it and have prepared themselves for it, the elect. And what is the message? Written on the tiger's face we read *"El secreto"* (The secret). But this expression does not tell us anything we did not know already, namely, that the god has revealed a secret on the tiger's hide. It does not reveal the secret, which remains hidden from anyone who is not prepared to understand. The secret, the revelation, and in the Jewish faith the Messiah, is still to come and only those chosen by the god will recognize him. If the tiger is the very symbol of the Messiah, he will be known only by those ready for that knowledge. The secret is not written on the tiger; rather, the secret is the tiger. His name is written on the markings of his head because he is the secret, and only by understanding and accepting him can the salvation that the priest craves be achieved. When that happens, whether to the priest or to us, our individuality and anxiety cease and we find what we were looking for, which is that nothing else matters.

12

The Secret Miracle

From a philosophical standpoint, Borges's "The Secret Miracle" presents us with at least two interesting questions, one has to do with the nature of time, the other with divine power and the nature of miracles. Is time relative or absolute? Are miracles produced by divine power possible? Both questions have been the subject of much discussion, and disagreements about their answers have been frequent. For Aristotle, whose view of time dominated Western thought until the eighteenth century, time is the measure of motion and therefore relative, a by-product of the substances that exist. But for Isaac Newton, whose view supplanted Aristotle's, time was absolute, a kind of receptacle where things fit. In the twentieth century, Albert Einstein challenged this position, combining time and space in the famous theory of relativity.

Miracles have also been controversial. The empiricism and rationalism of the Greeks made no room for miracles. Nature moves according to laws that determine outcomes and a divinity, such as Aristotle's Unmoved Mover, who moves the world by being its object of desire, not by tinkering with events. The idea of a personal god who cares for the individual banalities of people was unthinkable. But the success of Christianity changed all that, opening the doors to an attempt to develop a view of miracles concordant with science. Augustine and Thomas Aquinas were instrumental in establishing this tradition until early modern skeptics, such as David Hume, challenged it. For Hume, miracles are not only impossible, they are incomprehensible.

The ostensive answers to the questions of time and miracles posed by Borges's story are, first, that time is relative and, second, that this makes miracles possible. However, if one focuses on the statement in the story, to the effect that unreality is essential to art, it is possible to interpret the main theme of the narrative as the divide between the real and the unreal.

The story takes place in Prague during the occupation of the city by the forces of the Third Reich. It begins on March 14, 1939, the day before the invasion occurs. The protagonist is Jaromir Hladík, a Jewish playwright and author of various works including an incomplete drama entitled *The Enemies*. Jaromir is dreaming of a long game of chess whose players are two illustrious families, and he wakes up at the moment in which the armored cars roll into Prague. On March 19, an informer accuses him and he is arrested. He cannot deny that he comes from Jewish blood and has written on Jewish subjects. He is summarily condemned to be executed by firing squad on March 29. This terrifies him and he relives the moment of his death repeatedly, sometimes hoping that this could prevent it, and at other times thinking that his imaginings could be prophetic.

As the day of his execution approaches, he impatiently begins to yearn for the shots that will kill him. But on March 28, his thought runs back to his play, *The Enemies*. As a writer he measures others by their work, and he regrets that he has not left any book that lives up to his expectations. This leads him to think that perhaps he could redeem himself by finishing *The Enemies,* but he does not have the time. The incomplete play has a convoluted plot that ends where it began, suggesting that the action in the play has not taken place.

In a moment of hope, he asks God to give him one year to complete the play. That night, he dreams that he is at the Clementine Library in Prague and hears a voice that tells him, "The time for your labor has been granted." In the morning he is taken to the front of the firing squad. A heavy drop of rain grazes his temple and rolls down his cheek. The sergeant gives the order to fire, and the universe stops. Everything is frozen, including Jaromir, with the exception of his thoughts. He wonders whether he is dead or mad, or whether time has stopped. But this last possibility could not be, since he is still able to think. In time he realizes that his prayer has been answered favorably. A miracle, secret in that it is known only to him, has occurred. He works from memory and completes the play by March 29 at 9:02 a.m., at which time he dies. He hears himself cry, shakes his head, and the bullets kill him.

In Mirta Kupferminc's *El milagro secreto*, the images appear dark and superimposed, conveying the impression of chaos and temporal dislocation of events in Borges's story. At the bottom we see a composition of some of the most important buildings in Prague infused with a greenish hue. And at the top, a darker version of the same images is represented upside down. In between top and bottom appear a jumble of images of buildings and objects, divisible into lower and upper parts, in which the upper one is more defined than the lower. The green hue is

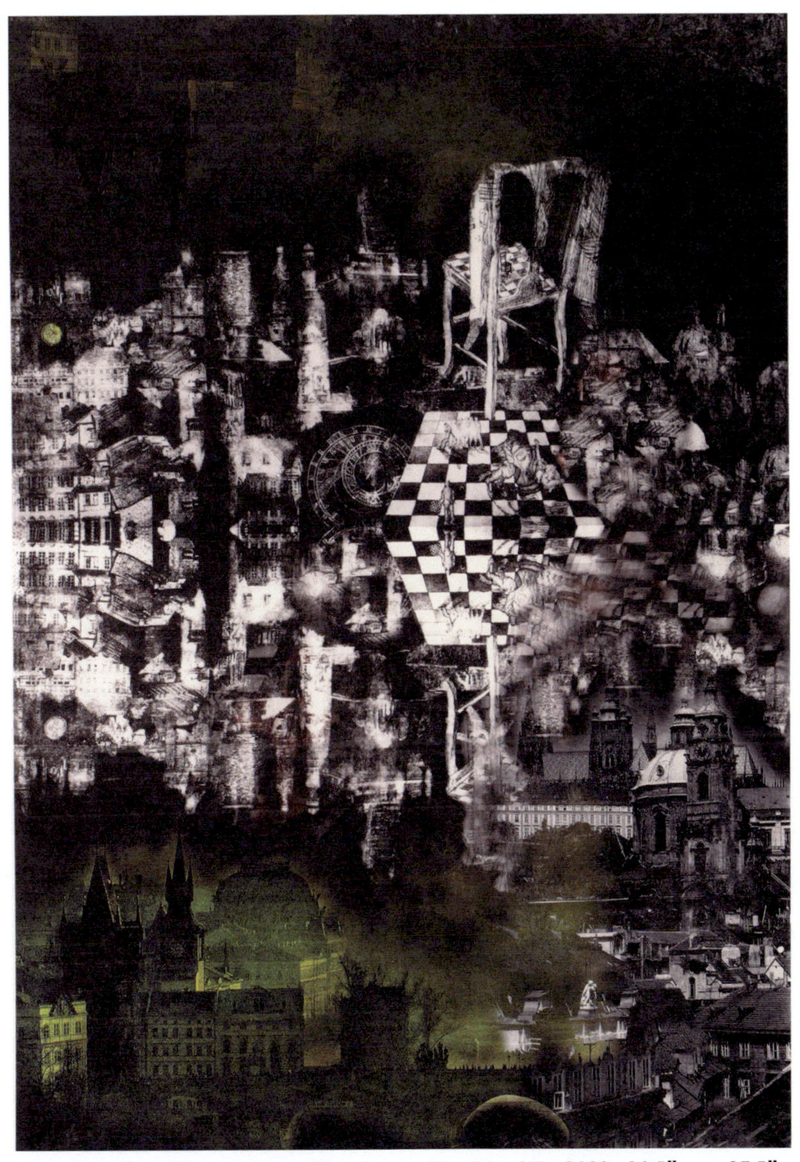

XXI. Mirta Kupferminc, *El milagro secreto* (The Secret Miracle), 4/5, 2008, 39.5" × 27.5", digital print.

missing here, except for the face of a clock that stands out in green, displaying wrong numbers. Somewhere on the lower part of these images one guesses at a pinkish hue, perhaps reminding us of the bloody denouement of the story. All this is flanked on the right by a chessboard, topped by a chair with its back to us on which, in turn, stands another chair. The chairs are quite different from each other; the bigger chair has wings and its seat looks like a chessboard. Are the chairs places for spectators or are they places for Hladík? The wings suggest a desire for flight from the grim reality that awaits the protagonist, but also an invitation for us, the spectators, to enter the story. They also signal the year of intellectual work the protagonist endures while he finishes *The Enemies*, and his wait for the end. Their sizes introduce another level to the work, the connection between the micro and the macro worlds, which as the chairs, are not different just in size, but also in other aspects.

As in the story, the role of the chess game is unclear. Borges speaks of a game of which Hladík dreams: of two families in conflict, of escape and destiny. Figures and objects resembling the pieces in a chess game are disorderly placed on the large chessboard, some upside down, others tumbled. And there are human figures at a couple of places. A single figure, most likely Jeromir, holds a chessboard on his hand, standing close to what appears to be a precipice, but which is the mirror image of the board in reverse. Behind him, further away, gather a group of people facing one who is falling to the ground. They most obviously refer to Jeromir and the firing squad that executes him, although the group could also stand for the soldiers that imprisoned him in first place.

A mirror image of the chessboard is folded down on the lower half of the work, following an axis all along the middle of the piece. To the right we see more buildings, quite distinct at the lower end, but more vague as we go up. There are towers and domes, images of buildings in Prague. The sense one gets is of motion; the images are moving at different times, superimposed on each other, and often lacking defined outlines, suggesting fluidity.

The division of the work into upper and lower parts suggests the two times at play in Borges's story: the time in which Hladík works on his play, and the time of the world outside his consciousness. The chessboard is the image with which the story begins, and which perhaps indicates an element of play or strategy. Time is most obviously present in the green clock and also in the scientific instruments of measurement found in the print. On the face of the clock we see four numbers: 3 (at the one-quarter of the hour), 39 (at the half hour), 44 (at the three-quarters of the hour), and 19 (at the hour). Hladík was taken prisoner on March 19, 1939, and Kupferminc has placed the numbers corresponding to the month, day, and year on the clock, as if they signified hours. The other number, 44, appears incomprehensible, but acquires significance when we learn that on the same month and day, but in the year 1944, Kupferminc's mother was taken prisoner and sent to Auschwitz. The imprisonment of Hladík and the imprisonment of Kupferminc's mother occur exactly five years apart. This brings together Hladík's story and Kupferminc's own past.

Kupferminc has tied her digital print to various elements of the story. She has sought to express the diversity of time and its relativity through symbols and by placing the images in contrary positions. She has also made references to Prague, the city in which the action of the story takes place. And she has introduced a dimension of waiting, observation, and expectation through the prominent use of the chair, which, as we saw in her *Con el fuego*, she frequently incorporates in her work. But she has omitted allusions to the particular actions of the narrative in the story, such as Jaromir's execution, the German invasion of the city, and Jaromir's imprisonment, except for the reference to its date. And, she has inserted a key reference to her own history that links Borges's fictional account to the real Jewish general plight during the Second World War and Jaromir's predicament as a Jew. This engages Borges's game of fiction and reality.

Nicolás Menza's *El milagro secreto* uses an entirely different approach to Borges's story from that used by Kupferminc's work. For one thing, it is only very loosely related to the story. Were it not for the title, it would be difficult to connect it with the narrative, although the connections are there, implicit and subtle.

The painting presents us with several distinct elements. The most significant is the image of a woman in profile whose shadow is cast over a wall. Her hair is gathered in a bun on top of her head. She wears a blue top that covers her neck. A red surface behind brings her figure into contrast, and her expression is firm and serious. Both the woman and the wall are common appearances in Menza's art.

Next to the woman we see a stand. Its top is yellow and the side of it that we can see is blue, picking up the color of the woman's sweater, although in a lighter tone. It is not clear to the observer whether we are seeing a table or a box with solid top and sides or a table or a box covered with a piece of cloth of different colors. On top of the stand lie two geometrical, tri-dimensional objects. One is a sphere and the other a cone. Like the woman's head, they also cast shadows, although these are projected on the stand, rather than on the wall. The side of the stand has a square-like hole on it, which appears dark.

Particularly intriguing is the background. It consists of a wall whose lower part, corresponding to the figures of the woman and the stand, is painted on an off-white color except for the places where the light does not illuminate it. It is fairly smooth but for a few

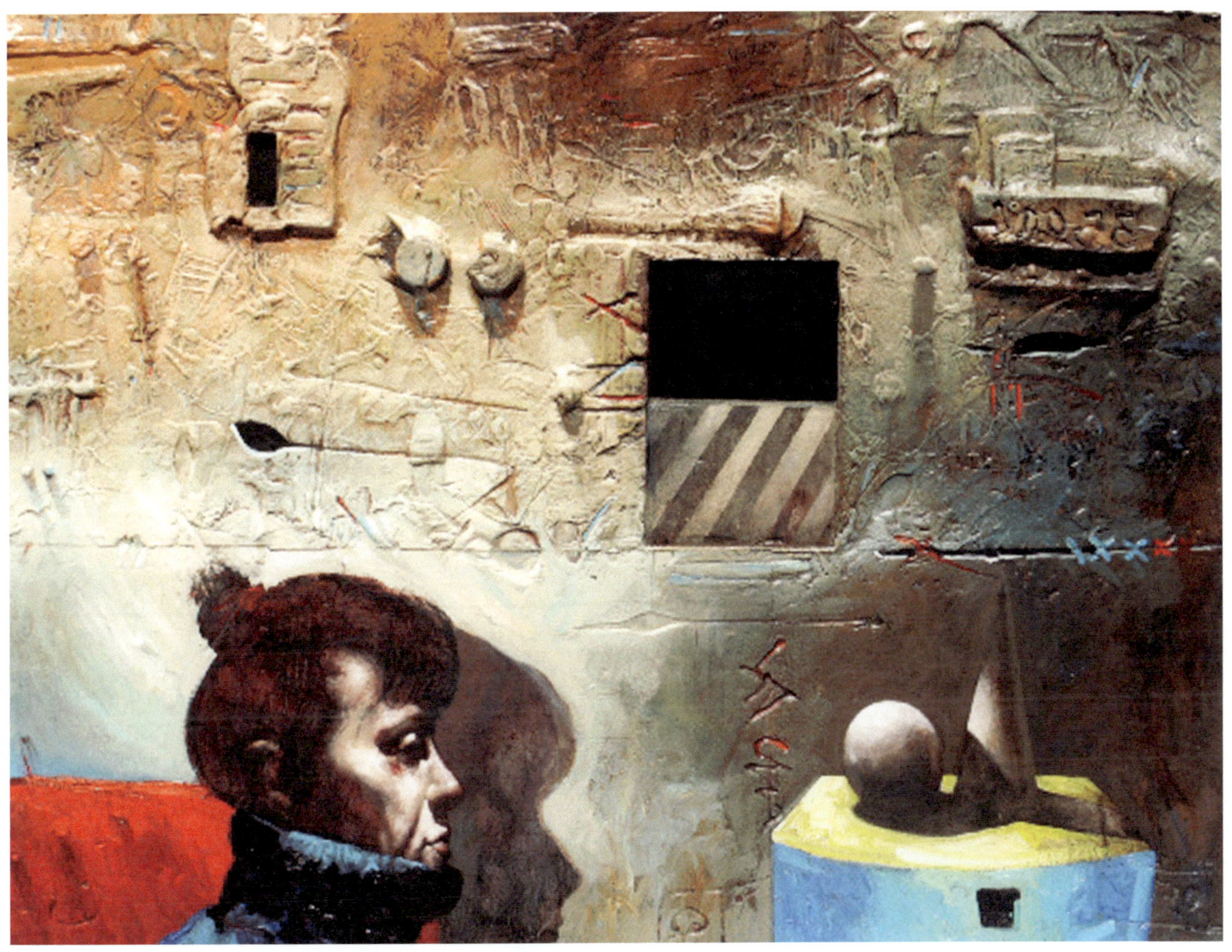

XXII. Nicolás Menza, *El milagro secreto* (The Secret Miracle), 2004, 27.5" × 39.5", goffering on paper.

marks around the center that appear to be scratches or designs on plaster. The upper part of the wall is more complicated and heavily textured. Impasto has been applied to it liberally. Part of it is smooth, but covered with irregularities of various sorts. Most prominent is what looks like a black rectangular hole in the middle of it, whose lower part seems to have been filled with a striped material. Other areas of the wall look like holes, pasted objects, figures, cracks, and enigmatic writings and symbols, but no definite writing or figures are discernible.

The painting is disconcerting. It is full of shadows projected by the various objects in it, but the shadows tend to undermine each other, lacking coherence. The shadow from the woman's head is projected on the wall and appears to be caused by light coming from the front, left, and top of the picture. However, the shadows of the geometrical objects on the stand are projected on the surface of the stand and their trajectories are not quite concordant with that of the shadow projected by the head. In addition, the shadows projected by the protuberances of it on the upper part of the wall also lead to conflicts. Most seem to come down, but there is some question concerning the large shadow visible on the right from the middle of the upper part of the wall all the way down to the end of the picture.

The use of shadows to create uncertainty, and open spaces for interpretation, is a frequent technique used by Menza and acquires particular significance in the interpretation of Borges's story. Perhaps shadows serve as signs of the temporal disconnect experienced by the protagonist in the story and the impossibility of the narrated situation. This brings me back to the woman and her expression. Is she in the kind of trance experienced by Hladík in the miracle? Does the textured background represent the world outside Hladík's mind, or is it a projection of his mind? The black holes painted on the surface of the work tease the curiosity of the audience, enticing them to look at them and construct a scene inaccessible to other observers. Is there a miracle? Yes, but it is a different miracle from the one Hladík experienced, although, like Hladík's miracle, it is inside the observer's head and inaccessible to anyone else.

Menza's usual strategy is to omit references to particular details of the stories he interprets pictorially except for the titles. This leads the audience to search for clues and to superimpose Borges's narrative on the painting. The aim is to open avenues of interpretation for an audience, who is asked to fill in the large blank spaces that exist between the story and Menza's work. As most creations of this artist, the focus is on a female figure whose expression is a rich field for interpretation. All of this fits well with Borges's own procedure in the stories.

13

The Gospel According to Mark

Borges's "The Gospel According to Mark" stays away from the supernatural, magical, and conceptual puzzles of which Borges is so fond. The story is quite clear and simple; it avoids references to obscure historical events, conceptual or physical labyrinths, paradoxes, and ambiguities. But when it comes to interpreting its meaning, matters are not so clear or simple. There are many ways of understanding its significance. Indeed, it is a treasure trove for the interpreter who can approach it from different interpretive perspectives.

The protagonist of the story is Baltasar Espinosa, whose last name means thorny and was also the name of a most celebrated Jewish philosopher in the seventeenth century, Baruch Spinoza. Baltasar's father is a freethinker and his mother a devout Catholic. He is characterized by a typical gift of oratory and "an almost unlimited goodness." He is, like Christ, thirty-three years old when the events narrated in the story happen, and also like Christ, he had accomplished nothing of note to that point.

He accepts an invitation from a cousin to spend the summer at a ranch in the *pampas*. The bailiff is named Gutre, which we are told later is a corruption of Guthrie, signaling a long forgotten family origin in Inverness. He lives with his son, who is particularly uncouth, and a girl of uncertain paternity. Their dwelling is not far from the main house.

Baltasar's cousin has to leave for Buenos Aires, but Baltasar remains at the ranch. A heat wave breaks in a colossal storm that isolates the ranch. The roof of the Gutres's place is threatened by a leak, and Baltasar allows them to move into a room in the main house, close to the tool shed. This brings all of them together. They have common meals and Baltasar tries to engage them in conversation, but with limited success. To pass the time, he attempts to read them passages from a famous book about gauchos in the *pampas*, a copy of which he finds in the small book collection of the ranch—the Gutres can neither read nor write. The bailiff, experienced in cattle ranching, finds the romanticized narrative inauthentic.

Baltasar lets his beard grow and speculates about what his city friends will think when he returns to Buenos Aires. One day, while exploring the house, he finds an old Bible, in English, with the Guthrie family history. The present Guthries had emigrated to the New World in the early nineteenth century, but had intermarried with Indians and had now forgotten both their origins and language. To try his hand at translating and to see if he could get them interested, he reads the Gutres some passages from "The Gospel According to Mark," and is surprised to find that they are fascinated by it. From then on, the Gutres anxiously look forward to the reading after dinner.

After Baltasar successfully treats the wound of a little lamb that is the girl's pet with standard medications, the Gutres show him extraordinary gratitude. They pamper him, follow him around the house, and obey his orders immediately. One day he catches them discussing him in respectful words. After finishing with the Gospel According to Mark, Baltasar tries to read them a different Gospel, but the bailiff asks him to read Mark again, so that they can understand it better.

One night Baltasar dreams of the Flood and wakes up at the sound of the hammering of the building of the Ark, but imagines it is thunder. The second storm takes place on Tuesday and, on Thursday, the girl comes into his room, naked and barefoot. She is a virgin.

The following day begins as usual, but the bailiff asks Baltasar whether Christ had undergone his death to save all mankind, including those who nailed him to the cross. Baltasar answers affirmatively, although he is not quite sure of the details of the Christian doctrine. Then they ask him to read the last chapters of the Gospel after lunch. Baltasar takes a siesta, which is interrupted by insistent hammering. Toward evening, the Gutres kneel on the floor in front of him and ask his blessing. Then they curse him, spit on him, and the men drive him to the back of the house, while the girl cries. When they open the door, Baltasar sees the sky and hears the cry of a goldfinch. They had taken the roof of the shed off and built "the Cross."

The meaning of this story is anything but clear, although the narrative of the events that occur is quite straightforward. At the outset, there are two ways of understanding it, depending on whether one takes it as a historical narrative of what actually happens or as a narrative of a romanticized nightmare by Baltasar. Both are possible as is usual with Borges's work, particularly in some stories, such as in "The South."

The significance of the events changes drastically if we interpret the narrative in one way or the other. If we take it historically, then the events can be seen in a social context: the ignorance of the Gutres, their isolation, and the character of the society in which they live. If we take the story as a dream, then the events can be understood to reflect the view that a young man from Buenos Aires has of the country and its people, a romanticized and prejudiced perspective on them and their culture. In both ways, the story could be taken as a criticism of Argentinean society with its vast disparities between the city and the country, the educated and the uneducated, the wealthy and the poor, the white and the mestizo, and the misguided pride of Argentineans regarding their social and racial superiority stemming from a European background. There is plenty in the story to support this view. We have the contrast, first, between the polished protagonist and the uncouth workers in the *estancia*—he is educated and sophisticated, and displays the kind of boredom characteristic of the superficial patina of culture prevalent among the Buenos Aires bourgeoisie, whereas the workers are illiterate and full of superstition and prejudice. Second, there is the contrast between the easy and pleasurable life in the city, suggested through the protagonist's friends, and the rough and hard life of the workers.

But we can also bracket the question of historicity and look at the story in its universal significance and what it says concerning religion and morality: religion, insofar as the story appears to be about sacrifice and redemption; and morality, insofar as it raises questions of violation and retribution. In the first sense we can interpret it as a criticism of religion in general or Christianity in particular. In the former, Baltasar is seen as a savior, a Christ-like figure, by the ignorant and credulous Gutres. Explainable events become miracles, and his horrible death a sacrifice. Is religion nothing more than a set of superstitions encouraged by ignorance in the context of particular circumstances? The repetition of the Christian story of atonement, sacrifice, and redemption in the context of a ranch in the *pampas* seems to point in this direction. The suggestion is that there is nothing supernatural in religion; it is purely a social phenomenon prompted by credulity and ignorance. How should we interpret the Christian story, then? Are Christian theologians right, or are the philosophers who dismiss their views correct?

If we take the story as a criticism of Christianity in particular, we begin to notice parallels between the story and the Christian narrative. Baltasar becomes an image of Christ, and some of the events in the story mirror events in the Gospels: the ignorance of the Gutres, the teaching by the master, the healing of the lamb, the passion of Baltasar, and the suggested crucifixion. But many elements are at odds between the two. Baltasar seems ignorant of what the Gutres think, and it is the Gutres who plan to crucify Baltasar; whereas the Christian crucifixion is carried out by Romans, and although the girl who offers herself to Baltasar resembles Mary Magdalene in some ways, there are significant contrasts between the two, a major one is that in the Christian story Mary Magdalene does not become Christ's lover.

Another way in which the story could be interpreted is as a criticism of the facile morality of Baltasar and his class. His piety consists in following his mother's advice, uttering the Lord's prayer, and crossing himself before going to bed, but at the same time, allowing himself to take advantage of a young virgin offered to him by credulous folks. The tale could be construed as a portrayal of Baltasar's life of leisure, without aim or direction, his guilt-ridden awareness of it, and its lack of meaning.

Héctor Destéfanis's *La decisión de los Guthre* depicts a moment in the presumed crucifixion of the story's protagonist, Baltasar, intended by the Gutres. Destéfanis uses subdued colors, giving a sense of the pathos of the moment. Instead of the location in the shed, where the action is supposed to take place, the artist has placed the composition on a terrain with a slight curvature on the horizon, probably intended to echo Golgotha, the location where Christ was reputedly crucified. Pervasive blacks, browns, and grays are only lightened by the subtle orange of Baltasar's shirt. The browns evoke the color of the earth and the silvery grays the rain that we are told has flooded the land. The hour is obviously dusk, when the sun is behind the horizon, leaving only traces of light in its deference to the oncoming darkness.

The main participants in the drama are Baltasar and the three Gutres, and all four are present in the picture. Daniel, Baltasar's cousin, is a ghostly character, a dandy concerned with superficial matters that disappears from the story quickly, as soon as he has been introduced, and he is omitted in the composition. At first, we tend to see only the four figures mentioned, but closer attention reveals a fifth. What looks like Baltasar's hat is actually a dark human shadow behind him. We can make out the outlines of a bowed head, and most importantly an arm stretched behind the figure of the Gutre son, all the way past him, ending with an open hand. On the right, behind the father's shoulder—we conjecture that the figure to whom the shoulder belongs is the father because of the graying hair in contrast with the son's darker hair—we see a darker line behind the back, and the tip of three fingers way up. The shadow is elongated, as shadows often are, and extends behind Baltasar, ending in a sort of bag wrapped around the lower parts of his legs and feet. One tends to speculate that it is Baltasar's shadow, but further attention indicates that this does not make sense. A shadow needs a surface on which to be cast, and there is no surface behind Baltasar. This leads to the surmise that it represents Christ, whose figure looms large behind the story, for Baltasar becomes a Christ in the eyes of his tormentors.

Baltasar is represented with a grown beard and European features. By contrast, the Gutre men have elongated eyes and native features, thick noses and mouths, revealing their mixed

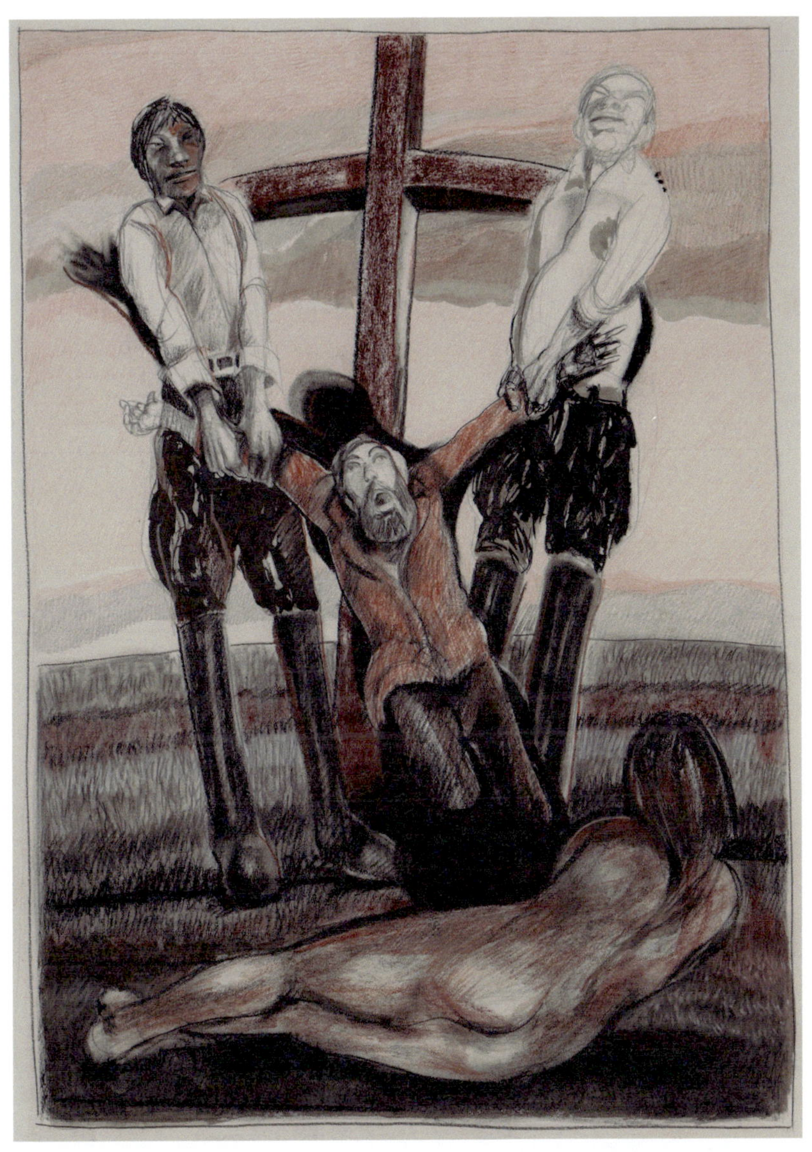

XXIII. Héctor Destéfanis, *La decisión de los Guthre* (The Guthres's Decision), 2009, 39.5" × 27.5", mixed media on paper.

ancestry. They are dressed in ranch attire, with the shirts, boots, and belts typical of the gauchos, the country folk that tend cattle in the *pampas*. The father has an expression of effort as he and his son drag Baltasar toward the cross they have built in the shed. In front of Baltasar lies the girl. She is nude, as she came into Baltasar's room the night when she offered herself to him. She is resting on her side, echoing the famous Ingres, seen from behind. Her voluptuous body contrasts with the desperate agony of the situation. The pose of relaxation and rest suggests unemotional involvement, and perhaps detached observation, which is surprising considering her behavior in the story, the gratitude she must have felt for Baltasar's healing of her lamb, and the intimacy they shared the night before. Does Baltasar's crucifixion have something to do with his sexual encounter with the girl? Is she an erotic object of desire at the center of an emotional storm? Why does she look rested and unconcerned, detached and comfortably observing the proceedings? In the story she is crying while the men drag Baltasar to the shed, but Destéfanis does not show her face, and her posture is not one that would normally be associated with sorrow. Is this unrealistic palette a sign that the key events narrated in the story, Baltasar's sexual encounter with the girl and his crucifixion, are no more than dreams projected by the protagonist's suppressed psychological desires and fears? Or is she in fact visually offering herself to him, is a reminder of their encounter, whether to palliate his present suffering or torment him for his ambiguous morality?

Perhaps none of the major events of the story occurred—the storm, the flood, the crucifixion, the encounter with the girl, the reading of the Gospel—perhaps reality is consigned to an emotional crisis in Baltasar prompted by solitude and a meditation of his meaningless life. Is he constructing, as the protagonist of "The South" does, a stage on which he becomes larger than he is in reality, a reality that gives his life meaning and romanticizes a rather puerile existence? Perhaps we are witnessing the crumbling of Baltasar's comfortable bourgeois world of the city prompted by the challenge of the raw countryside and its people, the loss of an illusory security when he is confronted with something entirely different from what he is used to and on which he relies for his psychical stability and contentment. After all, his veneer of sophistication, based on some meager understanding of positivist philosophy and the usual Argentinean contradictory attitudes toward France and the United States, receives a shock when he is confronted with the facts of the countryside.

For our purposes a salient aspect of Destéfanis's interpretation is that it focuses on an event in Borges's story that, paradoxically, is only a likely possibility, but does not take place or is described. Even if we take the story as an accurate narrative of what happens, rather than a metaphor for Baltasar's mental upheaval or a dream, the story ends with the Gutres dragging

Baltasar to the cross they have built in the shed, and Baltasar's coming to understand their intentions, not with the actual crucifixion. It is possible that their intentions are not realized. Baltasar's cousin, Daniel, might arrive at the ranch unexpectedly, as often happens in American westerns. Or Baltasar may be crucified, but not killed by the ordeal. Or he might convince the Gutres that what they are doing is absurd, and they will pay dearly for it. Or Baltasar may wake up and find out that it was all a nightmare, and he is comfortably sleeping next to the girl after an enjoyable coitus. All of this makes more sense, in an ordinary way, than the crucifixion, which is an act so bizarre that it appears surrealistic even in the rough and wild environment of the Argentinean countryside.

In fact, Destéfanis's interpretation seems to sidestep these questions, for it is focused on the decision of the Gutres, as the title of the artwork clearly indicates, rather than the Gospel or the crucifixion. The artist is well aware that he is depicting the Gutres's decided and intended action, not an event present in Borges's tale. He includes in his depiction something that is not present in the story and which he makes visible through the images of the artwork. In this he has gone well beyond the narrative, adding a denouement that could happen, but may not happen. And he has gone even beyond this by transplanting the location of the story to a place that echoes the historical landscape where Christ's crucifixion took place. But instead of the crying women of the traditional crucifixion, which he could have emulated by depicting a crying girl, he paints a nude, unconcerned, and relaxed, voluptuous woman. Whatever he is suggesting to us goes well beyond what Borges wrote and becomes a source of speculation and reflection by observers. He has added a fascinating wrinkle to what is already a most intriguing puzzle.

Ricardo Celma's *El evangelio según Borges* presents us with a central figure of a beautiful woman, dressed in a low-cut, white slip that reveals the shape of her enticing body. The fabric of the slip is a fine silk evident in the carefully painted folds as it revealingly clings to the body, its borders finished with delicate lace. The woman has brown hair, loose and falling freely around her face and covering part of her chest. She is looking fixedly at the observer who is thus drawn into the picture and becomes part of the scene. Her mood is serious, intent, and enigmatic, her clear eyes simultaneously revealing and concealing. What is she thinking? What does she want? She is kneeling in front of us, as if she were offering us something, which could be herself or the goldfinch she holds by the wings in a crucified pose. Although the bird appears to be dead, the legs hanging lifeless, the head is painted sideways and erect, contrary to what one would expect of death. No signs of a struggle are evident.

The head of the woman is surrounded by a gilded halo, in the style of medieval illuminations. Three inscriptions are visible. One appears just outside the halo and reads "Love

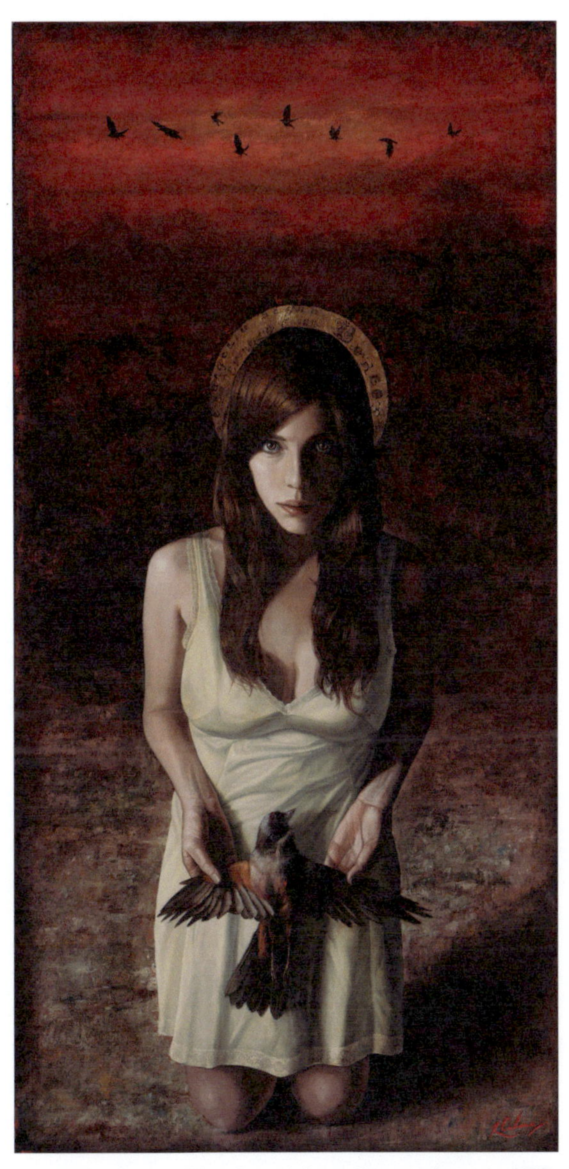

XXIV. Ricardo Celma, *El evangelio según Borges* (The Gospel According to Borges), 2009, 59" × 29.5", oil on canvas.

by Borges." On the halo itself, the inscription closest to the head reads *"Evangelio según Borges"* (Gospel according to Borges). This inscription is written in an elaborate script of the sort one would expect in an illuminated manuscript from the Middle Ages. Above part of this inscription, and parallel to the first two words of it, is also written *"evangelio según"* (gospel according to). This uses an ordinary, less elaborate, semi-uncial script.

The figure of the woman is located on an arid landscape, depicted in the colors of blood and earth. A red tinted sky, with an indistinct sun covered by clouds, suggests the beginning or the end of the day. Eight birds fly about the horizon in a kind of disordered arrangement, although they are all moving in the same direction. They appear too large in the distance to be goldfinches, and their dark color and body shapes reveal birds of prey, perhaps vultures scouring the landscape, waiting for the dead flesh usually hanging on crosses after crucifixions. The landscape itself is not clearly defined. A vague mountain stands on the left, and far away in the middle is perhaps a flooded plain. To the right we see the shadow of a cross. The mix of brown and red characterizing the landscape is graded, going from a mixed color in which brown predominates in the front, where the woman is kneeling, to one at the back where red is dominant. The bareness of the ground suggests a place from which flooding waters have retreated.

The techniques used in the figure of the woman and the goldfinch, on the one hand, and in the landscape and background, on the other, contrast sharply. The woman and bird are depicted in painstaking detail, in the context that some like to call *super realism*, but could be more aptly called *magical realism* in the style of Celma's work. The background is rendered in a rough, textured technique that contrasts strongly with the delicate brushwork used in the figures of the woman and the bird. The colors also clash: the white and subdued flesh tones used for the woman and the bird confront the somber and strong colors of the landscape.

Celma painted this work as an interpretation of Borges's story, but only a few elements are ostensively common to the painting and the story: most evident are the woman, the goldfinch, and the cross. In the narrative, the girl offers herself to Baltasar and we are told that the Gutres have built a cross; in the painting we have a woman who kneels in front of us holding a goldfinch, with the outlines of a cross far in the distance. The differences between the two works are obvious. The painting has no reference to the Gutre father and son, Baltasar or his cousin, or the Gospel according to Mark. The suggestion of a flood in the painting is unclear. And the goldfinch of the narrative is only heard by Baltasar, not seen or in any way connected with the girl, as it is in the painting. The girl of the story is a country girl, who comes naked and timidly to Baltasar, whereas the woman we see in the artwork appears to be sophisticated, dressed in a fine slip, and openly offering herself, the goldfinch, or both. She looks more like a sophisticated *porteña* than an uncouth servant. And the mountainous landscape and the birds on the horizon in the painting are missing in the story, which takes place in the flat *pampas*.

Yet, important elements in the painting tie it to the story. The goldfinch is a symbol of the passion of Christ because of the thistle seeds it eats, becoming a reference to the crown of thorns. This motif can be found in much art that has to do with Christ, most famously perhaps in Raphael's *Madonna of the Goldfinch,* in which the child John the Baptist presents the goldfinch to the child Christ as a reference to the future. The act of offering by the girl in the story is emulated in the painting, and the presence of the cross in both brings the piece and the Christian story together.

So what is the interpretation that the painting makes of Borges's story? It seems clear that it is focused on the girl and her connection to Baltasar. Borges writes that she offers herself to him on the night before the Gutres intend to crucify him. We also know that she is grateful to him for having cured her little lamb. And most important, we have a legend around the halo that reads "Love by Borges." From this we can infer that the painting is ultimately about the nature of love as exemplified in the girl's freely offering of herself to Baltasar. She is presented as a symbol of purity and innocence, in her white slip, who openly offers herself—she is kneeling. She does this fully knowing that Baltasar is going to suffer abuse and ultimately crucifixion at the hands of the Gutres, revealed by the symbol of the goldfinch she holds by the wings in a crucified pose and of the shadowy cross we see in the distance. Unlike offering a singing bird, which would be celebrating the event of her own offering to Baltasar, she holds a dead bird, or at least one that is trapped. The moment is sacred and serves to introduce the question of what the woman is thinking and the incapacity of a man to know it. If we become Baltasar, as the painting makes us do when we look at the picture, what do we know of the woman's thoughts? One thing is clear, she offers herself freely and expects nothing in return insofar as Baltasar's crucifixion has been decided. This is an unconditional gift, a present made with full consciousness of a future she is ready to embrace, although beyond this, we know nothing. In this, the interpretation is concordant with much of Celma's art, where the psyche of the female, and the masculine difficulty to understand it, is a regular topic.

At another level one could look at the painting as trying to present an interpretation of the story that harks back to the Gospel According to Mark. If we take this approach, the figure in the picture becomes Mary Magdalene, and this presents us with an interpretation of the biblical text in which Christ, played by Baltasar in the story, becomes her lover. However, this interpretative strategy is difficult to sustain insofar as the inscriptions on the woman's halo refer to Borges, not the biblical narrative. Rather, the painter has given an interpretation of Borges's tale and seems to have revealed to us one way of conceiving love, according to Borges. It is not the evangelist Mark and his doctrine that are under interpretation, but Borges's understanding of love as revealed in his story. In this respect the interpretation has gone well beyond the text, using as points of departure elements that are either present in, or suggested by, it.

Finally, does Celma's painting depict a reality or merely a dream of Baltasar? The answer to this question is unclear and perhaps irrelevant. The magical realism that inspires the work suggests that we are dealing with something that does not fit the categories of reality or unreality.

II

Identity and Interpretation

14

Literature, Art, and Philosophy

The artistic interpretations of Borges's stories presented in Part I of this book pose a number of interesting conceptual issues. The variety of media, approaches, and strategies they use raises questions that go to the heart of the hermeneutic task. Although all of the interpretations, except one, are versions of what might be called flat art, they differ in significant ways, going from painting to drawing, etching, and photography. The media they employ range from oil on canvas or plaster, to acrylic on canvas, to markers or ink, to etchings, to digital images, to coffee on paper. The styles are also very different; the artists use languages that are evidently their own. The art is figurative, but it ranges from versions of realism to works influenced by cubism, abstract expressionism, and surrealism. The color schemes also vary substantially; some of the art displays a muted appearance and has a limited spectrum of colors, whereas other art sharply impresses the observer with its variety and intensity. And although some of the works use traditional symbols and images, others turn their backs on the past in search for new venues of expression. All of this variety brings out the many possibilities of interpretation opened by the encounter between the art and Borges's stories.

A necessary step in understanding the complex relationship between an object of interpretation and its interpretation is to establish some parameters about the identity of both. In our case the objects of interpretation consist of the stories by Borges and the works of art that interpret them, and the interpretations consist of works of art and philosophical essays. I take up the identity of literary, artistic, and philosophical works in this chapter.

Identity

In a letter to his wife, to whom he dedicated the "Eighth Symphony," Mahler wrote:

> It is a peculiarity of the interpretation of works of art that *the rational element in them (that which is soluble by reason) is almost never their true reality*, but only a veil which hides their form. Insofar as a soul needs a body—which there is no disputing—an artist is bound to derive the means of creation from the natural world. But the chief thing is still the artistic conception. . . . [In *Faust*] everything points with growing mastery toward his final supreme moment—which, *though beyond expression, touches the very heart of feeling.*[1]

Mahler's use of the word 'interpretation' at the beginning of this text is misleading, for it may suggest that he is writing about what should peculiarly inform the *interpretation of works of art*. In fact, he has in mind what is peculiar to *works of art*, which for him is that they defy rationality and expression. By this he means that works of art are not reducible to ideas and, therefore, cannot be effectively translated.

If works of art are idiosyncratic in this way, then one would expect that this is also what distinguishes them from works of philosophy. Whereas art is irreducible to ideas and defies translation, philosophy is reducible to ideas and can be translated.

This is the standard modernist view of philosophy and art—and, by extension, of literature—which has been one of the points of attack by postmodernists. The argument is not only that art and literature are not reducible to ideas and therefore untranslatable, but that there is no distinction in this respect between art and literature on one hand and philosophy on the other. Philosophy is also art.[2]

Postmodernism has found a receptive audience in literary circles and especially on this point. Indeed, the view that there is no distinction between literature, in particular, and philosophy is often treated as dogma. I quote from a recent source: "[I]n fact, there is no substantial difference between philosophical discourse and literary discourse" in spite of "the boundaries that have been traditionally claimed to separate both discourses."[3]

The rationale behind this position has been well articulated in the last quarter of the twentieth century. Its expression in Latin America is especially pertinent here insofar as we are dealing with the interpretation of Borges's stories by Argentinean and Cuban artists. It takes the following form: Latin Americans have not produced, to date, a philosophical discourse that is recognized as such outside Latin America. The reason is that the criterion of what constitutes philosophy is modernist, that is, it draws a sharp line between philosophy and literature. If this criterion is rejected, and the dividing line between philosophy and literature is erased, however, Latin America cannot be said to lack philosophy. Latin America can be considered not to have produced philosophy only if one approaches this issue from the point of view of modernity. From the postmodern perspective, things are quite different. We must, then, change the way we approach philosophy and literature to make room for Latin America in the philosophical world.[4]

An author who, perhaps more than any other, is cited as proof of the absence of boundaries between philosophy and literature is, precisely, Borges.[5] And with reason, for Borges is widely known outside the Hispanic world and it would be very difficult to claim that his thought is not philosophical. Many of his stories, including the ones discussed in Part I of this book, appear to address profound philosophical questions. Indeed, many authors from different philosophical traditions have used them as points of departure for discussions that are generally regarded as philosophical. Earlier I referred to Michel Foucault and Arthur Danto as examples, but they are not the only ones by any means.[6]

For present purposes, determining the differences between philosophy, literature, and art is important insofar as the subject matter of this book is the interpretation of Borges's literary works in visual art. In order to investigate this topic I have adopted a philosophical standpoint in the analysis of both the stories and the art. The task, then, is to clarify the nature of philosophy, literature, and art to make explicit some of their main differences and similarities, although I do not by any means claim to have exhausted the list. My aim is more modest: I merely try to discover some of the differences and similarities that are pertinent in the present context, where the concern is with the visually artistic interpretation of literature and the philosophical interpretation of both art and literature.

Various ways of carrying out this task are possible, but for present purposes I focus on the identity of works of philosophy, art, and literature. To make things easier, in this book I use Borges's stories as examples of works of literature, the visual interpretations of the stories as examples of works of art, and my essays on them as examples of works of philosophy—although I also add a philosophical discussion of a Borges story by Danto and a philosophical discussion on *Las meninas* by Foucault. This narrows the field of art I discuss here to visual art; however, since my ultimate goal is to understand the visual interpretation of literature, this narrowing is appropriate. The pertinent questions are two: Can Borges's stories be considered works of philosophy, literature, or visual art? And, if they are not works of philosophy or visual art, as I argue, why, and more generally what distinguishes philosophy, literature, and visual art?[7]

To ask these questions in this way, however, is confusing, for the terms 'philosophy,' 'literature,' and 'art' are used in ordinary language to mean a variety of things. It is common to speak of philosophy, for example, as a discipline of learning, as an activity, as the thought of an author, and so on.[8] We find a similar variety of meanings for the terms 'literature' and 'art.' Moreover, because one of my ultimate aims is to establish the similarities and differences between Borges's stories and the works that interpret them, whether in art or philosophy, and such interpretations are both works and texts in the case of the stories and their philosophical interpretations, and works and pictures in the case of art, it will be useful to reformulate the general question as follows: What distinguishes literary works from artistic and philosophical works, and literary texts from philosophical texts and artistic pictures? The more specific question about Borges and the interpretations of his stories needs, then, to be also reformulated accordingly.

My thesis about Borges's stories is that they are literary works and texts rather than visually artistic or philosophical, but they share some interesting, and different, characteristics with philosophical works and texts. My thesis about philosophy and literature in general is that literary works are distinguished from philosophical ones in that they include the conditions of identity of the texts that express them, whereas that is not the case in philosophy. Moreover, literary texts are distinguished from philosophical ones in that they express literary works.[9] And, my thesis concerning visual artworks and the pictures that constitute them is that their identity conditions include those pictures. More generally, artistic pictures are distinguished from literary texts in that they express visual artistic works. Finally, works and texts of philosophy do not include the texts or the pictures of the objects that express them as identity conditions, and this distinguishes them from both literature and visual art.

As will become clear, this is an ontological, rather than an epistemological or a causal, claim. I assume that the question concerning the identity conditions of works and texts is not logically the same as the question concerning the conditions under which works and texts are known or are produced. This means that, in principle, knowing a work or text may entail certain requirements that are not part of the identity conditions of the work or text, and vice versa. And the same could be said concerning the conditions of their production. However, I also argue that, although some of the conditions of identity of literary works are not conditions of identity of philosophical ones, they may nonetheless be necessary conditions, in context, of knowing philosophical works, and some of the conditions of identity of visually artistic works that are not conditions of literary or philosophical works may also be necessary conditions, in context, of knowing literary or philosophical works. This is one of the important distinctions between my position and the standard modernist view and has important implications that I point out later.

Texts, Pictures, and Works

Let me begin by introducing some distinctions between texts, pictures, and works. This is a much disputed topic, but because I have no space to engage in a discussion of the relative merits of various current views in this matter, I proceed instead by presenting my own position.[10] This is not sufficient to establish it fully, but I hope it at least clarifies how I use it to articulate my view concerning the nature of literary and philosophical works and texts, and artistic works and pictures. I have chosen the term 'pictures' because the art included here, but for one piece, consists of pictures.

Texts

A *text* is a group of entities used as signs, selected, arranged, and intended by an author in order to convey a specific meaning to an audience in a certain context.[11] The entities in question can be of any sort. They can be ink marks on a piece of paper, sculpted pieces of ice, carvings on stone, designs on sand, sounds uttered by humans or produced by mechanical devices, actions, gestures, mental images, and so on. These entities, considered by themselves, are not a text. They become a text only when they are used by an author to convey some specific meaning to an audience in a certain context. Ontologically, this means that a text amounts to these entities considered as having a specific meaning, although what that meaning turns out to be depends on a variety of factors. The marks on the paper on which I am writing, for example, are not a text unless someone mentally connects them to a specific meaning. The situation is very much like that of a stone used as a paperweight. The stone becomes the paperweight only when someone thinks of it or uses it as a paperweight.

Texts are very much like the *signs* of which they are composed, but they can be distinguished from them in this way: the meaning of texts is in part the result of the meanings of the signs of which the texts are composed and the arrangement in which they are placed. But this is not so for the meaning of signs, even in cases in which the sign is composed of other signs. This is the difference between, say, the text 'My cat eats only Fine Feast cat food' and the sign 'cat.' The meaning of the first is the result of the meaning of 'My,' 'the,' and the other signs of which it is composed, in addition to the way they have been arranged. But the meaning of 'cat' is not the result of the meaning of 'c' 'a,' and 't,' and their arrangement, for the meaning of 'cat' has nothing to do with the meaning of 'c,' which is the letter 'c,' and the other signs of which the word is composed.[12]

The manner in which I have described texts and signs opens the way to think that pictures can be classified as texts. After all, a picture can be thought of as being composed of entities used as signs, selected, arranged, and intended by an author in order to convey a specific meaning to an audience in a certain context. However, generally we do not think of pictures as texts. We associate texts with words, that is with signs that are part of languages. In this sense we think of what is written on this page as a text, but not so of the images of the art reproduced in Part I of this book. To understand this difference we can point to a distinction between *word signs* and *image signs*, where the first are terms belonging to a language and the second are images that are not part of the vocabulary of any language. We could, then, reserve the notion of *text* for a composite of word signs and *picture* for a composite of image signs.

Some texts are presented in *scripts*, that is, compositions of *written words*, but others are presented as *utterances*, that is, compositions of *oral words*. Scripts and utterances are not like texts in that, by themselves, they do not have meaning, and they have characteristics different from those involved in meaning. For example, we may speak of a script as uncial, semi-uncial, or Gothic, and an utterance as loud or not, but texts and enunciations are none of these. We do not think of texts as uncial or of enunciations as loud. Scripts can turn into texts when they are used as signs with specific meanings, just as utterances can turn into *enunciations* when they are used as signs with specific meanings. For our purposes, however, only scripts and texts are relevant insofar as Borges's stories are expressed by texts, so we leave aside the complications dealing with utterances and enunciations.

Pictures seldom include scripts; they are generally composed of images that do not represent writing. And the *images* that constitute a picture are both similar and different from texts: they constitute groups of visual forms selected, arranged, and intended by an artist to convey a specific meaning to an audience. In spite of some similarities with texts, these images do not constitute texts insofar as neither they as a whole, nor their parts, function as linguistic signs; they are not words of a vocabulary put together according to established rules of usage to determine meaning. Although they may function as signs, and in some cases are arranged in established ways, the rules they follow are not fixed and have a very high degree of flexibility when compared with language, nor are they like the words that constitute the vocabulary of a language. Indeed, even when pictures contain images of texts, the texts do not always function as such and are placed in rich contexts of imagery that alter their functions. The function of the images in a picture corresponds to the function of words in a text. The *visual forms* that constitute the images that make up a picture correspond to the scripts, utterances, or mental images that make up written, oral, or mental texts, but they are neither the images they constitute nor the work of art. They become images when they are meaningfully used, that is, when they are used as signs.

Works

A *work* is the meaning of certain texts or pictures. Not all texts or pictures have meanings that qualify as works. 'The cat is on the mat' is a text as judged by the definition given, but it is not a work, and no one thinks of its meaning as a work. However, Borges's "The South," on the other hand, is both a text and a work. On the difficult question of which texts have corresponding works, and which do not, there is much disagreement in the literature.[13] The matter does not seem to depend on length, style, authorship, or the degree of effort involved in the production of the text. Fortunately, there is no need to resolve the question at this juncture. The pertinent point for us is that texts and works are not the same things: a text is a group of entities considered in relation to a specific meaning, whereas works are the meanings of certain texts. Meaning also is a contested notion—but I leave it open—for what I am going to say later does not depend on any particular conception of meaning.

In the case of Borges's stories, the texts are the marks on the pages we look at, the sounds we hear when someone reads them to us, certain images we imagine when we think about the marks on the pages or the sounds uttered by someone reading, and so on, as long as they are considered as signs intended to convey specific meanings. In contrast, the works of the stories are the meanings those marks, sounds, or images are intended to convey, that is, the stories. In the case of the visual art that interprets Borges's stories here, the pictures in the art correspond to the texts of the stories, and the artworks are the meanings those pictures have. And, in the case of the philosophical essays that interpret both the stories and the works of art, the texts are the words in English arranged according to usage, but the works are the meanings of those words and their arrangements, that is, the essays themselves apart from the texts. One important difference between literature and philosophy on one side, and visual art on the other, is that the actual physical object that embodies the artwork is part of it and therefore the visual artwork is subject to place and time. Delgado's *La otra* is a three-dimensional artifact that has a definite spatio-temporal location in addition to a meaning. But neither the scripts of works of literature or of philosophy, nor their texts, are in any way identified with the works and hence have no spatio-temporal location. Borges's "The Other" is not located in any place or time, such as UB library in Buffalo in 2010.

Following is a diagram that illustrates the structure of the relations among the various terms, and corresponding concepts, discussed above:

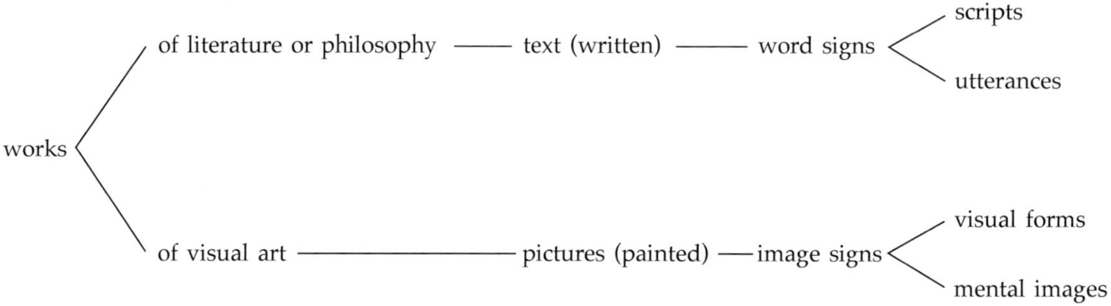

Literary and Philosophical Works and Texts, and Artistic Works and Pictures

Now that we have working notions of works, texts and pictures, word and image signs, and scripts and visual forms, we can go back to the issue posed at the beginning and ask, What is the distinction between philosophy, literature, and art?

The answer to this question is that there are distinctions between (1) works and texts of literature, (2) works and texts of philosophy, and (3) works and pictures of visual art. A literary work is distinguished from a philosophical one in that its conditions of identity include the text of which it is the meaning. This is to say that the signs of which the text is composed and the arrangements of the signs are essential to the literary work in question. This is the reason why no work of literature can ever be, strictly speaking, translated. It is in the nature of a literary work that the text that expresses it be essential to it. This is not the case with philosophical works. It should not really matter whether I read Kant's *Critique of Pure Reason* in German or English (in fact, many believe it is better to read it in English). What should matter is that I get the meaning.

The work is not essentially related to German, whereas Shakespeare's *Hamlet* could only have been written in English and Cervantes's *Don Quixote* could only have been written in Spanish.

Something similar to what applies to literature also applies to visual art and therefore sets visual art apart from philosophy. In art, the pictures that constitute what we see are essential parts of the identity conditions of the work. This means that visual art, like literature, and unlike philosophy, cannot be translated into a different art form. A painting cannot become a poem or a musical composition. But visual art also stands apart from literature in that rarely is the script of a literary work part of the work, whereas the visual forms of a picture are always part of the work of visual art.

With rare exceptions such as calligrams, the shape of a text or the kind of script it uses has no bearing on the identity of the literary work. *Don Quixote* may be written in Gothic or in uncial script, and that has no bearing on the work, that is, the meaning of the text. But the situation is different in visual art, because the visual forms that constitute the picture are always part of the work of art. Estévez's *Los jardines que se bifurcan* would not be the same work if the background of the picture were red, or the puppet at its center were drawn in geometrical patterns, or even if it had been painted with oils on canvas. An oil painting is a different work than a watercolor or a digital print, even if the images are alike.

So much, then, for the distinction between literary, artistic, and philosophical works. Now we can turn to the distinction between a literary text and a philosophical one, and between these and the pictures that constitute a work of visual art. But this does not prove to be difficult: a literary text is one that is essential to the work it expresses, whereas a philosophical text is not. Something similar can be said of a visual work of art. The pictures that constitute a visual work of art are essential to the work it expresses, whereas in a literary work, it is the text that is essential, and in a philosophical work only the ideas the text expresses are essential.

But perhaps I have gone too fast. After all, I have just stated my view and have not given any arguments for it. I could be wrong in holding that literary texts and works are distinguishable from philosophical and artistic ones. And even if not wrong about this, I could be wrong about the basis of the distinction.

To provide the kind of substantiation that this objection implies would take more space than I have at my disposal here, but I do need to say something in response to it. As a compromise, I offer some evidence to support my position, even if limited.

First of all, let me point out that those who oppose the distinction between philosophical and literary works and texts do so from at least two different perspectives. According to some, philosophical and literary works and texts are not distinguishable from each other because all philosophical works and texts are also literary works and texts. The distinction between them is artificial and based on a misunderstanding of the nature of works and texts. This is the kind of position that is quite popular these days in certain philosophical circles. All works and texts, and particularly philosophical ones, are to be viewed as literary or aesthetic ones; they are aesthetic or literary artifacts.[14] If this is so with respect to them, it should be obvious that the claim may also be applied to visual art.

Others, however, although also rejecting the distinction between philosophical and literary works and texts and visually artistic works and pictures, do so because they hold that all works, texts, and pictures are philosophical to the extent that they express ideas, and philosophy is about ideas. Thus, there is really no essential distinction between philosophy, literature, and visual art, but not because philosophical texts are literary or artistic, but rather because literary texts and artistic pictures are philosophical. This kind of position is not very popular these days, but one can find echoes of it in the history of philosophy beginning with Plato and his followers.[15]

Three pieces of evidence can be supplied against these positions. The first is that in practice we do make distinctions between at least some philosophical and literary works and texts and visually artistic works and the pictures that express them. Moreover, we treat them differently. That is, what we do with philosophical works and texts differs from what we do with the works and texts we regard as literary, and with works and pictures of visual art. This is a kind of pragmatic argument. The *Critique of Pure Reason* is studied in different academic departments, by different specialists, and in different ways than *Hamlet* and Michelangelo's frescoes in the Sistine Chapel. We do act as if these works, texts, and pictures are quite different in function and aim, and we use them for different purposes. Moreover, when we study them, we apply different methodologies. In the case of the *Critique of Pure Reason*, historians of philosophy and philosophers are concerned with the understanding of the ideas it proposes, the truth value of the propositions of which the arguments are composed, and the validity and soundness of the arguments it contains. We do pay attention to the language and the way Kant expresses himself, but the study of this language and the way Kant uses it is secondary to the main purpose of the study, which is determining the meaning and value of what Kant said.

Contrastingly, what we do with *Hamlet* is quite different. Here there may still be some concern about ideas, but there is no concern about arguments. No literary critic I know has ever tried to apply logic to discourses contained in the play. Moreover, the overriding preoccupation seems to be with the overall significance of the work and text, and by significance I mean the impact of the text on ourselves, others, society, and culture.[16] Likewise, when we approach Michelangelo's frescoes in the Sistine Chapel, we do so quite differently from what we do with philosophical works. The concern is with how Michelangelo has represented the story of the creation of Adam, for example, through imagery and color, and how this innovation puts a different light on that creation. The passive Adam, a masterful example of masculinity being awaken by God, and the active God, a masterful example of divinity creating Adam, are points of emphasis and discussion.

Still, it is obvious that, although we do use philosophical texts and works, literary texts and works, and artistic works and pictures in different ways, I could be wrong about what I have said. Someone could argue that we do so because we are following certain modernist traditions and customs well entrenched in our society, and there is nothing in the works, texts, or pictures themselves that justifies the different ways in which we treat them.

To this I respond with a second piece of evidence, namely, the case of poetry. Here is a kind of work or text of literature that seems clearly to fit the distinction I have drawn between philosophical and literary texts and works and stirs us in the direction of art. Some aspects of a poem make it quite different from prose, and although some philosophy has been presented in poetic form, most philosophy has not been so presented. Poetry involves certain structures, punctuation, and rhythm that stand out in contrast with the form of expression generally used in philosophical texts and works. Moreover, in poetry such factors are as essential for the identity of the work or text as the ideas expressed by the text.

In the case of visual art, and how it differs from philosophy and literature, we can return to the cited example of Michelangelo's frescoes. After all, here we have a series of paintings about a section of Genesis concerned with God's creation of the universe. The idea of creation in which philosophy is interested is quite different from the physical makeup and visual appearance of Michelangelo's masterpiece. The colors, the figures, the poses, the gestures, the gaze and expression of the figures, and their suggested motion or lack thereof are essential to the frescoes, but contribute little to the philosophy. Indeed, they are foreign to the literary work or text of Genesis. Consider the contrast with a poem on the same subject, such as John Milton's rendition of Adam's disobedience and sin in the first few lines of *Paradise Lost*. There the subject matter is presented with the great force of heroic English verse without rhyme, and burdened with references and implications present in the New Testament.

But, even if this piece of evidence were to convince us that at least poetic works and texts can be distinguished from philosophical ones, in that poetic texts are essential to poetic works, whereas this is not so with philosophical ones, the problem we still face is that not all literary works and texts are poetic. So what do we make of prose works and texts that are literary? How are we to distinguish them from philosophical ones, and vice versa?

My contention is that there is still a sense in that the identity of prose literary works depends on the texts they express, a fact which does not apply to philosophical works and which also affects the identity conditions of literary texts and works. The reason is not controversial. Indeed, it is generally accepted that the terms that constitute the vocabularies of different languages are not equivalent. Some are so, but the majority of terms are not equivalent in meaning or function. Still, many would hold that in a large number of cases one can find formulas in one language that would get across the meaning of the terms used in another. My point is that this is possible in principle in the case of philosophical works, but that it can never happen in the case of literary works. Therefore, we may ask, Why is this so? What are the differences between literary and philosophical texts and works that make literary meaning to be dependent on the text, whereas this is not so for philosophical meaning?

Many differences are at stake here, but I refer only to five for the sake of parsimony. Consider first the nature of the vocabulary used in literary and philosophical texts, how that vocabulary is used, and how the meaning of that vocabulary is treated. Philosophical vocabulary is overwhelmingly technical. This does not mean just that the terms used in philosophy are not generally used in ordinary discourse, whether spoken or written. It means that, even when terms that are commonly used are employed by philosophers, most of the terms acquire meanings different from those involved in common usage. Moreover, even when the meanings are not changed completely, philosophers circumscribe and limit the meanings. A word such as 'substance,' for example, which is commonly used in ordinary English, is a technical term in philosophy. Indeed, it is a technical term for most philosophers who use it, because they determine a particular sense in which they use it. On the other hand, the terms used in ordinary language have meanings that are frequently open-ended both because there are no strict criteria for their use and because their connotations vary. So much, then, for philosophy.

The situation with literature is very different from that in philosophy. In literary works and texts, terms are used primarily in an ordinary sense and their open-ended character is usually regarded as a good thing. Writers of literature do not generally define their terms or explain to us what they mean. They thrive on suggestion and connotation, leaving much leeway for the audience.

This brings me to a second difference that explains why the text is necessarily a part of the identity conditions of the work in literature but not so in philosophy. Most terms used in philosophy are rare, not because they rarely occur in common speech—if that were the case many pieces of literature would be indistinguishable from philosophy insofar as they too use words not commonly used in everyday speech—but because they are abstruse terms, which have meanings not directly related to common human experience. Consider, for example, the term 'substance' mentioned before. In common speech this means something like stuff, matter, or even money, among other things. But for scholastics who followed Aristotle, a substance is what is neither predicable nor part of something else, and the best example of it is God. By contrast, literature is precisely founded on common experience; that is one reason why the appeal of most literature is broad and takes little for granted in audiences.

The order of the words is also very important in literature, because literature aims to cause a certain effect on audiences which does not consist in the pure intellectual grasp of ideas. Literature is highly rhetorical. Each language has developed certain syntactical structures that produce particular effects in the audience that speaks the language of the text, and that are impossible or produce very different effects in audiences unfamiliar with that language. The audience plays a very special role in the case of literary works and texts.[17] The Latin periodic sentence, the epitome of elegance in that language, is generally a failure in English. In Latin, it is not only a sign of elegance, but is intended to produce a certain result. When one is reading these clauses and subclauses, not yet having arrived at the verb that puts it all together, one is supposed to develop a sense of anticipation which culminates in the grasp of meaning and in the relief one achieves when the verb is reached at the end. In English, it is impossible to put the verb at the end of a sentence in most cases, and the use of long periods of subordinated clauses, instead of causing anticipation, tends to produce confusion and frustration in audiences. A translation from Latin that tries to reproduce the Latin period in English is bound to have an entirely different effect on the English audience than the Latin had on the original Latin audience for which the Latin text was intended.

This brings me to style. Style is largely a matter of word choice, syntax, and punctuation, but style also depends very much on historical circumstances. Consider, for example, that a literary piece may be regarded as having an archaic style at a certain time, but as not having it at another time. A play written in the twentieth century in the style of Shakespeare is considered archaic, but a play written by Shakespeare during his time is not considered to have an archaic style. Style is always historically relative. It is also contextual insofar as it is relative to an audience. Now, style is of the essence in literature. The styles of authors are fundamental to the consideration of the authors and their work. But this is not so important, and some would say not important at all, when it comes to philosophy. In philosophy what matters is not the style of the author or the piece in question, but the philosophy, that is, the ideas the piece contains or, if you will, the claims it makes.[18] In this sense, although a text of philosophy may have a certain style, generally the work has little to do with it. This is another reason why the elements constitutive of texts are not part of the identity conditions of works of philosophy, whereas they are in a literary work.

Of course, one may want to argue that, since philosophy is expressed in texts, there is no way of avoiding style. And indeed, there are some philosophers who have insisted that the only way to present philosophy is in a particular format. This was certainly the case with Plato, for whom the proper philosophical form of discourse was the dialogue because this reflects the dialectical process leading to remembrance and truth.[19] And many other philosophers' writings can and are characterized stylistically, e.g., Russell and Hume. Indeed, even those philosophers who avoid stylistic peculiarities, like Aquinas, can be said to have a certain style that is clear or obscure, direct or indirect, and so on. Moreover, they use certain genres in their writing, such as the article form, the *quaestio* form, the commentary, and so on, and genre is bound up with style even if it is not the same thing. So it is difficult to argue that philosophy does not care for style, although one might argue that it does not care for a particular style.

Still, the point I am making is not that philosophical writing lacks style, or even that the style is always unrelated to meaning. My point is that philosophers do not generally think that what they are doing is essentially related to the style they use. Of course, not all philosophers have thought this way. The aforementioned case of Plato is a clear exception, but this attitude is rather the exception than the rule.[20]

Finally, let me turn to the use of cultural symbols and icons. In literature, these are most important; they are essential for both the work and the text of literature. Symbols and icons are particular to societies and are supposed to speak to their audiences in ways that are not always expressible in discourse. But this is not generally the case with philosophy. The language of philosophy is supposed to be transcultural and universal. Philosophers aim to communicate with the whole world independently of elements peculiar to particular cultures.

So far in this section I have been speaking of literary and philosophical texts and works and artistic pictures and works, but we should not forget two other important elements. In the case of literary and philosophical texts we should consider scripts, that is, the lines and drawings that are used to form the signs that make up texts. One cannot have written texts without them, but although the shapes of the letters that make up written words are necessary conditions for those written words to exist, and their particular shapes are essential for the recognition of the letters and words that are part of the text, they have nothing to do with the meaning of the texts. For this reason one should not expect that they would be part of the conditions of identity of the works of literature or philosophy that the texts express.

In philosophy this is clearly so, insofar as a philosophical work has nothing to do with the script of the text that expresses it. However, the situation in literature is not always so. Just as in the works of literature the texts that express the works are part of those works, there are some works of literature that include scripts as conditions of their identity. These particular works of literature have something in common with visual art that also adds another important difference with works of philosophy. For in visual art it is generally true that what corresponds to the script of a text, namely, the visual forms constituting the images used in a picture to express artistic meaning, is essential to the work of art. Here the very colors, shapes, drawings, and so on, are of the essence. Indeed, the situation in visual art goes even beyond this, for the very physical artifact that embodies the work is essential to the conditions of its identity. Franco's *La escritura de Dios* is not the image reproduced in this book, or a copy made by a student of art, but the very physical painting that Franco has hanging in his atelier in Buenos Aires. And this certainly differentiates the works of visual art from the works of literature and philosophy, because in neither philosophy nor literature are the physical artifacts that embody the works essential.

All this sounds perhaps too general and theoretical, so some concrete illustrations are in order. I provide four. In the next section, I give one illustration of a literary work whose conditions of identity include its text. Next I present an example of a philosophical work that uses a literary work to make a philosophical point but whose conditions of identity have nothing to do with the text that expresses it or the scrip that embodies it. This is followed by an illustration of an artwork whose conditions of identity include both visual forms and the physical artifacts in which it is embodied. And finally I add an illustration of a philosophical work that uses an artwork to philosophize and is independent of all conditions having to do with the visual forms of the work or the physical artifact that expresses it. The discussion of "Pierre Menard" is much longer than the others because it is meant to show how literature is different from philosophy, and this is a hotly contested issue. The other cases are less contested and more obvious, so shorter discussions seemed sufficient. Let me, then, put some flesh on the bones of my theory.

Borges's "Pierre Menard"

Let me begin with "Pierre Menard," a story that I have explored elsewhere and has the virtue of having been influential in contemporary discussions of the identity of literary works. In order to avoid the accusation that I concentrate only on certain passages of the text that particularly suit my view, I turn to the first two sentences of it to show how a translation of "Pierre Menard" into English does not do justice to the text or work "Pierre Menard" in Spanish. The point of all this is to show that in "Pierre Menard" in particular, and in all literary texts and works in general, elements of the text are essential to the meaning, that is, the work.

In the very first sentence of the translation I am using, there are at least three English words that fail to carry the full meaning of the words in Spanish.[21] The full sentence reads as follows:

La obra visible que ha dejado este novelista es de fácil y breve enumeración.

The visible work left by this novelist is easily and briefly enumerated.

The first two words of the English translation that create difficulties are 'easily' and 'briefly'; they translate *fácil* and *breve*. The Spanish words in question are adjectives whereas the English words are adverbs. This changes the force of what is being said in subtle ways. For one thing is to do something in a certain way—the adverbial modification—and another is to have something that is easy and brief. There is also a problem with the word 'easily' insofar as the English term has no negative connotation. If anything at all, it has a positive one: to do something easily is a good thing. But in Spanish to say that something is *fácil* sometimes carries the notion that in English is expressed by the term 'facile.' Things that are *fácil* are not always good things. Now, insofar as Borges is one of the greatest ironists of the Spanish language, one would expect that the use of words like *fácil* for him will carry with them all possible ambiguity.

Another word that creates difficulty is 'enumerated,' which translates the Spanish *enumeración*. The English term is a verb form, but the Spanish term is a substantive. This again paints a different picture, we might even say a different ontological picture. In one case, an action, or the remains of an action at least, are involved; in the other, we have a more substantial entity. But this is not all, for again the connotations of the English and Spanish terms are different, first because the use of the Spanish term in a context like this is not unusual. Indeed, the very term *enumeración* in Spanish is not an unusual term. But 'enumeration' is rare and rather pedantic in English. When was the last time you, reader, said that you were enumerating anything? For English speakers, this is a word of foreign origin, a learned term derived from Latin; they prefer to count, not enumerate. We, in Spanish, *enumeramos* as much as *contamos* (the counterpart of 'counting').

The second sentence also presents us with difficulties.

Son por lo tanto, imperdonables las omisiones y adiciones perpetradas por Madame Henri Bachelier en un catálogo falaz que cierto diario cuya tendencia protestante no es un secreto ha tenido la desconsideración de inferir a sus deplorables lectores—si bien éstos son pocos y calvinistas, cuando no masones y circuncisos.

Impardonable, therefore, are the omissions and additions perpetrated by Madame Henri Bachelier in a fallacious catalogue which a certain daily, whose *Protestant* tendency is no secret, has had the inconsideration to inflict upon its deplorable readers—though these be few and Calvinist, if not Masonic and circumcised.

The first area of difficulty with this sentence is its length: it is approximately five lines long, depending on the type that is used. This, by English standards, is too long for a sentence. But by Spanish standards, which often derive from Latin, it is not particularly long. Moreover, judged by English standards, the sentence is rather convoluted and confusing, calling for certain modifications in the translation—note, for example, the addition of two commas. For a Spanish audience, on the contrary, the sentence is quite elegant, revealing the dexterity in the language that one would expect in the writer of the piece.

The second source of difficulty concerns the first word in the sentence. The first word in the English translation is 'Impardonable,' and in Spanish it is *Son*. The emphases of the two sentences, then, are quite different. In English, the character of the omissions and additions is paramount; the position of the adjective suggests that this is a great fault. In Spanish, the use of the form of the verb 'to be' at the beginning suggests no such force, particularly when one considers that in Spanish one could also have placed *imperdonables* first. Of course, the translator in English had no alternative but to place 'Impardonable' at the beginning, for he could not very well have begun with 'Are,' not so much because it is ungrammatical as because it is inelegant, and this sentence is, without a doubt, intended to be 'elegant.'

The word 'fallacious' in English creates a different problem, for, although it does accurately translate the word *falaz*, the latter is a more common word in Spanish and one whose connotation is not as technical and narrow as fallacious. Generally, when people use 'fallacious' in English, they are thinking of arguments of some sort, but in Spanish the word *falaz* is often used to mean simply false, or incorrect. The translation of *desconsideración* by 'inconsideration' also poses problems. *Desconsideración* is a rather common word in Spanish, but the English cognate is rare. Again, it smacks of learning and pedantry. Finally, there is the subjunctive translation of *son* as 'be.' Borges is saying that the readers are in fact few, etc., but the subjunctive introduces a certain hesitation missing in the original text.

In short, the translation of the two sentences of "Pierre Menard" we have before us misses much that is essential to the work of the Spanish text. And yet, the translation is very good, indeed. In many ways, it is so good that it cannot be improved. Now, if we were trying to be faithful merely to the ideas expressed by the text, I am sure we could find circumlocutions that would do the trick. Or we could add learned notes that would make possible for us to understand precisely what the Spanish says. But if we do this, we lose "Pierre Menard," for we lose tone, emphasis, elegance, irony, rhythm, and particular connotations, to mention just a few essential elements to it. Indeed, to do this would be like putting a commentary or gloss in place of "Pierre Menard," or to use another example, to put St. John of the Cross's *Commentary on the Spiritual Canticle* in place of the *Spiritual Canticle*. And probably much worse, because the commentator of Borges would not be Borges or someone as gifted a writer as Borges, but some scholar of Borges who would never dream of writing a sentence such as Borges would write. But the commentator of St. John's poem is St. John. In short, a translation of Borges's "Pierre Menard" is not "Pierre Menard" and cannot do for it. This suggests that "Pierre Menard" is a literary text and work rather than a philosophical one.

Danto's Discussion of "Pierre Menard"

Arthur Danto's discussion of "Pierre Menard," in Chapter 2 of *The Transfiguration of the Common Place,* is a good example of how a philosophical work involves conditions of identity that are different from those that apply to literature or art. That Danto's piece is philosophical is quite clear from its place in the book and Danto's own words about it. As he points out at the very end of the book, he is "speaking as a philosopher."[22]

It is not only what Danto tells us that vouches for the philosophical character of the discussion, but the very nature of the discussion. Danto uses "Pierre Menard" as the jumping off point for formulating and addressing the philosophical problem of the indiscernibility of some artworks, and credits Borges with first identifying this problem in the context of literary works. In the story we are confronted with the possibility of there being two works that cannot be told apart, even though they are different works and have different authors with different nationalities and different literary intentions, different meanings, different styles, and different degrees of originality, in addition to having been written at different times and in different circumstances. One is the work of the Spaniard Miguel de Cervantes, produced in the sixteenth century with the intention of parodying the popular literary genre of chivalry romances; it is written in a Spanish style current at the time and displays both originality and considerable coarseness. The other is the work of the Frenchman Pierre Menard, composed centuries later with the intention of creating the *Quixote;* it is written in "an archaic style" that "suffers from a certain affectation," and displays infinitely more subtlety than the work of Cervantes and probably more originality than any other work in the history of literature. For Danto, this raises the general question of what it is that "separates any artwork from a mere object which, though it may resemble it precisely, happens not to be a work at all."[23]

In short, Danto's discussion of "Pierre Menard" is informed by the primary aim of positing the problem of indiscernibility in the case of artworks and ultimately, through that, addressing the question of their nature. This leads him to focus on the difficulties that Borges's fictional scenario raises for the philosopher, and in turn to a discussion of examples and counterexamples and the interpretation of hypotheses and arguments. He introduces philosophical doctrines, such as his own formulation of Leibniz's Principle of the Identity of Indiscernibles, according to which things that share the same properties are in fact the same thing, and argues that Menard's work cannot be considered a repetition, a copy, or a quotation from Cervantes's work.

To this must be added that Danto's discussion quotes texts from the story, adopts an exegetical tone at times, and is written in Danto's voice. These are common traits that characterize philosophical pieces that interpret others texts. A quotation is the best way to focus on a passage or expression that requires elaboration and distinguishes Danto's discussion from Borges's story—Menard does not quote Cervantes. The exegetical tone is appropriate because Danto is concerned with the meaning of the story and its implications, rather than with writing a story. This again is atypical of literary fiction. Finally, the voice Danto adopts is his own, whereas the voice in which the story is told is not clearly that of Borges, even if we know Borges is the writer, a reason why Borges, unlike Danto, is not putting forth a position he wishes to defend. This again, makes Danto's discussion quite different from "Pierre Menard."

The emphasis of Danto's piece is on clarity and argumentation, not on style. Ambiguities are generally missing, and when present appear to be unintended, to which must be added that the discussion is explicit and filled with examples, so as to avoid vagueness, suggestion, and allusion. Indeed, this is a good example of a work in aesthetics from the analytical philosophical tradition. What counts is the content, rather than an embellished form, and that is what identifies the meaning of the text.

Kupferminc's *Con el fuego*

Kupferminc's print, *Con el fuego*, is an interpretation of the Borges's story with the same title, but the conditions of its identity are not and cannot be, or could not be, part of a work of philosophy or of a work of literature. Consider, for example, the artifact that constitutes the work. This is a physical object with spatio-temporal dimensions; it has volume and weight; it is made up of particular materials; and it is an individual thing that can be carried, destroyed, or lost. None of this is possible with a work of literature or a work of philosophy. The pages of a book on which a work of literature has been written can be destroyed, but that does not affect the work itself, only the instrument through which audiences have access to it. And the same is true of philosophy. It is true that we speak of a lost work of literature, a Beethoven partiture, a story by Cervantes, and a dialogue by Plato. But what we mean by this is not that the work is a physical object that is lost; we mean that the physical object through which we could have access to the work has been lost or misplaced. The works by Beethoven, Cervantes, or Plato are not lost except in a metaphorical sense; they cannot be misplaced because they are not physical entities. Works of visual art, however, are physical entities: a reason why critics refer to them as embodied.[24] Like you or me, they have bodies and are individual, and this is clear in Kupferminc's *Con el fuego*.

A second point to note is the color. When we look at this particular work of art we see circles of fire depicted in oranges, reds, and blues, and those very colors and their shades constitute intrinsic parts of the work and are essential in order to grasp what the work is about. The perception of the intermingled shades of orange and blue gives rise to a unique experience based on a unique exposure to a phenomenon that is visible and different from others. For example, it is different from taste. If we were to stick our tongues out and pass them through *Con el fuego*, we would experience a certain taste, but that taste would have nothing to so with the work. It is the sight of the colors that matters. And in thinking about the colors, what matters are the visual images that we construct in our minds, not the words, sentences, or descriptions that we say or compose. Nor could we possibly be able to reproduce the sensation of the colors through descriptions of them. We could, by manipulating the brain in various ways, produce similar sensations to the ones we have when we look at the work of art, but we could not know that these sensations are of similar colors as those used in the piece unless we have access to the colors in the work. This makes the colors essential to the work and its grasp.

As a third point, we also need to note that there are some things that can be done with words that cannot be done effectively with visual images. Consider Borges's description of the god to whom he refers in the story. He tells us that originally it appeared to the sorcerer as a horse or tiger, and later as a horse, tiger, bull, rose, and tempest. In this description there is no suggestion that the appearances in the various guises were sequential; rather they appear somehow to have been combined. However, visually this is impossible for an artist to depict. A common attempt to picture composite animals consists in combining parts of all the animals into one overall monstrosity. But these composite entities made out of parts from various animals do not render the entire animals from which the parts are taken. Artists cut out parts of the animals and give the product the head of one animal, the tail of another, the legs of another, and so on. In *Con el fuego*, Kupferminc chose another course. She presents us with an image that is vague and suggestive, but that is not easily identifiable with anything in particular. This is quite successful, but obviously something different from what Borges tells us in the story.

Foucault's "Las Meninas"

A good illustration to bring out the differences in identity conditions of philosophical and artistic works is the case of a philosophical work concerned with a work of art. A very famous one is Foucault's interpretation of *Las meninas* in the first chapter of *The Order of Things*. It is particularly effective because Foucault's style has some literary qualities that might lead some to argue that his piece demonstrates that there are no boundaries between philosophy and literature.

Several things stand out at the outset. The title of the chapter is "Las Meninas," which is also the title of Velázquez's painting, so, presumably, the chapter is about the painting that Velázquez did of the princesses of the Spanish court during the reign of Philip IV. But curiously, although the chapter discusses the painting in great detail, Foucault does not refer to it by its official title. One reason is that an important thesis of the chapter is that the painting, in spite of its title and the images it presents to us, among which the princesses figure prominently, is not about the princesses. Foucault claims that the painting is in fact about the King and his Queen, who appear in the reflection of a mirror at the back, and who are the real subjects of the portrait whose back is pictured on the side of the painting we see. For Foucault, Velázquez's work is a portrait of something invisible in the work, something that is outside of it and coincides with the spectator's location and gaze.[25]

This leads Foucault to another significant thesis, which is the most important one, although made explicit only at the very end of the chapter: The painting illustrates a philosophical truth by showing "the necessary disappearance of that which is its [representation's] foundation—of the person it resembles and the person in whose eyes it is only a resemblance." The consequence is that we come to understand how "representation, freed finally from the relation that was impeding it, can offer itself as representation in its pure form."[26]

The purpose of Foucault's essay is to illustrate a philosophical position whose defense is given indirectly through his illustrative interpretation of *Las meninas*. Velázquez's painting serves to show how representation is best understood as independent of what many have considered essential to it, a foundational object that it represents. In this Foucault echoes views that he and others had voiced elsewhere: signification is disconnected from any *significatum*. Signs stand on their own, independent from the objects that they have been frequently taken to signify.[27]

The centrality of the philosophical thesis for the chapter is further supported by its place as the first chapter in *The Order of Things*. The Preface of this work makes clear its overarching goal. Foucault wants to show how the category "man" is an invention. This particular goal is laid out through the more general claim that all categories are inventions, a point Foucault makes by quoting from a Chinese encyclopedia to which Borges refers in "The Analytic Language of John Wilkins."[28]

So here we have the first important condition of identity of Foucault's philosophical work, namely, a philosophical thesis. This is essential to the essay. Nor is this the only thesis that has philosophical import in the chapter. The text is peppered with reflections and asides that are clearly philosophical. Two prominent ones should suffice to illustrate the point. The first concerns reflection. As Foucault tells us, ". . . the function of reflection is to draw into the interior of the picture what is intimately foreign to it: the gaze which has organized it and the gaze for which it is displayed."[29] The second is one to which I have referred earlier, namely, that "Neither [words nor the visible] can be reduced to the other's terms."[30] But these and other comments are intended to bolster the overall philosophical point of the chapter and the book.

Now, *The Order of Things* was originally published in French with the title *Le mots et les choses*. Apart from the different title, it should be clear to anyone who reads the French version that the style and texture of the text are different from the English one. But it also becomes clear that the philosophical content of the French original and the English translation are not different when it comes to the philosophy. Yes, they have different styles, their flavor is different, and in some cases the French is more effective in conveying the philosophical meaning, whereas in other cases the English is better. But none of the linguistic idiosyncracies of the words used, their sound quality, and the different syntax of the languages matter. Foucault's language, even when discussing Velázquez's painting is not intended to evoke visual images or feelings in readers, nor is the text meant to be ambiguous and suggestive as in Borges's story. There is a purpose of description and argument, a kind of pragmatic directive, that informs the text and distinguishes it from that of a story by Borges or a painting that interprets a story. This is why this text is translatable, and why it is a text of philosophy rather than of literature. The conditions of its identity do not include anything that has to do with the text.[31]

Two Questions

According to my thesis, the difference between literary and philosophical works is that for the former the texts that express them, and in some cases even the scripts, are part of their identity conditions, whereas for the latter they are not. With respect to texts, I have proposed that those which are philosophical differ from literary ones in that they do not have corresponding works in which the texts count as part of the identity conditions of the works, whereas in literary texts it is otherwise. Moreover, the differences between visual works of art and philosophical works is that the conditions of identity of the first include the pictures, images, visual forms, and even the physical artifacts, of which they are constituted, whereas the conditions of identity of the second do not include their texts, signs, scripts, or physical artifacts. Finally, I claim that the differences between literary works and visual artistic ones are two. First, literary works are constituted by texts that provide essential conditions of identity, but not by scripts or visual forms, except in rare cases in which the visual forms of the scripts are purposefully included as part of those conditions; whereas visual works of art always include as conditions of identity the pictures, images, and visual forms of which they are constituted. Second, the physical artifacts through which we become aware of literary works are never considered to be part of them, but they are part of visual works of art.

    I illustrated these claims by reference to Borges's "Pierre Menard," Danto's discussion of the same story, Kupferminc's *Con el fuego*, and Foucault's chapter on *Las meninas*. "Pierre Menard" is literary because its text is part of its identity conditions, with the result that it cannot be successfully translated. Its translations are more or less close approximations, rather than faithful renderings of the original. The text of "Pierre Menard" is literary because the work it expresses depends on it essentially. The language and the very words and syntax of the text that expresses it are fundamental to it. In Kuperminc's *Con el fuego* we found something similar in that there are conditions of its identity that defy the expression of the work in another medium. We saw, for example, that the very artifact used in the work and the visual forms and images the artist employed cannot be rendered in words, for they do not have the same effect in the audiences that are supposed to grasp the meaning. Moreover, we noted how art has some limitations that are not characteristic of other media. The combination of certain concepts, quite effective in writing, for example, is not always effectively rendered in a visual image. Finally, the works of philosophy by Danto and Foucault show that their aim is overwhelmingly the presentation and defense of philosophical theses, and this in a language that is unambiguous and direct.

At this point two questions arise: First, is the view I have proposed anything more than the stale, Platonic-based, position that philosophy is independent of the medium in which it is presented, whereas literature and visual art are not?[32] Second, is not the criterion for philosophy being used so strong that most of what we call philosophy is left out? Fair enough. These are good questions that I must address if my view can claim any originality and credibility. (Not that I am very concerned with originality. I would rather get things right than be original.)

The answer to the first question is that, indeed, my position has much in common with the position described, provided that position is understood clearly and adequately. However, even then, there are elements in my view that do not coincide with it. I do not claim, for example, as some Platonists do, that the ideas philosophy is all about are independent from the texts that express them in the sense that their ontological status is independent of those texts. Perhaps they are, but nothing I have said requires such a claim. My position is more modest. I merely claim that philosophical works, unlike literary and visually artistic ones, are not supposed to be tied to particular texts or pictures. In principle, philosophical works, unlike literary ones, ought to be able to be presented, expressed, or conveyed through different texts, and the different texts should not alter their identity as works. In short, the translation of philosophical works into other languages should be possible, whereas it should never be possible for a literary work.[33] Indeed, the styles and genres used by philosophers are usually those that make translation possible, whereas the literati use forms and structures so bound up with their meaning that any attempt at translating them becomes impossible. The philosophical text is not entirely superfluous or merely instrumental to the work, but it is essential only insofar as a certain text or type of text is conducive to the independence of the work, whereas others are not.

Moreover, no work of philosophy does or can exist unless there is a text that expresses it, and this is quite contrary to the Platonic position. To my knowledge, there are no works, ideas, meanings, or the like, floating around anywhere. In this I concur with both Quine and Foucault. The relation between visual art and philosophy is similar to that of philosophy and literature, except for the fact that, instead of texts, visual art is constituted by images. One could say that art is literature in images and literature is art in words.

Finally, I hope it is obvious that the elements that constitute texts are essential both for philosophical and literary texts. German words are essential to the text of the *Critique of Pure Reason*, just as Spanish words are essential to the text of "El otro." But German words are not necessary for the work *Critique of Pure Reason*, whereas Spanish words are for the work "El otro." Particular literary contents are inseparable from particular signs, whereas particular philosophical contents should be separable in principle from particular signs, even though they are not separable from all signs. To this we need to add that the script and physical artifact are not essential to philosophy; the script, but never the artifact, is sometimes essential to literature; and in visual art both the images and the artifact are essential.

I answer the second question, namely, "Is not your criterion of philosophy so strong that most of what we call philosophy is left out?" as follows. If applied strictly, the criterion I have suggested appears to disqualify much that is considered philosophy and make it literature. Indeed, as stated at the beginning, I believe this is one of the reasons some philosophers wish to see philosophy as literature. If we were to apply strictly the criterion I have suggested, we might have to leave out of the philosophical canon many works that are part of it. Out would go such works as Pascal's *Pensées*, Montaigne's *Essays*, and even perhaps Descartes's *Discourse on Method* and Wittgenstein's *Philosophical Investigations*. And not only this, but we might have to develop a technically precise language to be used in all philosophical texts. Yet, I do not think any of us, except for a very small group of ideological purists, would want to do this. The time of the Vienna Circle and the search for an ideal scientific language in philosophy is over, at least for the moment. So what do we do?

Identity, Identification, and Causation

Part of the problem arises because so far I have not distinguished between identity, identification, and causation. I have been speaking of conditions of identity, and these conditions concern the identity of philosophical and literary works and texts, and of visually artistic works and images, considered apart from the knowledge we may have of them and the causes that bring them about. But we can also speak of the conditions under which we know philosophical and literary works and texts, and visually artistic works and images, and of the conditions under which they are produced. The distinction between identity, identification, and causation is standard, and I trust does not need much elaboration. I assume that the conditions of being X, the conditions of knowing X, and the conditions of there being an X are not necessarily the same. One thing is to be human, another to know that something is human, and still another to cause something human.

The application of this distinction to philosophical texts and works allows us to draw certain significant inferences. First, by keeping causal conditions separate from conditions of identity and identification, we can understand how the distinction between literary works and texts can still be made in terms of the character of the texts and works themselves in spite of the fact that the causes that produce them include factors other than the texts and works. Consider that a text is a human artifact. A text is a group of entities *used* as signs, which are *selected*, *arranged*, and *intended* by an author *to convey* a specific meaning *to* an audience *in* a certain context. This means that a text is causally dependent on its author, audience, and context. It depends on the author because the author does the using, selecting, arranging, and intending. It depends on the audience at least insofar as the audience is the target of the communication and, therefore, determines to some extent the choices the author makes (its dependence on the audience may actually be stronger, but this is another issue). And it depends on the context because the context alters the conditions of receptivity for the text. The entities that constitute a text by themselves are not a text. The lines, sounds, and so on, that an author uses to compose a text, are not by themselves a text. They merely make up a script. To be a text they have to be used for a definite purpose related to an audience and a context. This means that the conditions of the existence of a text involve factors outside the text, for a text does not come to be by itself. The conditions of being a text and the conditions required to bring a text into being are not the same. And something similar can be said about meaning. The meaning of a text is determined by factors that are other than the entities that constitute the text, for the meaning is not naturally tied to those entities. It becomes tied to them through the use that the author and the audience make of it in context.[34]

This has important consequences for the matter we are addressing here. It entails that the distinction between literary and philosophical texts and works in general, and of particular literary and philosophical texts and works, can be made in terms of the texts and works themselves. But it also allows one to hold that these distinctions are caused by what authors and audiences do in particular contexts. It is the uses and practices of authors and audiences that are responsible for texts and works and for the connection between particular meanings and the entities that constitute the texts. That the identity conditions of the meaning (i.e., works) necessarily include reference to the entities that constitute the texts, whereas in others texts they do not, is a result of the actions of authors and audiences in context. Moreover, that some texts express works like these, and others do not, again is a result of the actions of authors and audiences in context. But this does not reduce the conditions of identity of texts and works to their causes. It is a mistake to reject the distinction between philosophical and literary texts and works based on the consideration of their character because texts and works are artifacts, that is, results of human activity and design. The conditions that make a coat hanger what it is are logically independent of the fact that someone invented and made the coat hanger.

What I have said about philosophical and literary works and texts can be applied mutatis mutandis to them vs. visual artworks and pictures. Thus I need not repeat much that has already been said.

Now let us turn to the distinction between identity and identification. This distinction is important for my purposes because, when applied to texts and works, it explains how, although it is essential for the *identity* of a literary work to include the corresponding text and for a visual artwork to include the corresponding pictures, it is not the case that a philosophical work or text includes its text; there is no reason why the conditions of the *knowledge* of a philosophical work cannot include precisely the conditions of identity of a literary or visual artwork, at least in some cases. Indeed, I propose that they do for many reasons, at least three of which I would like to mention. First, many philosophical claims and issues are too profound and abstract to be grasped without heuristic devices that make them clear. We need to give them flesh and blood, as it were; that is, we need to make them concrete in order to render them intelligible. Second, humans are not mere rational faculties; they are complex entities with passions and feelings. This makeup influences their capacity to understand, so that often they need to have their feelings and emotions moved in order for them to understand. Third, all works are known through texts or pictures, and texts and pictures are made up of entities and structures that are cultural, and this has repercussions for our understanding.

In short, the conditions of our knowledge of philosophical works include textual elements, for without some of these elements we might not be able to know them at all, or if we are able to do so, we might not be able to know them effectively. So, although philosophical works do not in principle include these conditions among their conditions of identity, they may and often do include them among the conditions of their being known.

This looks fine at first glance, for it amounts to a distinction between a philosophical work and how we know it. But there is a difficulty. A philosophical work, as I have proposed, is the meaning of a certain text, and now we have found out that in order to know the philosophical work, the text must include elements that are characteristic of literary rather than philosophical texts. Moreover, since every literary text expresses a literary work, then it turns out that those philosophical works that require the inclusion of literary devices in their texts in order to be known entail the existence of literary works as well as texts.

Consider Descartes's *Discourse on Method*. If what has been said is correct, then in the *Discourse on Method* we have: (1) a work of philosophy; (2) a text of philosophy; (3) a work of literature; and (4) a text of literature. This creates two problems. One problem is ontological: it appears that the *Discourse on Method* is two works and two texts rather than one work and one text. The other problem is epistemological: we cannot easily determine who is to separate them or how they are to be separated. In the face of these difficulties, why not give up the whole thing? Why not go with the postmodernists or the Platonists after all?

Two viable responses can be given to the ontological difficulty. One, which I call the Two-Text/Two-Work Alternative, is to say that the *Discourse on Method* is two works and two texts is not such a bad thing after all. The philosophical work is a certain meaning that does not include a text among its conditions of identity. The philosophical text is the text whose meaning is the philosophical work. The literary work is a certain meaning that includes a text among its conditions of identity. And the literary text is the text whose meaning is the literary work. Presumably, then, only the philosophical work is translatable; the literary one is not. This sounds a bit strange, but it does make sense to this extent: it allows us to maintain that there is something about the *Discourse on Method* that is translatable and something that is not. And this is, indeed, a fact that anyone familiar with the French text should know. Moreover, it allows us to hold that what is translatable is the philosophy, whereas what is not is the literature. And this, again, makes sense in terms of our common intuitions and practices.

The other response, which I call the One-Text/One-Work Alternative, is that there are in fact only one work and one text in the *Discourse on Method*, for the literary textual devices required for the knowledge of the philosophical work are merely ancillary and do not form part of the identity conditions of a separate literary work. And, of course, if there is no literary work, there is no literary text. This ancillary relationship is similar to the relationship that exists between a sentence written on a white paper and the color of the ink with which it is written. The color is black in order to make the sentence visible, but the color is not part of the sentence or its meaning.

This response has at least two advantages over the first: it is more economical and it solves the epistemological problem raised above. If there are not two works and two texts, then we need not devise a way of distinguishing them. All the same, even if we adopt this second alternative, we are still left with an epistemological problem, albeit a different one. For how can we tell when we have a philosophical work expressed by a philosophical text accompanied by literary devices, or a literary work and a literary text? That is, how can we tell when the literary devices are not essential to the work and when they are? The answer is that it is probably a matter of degree. Some works have so little relation to anything textual that clearly they are philosophical. This is the case of Suárez's *Metaphysical Disputations* and Kant's *Critique of Pure Reason*. At the other extreme some works are so tightly related to their texts that clearly they are literary. This is the case of Shakespeare's *Hamlet* and St. John of the Cross's *Spiritual Canticle*. And there are many works that fall in between, and here it is not clear whether we have a philosophical work or a literary one. This is the case of Montaigne's *Essays* and Pascal's *Pensées*. But surely this does not undermine the distinction we have drawn between the literary and the philosophical, just as the existence of gray does not undermine the distinction between black and white.

Back to Philosophy, Literature, and Visual Art

So, what do we make of Borges's stories? Are they like Kant's *Critique of Pure Reason*, Shakespeare's *Hamlet*, or Montaigne's *Essays*? I tend to think they are more like Shakespeare's *Hamlet*, but this is not an incontestable conclusion. I am not absolutely certain of it. But I am quite certain of several other things as a result of the foregoing reflections, and regardless of whether one adopts the Two-Text/Two-Work Alternative or the One-Text/One-Work Alternative. First, I am certain that the uncertainty about the literary or philosophical nature of Borges's stories does not undermine the distinction between philosophical works and texts on one hand and literary ones on the other. Second, we need not reject the distinction between philosophy and literature in order to make room in the philosophical canon for such works and texts as Montaigne's *Essays* or Pascal's *Pensées*. And, third, we do not need to reject this distinction in order to legitimize Latin-American philosophy. Indeed, I believe the argument that seeks to legitimize Latin-American philosophy by eliminating the distinction between philosophy and literature is counterproductive in this sense, namely, that it assumes that Latin-American philosophical works and texts do not pass muster if one maintains a strict distinction between philosophy and literature. But this is nonsense for two reasons. First, because there is much philosophy in Latin America that meets the strictest standards of a philosophical work or text. And, second, because the reasons why Latin-American philosophy is generally disenfranchised, particularly in the United States, are quite different. But that is another story that I have told in part elsewhere.[35]

It is also clear from the discussion that Borges's stories, the visual works of art that the artists claim are their interpretations, and my own philosophical analyses as well as the discussions by Danto and Foucault are works with entirely different identities and of very different kinds. Borges's stories include as conditions of their identity their texts; the artistic interpretations of those stories do not include in their conditions of their identity any texts other than their titles, but they do include the pictures that express the works and the physical artifacts that embody them; and the philosophical essays include in their conditions of identity neither texts nor pictures.

For these reasons, the philosophical essays are translatable into texts of languages other than the original English or French in which they were written, whereas neither Borges's stories nor their artistic interpretations are translatable. Indeed, it is difficult to conceive that it is possible to translate literature into visual art and both literature and visual art into philosophy, when their conditions of identity are so different. How, then, can a story by Borges be painted? And how can a story and a painting be put into the language of philosophy? If translation is impossible in their cases, is interpretation also impossible, insofar as an interpretation is a kind of translation? Are the works of art contained in Part I of this book counterfeit interpretations and their authors forgers or confused?

The artists who produced the artworks reproduced here, and claim to have interpreted Borges's stories, engaged into many different procedures in order to produce their interpretations. They focused, cut, and added, among other things. But now we find that, in addition, they have created something very different from the things they were interpreting. It is one thing to produce pictures and another to produce a text. The challenge these interpreters faced appears to be similar to the challenge of translating the seen into what has been smelled, and what is smelled into a visual image that can be seen, or of translating what has been heard into something that can be tasted. We could put it in terms of the senses themselves, by asking whether the sense of smell can be translated into the sense of hearing or touch. Can I smell a visual image or see a smell? Can I hear a taste or taste a noise? How can I express what I smell through sight, or what I taste through hearing? The first step toward finding a solution to this puzzle is to develop an understanding of interpretation, to which I turn in the next chapter.

15

Interpretation

The last chapter presented a view concerning the identity of works of philosophy, literature, and visual art. This was a necessary step toward understanding the difficulties involved in the interpretation of literature by works of visual art. Another necessary step has to do with the proper understanding of interpretation, which is the topic of this chapter. I begin with a discussion of the structure of interpretation, both internal and contextual, and then briefly discuss various phenomena often confused with interpretation, before turning to the aims and kinds of interpretation.[1]

Internal Structure of Interpretation

To say something like "The event was an accidental crash," "Genesis is a story of creation," and " 'The Other' is a story about identity," is to give interpretations of an event, Genesis, and Borges's "The Other." The general structure in each case resembles the structure of a definition, in which a *definiens* is added to a *definiendum*. In a definition, such as "Humans are rational animals," the *definiendum* "humans" and the *definiens* "rational animals" together make up the definition. But not all interpretations are definitions. When I say, " 'The Other' is a story about identity," I am giving an interpretation, but not a definition.

Nonetheless, definitions and interpretations have in common a reference to something about which they make a claim. To interpret is always to interpret something, just as to define is also to define something. In this vein, adapting the terminology of definition, I call the object of interpretation *interpretandum* and the defining item *interpretans*. "The event," "Genesis," and "The Other" are the interpretanda of the three interpretations given, and "an accidental crash," "a story of creation," and "a story about identity" are interpretantia that interpret the interpretanda. Although an interpretandum is required for an interpretation, it is not always explicit in interpretations. Often it is taken for granted and the reference to it is implicit or made through context. I do not have to repeat that I am talking about Genesis when someone else has already referred to Genesis in our conversation and it is clear that I am responding to her comments. Still, in order for something to qualify as an interpretans, and for an interpretation to take place, there has to be an interpretandum.

Apart from an internal structure involving interpretandum and interpretans, it is also important to note that an interpretation is a kind of understanding or an instrument that causes such understanding.[2] I say "a kind" of understanding because we often associate understanding with reasoning, discursive processes in the mind, and propositional states, while excluding flashes of insight, intuitions, and non-propositional states of awareness. But the acts in which we engage when we interpret include a large variety of phenomena and are not restricted to those listed. For example, when I see a suspicious character in a dark alley move his hand into his coat pocket and I run for cover, I have interpreted his act to mean that he is about to draw a weapon, but most likely I have not formulated any kind of proposition or engaged in a conscious inferential process. My reaction is more like an intuitive response similar to the one I have when I touch something very hot and pull back my hand.

Now, when I interpret Genesis as a story of creation, I also engage in an understanding of it, but when I say to Carlos, "Genesis is a story of creation," I have also done something else: I have created an instrument—the sentence I uttered—through which I can cause Carlos to have an understanding that may be more or less similar to the one I have. We generally refer to both of these as interpretations. We speak of Foucault's interpretation of *Las meninas* as what we think Foucault understood about this painting, and also about the text of Chapter 1 of *The Order of Things* in which Foucault expresses his understanding of it.

The internal structure of interpretation may be diagramed as follows:

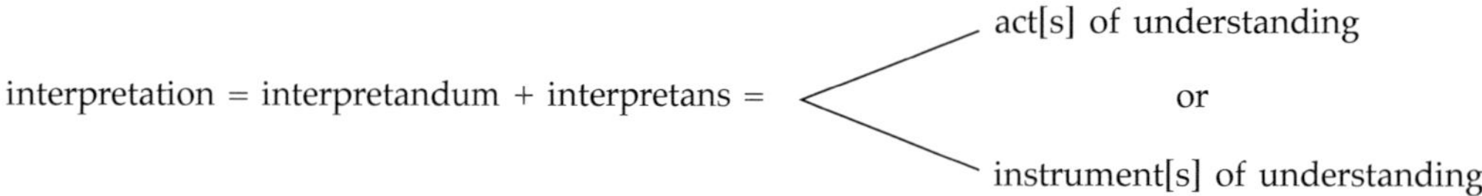

Because interpretations may be acts of understanding or instruments of understanding, I refer to the first as *understanding interpretations* and to the second as *instrumental interpretations.* The internal structure of interpretations and their division into these two types are important for clarifying what an interpretation is and how it functions. However, these are not the only things we need to know in order to do so. It is indispensable also to grasp the structural context within which interpretations occur, because it reveals other factors that are closely related to interpretations and plays a role in them.

Contextual Structure of Interpretation

Some contextual factors pertinent for the understanding of interpretation are common to all interpretations, whereas some are common only to some kinds of interpretations. Among the first are the interpreter and the context of the interpreter, the interpretandum, and the interpretation, as well as one or both of the two forms mentioned that interpretations can take, as understandings and instruments of understanding. The elements that are not common to all interpretations are the author and audience (other than the interpreter) of the interpretandum, the audience of the instrumental interpretation, and their respective contexts. These last three factors are involved only in cases of interpretanda that have authors and audiences and in instrumental interpretations that have audiences. I will return to the difference between the audience of the interpretandum and the interpreter later, but for the moment, let us regard the audience and the interpreter as playing the same role.

Because interpretations are of the two types previously mentioned, it is possible that the context of an interpretation that is an understanding is not the same as the context of an interpretation that is an instrument of understanding. Here is a diagram of the major factors in the contextual structure of interpretation, called Case A, when the interpreter/audience of an interpretandum merely interprets it in the sense of understanding it, and does not proceed to create an instrument to cause further understandings of it in others:

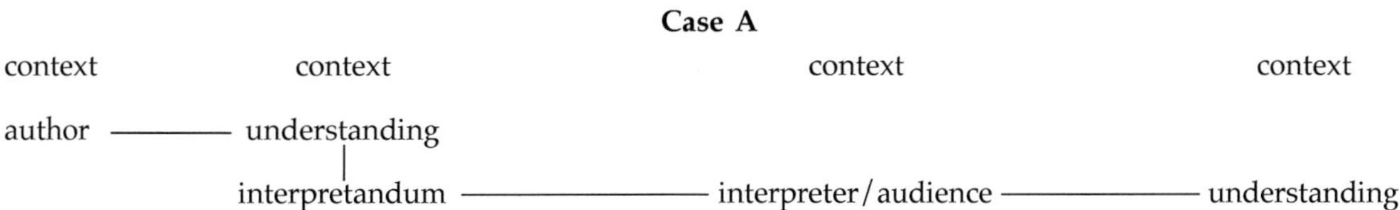

A slightly different structure occurs, Case B, when the interpreter/audience does not only interpret the interpretandum in the sense of having an understanding of it, but goes beyond that to create an instrument to cause an understanding of it in some other interpreters/audiences:

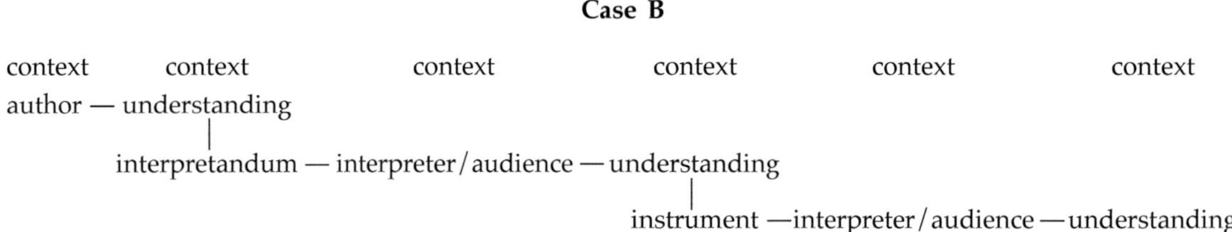

Interpretandum

The interpretandum is the object of interpretation.[3] In the case of any of the artistic interpretations found in this book, the object ostensibly consists of a story by Borges. However, the matter is not so simple in that the interpretandum, even in this case, may in fact be at least three different things: the object with which the interpreter is presented, which in this case is most likely a script (it could also be a series of utterances made by a reader of the script); the text, which is the script considered as endowed with meaning; and Borges's story, which is the meaning of the text. In the previous chapter I identified the last one with the work.

The *script* is the copy the interpreter has of the autograph produced by Borges. As an individual copy it is both non-instantiable and an instance of the universal script of which it is an instance. The individual copy is the object with which the interpreter comes into contact, and the universal is the instantiable of which the individual script is an instance. As we saw in the previous chapter, the individual script, with few exceptions, is not part of the identity conditions of a work of literature, and therefore it is not relevant for us here. We are only concerned with the universal script. Indeed, it makes no difference which copy of the script I use. I can photocopy the script ten times and any one of those copies, if it is an exact copy, is good enough. Put in a terminology favored today, it is not the token that matters, but the type.

Let me call the script available to the interpreter *contemporary script*, to contrast it with the script Borges produced—which we might call *historical script*, or as many prefer, *autograph*. In addition to the contemporary script, there may have been other scripts of each story that are no longer available, and may have functioned as intermediaries between the autograph and the contemporary script. A script is usually composed of lines and drawings used as letters that compose words and signs in a text. It is the object we see in the case of writing, although a script may also be composed of touchable surfaces, tastes, sounds, and smells, all of which could be used to make up texts.[4] It appears odd to refer to these other entities as scripts insofar as the term 'script' refers to writing, but this issue is not significant here. In our case the script is made up of lines and drawings in the form of writing, and so I dispense with reference to the other forms it could take.

The script contemporary with an interpretation is usually an edited version of the author's autograph, when there is one, and therefore more or less different from it, although in some cases there is no autograph, as happens, for example, when the text is dictated by the author. The differences between the two arise because many people may have been involved in the production and shape of a contemporary script. Mistakes may have been made, for the autograph may have been lost, or it may be unclear, or it may have been changed at some point either by the author or by others. So it is not always certain that the contemporary script of a particular story by Borges is an accurate copy of the historical script or autograph. Nor is it always the case that there is only one scribe of it, since many persons may have been involved in producing the version of it we have. Moreover, there may be more than one contemporary script of each story as a result of the production of different editions and copies. All of this complicates matters substantially, particularly because different scripts may give rise to different texts, and different texts may have different meanings, thus producing different versions of the same story or perhaps even different stories, that is, different works.

The *text* is the script considered as having meaning, although not any particular meaning. It is composed of words and signs arranged according to certain rules of grammar and rhetoric for the purpose of expressing meaning. Because the foundation of the text is the script, we can also speak of a *contemporary text*, namely, the script we have today considered as the bearer of meaning. When we speak of a text, there is always a particular language involved. In the case of Borges, it is Spanish. But we may also speak of translations of it, which are different texts from the Spanish text. These translations are in fact different works, according to what I claimed in the previous chapter, because Borges's stories are works of literature, and the conditions of identity of literary works include their texts and the peculiarities of their languages. Still, we need not worry about translations here insofar as the artists who produced the paintings whose images are reproduced in Part I of this book read Borges in Spanish. But we should entertain some worries in the case of the interpretation by Danto discussed earlier because he seems to have used an English translation of "Pierre Menard."

The *work* is the meaning of the text. In the case of Borges's stories, because they are literary works, the *work* consists of the stories themselves as told through the Spanish text. This meaning is frequently the focus of interpretation as is clear from many of the artworks reproduced here. The artists are not concerned with the scripts as such, or even with the texts as meaningful scripts apart from particular meanings, but rather with particular meanings of the texts of Borges's stories. They are not interested in the physical appearance of the words written by Borges, but with the meanings that the words have.

There are at least five ways to understand the meaning that constitutes a work: as significance, reference, intention, ideas, and use.[5] This raises the question of which of these is pertinent for an interpreter. Significance has to do with importance, relevance, and consequences, and interpreters may in fact try to determine the importance, relevance, or consequences of the works they interpret. For example, they may be concerned about other writers and how Borges's works influenced them. For Borges scholars interested in "Pierre Menard," it may be deemed important to note the great attention it has received by philosophers such as Danto and Foucault. Reference has to do with the persons or events to which a work refers. Thus Pereda is interested in Juliana, a fictional character in Borges's "The Interloper." Intention refers to what the author may have had in mind to say. In "The House of Asterion," was Borges concerned with death and the deliverance it may entail, as Sierra seems to have depicted, or did he intend to explore the mental labyrinths in which we trap ourselves, as Azaceta's work suggests? Ideas involve the conceptual claims that may be implicit in the works. Perhaps the point of "Funes, the Memorious" is that a nondiscriminating memory is as good as a collector of garbage, as Delgado leads us to think with her painting. Or maybe the point concerns the use to which a work can be put. For Rey, "The Rose of Paracelsus" concerns an existential struggle with faith that echoes his own.

Apart from these ways to understand meaning, we also need to take into account four possible sources of it: the author, the audience, the text apart from the author or audience, and the meaning together with its implications. Are the artists in this book searching for the meaning of the stories as understood by Borges or by any particular audience or audiences, as present in the text and independent of what the author or any particular audience may think, or as the meaning understood in any of these ways and considered together with its implications? The result of considering these different alternatives may be very different. What Borges understood the meaning of what he wrote to be may be quite different from what someone else might think it is, or what the text actually says. And he, or particular audiences, may not be aware of the implications of that or other meanings. This indicates that the interpreters of the works could be searching for different things, whether they are aware of it or not. Menza, for example, seems to pay little heed to the actual meaning of the stories he interprets, or to what Borges may have had in mind by them. In *El milagro secreto* and *Ruinas circulares II*, he appears to be more interested in drawing certain pictorial implications of Borges's stories. Kupferminc relates "The Secret Miracle" to her mother, and Cámpora uses "The South" to point to a state of doubt that goes well beyond anything that Borges may have intended or the text mentions or implies.

Finally, we need to consider the various aspects of an interpretandum that may become significant for an interpretation. One of these is its title.[6] For example in *"Si la querés, usála"* (If you want her, use her) Pereda not only signals that her work has to do with Borges's "The Interloper" insofar as this is a line in the story, but also that the focus of her interpretation is the way Juliana is treated in a rough society dominated by males. In *Asterión*, Sierra not only signals a connection with Borges's "The House of Asterion," but also his interest in Asterion himself. And Rey's title, *Doubting of St. Thomas* ties his work to Caravaggio's *The Incredulity of St. Thomas*, focusing attention on the issue of faith rather than some of the other themes explored in the story, whereas Estévez's interpretation in *La rosa de Paracelso* turns to entirely different themes.

Apart from the title, other components of a work may also be significant. These include descriptions of such things as events, characters, relations, dialogues, feelings, ideas, intentions, views, memories, images, actions, and symbols, to name just a few that stand out. All these are present in Borges's stories and have been used in the interpretations given in this book.

Interpretation

An *interpretation* can be either an act of understanding or a product of that act created to cause other acts of understanding in an audience. When the interpretation is not an act of understanding, it can be anything, such as a text, a picture, or a gesture, to name just three possibilities. And it is not necessary that it be something physical, external to the mind. I can create a mental image or a mental text that serves the purpose of reminding me of my understanding of the interpretandum, or that helps me develop further the understanding I had of it in the first place, and this does not need to be anything accessible to anyone but me.

This book includes my own interpretations of Borges's stories, the artists' interpretations of the stories, and my interpretations of the artists' interpretations. The first are texts that I have produced; the second are the works of art produced by the artists who have interpreted Borges's stories; and the third are the texts I have written as interpretations of the works of art. All three are instruments that the interpreters—the artists and I—have created to cause certain understandings in others. Apart from these interpretations, we can also speak of the understanding of Borges's stories the artists or I have, but these are not in the book; they were, or are, present in our minds and are not accessible to anyone except those who have them, unless we create instruments through which they can be accessed. For my purposes, the instruments, rather than the understandings that the artists or I had, are the relevant interpretations; my concern is with instrumental interpretations.

Interpreter

The *interpreter* is a member of the audience of an interpretandum who may have an understanding interpretation of an interpretandum and who may also be the author of an instrumental interpretation of it. As such, the interpreter may be considered part of what below I call *interpretive audience* to distinguish it from other audiences.

The identity of the interpreter is not as clear as it might appear at first. Indeed, the interpreter may be a historical person or persons who actually produced an interpretation, or it may be a composite idea in someone's mind about who that person or persons are. The first is what I call the *historical interpreter*, adapting a terminology I developed elsewhere concerning authors.[7] Historical interpreters are the persons who produce interpretations at particular times. In the present case, for example, they are the authors of the artworks that interpret Borges's stories here. The artists are the creators of the art pieces used here, so they are the historical interpreters of these interpretations in that they produced the interpretations at particular junctures in history.

We may also speak of the *pseudo-historical interpreter*. This may be taken in two ways. In one, it is a composite of what we know or think we know about the historical interpreter. In another, it is the *persona* the historical interpreter wishes others to think about him or her. For us, the pseudo-historical interpreters considered in the first sense are composites of what readers of this book know or think they know about the artists and other interpreters who present interpretations in it. The pseudo-historical interpreters in the second sense are the *personae* that the interpreters have manufactured for the audience. This applies to all interpreters, the artists, Danto, Foucault, and me.

In addition, one may speak of the *composite interpreter*. This is a composite of all those persons who had something to do with the production of an interpretation. In the present situation, there is only one artist per work of art, so we have one interpreter per interpretation, but in principle there could be more than one, just as it may happen with any product of authorship. The interpreter may, in fact, be more than one person in situations where various people cooperate in producing the interpretation. Whether one or many, the historical interpreter is a historical reality. Moreover, as with the texts of Borges's stories, the images of the artworks that interpret the stories are seldom autographs. Even in cases in which the interpretation is a text, the text is rarely exactly like the text produced by the historical interpreter. We could expect that copyeditors, printers, and others will have a hand in the production and this creates something quite different from the original autograph. In some cases, the differences are minor and can be ignored, but in other cases, a comma, for example, may create an ambiguity of such proportions that the original meaning of the text is completely altered. And the same occurs with the images of works of art. These works themselves are like autographs, but the pictures we see on the pages of a book are very different from what the artists created. In some reproductions the color and texture are different, essential items for some works of art. The composite interpreter is composed of all the persons who have had a hand in the production of what is presented to an audience. This notion serves to remind us that what we often regard as an interpretation by a certain interpreter may in fact be different from what the interpreter produced.

Apart from the identity of the interpreter, it is important to take into account the various factors in the interpreter that affect the interpretation. Among these are acts of understanding, intentions, ideas, mental texts, feelings, views, memories, images, and the subconscious. All of these were at play when the artists whose works are discussed here produced artistic interpretations of Borges's stories and affect the interpretations in various ways. For example, Ferrari's interpretation of "The Immortal" is influenced by his naturalistic view of the universe and his rejection of any kind of personal immortality.

Context

Context is important in that it plays a key role in all the elements included in the structure of interpretation. There is never an interpretandum, an interpretation, an interpreter, or an audience of an interpretandum without a context. And context often alters the meaning of interpretanda and interpretations as well as of their understanding. Consider the case of a text such as "Fire!" One thing is to read it in *Jane Eyre*, another to hear it shouted by a commander of a firing squad, and still another to hear it shouted by a punk at the back of an auditorium in a falsetto voice. In each case, it means something different and is taken to mean something different.

The contexts pertinent to interpretation include the contexts of the author, interpretandum, the audience of the interpretandum, the interpreter, the interpretation, and the audience of the interpretation. Only elements that can make a difference for any of the factors involved in interpretation should be considered part of its context. It makes no sense to take into account a one degree Fahrenheit temperature variation in the room where the interpretandum is located for the interpretations by Kupferminc and Menza of Borges's "The Secret Miracle." But it is certainly important to take into account the background of the two artists, for in the case of Kupferminc it prompts her to bring into the picture elements associated with her Jewish heritage that are missing in Menza's work.

Author

The *author* is the creator of the interpretandum.[8] Here, as we saw with the interpreter, there are various possibilities: the *historical author* is the author of the historical interpretandum, who is Borges in our case; the *pseudo-historical author*, also called by some the *postulated author*, is what we know or think we know about the historical author, that is Borges, or what he has succeeded in making us think about him; the *composite author* is the group of persons who had a hand in producing the interpretandum as we have it, that is Borges's stories; and the *interpretive author* is none other than the interpreter, whose understanding introduces elements into the interpretandum that may modify it, as happens in translations. The author of the interpretandum is one of two factors included in the structure of interpretation that is not essential to interpretation. An interpretandum may lack an author insofar as it can be a natural object such as a sunset, or a product of an unintentional event, such as an automobile accident, although here it is present and it is Borges.

As with the interpreter, it is important to keep in mind the factors in the author that play a role in interpretation, such as acts of understanding, intentions, ideas, mental texts, feelings, views, memories, images, and the subconscious. All of these were at work when Borges wrote his stories and, depending on the kind of interpretation an interpreter aims to provide, they may become essential. For example, when the interpreter wishes to provide an interpretation that makes us understand the relation of Borges's personal experience to one of his stories, as happens with "The South," it is essential to bring into the interpretation the fact that Borges suffered an accident similar to the one experienced by the protagonist.

Audience

The *audience* can be any person or group of persons that have access to the interpretandum.[9] One of these is the person or persons that had access to the interpretandum at the time it was produced, call it *historical audience.* Another is the audience intended by the author, call it *intended audience*. Another is the interpreter, who often functions as audience in the process of interpretation, call it *interpretive audience*. In the present case, the first is the audience at the time Borges produced his stories, the second is the audience he intended for the stories, and the third is composed of anyone who has interpreted Borges's stories, including those persons who have offered interpretations of them in this book. The audience can be anyone who has access to this book, to the works of the artists who produced interpretations of Borges's stories, or to Borges's stories.

The audience intended by authors may be contemporaneous with them or not. They may also be restricted by certain languages, such as Spanish or English, by certain places, such as Argentina or the United States, by certain faiths, such as Christianity or Judaism, by certain institutional affiliations, such as the faculty of a college or members of a club, and so on. Authors may have all kinds of audiences in mind, and restrict them according to a large number of parameters. Likewise, the audience contemporaneous with the author may be divided into various kinds, depending on the understanding of the person or persons involved.

Interpreters themselves may be audiences of their interpretations while they are composing them or after they have finished doing so, just as they are authors of the interpretations they create. The process of creation takes time and involves many steps, and during all these it is necessary for interpreters to consider what they have already done and what they are going to do next. And after an interpretation has been completed, frequently the interpreter will come back to the interpretation and, even if modifications cannot be made, consider it, functioning as an audience of it in the process.

Apart from the interpreter, however, we may also speak of the audiences intended by the interpreter. These are the audiences that interpreters have in mind for their interpretations. For example, consider the students in my classes for whom I compose a lecture. There are also the audience contemporaneous with the interpreter and audiences that are not so, but have access to the interpretation in the future.

An interpretation may actually lack an audience other than the interpreter, although it may in principle have many possible audiences. An interpretation may be destroyed at the moment of completion, for example, and not be available to anyone but its creator. Of course, in principle there is always an audience in that the interpreter may have one in mind, either specifically or in general. We could also refer to this as an *intended audience*. An actual audience is not necessary for every interpretation.

Audiences, like interpreters, have various factors that play roles in their understanding and instrumental interpretations. The list of factors is similar to that given earlier in the case of the authors of the interpretandum and interpreters, so it need not be repeated.

Phenomena often Confused with Interpretation

The structure of interpretation makes clear some of the essential elements of every interpretation; thus, it helps us grasp the nature of interpretation and prepares the ground for the discussion of its aims and kinds. Before I turn to these, however, we need to touch briefly on some phenomena that are closely connected to, and often confused with, interpretation. This should help prevent some misunderstandings.

Among the most common of these phenomena are illustration, representation, description, rendition, adaptation, portrayal, exemplification, instantiation, manifestation, and depiction. Some of these are more common than others in certain media. For example, *illustration* is very often found in art. It is frequent to find illustrations of stories, novels, and scenes from stories and novels. How many illustrations of *Don Quixote* have been made, for example, that consist of paintings of Don Quixote and the windmills and other events narrated in the novel? The same is true of *representation,* although it is not surprising that this term is often used to refer to performances. We speak of a representation of Shakespeare's *Hamlet,* for example. *Adaptation* is more common in film. Producers often refer to their film versions of literary works, such as those of Bram Stoker's *Dracula,* as adaptations in order to emphasize changes in medium and their implications. This frees them from possible criticisms about not being true to their sources.

Description is usually confined to texts that render nonlinguistic phenomena, such as events or pictures, into language. Thus art critics often describe Leonardo da Vinci's *Last Supper* or the events that happen in a play. *Portrayal* very often refers to persons. Artists paint portraits of subjects, such as Goya did of the Count of Alcutra. *Exemplification* involves giving or adding an example. This usually does not apply to particular pieces of literature or art, but to such things as literary genres. One may give examples of a novel, but not of *Wuthering Heights.* And something similar applies to *instantiation.* This applies to situations in which a universal type, such as "oil painting," is instantiated in particular instances such as Leonardo's "La Gioconda." Unlike an interpretation, a *manifestation* is independent of an interpreter. Fear, for example, manifests itself in a certain facial expression. And a *depiction* is more like a pictorial description, as when a drawing of an accident is made on an insurance form.

For our purposes, the most pertinent of these phenomena are illustration and representation. Both of these are interpretations of sorts, but not all interpretations are illustrations or representations. Illustrations try to stay within the confines of the object of illustration. To illustrate a story visually involves producing images that help an audience to visualize it, to see it. But interpretations may have aims that either are different than this or go beyond this. For example, painters select and cut elements from stories in their pictorial interpretations and add elements that are not present in them, as we have seen the artistic interpretations presented here do. But illustrators need to be more careful about selection, omission, and addition. Indeed, as noted, illustrators usually stay within the narrow confines of the objects they illustrate.

Something similar occurs with representation. This phenomenon often applies to visual images. Literally, a representation is a presentation of an object that is already present or has been present. Representing involves presenting something again, and it can consist of merely a copy, or be more elaborate, such as a picture, a photograph, a painting, a drawing, or a sculpture. A representation wants to be close to the original, although, unlike an illustration, its aim may not be to help an audience grasp the original. In this, a representation is different from an illustration, although an illustration may involve representation.

In this book, the works of visual art are intended as interpretations of Borges's stories, not as any of the other phenomena mentioned, and their aims are quite different for those particularly pursued in illustrations and representations. I turn next to the aims of interpretations and the various kinds of interpretations they produce.

Aims and Kinds of Interpretation

The aims of interpretations allow us to classify them into different kinds that are important both to understand what interpreters do and to judge the legitimacy and success of their interpretations. But what are these aims? What are interpreters trying to do when they produce interpretations? This has been an area of intense debate for many years, particularly when the aims are tied to the question of the interpretation's legitimacy.[10]

Interpretations involve both essential and nonessential elements that differ depending on whether the interpretandum is produced by a historical author or it is not. All the cases we are interested in here are cases that involve a historical author, so I dispense with situations in which there is not. But this is not all, for interpretations can be understandings and instruments of understanding as already noted and this has implications for the factors that are relevant for them. For interpretations that are understandings we need to consider the following factors: the historical author, the interpretandum, the understanding of the interpretandum by the historical author, the interpreter/audience, the understanding of the interpreter/audience, and the contexts of all these (see Case A above). For example, we may have a story such as "The South," Borges,

Borges's understanding of "The South," and Boim's understanding of "The South," in addition to the contexts of all of these.

When the interpretation is an instrument to cause understanding, we need to consider the following factors: a historical author, the interpretandum, the historical author's understanding of the interpretandum, the interpreter/audience, the understanding of the interpreter/audience, the instrument created by the interpreter/audience to cause understanding in other audiences, the interpreter/audience of that instrument, and the context of each and every one of these factors. Of course, there may also be interpreters/audiences of the interpretandum that may produce instruments of understanding, which in turn may give rise to further understandings by other audiences (see Case B above). For example, we may have a story "The South," Borges, Borges's understanding of "The South," Boim's understanding of "The South," Boim's instrumental interpretation of "The South" (i.e., the painting *El sur*), my understanding of Boim's *El sur*, my instrumental interpretation of Boim's *El sur* (i.e., what I said about it in Part I of this book), and the various contexts of all of these. This structure repeats itself, moreover, in other audiences, such as that of this book, and so on *ad infinitum*.

The aims of interpretations that are understandings either have themselves as aims or have some other aims. Understanding can be its own end; we understand because we aim to understand. Of course, one might object that understanding in this sense might have the aim of satisfying curiosity, as Aristotle thought, but this does not get us very far away from understanding, for although the curiosity in question may be the motivation of understanding, it is the understanding that is wanted and where the inquiry rests. The aim of understanding that $2 + 2 = 4$ may be just to understand it, and the same may apply to the understanding I seek when I read "The Interloper." Of course, there are many other possible aims, such as power, money, fame, and so on.

The primary aim of instrumental interpretations is to produce understanding in some person or persons other than the interpreter. The most common situation is that in which interpreters have already developed understandings of the interpretandum in their minds, that is, interpretations of it in the first sense, and produce instruments through which they cause further understandings in audiences. Pereda is trying to produce an understanding of Borges's "The Interloper" in anyone who looks at her painting "*Si la querés, usála.*" In some cases the audiences are the interpreters themselves. We often create pictures, diagrams, narratives, and other tools to facilitate our own understanding of something. I may, for example, draw a Venn diagram to grasp better the logical relations among certain classes. And the same can happen with a story of Borges. I might make a list of the characters in a particular story, list the main events, and so on, in order to have a better insight into it. Nizzero could have produced his piece on "The Other" in order to get a better grasp of Borges's story. Or I may produce an instrument of understanding in order to have something that would at some point in the future bring me back to an understanding I have forgotten. We certainly write notes to ourselves, and sometimes draw pictures of something that has happened, to achieve such an aim. All of these are instrumental interpretations.

From these aims, we can infer that, in addition to understanding and instrumental interpretations, there are two other general kinds of interpretations—meaning and relational— which, as we shall see, are themselves divisible into various other kinds.

Meaning Interpretations

In meaning interpretations, interpreters try to understand the meaning of an interpretandum or to create instruments that will create an understanding of it in audiences. But what is the meaning of an interpretandum? This can be taken in at least four ways: the meaning determined by the author of the interpretandum, the meaning determined by a particular audience or interpreter, the meaning determined by the interpretandum independently of whatever the author or a particular audience or interpreter thought, and the meaning taken in any one of these senses and including its implications. Let us call interpretations that claim to be understandings of the meaning determined by the author of the interpretandum *authorial interpretations*; those that claim to be understandings of the meaning determined by a particular audience or interpreter, *audiencial interpretations*; interpretations that claim to be understandings of the meaning determined by the interpretandum independently of whatever the author or particular interpreters/audiences thought *work-based interpretations*; and interpretations that claim to be understandings of the meaning (in any of the ways mentioned) together with its implications *implicative interpretations*.

AUTHORIAL INTERPRETATIONS

The aim of *authorial interpretations* is to produce an understanding of the historical author's own understanding of the interpretandum (e.g., Borges's understanding of "The Immortal"), either in the interpreter (e.g., D'Leo or Ferrari), or in an audience for which the interpreter has produced an object of interpretation (e.g., readers of this book).[11] Accordingly, the aim of the works of art in this book is, or should be, to recreate what Borges understood when he wrote the stories. This is often expressed as "the intention of the author," because what the author thought the story means is taken to be precisely what he/she intended by it. In our case, the aim of the interpreter is to understand or cause an understanding of what Borges intended to say in his stories. At others times this is expressed as "the author's meaning": the aim of an interpretation of Borges's stories is to get at what Borges meant by his stories. The position of those who think in terms of what I call *the historical author*, namely Borges, is often known as *actual intentionalism*, and that of those who think in terms of what I call *the pseudo-historical author*, namely the Borges we have constructed, is known as *hypothetical intentionalism*.[12] For the sake of parsimony, and because the problems hypothetical intentionalism faces are even more serious than those of actual intentionalism, I dispense with hypothetical intentionalism here.

Authorial interpretations reduce the meaning of an interpretandum either to the understandings interpreters have of what the authors understood or intended to be understood in the case of understanding interpretations, or to the intentions interpreters have to produce understandings of what authors understood or intended to be understood in their audiences through the recognition of those intentions. In addition to what the author understood, however, the author also had all sorts of other factors at play during the process of creation, such as feelings, subconscious drives, memories, and so on. These are irrelevant if the aim of the interpreter is the development of an understanding similar to the author's understanding, although they may be useful in figuring out that understanding. Given that we have the interpretandum and the aim is to understand it as the author did, three possibilities come to mind regarding the focus of the interpreter's interpretation, all of which are states of mind:

1. What the author intended to say but did not say

2. What the author intended to say and said

3. What the author thought in addition to what he or she said.

In number 1 the meaning the interpreter is after is what Borges intended to say but did not say. The difficulties with this are at least three. First, in the context of Borges's stories it becomes unclear whether anyone but Borges could know the meaning of the texts of his stories. This would make the meanings of the texts private affairs, contrary to some of our most basic intuitions.

Second, it assumes that Borges did not use language properly, or that he made mistakes in its use. Now, it would be difficult to argue that Borges's knowledge of Spanish is worse than the knowledge of most of his interpreters. Moreover, although one might believe that Borges did make mistakes here and there, it would be absurd to assume that all he wrote is of the sort he did not intent. Borges was an extremely gifted and careful writer who took pains in his writing.

Third, how are we to get at what Borges intended when what we have is only what he wrote? Does it make any sense to think about this as anything more than a mere possibility? Indeed, it makes sense only if there is something wrong with the text we have from Borges: it looks incomplete or incoherent, or we know from some other source that the text of the story is not what he meant at all. But if we do not have this kind of information, it makes no sense to identify the goal of the interpretation with what Borges intended to say and did not say.

Let us now consider number 2 as the aim of the interpreter: the interpreter should try to understand what the author intended to say and said. If this is so, one could ask why we need an instrumental interpretation at all. It would appear that we only need an understanding interpretation, and anything an interpreter adds to the interpretandum would distort its meaning. This is what I called elsewhere "The Interpreter's Dilemma."[13] But there is a way out of this, namely, that the differences between Borges and his audience on the one hand, and the audience that interpreters have in mind on the other, are such that the interpreters need to add something to the interpretandum to make it understandable to the audiences. This is what happens, for example, when a translator renders one of Borges's stories into English for the sake of an English-speaking audience that does not know Spanish, or a teacher adds a gloss to a story for the sake of students who are inexperienced in reading these sorts of texts.

This also provides a rationale for number 3, an interpreter who, in order to understand Borges's stories and explain them to others, considers and uses what Borges said elsewhere in addition to what he said in the story with the aim of making it accessible to an audience for which it would not be accessible otherwise. Indeed, this justifies any historical research that may help the interpreter figure out what Borges intended. The justification for this kind of interpretation is that the differences between readers of Borges and an interpreter's audience are such that the interpreter is required to do two things: first, determine Borges's meaning through whatever means are available, and, second, create an instrumental interpretation that effectively makes the interpreter's audience grasp the meaning of Borges's story which, without its help, they could not.

These responses do not resolve all the problems of intentionalism. Some of these are evident in art. Consider Azaceta's *La casa de Asterión*. Does it make sense to say that the meaning of this work is the intention Azaceta had when he created it? Three reasons argue against it. First, the meaning seems to have to do with the work itself, regardless of any intention Azaceta may have had. Second, how can anyone but Azaceta have any access to his intention except through the very work in question? This is a particularly telling difficulty with visual art, especially if we accept the view defended in the last chapter, according to which the identity conditions of a work of visual art include not only its images, but also the physical artifact that embodies it. For how could the meaning of Azaceta's painting not include Azaceta's painting? And third, the meaning of the work does not seem to be anything in Azaceta's mind, whether an intention or any other state; the meaning of *La casa de Asterión* is the work *La casa de Asterión* as painted by Azaceta, and this does not appear to be anything mental.

If the aim of an artistic interpretation of a literary work were to produce an understanding of the intention of the author of the interpretandum, then the work of art would become a visual depiction of what the author of the interpretandum thought, that is, a kind of illustration. But the artists represented in this book do not consider their works to be that. Besides, this kind of understanding may not be what the texts of Borges, or even his stories, mean. For he could have written what he did not mean to write, and he could have failed to write something he intended, as already noted.

So far I have been speaking of authorial interpretations involving the historical author. But, as we saw earlier, this author is not the only one at play in interpretation. We could be concerned with the pseudo-historical and the composite authors, and this complicates matters considerably. If there are no historical authors as some have argued, and all we have are our ideas of them, how can we make sense of trying to recover their understanding of interpretanda? And if we turn to the composite author, matters are as bad, because whose intention are we going to take into account?

AUDIENCIAL INTERPRETATIONS

Some of the things that have been said concerning authorial interpretation apply, mutatis mutandis, to *audiencial interpretations*.[14] In both cases, for example, we have a person or persons whose understanding is the aim of the interpretations. The difference is that in the case of authorial interpretations, the target is the author's understanding, and in audiencial interpretations it is the audience's understanding. The pertinent audiences for this kind of interpretation are four: the intended audience, the historical audience, the interpretive audience, and any other audience whose understanding of the interpretandum interpreters seek to reproduce in themselves or in others.

Unlike authorial interpretations, audiencial interpretations have nothing to do with the intention of audiences, so interpreters need be concerned only with the identity of the audiences, what the audiences in fact understood (or perhaps could have understood had the audiences been exposed to the interpretandum), and factors other than understanding that may affect the members of the audiences. Insofar as audiences are composed of persons, just like authors they have in their minds other things in addition to their understanding, which may include not only thoughts, but also feelings, subconscious drives, memories, and so on. But these items are not the target of interpreters, although they may be helpful in getting at the understanding the audiences may have had of the interpretandum.

For example, the motives that led to the breaking of Ferrari's *El inmortal* are a legitimate target of understanding by an interpreter who wants to grasp the reasons of the current condition of the work. In this sense, the interpreter's primary goal is to understand the reasons that led a group of people to storm the gallery where the work was displayed and attack it. Obviously, this may shed some light on the work itself and help in its understanding, but the hermeneutical outcome would be very different for those interpreters who seek a different kind of understanding. This is a limitation of this kind of interpretation, that is, its marginal tie to the work.

WORK-BASED INTERPRETATIONS

Authorial and audiencial interpretations are aimed to reproduce the understanding of certain persons in others persons, that is, the understanding of an author or a particular audience in an interpreter or on an interpreter's audience.[15] But there are other aims that are not linked to authors or audiences. This occurs when the meaning whose understanding is sought by interpreters is identified as the meaning of the interpretandum, say a story of Borges, or a painting by Celma, independently of what the author or any audience may have understood it to be. This meaning is what I called the *work* in the last chapter. In the case of Borges's interpretanda, they are stories, and in the case of the artists, they are works of visual art they have created. In a story, the meaning is a result of the text Borges produced considered in a certain context, which can be historical or contemporary with the interpreter. The interpreter, for example, may want to understand or produce an understanding of "The Interloper" in the context in which it was created, such as the world of the outskirts of Buenos Aires. Or the interpreter may want to have or produce an understanding in the context of the inner city at the time. And this applies to any of the works of art in this book.

The problem with this kind of interpretation is that it is difficult to establish exactly what the work is independently of an author or an audience, for meaning appears always to be meaning to someone. What is the meaning of "The Rose of Paracelsus"? We can understand what it means for Rey and Estévez, although the meaning is different in each case. And we may try to understand what it means for each of us, or what it meant for Borges. But what is the meaning of it apart from what it means for somebody? Indeed, philosophers such as Quine, Foucault, and Derrida, among others, have questioned the very existence of meanings in the mind, let alone meanings independently of the mind, which is what the work would have to be if it is not identified with something in the minds of authors or audiences. Perhaps this could be considered an ideal entity of the sort Plato was fond of, but it raises all sorts of red flags.

IMPLICATIVE INTERPRETATIONS

Implicative interpretations aim to cause an understanding of both the meaning of the work considered in any of the particular ways mentioned above and of its implications—the aim is not to understand, say, just what Borges meant by his stories, or what some particular audience understood by it, or even what the text of the story means apart from what authors and audiences understand by it, but also the implications of any of these.[16] This assumes that meaning does not necessarily include implications, such as, for example, that the meaning of 'Men are animals and animals are mortal' does not include that men are mortal, even if that is a logical consequence of it. Some philosophers argue it does, whereas others maintain it does not. The disagreement hinges to some extent on whether meaning is approached logically or psychologically. If it is approached logically, logical implications must be included in it, but if meaning is approached psychologically, they must not. The meaning of 'Men are animals and animals are mortal' logically includes, because it implies it, the meaning of 'Men are mortal.' But to be psychologically aware of the first does not carry with it awareness of the second.

The implications of the meanings of literary texts or works of art are obviously important sources of interpretations. But it is also important to understand how implication is related to other kinds of interpretations and not to confuse them.

Relational Interpretations

In *relational interpretations*, interpreters try to understand the relation of the interpretandum or the instruments that express its meaning (i.e., texts or pictures) to something else interpreters consider. Because this "something other" can be practically anything, there are a great number of possibilities. Interpreters may seek to understand the relation between an interpretandum and many kinds of things. If, for example, the interpretandum is a story by Borges, here are some possibilities: (1) a work and another work—Borges's "The Other" and "Funes, the Memorious";

(2) a work and a date—"The Secret Miracle" and the date of the invasion of Prague by the German army; (3) a view expressed by a particular work and another view expressed by some other work—Borges's view about religion in "The Gospel According to Mark" and about faith in "The Rose of Paracelsus"; (4) a work and one or more historical events—"The Other" and Borges's stay in Cambridge and Geneva; and (5) a work and a person, whether the author or someone else—"The South" and Borges.

The same applies to visual art. One thing is to try to understand a work and another to understand the relation of the work to something else. In the case of "The Interloper," Pereda has interpreted the story as a spring for the understanding of the social condition of women, but other interpretations are possible. Gontard's painting seems to focus instead on the relation between the two brothers. And other audiences would probably have other understandings of it, including Borges himself. All this will depend on context and what interpreters aim to do and bring with them. Indeed, it is notable that for each of the stories discussed in this book, there are two artistic interpretations, but in no case have the artists focused on the same point.

Interpreters often intend to produce an understanding of a work rather than of its relation to something else, but nonetheless hold that the only way to produce such an understanding is through something outside the work that they bring into the process. A Freudian interpreter of Borges's "The Interloper" may ultimately want to understand the story but also hold that the only way to do so is in terms of Freudian theory: Freudian theory is the means necessary to get at the work, just as Spanish is insofar as this is the language in which the story is written. In this case, the interpretation intended is the meaning kind, but the interpreter has a view of the world, or of the method of producing interpretations, that makes it necessary to relate the work to Freudian theory. This kind of interpretation comes with a certain baggage, and the baggage can be put into a question: Does the use of Freudian theory really make sense in the interpretation of "The Interloper?" Is Freudian theory necessary to understand this story? Several issues are at stake: the interpreter's commitment to a certain theory, the interpreter's commitment to a certain theory as a proper means of interpreting a work, and the accuracy and effectiveness with which such a theory is applied. It is important to keep these in mind, and separate, when judging a relational interpretation of this sort.

The possible relata in relational interpretations have no limits in the sense that anything may be used by an interpreter in the interpretive process. For example, they may involve the discipline in which the interpretation is provided, personal experiences, ideological agendas, conceptual assumptions, sensory constraints, and so on. All of these are in use in hermeneutics, but those that involve conceptual schemes, sometimes referred to as theory-laden interpretations, are particularly controversial. What kinds of conceptual schemes are these? Here are some examples: feminist, Freudian, Marxist, Thomist, sociological, psychological, theological, and literary. One may, for instance, attempt to understand "The South" in psychological terms, thinking of the events narrated in the story as the hallucinations produced by the yearnings of the protagonist. Or one may understand "The Interloper" in homoerotic terms, referring to the relationship between the two brothers, rather than the situation of women or the love of the brothers for Juliana. In these cases, it is important to relate Borges's work to psychology and to explore how Borges's thinking, or the thinking of the characters of the tale, as revealed in the story, reflects psychological states of mind. The same can be applied in the other cases, as happens in art. We could look at Delgado's *La otra* or Pereda's *"Si la querés usála"* as a feminist statement.

Most interpreters engage in the interpretive process without a clear awareness of the distinction between meaning or relational interpretations, and their respective varieties, and often mix them. Meaning interpretations often contain relational elements. Most interpretations of Borges's works refer to historical facts about Borges that are not part of the texts and thus are brought into the interpretive process by interpreters. For example, interpretations of "The South" often refer to the autobiographical context of the story. The point to keep in mind, however, is that the establishment of the relation of these facts to the work need not be the primary function of the interpretation. And, indeed, if what we have is fundamentally a meaning interpretation, its function is rather to understand the meaning of the interpretandum, and the relations that the interpretandum has with these facts are used merely as ways to enhance that fundamental function. Only when these facts are brought in to produce some other kind of understanding, such as the relation of the interpretandum to a historical period or a literary current, for example, does the interpretation become relational. This happens, for example, when we try to establish how Borges's work fits within contemporary Latin American literature or the so-called Boom.

Most relational interpretations do not ignore the interpretandum or its meaning, but they are mediated through the primary aim of causing some other effect or achieving some other end, such as relating the interpretandum to a historical event. So, even though meaning and relational interpretations, and their varieties, are seldom found in isolation from each other, and there are relational elements in meaning interpretations and meaning elements in relational interpretations, it is still useful to keep this distinction in mind in order to facilitate the understanding of interpretations and their connection to the interpretanda they interpret. This will become clear in the chapters that follow.

16

Painting Borges

In Chapter 14, I argued that works of art, philosophy, and literature are different in significant ways. Works of visual art include not just the pictures and visual images that compose them, but also the actual physical artefacts in which they are embodied. Works of philosophy do not include the texts, let alone the scripts or the artifacts that express them in the conditions of their identity. And works of literature include their texts, only very seldom the scripts, and never the artifacts.

In Chapter 15 I argued that there are two main types of interpretations: understanding and instrumental. Hence, artistic interpretations of literature are either artistic understandings of literature or artworks that function as instruments to cause artistic understandings of literature. And philosophical interpretations of art and literature are either philosophical understandings of art and literature or philosophical works that function as instruments to cause philosophical understandings of art and literature.

In this chapter I address the problem of how these diverse interpretations function, considering the significant differences that separate visual art, philosophy, and literature. The main focus is the artistic interpretation of literature in visual art, that is, on "painting Borges's stories." I also discuss, to a lesser extent, the philosophical interpretation of visual art and literature insofar as this is a book of philosophy concerned with them, and the relation between visual art and philosophy on one hand, and literature, on the other, shed light on the relation between visual art and literature. I begin by posing the problems of interpretation in general and more specifically in the context of the artistic interpretation of literature. Then I turn to the core issue, which is the identification and discussion of the various interpretive strategies used by the artists in the interpretation of Borges's stories.

Problems of Interpretation

The differences between visual art, philosophy, and literature create various problems for the artistic interpretation of literature as well as the philosophical interpretation of literature and art. We may begin by considering a general difficulty common to all understanding. It has to do with the apparent gap, and how to bridge it, between an object of understanding and the acts of the interpreter that constitute the understanding of it. In our case, for example, one may question how it is possible to bridge the gap between an interpretandum and an interpreter when an interpretation, considered as understanding, is so different from the interpretandum. In one case we have, say, the text of a story by Borges and the mental acts either in an interpreter or in an audience of the instrumental interpretation. In another case we have a painting that interprets one of Borges's stories and the acts of understanding of the painter and her audience.

This problem applies not just to interpretation, but generally to all situations in which we have something known and a knower, when what is known is a different kind of thing from the means used by the knower to know it. Philosophers have grappled with this problem in various ways, but they often try to reduce both the object of understanding and the acts of understanding to the same metaphysical kind in order to bridge the gap between them. Thus, for example, materialists address this problem by conceiving both the objects of understanding and the acts of understanding to be material. And idealists do it by reducing both the objects of understanding and the acts of understanding to ideas. My concern here is with the more specific situation of interpretation and the particular problems that arise from it, so I have put aside the general problem and choose to focus rather on problems that arise particularly in the context of hermeneutics.

In the specific case of the gap between interpretandum and interpretation, a common strategy is to think of an interpretation as an understanding by an interpreter and identify a similar kind of object of interpretation, which usually is taken to be the understanding of the interpretandum by the historical author or the historical audience. In this way, metaphysical homogeneity is established and one can compare the interpretation to something of its same kind: understanding to understanding. This makes it possible to judge the legitimacy of an interpretation more easily. If the understanding of the interpreter matches, or corresponds to, that of the historical author (for those who favor authorial interpretations) or of a particular audience (for those who favor audiencial interpretations), then we have a legitimate interpretation, and if it does not, then we have an illegitimate one.

However, this strategy does not eliminate the more serious problem arising from a disparity between two different kinds of things that play roles in interpretation when interpretation is not taken as understanding, but as an instrument created by an interpreter for understanding. For example, one may question how the gap between an interpretandum and the understanding of the audience of the instrumental interpretation can be bridged when the instrumental interpretation provided by the interpreter for the benefit of the audience is different from the interpretandum. Two cases present us with different levels of difficulty. In one we have the same medium in the interpretandum and instrumental interpretation, and in the other we have different media. An instance of the first is the case of Borges's stories on one hand and the philosophical interpretations of the stories, such as those given here, on the other.

author — understanding
      |
    interpretandum — audience/interpreter — understanding
     (story) |
                   instrumental interpretation — audience/interpreter — understanding
                   (philosophical essay)

In this situation we have two items expressed by texts: the story and the philosophical essay share something important, a language, even if the texts are different. The literary text of the interpretandum may involve a narrative, for example, whereas the philosophical text of the instrumental interpretation may not. Indeed, even if the latter were to include narratives, these would not be the ones that are part of the former, or they would be told by a different voice and presented with a different force than the narratives in the story. In "The South," Dahlmann's descriptions of what is happening to him are presented as believed by him to be real. But the philosophical interpreter, even when she refers to, or reproduces, these narratives, does not give them the same credence. I, for one, take the descriptions to be the products of hallucinations, or at least possibly hallucinatory, whereas Dahlmann appears to accept them as products of real events. This changes the dynamic. But the fact that the interpretandum and instrumental interpretation are both texts is nonetheless significant and helps in some ways to bridge the gaps between them, for language functions in standard ways in both cases. Indeed, now we have two parallel cases that help create bridges: one is the understandings by both historical author and interpreter, and the other is the interpretandum and the instrumental interpretation. This can be easily seen in a diagram if we use bold (for the texts) and italics (for the understandings) to underscore the similarities:

author — *understanding*
      |
    interpretandum — audience/interpreter — *understanding*
    (story) |
              instrumental interpretation–audience/interpreter — *understanding*
              (philosophical essay)

A case of a situation in which different media are at play is that of a Borges story and one of the works of art that interpret it.

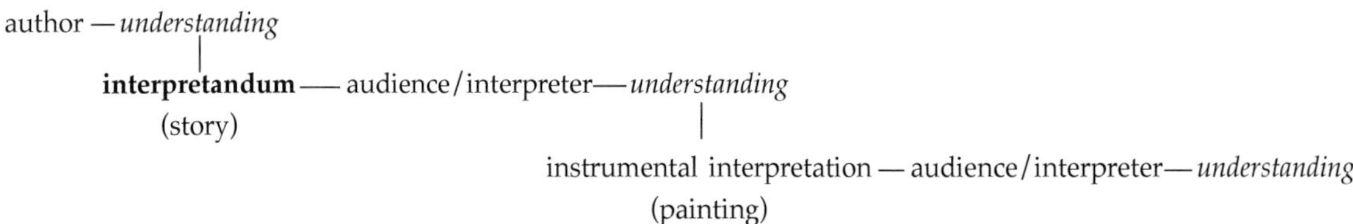

author — *understanding*
      |
    interpretandum — audience/interpreter—*understanding*
    (story) |
              instrumental interpretation — audience/interpreter—*understanding*
              (painting)

In this case there is no common medium shared by the interpretandum and the instrumental interpretation, so the differences multiply exponentially. Whereas the story by Borges is told through a Spanish text, that is, through Spanish words that are put together according to the grammatical rules of Spanish, the painting consists of visual images that do not function as Spanish words, are not organized according to grammatical rules, and are not Spanish. For example, in "The Interloper" Borges uses the Spanish of the Argentinean countryside to reveal the characters of the two brothers, their regard for each other and the way they consciously think of Juliana, as well as the fabric of the society to which they belong. But Gontard has no access to language in his painting and so he presents us with a context in which the positions of the characters reveal the complex relationships among them. The parallelism in the earlier case is consigned to the understandings of the author, interpreter, and audiences, but understandings are notoriously mysterious and thus not very helpful.

The number of all the possible differences between interpretanda and instrumental interpretations, whether they use the same medium or not, is too large to list here and too dependent on the types of media and other factors in question to be established with any degree of stability, let alone certainty. Still, it should be useful to come up with a few in order to illustrate the kinds of difficulties that interpreters encounter and how they manage them. We could consider such cases as a film interpretation of a novel (or vice versa), or a musical interpretation of a story (or vice versa), but given our context it makes more sense to restrict the examples to the cases we have at hand, that is, philosophical interpretations of literature or visual art, and visual artistic interpretations of literature. I propose, then, to use Borges's stories, their interpretations in the works of visual art reproduced here, and my philosophical interpretations of both for this purpose.

The sources of the differences between interpretanda and instrumental interpretations can be broken down in various ways, such as differences of genre, medium, style, time, space, context, aim, approach, focus, content, and voice. The works by Borges we are considering fall into the fictional short-story genre; the works of visual art are figurative paintings, drawings, or works of mixed genres; and my interpretations are philosophical essays. The medium of the stories and my essays is linguistic, although in the latter it is academic English and in the former it is literary Spanish that changes from story to story, and also within the stories themselves, depending on the characters and context; but the medium of the works of art ranges from oil or acrylic on canvas or plaster on wood, to pencil, watercolor, pastels, tempera, etching, print, and mixed media. The style is unique to each author: Borges often displays a parsimonious magical realism; the art ranges from magical realism to figurative expressionism; and my essays are characterized by a traditional, philosophical approach. The stories vary in length, my essays are short, usually covering one or two pages, and the dimensions of the artworks vary substantially and in at least one case are part of an ensemble. With respect to time, the stories were produced at different times and the events in them expand different times as well. Similarly, the philosophical essays and paintings were produced at different times, but the paintings try to include temporal elements, while the philosophical essays pay little attention to time.

The context of all three types of works is both similar and different. All three were produced over a period of time in different contexts and survive as texts or artifacts that can be read or observed in other contexts; but the contexts in which they were created are very different. The Borgesian context, which so often involves Buenos Aires and the Argentinean milieu in which he lived and wrote, resembles the context of the Argentinean artists, although historically the Borgesian context and that of the artists differ substantially from the context of the Cuban artists, and from mine, in that we are persons of Cuban origin, but writing and living in the United States with one exception (Franco). The aims and approaches are quite different in each case. Borges's aim was probably to tell a story; the artists tried to create works of visual art that interpret Borges's stories; and I tried to present a philosophical take on the stories and the artworks to explain how the works of art relate to them. The matter of focus is difficult to determine, but it seems different in most cases. Some of Borges's stories appear to be focused on one central theme, but the works of art often focus on peripheral themes in the stories, and my focus is always permeated by a philosophical interest, although sometimes I present a more comprehensive picture.

Content varies drastically in that the stories involve narratives, dialogues, and descriptions of the physical appearances and invisible thoughts of the characters; the artworks present us with visual images and depictions of events and persons, and with visual expressions of mental states; and, although I refer to events and other factors that play roles in the stories, I dispense with most details concerning these. Finally, the voices are also different. In Borges's stories, he is often the narrator either explicitly or tacitly, but there are many other voices at play; in the cases of the artworks the voice is not always explicit, except as a signature, and implicit in the point of view; and in my essays my voice is explicit throughout in addition to being confirmed by my signature.

In sum, the differences between interpretanda and instrumental interpretations noted are deep and extensive. How can they be bridged, then? How can philosophical interpretations produce legitimate understandings of the visual art and the literature, and how can interpretations in the artworks produce legitimate understandings of the literature?

A comparison to the senses at the beginning of this book should help us see the problem more clearly. We commonly think about what we see, hear, touch, taste, or smell in terms that are not visual, auditory, gustatory, tactile, or olfactory. I talk about what I see or taste in sentences that express concepts, not in sensations of sight or of sounds. I translate claims to pictures: "Mary wears a blue blouse" becomes a picture of Mary wearing a blue blouse; "Mary had a bitter taste in her mouth" becomes a picture of Mary's face with an expression associated with bitter taste. These approaches appear to be effective in some cases, although in some others they are clearly not. It is difficult to translate "He concluded that the world is infinite" into a visual image, let alone a sound, a taste, a touch, a smell, or a sight. Indeed, there are certain things that cannot be expressed through sensibilia, such as universals (all pictures are of individual things), nonphysical objects (all pictures use physical images), abstract entities (all pictures involve concrete objects), and states of mind or feelings (all pictures use visible forms). So, how is it that those approaches that work do, and why do they work?

In many ways, this problem is similar to that of translating different sensibilia into each other, although it is concerned in particular with the relation between visual art, philosophy, and literature. Let me briefly go back, then, to the discussion of what constitutes the identities of philosophical, artistic, and literary works in Chapter 14. This should help us understand further the challenges interpreters face, explain the ways interpreters manage them, and clarify how their interpretations can be better understood.

Back to the Identity of Works of Visual Art, Philosophy, and Literature

A philosophical work is expressed by a text, but the text, let alone the script, is not generally part of its identity. And a philosophical work is composed of such elements as arguments, claims, reports of views and facts, universal concepts, and particular examples, among others things. It also tends to adhere to certain rules such as the laws of logic, respect for facts, and the use of the voice of the author, but it is often oblivious to time and location, except in the context of examples it uses for purposes of illustration.

All of these features are easily illustrated by the essays that interpret Borges's stories in this book. The essays are written in academic English, but neither the English text nor the script is essential to them. What counts are the ideas in them, a reason why, for all intents and purposes, their translations into Spanish, for example, will do.

Like a work of philosophy, a work of literature is also expressed by a text, but in this case the text is part of its identity, and in some cases even the script is. The text of Borges's "Pierre Menard" is in part what makes "Pierre Menard" what it is. The work is the story and the story is told in Spanish. In this sense, the very Spanish words that Borges uses are essential to the work, and so are the punctuation and style. Also essential to the work is the description of the characters and the use of symbols in addition to signs, a location, and time. It is essential to the story that Pierre Menard is a twentieth-century man, whereas Cervantes lived more than three hundred years before. But none of this is the province of philosophical works, although there are exceptions. Literature also is less about arguments and claims, the voices in the literary work are usually the voices of the characters, and not of the author, except indirectly, although the author sometimes does appear, as Borges does in "The Other." The views reported are also those of characters, rather than of the author, thus leaving open the question of what the author may hold. Facts and logic are often disregarded in order to create an effect. Thus, for example, we frequently find the use of terms such as 'infinite' in Borges's stories to create a certain impression rather than literally to refer to a fact. This is something that most philosophers would avoid; they shun the use of such words as 'infinite' unless they use them to mean what the words normally do or they give a technical understanding of them.

Literary fictional works focus on the particular, narrate events, and generally favor an implicit, rather than explicit, approach characterized by suggestion rather than statement. This is part of their attraction and function. In literature we are looking for insight rather than information. And if in both we might be looking for truth, the truth in question is quite different in each case. Consider "The South" and compare it to the philosophical interpretation I give of it. My interpretation is intended to present a clear, coherent, and sustainable, if brief, understanding of the story. Thus I suggest, for example, that Dahlmann is hallucinating when he thinks he is going back to the South, where he gets killed by a gaucho, when in fact he lays on an operating table. But Borges's story contains no such a clear claim. Indeed, it is part of its interest that, when readers get into it, they might come up with different, but nonetheless defensible conclusions.

Finally, a work of visual art does not generally include a text in its conditions of identity, but it always includes the very artifact or artifacts that embody it. This distinguishes it from both literature and philosophy, although in different ways. Visual art, like literature, uses symbols and the particular, but in this case these take the form of visual images. Also like literature, visual art uses an implicit, rather than the explicit, approach of philosophy. Visual art contains no arguments, claims, reports of views, or universal concepts, and its voice is generally that of the artist. In some cases it uses time, but it often disregards facts and logic, whereas location is generally very important both for, and in, it.

Consider the dislocations in the figures presented in Kupferminc's *El milagro secreto*. There cannot be such a reality as that depicted in the picture. Buildings cannot exist on top of each other and upside down, and clocks do not have dates for numbers. Indeed, most of what is presented in the work makes no sense if taken as a depiction of reality, yet it makes eminent sense in the Borgesian context, even though Borges's story does not refer to anything like it, because Borges's stories are narratives that blur the boundaries between fiction and reality.

The conditions of identity of works of visual art, philosophy, and literature are behind many of the differences noted above between interpretanda and instrumental interpretations.

In order to understand how they make sense in a hermeneutic context, we need to turn next to the strategies that interpreters use to bridge the gaps created by these differences. Since my main concern in this book is with the interpretation of literature in visual art, I now turn to the strategies used by artists whose work is included here to bridge the gaps between literary works and their visual interpretations.

Interpretive Strategies

The aim of the interpreter is to make possible that the audience of the instrumental interpretation achieve the understanding of the interpretandum the interpreter wishes to cause. The possible strategies seem endless, but we might get an idea of their various kinds and how they function by considering some of those used by the artistic interpretations presented in this book.

Here are some of them: reference and title, focus, literal and metaphorical readings, transposition, elimination and addition, translation, appropriation, symbolization, and picturing. Direct or indirect references and a title are used to indicate a relation to the interpretandum. A focus helps simplify a complex interpretandum. The literal approach takes the text of a story literally, to mean what it says, and helps to maintain accuracy. The metaphorical approach ignores what the story says literally and interprets it metaphorically to mean something else; what is presented in the story is mirrored through an image that is very different from the original but helps deepen our understanding. In transposition the story, or some aspect of it, is moved from its original context and located in a different one, although keeping what the artist thinks is essential, providing a reference that would otherwise be missed. Elimination allows artists to cut out from their interpretations any elements they do not think fundamental in the story or its interpretation, thus helping to develop an emphasis. Through addition, artists supply elements not present in the story to either get closer to what they think is important in it or in order to give it a twist that reveals an application or understanding of it. Artists also translate the stories and their elements into different media, using styles of their own to express them, and they also appropriate them in various ways by taking from them what seems to be personally pertinent to them. The use of symbols helps artists evoke meanings, and picturing presents the audience with visual images of literary descriptions. None of the artists seems to use only one of these various strategies, although it is clear that some artists favor some strategies over others.

I argued that the interpretandum is an essential part of an interpretation insofar as an interpretans makes no sense apart from it, just as in a definition a definiens makes no sense apart from the definiendum. So the first step that needs to be taken in an interpretive process is to establish a connection between the interpretandum and the instrumental interpretation. There are various ways in which this can be done textually. For example, in a philosophical interpretation of a literary work or an artwork, the interpreter may simply *refer* to the interpretandum by saying something like "This essay concerns Borges's 'The Immortal' or Kupferminc's *El milagro secreto*." But when the interpretation is not textual, as happens generally with works of visual art, this solution is not readily open to the interpreter.

An alternate common and effective way of referring to the interpretandum is through *the title* of the interpretation. All the works of art in this book, except one, use this method. In some cases the title given to the interpretive work is the title of the interpretandum. Azaceta's *La casa de Asterión* has the very title of Borges's story. At other times the title of the story is modified, as happens with Sierra's *Asterión*, which interprets Borges's "The House of Asterion," and Delgado's *La otra* or Estévez's *Los jardines que se bifurcan*, which are modified versions of Borges's titles "The Other" and "The Garden of Forking Paths." In other cases, it is not the title of the story that is used, as in Pereda's "*Si la querés, usála*," but a line taken from the story.

The title is extremely important in interpretive visual artworks. Indeed, consider the difficulties that arise when one does not use this way of connecting the interpretation to the interpretandum. Take, for example, an artwork that has no significant title, say "Untitled." How could this be understood as an interpretation of a particular literary work? Imagine that this were the title of Azaceta's *La casa de Asterión*. In the first place, how would an audience know that the artwork has to do with a story by Borges, let alone that it has to do with Borges's "The House of Asterion?" There is nothing in the artwork that clearly connects it to Borges, his stories, or this particular story. Azaceta's piece depicts what looks like a labyrinth, so one could surmise that the work means something about this. And one could go further and see in it a mental labyrinth insofar as the painted labyrinth seems to be inside of a head. But this does not connect the work to Borges, his stories, or this particular story. It is true that Borges was fascinated with labyrinths and that they figure prominently in some of his stories, but there is nothing in the labyrinth depicted in Azaceta's work that relates it to any of the Borgesian labyrinths, and there are many other writers who have used this motif in their art. The context could help relate the work to Borges, but only if it were quite specific, and even then there would always be a doubt, for it is possible for the audience to misinterpret the significance of the context. Matters are even more difficult in a work such as Menza's *El milagro secreto*, which has nothing in it that ostensibly relates it to Borges's story. Once we have a title that is sufficiently specific, however, it becomes clear that the works by Azaceta and Menza are related in some way, and most likely as interpretations, to Borges's stories with the same titles. Moreover, the titles provide not only a connection, but also an ontological bridge between the art and the literature insofar as they are texts, just as the stories are.

Focus

Focusing on some ostensive aspect of the interpretandum is generally an effective way to connect an interpretation to it. This strategy also serves to draw attention to an aspect of the interpretandum that the interpreter deems important while avoiding the problems posed by the representation of many of the details present in a complex object of interpretation. Some interpreters are content to concentrate on one focus, but others choose more than one. At least six different kinds of foci are easily identifiable in the artworks included in this book: a line from the text, a figure, an idea, an inner state, an event, and the plot. The line can be a phrase, a sentence, or a word taken from the interpretandum. The figure may refer to a person, animal, or object that plays a role in the story. The idea may be a notion or thought that encapsulates something important in the story. The inner state may refer to a feeling or attitude of a person presented in the story. And the event could be anything that happens, whereas the plot usually consists of a series of events narrated.

Some artists pick a line or phrase from the story as a focus, which is sometimes used in the title, or subtitle, of the artwork, giving us an insight into what they wish to emphasize. This is the case with Pereda's *"Si la querés, usála"* and Delgado's *Funes, vaciadero de basura II*. For Pereda, Borges's "The Interloper" is about a woman, who is the object of both love and resentment by the Nilsen brothers, and about her feelings, social situation, and ultimate death at the hands of one of the brothers who wishes to reestablish an original filial relationship that had been lost when she came between the brothers. For Delgado, the metaphor expressed in the phrase captures the nature of a memory so perfect that it cannot discriminate and distinguish between what is important and what is not.

The emphasis on a figure or figures is common in the artistic interpretations in this book. Figurative art uses representations of humans, animals, or objects. For some art, the human figure becomes the focus. This is evident in Boim's *El sur*, where Dahlmann is given center stage in a kind of surrealist space. Celma's *El evangelio según Borges* displays the virgin with whom Baltasar has intercourse. And Cámpora's *La duda* prominently pictures Dahlmann at various stages of his life, although the painting also includes depictions of a cat, two ravens, a dove, and some inanimate objects, such as books, a train, and a toy horse. D'Leo focuses on the immortal, who represents all humans, in *El inmortal,* although he surrounds his figure with various architectural motifs and water plays an important role in the painting. Gontard includes all three major characters—the two brothers and Juliana and the minor character of the madam—in *La intrusa.* Menza has a central figure of a nude woman in all three works included here—*Ruinas circulares II, El jardín de senderos que se bifurcan,* and *El milagro secreto*—although he provides settings that locate them differently and in the second painting he adds some elements suggested in the story. Both works by Nizzero include human figures. In *El otro,* Borges is portrayed as young and old, and in *Funes,* the unfortunate protagonist and a peeping Borges are present. Kupferminc's *La escritura del dios* displays a long procession of human figures walking on the back of the tiger that is the focus of her work, and *Con el fuego* has the images of men or women in the background and the back of a chair, and of two small men sitting on the rungs of the chair. The centerpiece of Pereda's *"Si la querés, usála"* is the body of Juliana, laying down on a kind of bed or table. Franco depicts the outline of a humanoid symbolizing God, a priest, or humankind in *La escritura de Dios.* Rey focuses on the human hand of St. Thomas exploring the wound in Christ's chest in *Doubting of St. Thomas.* In *Los jardines que se bifurcan,* Estévez displays one of his puppets in a meditative position, and in *La rosa de Paracelso* uses anthropomorphic plants to represent Paracelsus's presumptive disciples.

Animals are less frequent, in part because they do not figure much in the stories that we are considering. Only five artists include them in their art, and it could be argued that only one, if any, makes them the focus of attention. For Cámpora, the cat he depicts in *La duda* reproduces a reference in Borges's story, but does not take center stage, and something similar applies to the ravens and dove to which I referred earlier. Franco's *La escritura de Dios* has two jaguars in it, but the central figure is a humanoid, although it is the skin of the jaguars that is supposed to reveal the divine message and it turns out that it is their whole presence that most effectively makes the point. Celma paints the young woman who is the focus of his piece holding the goldfinch to which the story refers. Ferrari's cockroaches in *El inmortal* signify both immortality and a return to nature. Only Kupferminc's *La escritura del dios* appears to make a tiger central, although the procession of humans on its back shares the spotlight. And Sierra's Asterion, in *Asterión,* has the head of a bull.

Objects, a category in which I include landscapes or parts of them, are seldom the focus of the works of art in these interpretations, serving only a secondary role or simply functioning as context. This is the case in the works by Boim, Cámpora, Celma, Destéfanis, D'Leo, and Estévez. Boim's *El sur* includes a picture of a building that could be the house associated with Dahlmann's childhood memories or the restaurant where he presumably meets his fate. In *La duda* Cámpora locates his figures in a complicated setting that includes a train symbolizing Dahlmann's trip, as well as various objects of reminiscence, such as a toy horse and books, to some of which Borges refers in the story. Celma includes a cross in a vast landscape that serves as a background for the central female figure in *El evangelio según Borges*. Destéfanis also has a cross in *La decisión de los Guthre* where Baltasar is to be crucified. D'Leo pictures various architectural motifs and words that allude to a Greek background in *El inmortal*. Gontard's *La intrusa* places the three main characters of the story in a room, and locates the bordello's madam beyond it, looking in through a barred window. Menza surrounds the woman that is the central figure of *El milagro secreto* with various objects, but these do not seem to have an essential connection to the story. Nizzero adds a rough surrounding on both of his works, *El otro* and *Funes*. Pereda places Juliana on a kind of bed or table in "*Si la querés, usála.*" Rey works in some detail the robes of the participants in *Doubting of St. Thomas*. Sierra locates the Minotaur among nasty and bloody looking giant weeds against a background of stars, in *Asterión*. And Ferrari fills his transparent prism with plastic vines and flowers.

Still, a few works make objects central. Azaceta's *La casa de Asterión* depicts a castle-like building with a human profile. Delgado's *Funes, vaciadero de basura II*, presents a utility room full of objects of refuse. Kuperminc's *El milagro secreto* consists entirely of parts of the cityscape of Prague, together with a very large chair, a chessboard, and various instruments that keep time, and *Con el fuego* includes several circles of fire and a chair. Two of Menza's works contain objects that are essential to the story, even if they are not quite the focus of it. In *El jardín de senderos que se bifurcan*, the garden appears in the background as a forest, and in *Ruinas circulares II* he paints circular ruins on the upper left-hand corner of the wall behind the main figure. And an architectural building of large proportions takes the place of the puppet's cranial area, perhaps representing the figure's mind, in Estévez's *Los jardines que se bifurcan*.

Literal and Metaphorical Readings

For some artists, it seems important to maintain a *literal* connection to the story, its plot, characters, and setting, even if these are sometimes modified in ways that suggest a *metaphorical* rendition. This is clear in Azaceta's *La casa de Asterión* where we see a labyrinthine building as the focus of the piece, although with a shape of a human face. Destéfanis's *La decisión de los Guthre* emphasizes the crucifixion of Baltasar, which is supposed to be the dramatic, although left undescribed, denouement of Borges's "The Gospel According to Mark." He presents it in a way that emphasizes the figure of the girl that Baltasar takes, making her a symbol of guilt and eroticism. Franco's *La escritura de Dios* depicts marks on the skins of the jaguars that could be understood as the writing through which God is supposed to have revealed the key to ending the suffering of the universe in Borges's "The Writing of the God," but they become symbols of the divine call for a return of humans to nature. Gontard's *La intrusa* includes all the main characters of "The Interloper," although he modifies them in substantial ways in order to reveal their relations and roles—the younger brother becomes a negative image, indicating his subservience to the will of the older; the older brother appears to express his feelings for the younger in a gesture associated with love; Juliana is seen as a coquette, appropriate in her role as object of desire; and the madam is depicted as a monstrous figure behind bars, like one would expect of a brutal animal in a cage or a jailer looking from behind or within a jail or, alternatively, a woman trapped by a society that forces her to become a monster as her only way to survive. And Azaceta includes both a labyrinth and a human Minotaur in his work, but makes the labyrinth mental and the Minotaur human.

Kupferminc's three pieces—*Con el fuego*, *El milagro secreto*, and *La escritura del dios*—display some of the fundamental elements of the Borges narratives: the fire, smoke, burned paper, and circular structures of "The Circular Ruins" in the first; the cityscape of Prague and a clock, among other things, in "The Secret Miracle"; and the jaguar, rendered as a Bengal tiger, with the markings on its hide, from "The Writing of the God." But they become metaphors for something else: the fire, smoke, and burned paper of the first turn into images of women or men that, like the priest of the story and his creation, are both real and unreal; the upside-down cityscapes of the second indicate the duality of time and one of the clocks is used to signal a personally significant time for Kupferminc; and the tiger becomes a symbol of the Messiah. Nizzero's *El otro* and *Funes, el memorioso* present the events and their settings described by Borges in "The Other" and "Funes, the Memorious"—in the first, the park and bench with the young and old Borges, and in the second, Funes on his deathbed, enclosed in a room of memories. But Nizzero draws them in ways that evoke something different: in the first youth and old age, the present and the past; and in the second the room becomes a metaphor for Funes's imprisonment in his memory. Celma draws the goldfinch mentioned by Borges, but turns it into a more open metaphor of a crucifixion by having it held by the girl in a cruciform pose. Ferrari reproduces the complete text of "The Immortal" in his piece, but he writes it on a prism of fiberglass that encloses an ensemble of vines, flowers, and bugs that stand for the resilience of nature. And Sierra paints Asterion as the Minotaur, a man with a head of a bull, dead after Theseus's attack, a metaphor for loneliness and desperation.

Transposition

Several artists use the technique of *transposition*, changing the setting of the story to a different context and a different application of a central theme. The advantage of this method is that it moves a theme, idea, or motif present in the story to a new context, thus allowing the artist to change its dialectic and significance. This opens more interpretive alternatives to the artist and the audience of the painting, allowing them to reveal something that might not have been pertinent, or perhaps is pertinent but not easily grasped in the original story.

Cámpora does it in *La duda*, where Dahlmann is presented as challenged by a choice of what he would like vs. what is, but the desired reality and the actual reality of the story and the painting are different. Both may be places in Argentina, but they are very different places. The times have clearly changed. Indeed, the location depicted in the painting suggests a surrealist space, something possibly inside Dahlmann's head, rather than an actual location that could exist at some time. A similar approach is used by Rey in *Doubting of St. Thomas,* for the question of true faith is moved from the setting of Paracelsus and his possible disciple to that of Christ and some of his apostles, including St. Thomas, although the painting depicts only Christ's wound and St. Thomas's hand. The idea of doubt is present in both, but nothing in the story is represented in the painting. Indeed, Rey moves even farther in this transposition because he goes back to a work of another artist, Caravaggio, to find a suitable context, thus opening a path to the past of both the idea and the history of painting. In *La otra,* Delgado transposes the Borges sitting on a bench in Cambridge to a girl sitting in a dark space, and the room where Funes narrates his story in *Funes, vaciadero de basura II,* becomes a utility room full of junk. This not only opens new avenues of interpretation, but also changes the dynamic of the tale, for now the issue becomes self-depiction rather that identity through time. The idea is there, in Borges's story, but it is wrapped in other ideas so that it is hardly clear, whereas it is quite evident in Delgado's work. The works of Cámpora, Rey, and Delgado are the most dramatic cases of the use of transposition, but other artists also use this strategy, although in less poignant ways.

Elimination and *addition* go hand in hand with focusing and are essential strategies for the visual interpretation of literature. Elimination serves the purpose of drawing attention to something that the artist thinks is significant by eliminating superfluous details. It also facilitates bridging the gap between a painting and a long and complex narrative.

One may focus on a variety of ways, but eliminating references to parts of the interpretandum is particularly effective. At the same time, adding elements in the instrumental interpretation serves to complete a picture of what the interpreter wishes to emphasize.

Although most works of art we are considering engage in these techniques, eliminating what the interpreter considers unnecessary distractions and adding elements to emphasize various aspects of the interpretandum, a few of them do so in a particularly obvious and vigorous way. All of Menza's pieces—*Ruinas circulares II, El jardín de senderos que se bifurcan,* and *El milagro secreto*—do it, but the first and the third do it dramatically. In the third work, we find nothing but the facial expression of a nude woman that can be used to tie the painting to the story. The first is less drastic, including also a prominent reference to the circular ruins of the story. And the second is most closely tied to the narrative because of its depiction of a garden in the form of woods with forking paths. In all three works most elements of the stories have been left out, and some other elements, unrelated to the story, have been added.

The strategies of elimination and addition are also evident in D'Leo's *El inmortal.* The painting focuses on the immortal and the water of the river mentioned in Borges's text. But depictions of Greek buildings and words are placed on the background, because these are elements that do not stand out in the story, and much of what occurs in Borges's narrative is ignored. Pereda's *"Si la querés, usála,"* eliminates everything from the story except the important figure of Juliana, and Celma's *El evangelio según Borges* does the same except for the girl and the goldfinch and background references to the cross and the flood. Estévez's *Los jardines que se bifurcan* omits references to the story's plot and its characters, and *La rosa de Paracelso* adds extraneous elements, such as plants, a vase, a mechanical looking body, and various heads. Delgado's *La otra* and *Funes, vaciadero de basura II* ignore most details of the stories, adding in the first the figure of a girl drawing herself, and in the second a room full of trash. Although Destéfanis's *La decisión de los Guthre* contains the characters of Borges's piece and a detailed event suggested in it, the setting, plot, and Mark's Gospel are not included. Franco's *La escritura de Dios* has no reference to the cell in which the priest is trapped, but includes two jaguars rather than one. Kupferminc's *Con el fuego* omits the main character and adds images of women, poets, and a chair, among other things. And Ferrari's *El inmortal* is most evidently tied to the story through the idea of immortality, which is ostensibly the reason for the plastic cockroaches in the work, and more subtly related to the representation of nature.

Translation

The technique of *translation* appears in two modalities. First, it occurs in the translation of a story expressed through a text composed of words into a visual artwork in which pigments and images are the media. On the one hand, we have words belonging to the Spanish language, and on the other we have visual images in which shapes and colors are the means of expression. The second modality involves the translation of the story into the particular style of the artist. Most of the artists whose work is presented here have definite styles that inform the way in which they interpret the stories.

Azaceta's work is dominated by a drawing technique in which figures are rendered through simplified lines, in a sort of comic book style, with a certain exaggeration typical of caricatures and including certain motifs, such as visual conundrums and labyrinths. All this is quite evident in *La casa de Asterión,* where the Minotaur's house is presented as a puzzling maze, crowned by a profile of a caricatured Asterion. Boim favors a certain dark coloring where humans stand out as if floating, quite evident in *El sur.* Cámpora uses solid colors, landscapes, and thoughtful, even grim figures, to express his concerns with the human condition, and he frequently uses symbols to emphasize a message, such as certain kinds of birds. In *La duda* these elements are quite clear: the train, the ravens and the dove, the assemblage of objects, and the thoughtful countenance of the figures.

Delgado exploits her penchant for children and realistic painting in *La otra,* where a girl and a drawing of herself are used to refer to Borges's encounter with himself. Her preference for vivid colors and the integration of cloth and certain materials are utilized to reveal the useless nature of Funes's memory in *Funes, vaciadero de basura II.* Destéfanis's drawing technique with a mix of media, and the simplification of features and shapes, are displayed in *La decisión de los Guthre.* D'Leo's geometrical, almost Cubist, style, in which strong lines delineate boundaries, and solid colors fill spaces, together with a preference for facial expressions of despair and anxiety, is clear in *El inmortal.* Estévez's art is characterized by an interest in puppets, machines, and architectural motifs that come together in *Los jardines que se bifurcan* and *La rosa de Paracelso.* His strong drawing technique clearly informs his vision of Borges's stories.

Franco's *La escritura de Dios* reveals his concern with texture and the variety of designs of animal hides. His interest in nature and visual texture is common in his work. Kupferminc has a preference for the dramatic that can more easily be achieved through digital images and etchings, and so she uses photos in *El milagro secreto, Con el fuego,* and *La escritura del dios.* She also often develops themes tied to her Jewish heritage in the mentioned works. The presence of nude women, geometrical objects, and large expanses of color are typical of Menza's paintings, and are present in all three works used here: *Ruinas circulares II, El jardín de senderos que se bifurcan,* and *El milagro secreto.*

Nizzero's style is characterized by large swaths of brush work, a narrow range of color, ink drawing, and the use of unconventional media, such as coffee. In the two works we have from him—*El otro* and *Funes*—all three features are evident. Pereda has developed an approach in which geometrical lines, tied to the realistic but parsimonious depiction of human bodies, is used to reveal internal states of feeling. These are prominently applied in *"Si la querés, usála."* Rey is a multifaceted artist, with a strong realistic bent in recent years and an interest in relating his work to that of past masters. In *Doubting of St. Thomas,* he goes back to Caravaggio's *The Incredulity of St. Thomas* to find inspiration and presents us with a new rendition of a section of that painting. Celma also turns to realism in *El evangelio según Borges,* but his is a magical realism that blurs the boundaries between reality and appearance. Sierra is known for his lush plants and landscapes, strong colors, and a surrealistic emphasis, and in *Asterión* he effectively mixes all these elements in a dramatic depiction of the dead Minotaur. And a good portion of Ferrari's work involves fiberglass, plastic objects, wire, and writing, all of which figure prominently in *El inmortal.*

Appropriation

Appropriation is another strategy that the artists have used in at least two ways. First, they have taken from the interpretanda what appears relevant or important to them, to their personal concerns and lives, what resonates with their experience. Second, they have ignored, discarded, or glossed over much that is present in the stories, but which for them has no meaning, or they consider distracting because it takes away from what they think important. The result is that there is a significant element of *selectivity* based on personal interest in the works of art. In part, of course, selectivity could not have been avoided. Stories have plots, describe many events, usually involve various characters and settings, and reveal the inner states of the characters through descriptions of their thoughts. A work of visual art can hardly do all these things. It is circumscribed by the space it uses and the media it employs. So it is inevitable that the artists select and cut. We already saw earlier that focusing, elimination, and addition go hand in hand.

But to this we need to add the element of selectivity governed by appropriation, by trying to pick from the interpretandum something that makes the work they are creating resonate for themselves, making it their own.

In *La casa de Asterión,* for example, Azaceta appropriates the labyrinth to a concern with existential *angst.* Boim captures the Argentinean countryside in *El sur.* Cámpora picks on Dahlmann's doubt in *La duda.* Celma searches for the meaning of true love in *El evangelio según Borges.* Delgado selects the idea of identity and self-revelation as the center of *La otra,* and substitutes herself as a child for Borges. Destéfanis focuses on the purported crucifixion in *La decisión de los Guthre.* D'Leo chooses the plight of the immortal in *El inmortal.* Estévez attends to the difficulty of discipleship and communication in *La rosa de Paracelso* and the infinity of choice in *Los jardines que se bifurcan.* Franco is interested in the way in which nature, in the form of animal skins, reveals the way in which humans can get back into harmony with their surroundings in *La escritura de Dios.* Gontard seizes on human relations in *La intrusa.* In two of her works, *El milagro secreto* and *Con el fuego,* Kupferminc brings Jewish motifs into her interpretations, including a family relation. Menza turns to the female figures present in many of his creations. Pereda focuses on the condition of women in *"Si la querés, usála"* because of its significance for herself as a woman. For Rey, it is the question of faith that takes center stage, responding to his own struggles, in *Doubting of St. Thomas.* For Sierra, death captures his attention in Asterión, a topic related to personal preoccupations. And Ferrari gives us a completely naturalistic picture of immortality concordant with his personal worldview in *El inmortal.*

Symbolization

An important function of a *symbol* is to evoke a certain understanding in those presented with it. A symbol differs from a sign in various ways. Both signs and symbols are cultural entities, but signs have more strict and limited meanings than symbols. Symbols are open-ended; they point rather than define, and pointing, unlike linguistic definitions and definite descriptions, lacks precise boundaries. Symbols belong to the world of suggestion and allusion. This is one reason why symbols are often used in literary and artistic works but are generally avoided in scientific or philosophical discourse. However, not all literature or art uses symbols, a fact well illustrated in the work of the artists considered in this book.

Still, many of the artworks included here use symbols in order to reveal the meaning, sometimes illusive, of Borges's stories. One that clearly does is Cámpora's *La duda.* The image of the train in it may literally refer to the train in which Dahlmann travels to the country, but it may also stand for his life's journey. Ravens often are related to death, so the two in the painting may indicate Dahlmann's imminent demise. The black cat could just be a reference to the cat in the story, but it may also indicate catastrophe. The bridge over the precipice toward which one of the representations of Dahlmann is close, brings to mind danger and risk. And the dove may point to the peace and resolution that characterize Dahlmann's courageous choice.

In Sierra's *Asterión*, the shape of the leaves of the plants that surround the Minotaur recall a sword, and the red coloring of their tips suggests the Minotaur's blood. Gontard has used symbolic gestures to give an idea of both Juliana's mental state and role and the relation of the brothers in *La intrusa*. Juliana is fixing her hair, a symbol of coquetry and her position in the story—she must appeal to the desires of the brothers. And the older brother's position of the left hand over his heart reveals a deep feeling for his younger brother. In *La casa de Asterión*, Azaceta uses a ceiling lamp with an uncovered lightbulb—traditional symbols of illumination and understanding—to indicate Asterion's way out of the labyrinth in which he is trapped. Kupferminc's clock and timing devices, in *El milagro secreto*, draw our attention to time and its passage, a central focus of the narrative. And the chair that she uses in that same story, and in *Con el fuego,* ties the work to the Jewish traditions and its rituals connected to death.

These symbols evoke and lead, although they do not explain or narrate. They merely make suggestions, or better still, open avenues of understanding that audiences may pursue and which are rooted in the ambiguities and allusions present in Borges's stories. No symbol delivers an unambiguous message. A train may refer to an actual trip but also to life's journey; a leaf may be what it is and also a representation of a sword; red may be just a brilliant color in a composition or a reference to blood; a clock may be an instrument pointing to a particular time but also an indication of time itself; and a chair may be a piece of furniture and a reference to death. These symbols serve not only to connect audiences to interpretanda, but also become interpretanda themselves that engage audiences in a process of understanding.

The symbols that are used in the paintings included here are of two main sorts: some belong to the stories themselves and aim to provide a closer interpretation of them. Others are not present in the stories, in which case they introduce a more free understanding of them. Kupferminc's images of chairs are symbols of the second sort. With the introduction of these objects the artist brings into the interpretations a dimension that is not present in the stories. But Celma's use of the goldfinch in *The Gospel According to Borges* is a symbol of the first sort, because Borges's story mentions the bird.

Picturing

One could argue that everything that painters do when they interpret a literary work is *to picture* it, but this is not quite right. Picturing a literary work as a whole, or any of the events to which it makes reference or characters that play roles in it, is to create an illustration rather than an interpretation. An interpretation is something different, because it is both more and less than an illustration. For example, Destéfanis's interpretation of "The Gospel According to Mark" is much more and much less than the story. It is much more because it depicts an event that is not described in the story but merely hinted at—Baltasar's crucifixion—and it is much less because it leaves out all the events that unfold in the narrative. Still, part of the task of artists who interpret literary works is to turn descriptions found in the interpretanda into visual images: picturing them. This involves a process of imagining or mentally depicting something which is then transferred to a physical medium.

This procedure is used in one way or another in most of the artworks we are considering here, although to very different degrees. In *El sur*, Boim presents us with pictures of Dahlmann, the Argentinean countryside, and a building that could represent either the memory of Dahlmann's childhood countryhouse or the restaurant where he meets his actual or imaginary end. But the labyrinth depicted by Azaceta in *La casa de Asterión* is very different, lacking most of the realistic elements of Boim's picture, and presenting us with complicated and purposefully impossible sets of passages, doors, and stairs that appear to be inside a head. These two examples should suffice to give an idea of the breadth and depth of the picturing that takes place in the instrumental visual interpretations that the artists have created in their understandings of Borges's works.

Some Loose Ends

From all this, it should be clear that the range of approaches used by the artists in providing their interpretations of Borges is extraordinary. It should also be clear that the artists were quite aware that what they were doing, or were supposed to do, were interpretations. In all cases they were consulted, and most of them produced new works. So we cannot attribute the range and differences in strategies to the fact that some of them may not have been aware that their works were supposed to be interpretations. Indeed, the works they have produced constitute de facto unambiguous statements as to what they consider an interpretation to be.

This suggests some questions that I have not yet addressed but are at the core of this inquiry. For one, we may ask: Should all the visual works that claim to interpret Borges's stories be legitimately considered interpretations? Do all of them qualify as interpretations or are there some that should be disqualified as such? This is another way of asking whether there are limits to interpretation and if there are, what they are. For another, if they are legitimate interpretations, we may want to know the kind of interpretations they are, and their degree of success. I turn to these questions in the next and final chapter.

17

Limits of Interpretation

The question of whether there are limits to interpretation is one of the most debated issues in hermeneutics today. The issue is not a matter of whether de facto there are limits to what interpreters can do, but rather whether there are any boundaries beyond which interpreters should not go. Are interpreters completely free to understand, and create instruments of understanding of, interpretanda in any way they want, without any constraints imposed on them, whether by the author, audience, context, or the interpretanda themselves? Or are interpreters limited in the ways they should legitimately understand, or produce understandings of, interpretanda so that, if they go beyond certain boundaries, their interpretations are no longer understandings, but rather misunderstandings?

Among the many views in the current literature that have attracted attention are two extreme positions that I call the Strict-Limits View and the Loose-Limits View. Both are flawed. Apart from these two extreme positions, many others fall in between, often doing greater justice to the facts of experience. It would not do, however, to discuss even a fraction of these positions here, for that would take more space than I have at my disposal. Instead, I propose to present a brief and general discussion of the Strict-Limits and Loose-Limits Views and then use some of the points made and clarifications introduced in earlier chapters to help us find a satisfactory answer to the question of the limits of interpretation. I call the view I advocate the Conditional-Limits View. With these considerations in mind, we are in a better position to judge the value of the artistic interpretation of Borges's stories included in this book.

This position holds that there are strict limits to the understanding of interpretanda and that understandings that do not respect those limits are misunderstandings to the extent that they do not. In principle, the source of the limits can vary; it could be related to the historical author, a particular audience, or even the interpretandum itself. But in fact, most of those who adhere to versions of this position regard historical authors as the source: the limits are imposed by the historical authors of interpretanda at the time of creation, so that understanding interpretanda in ways other than the way in which they were understood, or intended to be understood, by the historical authors at the time of creation, implies misunderstanding them.[1] Interpretanda, such as the ones discussed in this book, so the argument goes, are instruments authors use to convey particular meanings, and to understand them differently than their historical authors is inappropriate, leading to historical inaccuracies that are downright pernicious and certainly unfair to the authors. Authors have a proprietary interest in interpretanda, having created them, and thus interpreters must submit to their authority.

The reasons for adopting the view that interpreters should understand historical interpretanda as their historical authors understood them, or as they intended them to be understood, appear prima facie quite sensible and are rooted both in a desire to respect the wishes of historical authors and in a concern for historical accuracy and effective communication. To ignore the understanding historical authors had of interpretanda in the historical contexts in which they were produced, appears to imply giving up on scientific objectivity and historical accuracy. Indeed, the consequences of this rejection go so deep that they seem to undermine the very foundations of communication in the minds of many, leading inevitably to a tower of Babel or to silence.

In spite of these merits, however, the Strict-Limits View approach fails to take into account at least two important facts concerning interpretation. One is that we do not always interpret for the same reasons, and certainly not always in order to find out what an author understood by an interpretandum. Indeed, we do not even always want to understand what a particular audience understood by interpretanda, or their meaning or implications. In many cases we do interpret with those aims in mind, but in many others we seek to achieve other goals, such as playing with ideas, enjoying ourselves, making money, showing off, lying, hurting someone, and so on. Many of these aims do not involve understanding what the historical author of the interpretandum understood, or intended to be understood, by it. And the same applies, mutatis mutandis, to cases of the understandings of particular audiences or the meanings and implications of interpretanda.

The second fact that the Strict-Limits View overlooks is the substantial disagreement that occurs when we come to the understanding of interpretanda. Although there is frequent agreement concerning some of them, many interpretanda, particularly complex ones, become subjects of substantial disagreement, and even of contradictory interpretations, How can this be explained? Surely not easily if the limits of interpretations are strict, as this view proposes. Only a position that allows for flexibility in interpretation can effectively account for the richness in the variety of understandings to which interpretanda are regularly subjected.

Loose-Limits View

At the opposite extreme is the Loose-Limits View, according to which interpreters have freedom to understand or produce understandings of an interpretandum.[2] They tend to think of interpretanda as entities independent of their historical authors, intended and contemporaneous audiences, and the contexts in which they were produced, and tie them closer to their interpreters. Not that they always hold this entails complete license. Some of the proponents of this point of view would grant, for example, that a text in English cannot be understood as if it were in French, even if the scripts of the texts were similar or even the same. The point can be easily illustrated with signs, for there are some French words that look the same as English words yet mean something different. Most adherents to this position grant that there are some constraints on the understanding of interpretanda, but they insist that the constraints are to be found in the interpretanda themselves, not outside them. They particularly object to constraints that involve historical authors, their contemporaneous audiences, and the historical contexts in which the interpretanda were produced. Indeed, many of those who adopt this view are especially concerned with what they consider to be the excessive importance given to the historical author and the historical context in the understanding of interpretanda. They are also concerned with the misuse of authority granted to historical authors, in that this authority may be abused and serve to perpetuate alienating social structures in which groups of persons are marginalized, not only intellectually but also economically and socially, when certain views are used ideologically to preserve an unjust status quo. To prevent such abuses, interpreters must be granted the freedom to understand interpretanda as they wish within very general parameters.

The Loose-Limits View has the advantage that it accounts for the frequent disagreements that occur when it comes to the understanding of interpretanda. Indeed, there appears to be no interpretandum of any consequence whose meaning cannot be the subject of a dispute. Even words are subject to different understandings, becoming sources of disagreement. The lack of closure when it comes to the understanding of interpretanda, so the argument goes, must be recognized in hermeneutics by regarding interpretanda merely as loci of multiple understandings. There can be no single, definitive, and univocal interpretation of interpretanda. Indeed, some contemporary literary theorists go so far as to hold, ironically, that every understanding of a text cannot help but be, in fact, a misunderstanding of it.

In spite of the mentioned advantage, this view does not fare much better than the Strict-Limits View. Its main problems are precisely the reverse of those faced by that view. One is that it fails to recognize that, although there may be many different aims of interpretation, many interpretations have the same aims. Not every interpretation is *sui generis*; considerable overlapping and unity in interpretations is common. It is clear that many interpreters seek the same aim of, for example, understanding the intention of the historical author of an interpretandum, or the way a particular audience understood an interpretandum, or even the meaning of the interpretandum and its implications.

The second fact that this view fails to take into account is the considerable agreement among interpretations. Entire groups of people seem to agree that a certain interpretation of this or that interpretandum is appropriate and some other one is not. And this cannot be explained by just saying that this agreement is accidental if, in fact, there are no limits to interpretation. Yet, we do want to issue judgments as to the value and legitimacy of interpretations, and often very strong ones. Indeed, it is ironic that some of the more strident defenders of the Loose-Limits View themselves take strong exception to some interpretations of their own texts, considering them to be misinterpretations!

Conditional-Limits View

The Strict-Limits and Loose-Limits Views of interpretation fail to provide effective accounts of interpretation. In order to identify the source of their difficulties and formulate an adequate view, I submit that the rationale for both is rooted in part in considerations that are external to hermeneutics and in some cases have a moral dimension. In the Strict-Limits View, the moral dimension concerns the rights of the author when the interpretation in question is authorial, although it can also be related to an audience with appropriate authority, or even to the work insofar as it is arguable that it should not be defiled. In the Loose-Limits View it is regarded as the pernicious consequences of limiting the understanding by interpreters, when this is used to support the social status quo. Both positions adopt an answer to the question of the limits of understanding interpretanda based in part on certain views external to interpretation, thereby ignoring interpretanda and their function. One might even say that, in a sense, these solutions are ideological, if by ideological one means views whose adoption is based on their use to carry out certain programs of action rather than a concern for truth.

The most telling error that both of these positions make is that they neglect two factors essentially tied to interpretation, namely, context and aim. To neglect them leaves out of consideration two factors that have much to do with the function of interpretation. These positions ignore context in that they treat all interpretations as if they were meant to function under the same circumstances, and this is inappropriate. Consider the case of Borges's "The Rose of Paracelsus." We saw earlier that the interpretations of it provided by Rey and Estévez are radically different. For Rey, the heart of the story is the nature of true faith: "Does faith require to be buttressed by evidence, or is faith independent of evidence"? Rey's reading is based on what is pertinent for him. His preoccupation, founded on his personal circumstances, lead him to this understanding.

With Estévez the situation is quite different. His interpretation of the story involves the misunderstanding of Paracelsus by presumptive disciples, those around him who are supposed to admire his genius, but instead miss its true character and value. Estévez understands the story as concerning the artist whose art is misunderstood. And the reason, as with Rey, is that Estévez is reading the story from a particular point of view and a set of concerns. These lead him to see in it something Rey did not. Estévez's context changes the interpretive dynamic, giving us a completely different understanding of Borges's tale.

Something similar happens with the neglect to consider the aims of interpretation. Not all interpretations have the same aim, and therefore not all interpreters use the same hermeneutic approach. Consider the case of Borges's "The Immortal" and the two interpretations used here. Ferrari's work focuses on the notion of immortality as it applies to nature. He wants the audience to understand that "the immortal" is nature, the universe as a whole, and not particular humans, or even humanity as a whole, and certainly nothing that smacks of divinity. Thus he picks both vegetation, a wild entanglement of vines and flowers representing the richness of the universe and its beauty, and one of the lowest, and most despised, creatures in it, the cockroach, which thrives in this lush environment. There is no sign of humanity or culture in the piece, except for the writing, which represents the universe of the story, the universe of discourse that sets the boundaries of the narrative. It is not humanity and its creations that survive, not even Ferrari's own art; it is nature. This is quite concordant with Ferrari's naturalistic outlook, and perhaps his age. When he created this work he was approaching ninety years of age, and thus contemplating the not-very-distant end of a rich life. These thoughts may have brought him back to his basic, naturalistic outlook. He leaves us with a message of hope, but it is not a message of personal immortality, or even of cultural immortality.

D'Leo's painting has an entirely different aim that strongly contrasts with that of Ferrari's work. It focuses on the moment of communication in the story and the unity of humankind that it involves. The point is the discovery of the unity of all knowledge and, in this, of humankind. This is the moment in which Marcus realizes that he is not alone, for he becomes all humans in virtue of the universality of knowledge. For D'Leo, with his strong social concerns and his desire for justice and fellowship, this is an important message in Borges's story. It is a message of redemption that the artist has represented through the tattered image of the immortal, who is Marcus, Homer, and ultimately humankind in its struggling trek through history.

The neglect to consider context and aim leads proponents of the Strict-Limits and Loose-Limits Views to confuse the general aim of all interpretations with particular aims and to ignore the contextual importance of interpretation. This in turn leads them to the formulation of a false dilemma. The key to a proper understanding of interpretation is to realize that there is neither only one general aim for all interpretations nor many particular aims. Rather, we need to recognize that there is a general, overall aim for all interpretations, a number of specific aims resulting from various kinds of interpretations, and particular aims resulting from the diverse contexts and situations in which interpretations take place.

As an understanding, an interpretation is a mental act (or acts) that an interpreter has in relation to an interpretandum and that may lead in turn to the creation of an instrument to cause mental acts in others. Note that I have not called this act (or acts) "knowledge," for knowledge imposes constraints that do not necessarily apply to understanding. Knowledge may have to be true, justifiable, and so on. But an understanding need not have any of these characteristics. An understanding may be accurate or inaccurate, appropriate or inappropriate.

As an understanding, an interpretation may have itself for aim insofar as understanding can be its own aim, or it may have for aim something other than itself. There is no specific or particular aim that all interpretations have other than themselves. And if instead of understandings, interpretations are taken to be instruments of understanding, that is, instruments that cause understandings in ourselves or in others, the same applies, mutatis mutandis. An instrument of understanding may have itself as aim or it may have as aim the understandings to which it is supposed to lead, or it may have still other specific and particular understandings as aims. The general aim of instrumental interpretations is either themselves or the various understandings they are intended to cause.

The specific aims that interpretations may have in either one of their two modalities are related to their various kinds. We saw these in the previous chapter. Meaning interpretations have as aim the understanding of the meaning of interpretanda, and are divided into authorial, audiencial, work-based, and implicative, depending on whether the meaning is taken to be determined by the author, an audience, the work, or by any of these and their implications. Relational interpretations, by contrast, have as aim the understanding of a relation between the interpretandum, or its meaning, and something else that the interpreter brings into the hermeneutic process. Relational interpretations are infinite in kind, since an interpretandum may, in principle, be related to anything whatever.

We also need to realize that within these specific kinds of interpretations and their aims, contexts lead to further particular aims for interpreters. For example, a Freudian interpretation may be given a particular twist because the interpreter wishes to have a particular kind of understanding of the interpretandum. All this brings variety and flexibility to interpretation.

I call the position that takes into account contexts and aims, the Conditional-Limits View because, according to it, interpretations depend on their aims and the contexts in which they are given. Now, if we accept the taxonomy of aims and the variety of contexts mentioned, it should be clear that there are not, and cannot be, any limits to interpretation. The reason is that there are no limits to the contexts and kinds (specific and particular) of interpretations.

But does this mean that the Conditional View is after all not different from the Loose-Limits View, in that interpreters are considered to have unlimited license to interpret in any way they wish? The answer is no. It is true that no general conditions need apply to all interpretations other than the ones mentioned above, but it is also true that specific and particular kinds of interpretations, as well as particular contexts, impose limits, sometimes very strict, on interpretations. For example, if the interpretation wanted is authorial, clearly there are conditions to this understanding that would make certain interpretations legitimate and others illegitimate. An authorial interpretation that confuses the author of an interpretandum with some other historical figure would be clearly illegitimate. And an interpretation that proposes to give a Freudian understanding of a work by Borges and uses Marxist theory instead of Freudian theory to carry it out, clearly is not an adequate Freudian interpretation.

Now, in order to address my next task, namely, to judge the value of the interpretations that have been presented in this book and thus illustrate how this theoretical framework functions in practice, I need to determine the kinds of interpretations they are. Before I do this, however, I should make sure that we correctly identify the interpretanda and interpretations in question.

Interpretanda and Interpretations

The main interpretanda of this project are stories by Borges and the artworks reproduced in this book, although I have also discussed Foucault's interpretation of a painting by Velázquez, Danto's interpretation of "Pierre Menard," and my own interpretation of the art. However, we need to keep in mind that the interpretations of these interpretanda themselves become objects of interpretation, that is interpretanda. Moreover, the answers to the questions regarding the kinds of interpretations they are themselves also become interpretations; insofar as we are seeking to determine the kind of interpretation that these interpretations are, we are engaged in providing interpretations of them. This in turn entails that the very interpretations we seek can be classified according to the taxonomy provided above.

For the sake of illustration, let us consider three examples: (1) an interpretation of a story by Borges in terms of visual art given in this book, such as Destéfanis's *La decisión de los Guthre*; (2) Danto's philosophical interpretation of "Pierre Menard"; and (3) Foucault's philosophical interpretation of *Las meninas*. Our task is to determine, first, whether Destéfanis's *La decisión de los Guthre* is an authorial, audiencial, work-based, implicative, or relational interpretation. And the same applies to Danto's interpretation of "Pierre Menard" and Foucault's interpretation of *Las meninas*. This task involves considering the interpretations by Destéfanis, Danto, and Foucault themselves as interpretanda, and the discussion and conclusions about them that I reach as their interpretations. Moreover, as interpretations, what I say about them is subject to classification in terms of the hermeneutical taxonomy provided: Are the interpretations I give to be considered authorial, audiencial, work-based, implicative, or relational? The same applies to the understanding that the readers reach when they interpret my interpretations. Here is a diagram of the situation:

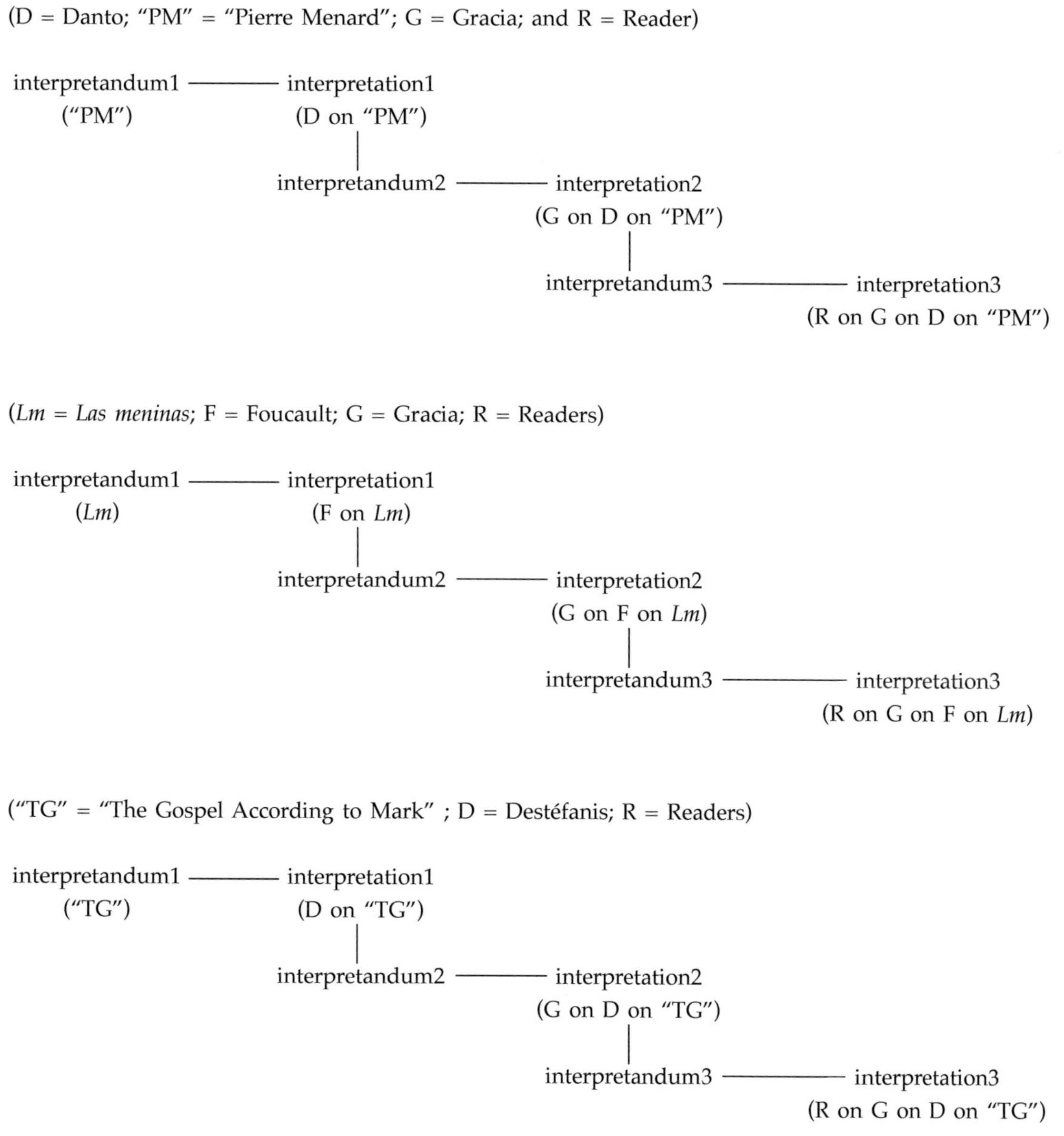
(D = Danto; "PM" = "Pierre Menard"; G = Gracia; and R = Reader)

interpretandum1 ———— interpretation1
("PM")   (D on "PM")

interpretandum2 ———— interpretation2
                     (G on D on "PM")

interpretandum3 ———— interpretation3
                     (R on G on D on "PM")

(Lm = Las meninas; F = Foucault; G = Gracia; R = Readers)

interpretandum1 ———— interpretation1
(Lm)   (F on Lm)

interpretandum2 ———— interpretation2
                     (G on F on Lm)

interpretandum3 ———— interpretation3
                     (R on G on F on Lm)

("TG" = "The Gospel According to Mark" ; D = Destéfanis; R = Readers)

interpretandum1 ———— interpretation1
("TG")   (D on "TG")

interpretandum2 ———— interpretation2
                     (G on D on "TG")

interpretandum3 ———— interpretation3
                     (R on G on D on "TG")

Classifying the Interpretations

With the previous discussion in mind, we can turn to the classification of interpretations in this book. This is important because, on the basis of this classification, we should be able to determine what interpreters seek and whether they succeed. In other words, this procedure will allow us to judge the effectiveness and success of the interpretations in terms of their aims.

Are They Authorial?

Let me begin by asking whether the interpretations by the artists, Danto, Foucault, and me, are authorial. This involves determining whether the interpreters intended to produce instruments of understanding for audiences that would cause understandings in them similar to the understandings of the authors in one or more of their various modalities (historical, pseudo-historical, composite, or interpretive), although here I mainly consider historical authors for the sake of parsimony. In order to do this we need in turn to ask what kinds of evidence we would need in order to reach a correct answer to this question. Several possibilities suggest themselves. For the determination of whether they are interpretations that seek to understand what historical authors understood, we would need references to the authors, such as statements saying that, for example, Borges thought this or that, or intended this or that. In cases in which the names of the authors are not used, definite descriptions that fit them would be sufficient in context, such as "the author of *Ficciones.*"

Finding such references in a text would likely indicate authorial interpretative intent, but a lack of such references does not indicate a lack of it. I may have an authorial intent in mind and not express it. An interpreter of my interpretation might conclude that, based on the absence of reference, I am not interested in what the historical author understood, and yet that might be exactly what I have in mind.

In cases in which the interpretations are texts, as in those given by Danto, Foucault, and me, it is fairly easy to determine the presence of references to the historical author. Some mention the author's name and a report of what the interpreter thinks he understood or intended. This is clear when Danto says at the outset ". . . the possibility was first recognized, I believe, in connection with literary works, by Borges, who has the glory of having discovered it in his masterpiece, 'Pierre Menard . . . ,'" and makes further references to Borges, what he wrote, and what Danto thinks he was trying to do. Although the situation is not as obvious in Foucault's interpretation of *Las meninas*, he does refer to Velázquez and to "the painter" at various junctures, and in some places includes definite descriptions that in context are as good as direct references. Neither Danto nor Foucault are good at providing identification information in footnotes, claims the authors may have made elsewhere, historical details, accounts of interviews, and so on, that would indicate authorial intent, but other interpreters frequently supply this kind of information. And what has been said about the interpretations by Danto and Foucault may be applied to mine. In any case, this suggests that there is an authorial interpretative aim in terms of the historical author in the philosophical interpretations of Borges's stories, Velázquez's *Las meninas*, and the artworks discussed in this book by Danto, Foucault, and me, even if that aim may not be exclusive of others.

To determine whether visual interpretations have authorial intent is much more difficult than it is in the case of textual interpretations, because artists do not often include the authors of the works they are interpreting in their visual interpretations. One artist who does is, precisely, Velázquez, who paints himself painting *Las meninas*. But this is rare, and it is even more so when the interpretandum of which the artist provides a visual interpretation is not the work of the artist, as is the case in this book. In the artworks used here, two artists include images of what appears to be Borges. Nizzero does so in both *El otro* and *Funes, el memorioso*, and Boim includes an image that looks like Borges in *El sur*, although this is done indirectly, through Dahlmann, the protagonist of the story. This could be interpreted as an authorial intent in both of these artists. However, the images Nizzero presents us with are not of Borges, the historical author of the stories—in neither of the two works by him are they portraits. The images are of Borges a character in the stories—in the first it is Borges himself, but in the second it is Borges as narrator. This may indicate after all that it is not the historical author Nizzero has in mind, but rather the pseudo-historical author, that is, the *persona* that Borges reveals to us in the stories. In the case of Boim, establishing authorial intent is also complicated, for the image in the painting is not supposed to be Borges, but Dahlmann, although we know that the story is partly autobiographical and Dahlmann may represent Borges, to which must be added that there is a certain resemblance between the painted Dahlmann and the real Borges.

More explicit is the case of artists who write the name of the historical author in the title of the artworks, as Celma does in *El evangelio según Borges*. Or artists who write the name of the author in some part of the work as both Celma and Pereda do. Celma writes it on the halo that surrounds the main figure in the painting, adding outside the halo: "Love by Borges," which presumably unpacks the reference to Borges's view given in the title. And Pereda does it in a dedication included in the painting. In both cases it appears that the artists are trying to convey an understanding that Borges had: his view of love in the case of Celma and his take on the condition of women in the case of Pereda.

So, what do we make of all this? Are the interpretations by Nizzero, Boim, Celma, and Pereda authorial or not? The answer is not clear in the first two, for we have no obvious connection between the figures depicted in the artworks and any particular understanding that the artworks are supposed to produce in their audiences. For this reason I favor the simpler explanation and, therefore, the most believable if we are to adhere to the Principle of Parsimony, namely, that these are examples in which we have some, although not strong, authorial interpretative intent, whether in terms of the historical author or the pseudo-historical author.

Concerning Celma and Pereda, the case for authorial intent is stronger, but again, not beyond question. So, again, for the sake of simplicity, I am comfortable with accepting some authorial intention. Moreover, in none of the four cases mentioned—those of Nizzero, Boim, Celma, or Pereda—does this prove that authorial intent is the only aim for the interpretations that the artists have given, or that this applies to other interpretive artworks discussed in this book. Indeed, I do not find any other of the artworks under consideration here where the artists have included the author of the interpretandum, in any modality, in the works of art, either as an image or by way of a reference.

Of course, as I mentioned in the case of the interpretations by Danto and Foucault, for example, we could also consider other sources in order to determine the intent of the artists, such as notes, historical data, interviews, and so on. Some evidence of this sort is in fact available for the artists in the filmed interviews I conducted with them, but these interviews do not contain any evidence of authorial intent. Indeed, the artists emphasize their intent to present something that is quite their own—their particular understanding of some aspect of the story. The absence of evidence to the contrary, then, leads me to surmise that it is likely that none of the artistic interpretations we have in this book are strictly or strongly authorial in intent.

Are They Audiencial?

What has been said about authorial interpretations may also be said about audiencial interpretations. In their case, however, the references that support them are not usually to persons, but rather to historical contexts. They may take the form of references to what particular people or groups of people thought the interpretanda mean. In some instances, they involve references to scholarly works such as learned treatises and, in other instances, references to popular sources such as newspapers and media. They may also consist of references to what other authors of the times may have noted. In the philosophical interpretations of Borges's stories, for example, interpreters often refer to other interpretations. Although, none of the philosophical or artistic interpretations of the stories we have been considering here contains such references, many others do, although this is of no help to us in order to determine the character of the interpretations we are considering.

Another way to tie a story to a particular audience is by historical contextualization. Factors such as clothing, architecture, and landscape may be used by interpreters to indicate an audience they have in mind, whether historical, intended, or interpretive. The works of Kupferminc, Boim, and Destéfanis, for example, contain such motifs, so one could argue that this may reveal some audiencial intent in them. The references to Jewish motifs in Kupferminc's works suggest that she may have in mind a Jewish audience that may be able to understand these motifs. Boim's depiction of a landscape with some typical motifs from the Argentinean south in *El sur* may indicate that he wishes to speak to an Argentinean audience. And something similar could be mentioned in the case of Destéfanis's *La decisión de los Guthre*, in that he dresses his characters in the typical clothing of the Argentinean gaucho.

Another factor is the use of a certain style of writing that may restrict the audience of an interpretation. For example, the analytic style used by Danto is unpalatable to a philosophically Continental audience, thus limiting the appeal of his interpretation to it. And the reverse is true of Foucault's interpretation of *Las meninas* which, because of the style, makes many analytic philosophers exclude themselves from considering it.

Still, none of these depictions may actually have an audiencial aim, but rather be trying to render accurately what the interpreter understands the interpretandum to mean. In Kupferminc's *El milagro secreto,* the protagonist is Jewish, so it makes sense for any audience to expect some Jewish motifs. And Boim and Destéfanis may just be trying to depict the clothing and landscape appropriate to the stories. Hence, it is far from clear that the use of any of these motifs can be considered evidence that an interpretation is audiencial.

One factor that could add significance to context would be a change in time or place. For example, setting the opera "Carmen" in the context of the Spanish Civil War seems to mark a clear intent to change the audience from its historical one to a later period, for the reference to this war would have made no sense to the historical audience. But even here, the aim may have nothing to do with the audience, but rather with something else that the interpreter has in mind, such as politics.

However, contextualization is not at play in any of the philosophical interpretations of Borges given here, although it may be a factor to consider in at least a couple of the artistic interpretations. One is Rey's use of Caravaggio's insight in *Doubting of St. Thomas*. Rey has picked a section of Caravaggio's painting, *The Incredulity of St. Thomas*, and used it to convey a message. But the use of this device established parameters for the prospective audience, for its significance is plain only to those who know the biblical story or are acquainted with Caravaggio's painting. The reason is that there is nothing else in Rey's painting that relates it to Borges's story, not even the title. Audiences that are not acquainted with the biblical story or the Caravaggio necessarily would miss the significance of Rey's work and the connection to the story by Borges. The only other way in which they could relate Rey's work to the story would be through some external context, such as its inclusion in this book. This suggests that, consciously or unconsciously, Rey had a certain audience in mind when he created his interpretation.

Something similar might apply to Delgado's *La otra*. Again, as with Rey's work, this painting has no ostensive relation to Borges's "The Other," although in this case there is a stronger parallelism between the story and the painting insofar as the latter is clearly about identity. This may suggest some particular audience, although it is by no means clear which. In short, a narrow audiencial intent does not seem ostensibly present in any of the artistic interpretations we are considering except perhaps in Rey's work.

Are They Work-Based?

Next I turn to work-based interpretations: Are the philosophical and artistic interpretations that concern us here work-based? Do they aim to provide an understanding, or cause an understanding, of the meaning of the interpretanda in question, apart from what their authors or particular audiences may have understood by them? Let us begin with the philosophical interpretations of both the literary works and the artistic ones.

Danto's interpretation refers to the work of Borges, but it gives a prominent role to the author. We saw earlier that one could surmise that the interpretation is strongly authorial. However, Danto also quotes from the text and refers to its meaning without always pointing to the author as the source of that meaning. So it would be possible to argue that, even with a strong authorial component, there is also room here for considering Danto's interpretation of "Pierre Menard" to be work-based.

In the case of Foucault, the interpretation mentions Velázquez only a few times, and emphasizes the painting rather than the author. This makes sense insofar as it is one of Foucault's main views that the historical author of a work is unimportant for the interpretation of the work. So, presumably, he must consider his interpretation of *Las meninas* to be work-based. But this, of course, does not compel us to agree with him unless we hold that Foucault, qua author of his interpretation of *Las meninas*, should be the determining factor on our understanding of the chapter of his book. And if we look at the chapter, there are some references to Velázquez, and therefore one could argue that the chapter itself is not merely a work-based interpretation but also has an authorial intent.

This brings me to my own interpretations of both the stories and the works of art. Even a cursory look at the first indicates that they refer both to the author of the stories and the artists, and thus presumably have an authorial aim. But also they often explicitly go beyond what the artists may have had in mind to construct understandings that are suggested by the works themselves. Indeed, even when the artists are brought in to enlighten us about the meaning of a text or a feature of a work of art—as when I say something like, "this is a motif that is frequently explored by Borges or the artist"—they are brought in as ways to help understand certain features of the work and reaffirm a reading of it, rather than as an ultimate aim. This means that in my interpretations it is the work that is considered fundamental, and the authors' understandings are used only as corroborating evidence of certain understandings of the works.

The aim of the artists is even more difficult to establish. In the first place, very few artists refer to Borges in the titles of their works or the works themselves, and this would indicate that they are not concerned with providing an authorial interpretation. Even in the cases of those that do, like Celma and Pereda, it is not clear that they have an authorial intention. Moreover, very few artists include the image of the author in their works. Only Nizzero and perhaps Boim do, but again, it is not evident that this indicates authorial intent. The case for a substantial audiencial aim is feasible only in Rey's *Doubting of St. Thomas* and perhaps Delgado's *La otra*. So there would seem to be nothing standing in the way of inferring that these interpretations are fundamentally work-based.

However, matters are not so easy for two reasons. First, there is much in the works of art that is not present in the original text of the stories, and second, they often neglect to incorporate elements from the stories. Just consider the works by Azaceta, Delgado, Destéfanis, D'Leo, Estévez, Ferrari, Franco, Kupferminc, and Menza. Indeed, not only are the techniques of elimination and addition discussed in Chapter 16 strongly at work in them, but most of the other strategies that undermine a work-based interpretation, such as focusing, metaphorical reading, transposition, translation, appropriation, and symbolization are present. Even works such as Gontard's *La intrusa,* Boim's *El sur,* Sierra's *Asterión,* and Nizzero's *El otro* and *Funes, el memorioso*, that have strong descriptive dimensions, and in some cases refer to various elements present in the stories, go well beyond the stories, so that it is difficult to argue that they should be considered strictly speaking work-based.

Are They Implicative?

This brings me to implicative interpretations, which are concerned with the understanding of the implications of an interpretandum's meaning. All the philosophical interpretations we have considered have a strong implicative component, for they all involve understandings, or cause understandings, of the perceived implications of the meanings of the interpretanda, whether that meaning is conceived in terms of the author, the audience, or the work. Danto's interpretation draws implications of Danto's basic understanding of "Pierre Menard" that apply to the identity of all literary works; Foucault draws the philosophical implications of his reading of *Las meninas* for a theory of interpretation in general; and my interpretations of Borges's stories and their artistic interpretations draw implications for a general theory of the interpretation of literature through visual works of art.

The situation with the interpretive artworks is not as clear perhaps, but can be gathered from a closer analysis. In some cases, as in Destéfanis's *La decisión de los Guthre*, the implication is obvious, insofar as the artist depicts an event that is indirectly referred to, but does not occur, in the story. Celma's *El evangelio según Borges* gives us a picture of love that is not explicit in the story. Pereda's "*Si la querés, usála*" is a stark depiction of a woman as object, although the story itself does not quite say that. Ferrari's universe in *El inmortal* is nothing if not an implication of what is certainly not evident in the story. And the same appears to be the case with the other works of art. They all seem to thrive on implication, although the source of the implication is not always uniform. For some, it is what the historical author may have understood, whereas for others it is what a particular audience might understand or what the work itself reveals. It is appropriate to conclude, then, that most of the interpretations we consider here are implicative, although this aim is not their primary focus.

Are They Relational?

A relational interpretation is not an understanding of the meaning of an interpretandum, but rather of a relation between the interpretandum and something the interpreter brings into the hermeneutic process, or alternatively it is an instrument intended to cause that understanding.

Foucault's interpretation of *Las meninas* is a good example of a relational philosophical interpretation. Although he presents us with a very detailed discussion of Velázquez's work, he explores only some very limited aspects of the painting, namely those that substantiate his take. He focuses only on elements in it that are related to the philosophical point of view he brings into the picture: a painting reveals what is not in it, what is hidden, rather than what it is plainly in view. This point of view is by no means universally accepted. Foucault is engaged in a relational interpretation in which he presents us with an understanding of the relation of his particular philosophical theory of art to a work of art, rather than on a meaning interpretation that seeks to understand the philosophy *in* the picture.[3]

The case of Danto's interpretation of "Pierre Menard" is not as clearly relational, for he argues that the view he finds so significant is in fact explicitly presented by Borges in the story. Nonetheless, one could make a good case that Danto, like Foucault, is not really trying to understand what Borges understood, but rather to show how what Borges says in the story matches a philosophical position that Danto finds significant and proposes in his own work. In other words, he is interested in using an understanding of this position and its relation to the story and Borges's understanding of it. The interpretation, thus, can be considered relational in this sense.

The same ambiguity that we see in Danto can be detected in my own interpretations in this book. They do not reveal an overriding interest in trying to understand what Borges understood, whereas there is some clear interest in producing understandings of the works of literature or of art that match a certain point of view that, as a philosopher, I hold. If so, the overriding thrust of the interpretations must be considered relational.

When we come to the artistic interpretations of the stories, they seem to reveal the same kind of emphasis on a relation of the story to something else that the artists bring into the process. In *La casa de Asterión*, Azaceta introduces into the hermeneutic process his existential concern with the mental anguish caused by the human predicament—his interpretation consists of an understanding of the relation between this concern and "The House of Asterion." Cámpora's *La duda* is an exploration of how doubt and its resolution are related to "The South" and the choice that Dahlmann faces in it. Celma seeks to express the relation between his interest in the mystery of womanhood and love to "The Gospel According to Mark." In *La otra*, Delgado delves into the relation between her interest in self-revelation and "The Other," and in *Funes* she draws the connection between good and bad memory to "Funes, the Memorious." Destéfanis investigates guilt and eroticism in "The Gospel According to Mark" in *La decisión de los Guthre*. In *El inmortal*, D'Leo reads into "The Immortal" his belief in the true immortality of human knowledge. In *Los jardines que se bifurcan*, Estévez translates Borges's ideas about time and possible universes into bodily and mental states, and in *La rosa de Paracelso* he relates "The Rose of Paracelsus" to the predicament of the misunderstood artist. Ferrari, in *El inmortal*, connects his naturalistic view of the universe and the insignificance of humanity to "The Immortal." Franco's *La escritura de Dios* explores the relation between the need for humanity to go back to nature and overcome excessive technology to "The Writing of the God." Gontard finds in "The Interloper" a message about brotherly love that he expresses in *La intrusa*. Kuperminc connects "The Secret Miracle," "The Circular Ruins," and "The Writing of the God," to her ethnic heritage and even family experience in *El milagro secreto, Con el fuego,* and *La escritura del dios.* Menza's *Ruinas circulares II, El jardín de senderos que se bifurcan,* and *El milagro secreto* uses motifs he explores in many of his works to express "The Circular Ruins," "The Garden of Forking Paths," and "The Secret Miracle." In *"Si la querés, usála,"* Pereda's concern is to draw a relation between the condition of women to "The Interloper." Rey draws a connection between the Christian story as rendered by Caravaggio and "The Rose of Paracelsus" in *Doubting of St. Thomas.* And Sierra's *Asterión* brings together the artists' preoccupation with death in "The House of Asterion."

In all these cases the artists have brought into the hermeneutic understanding something they thought important—an idea, an image, a thought, a feeling, a concern—and related it to Borges's stories. Thus, the understanding is precisely of that relation and, through it, of both what the artists brought in and the story written by Borges.

The Limits of Interpretation

From this discussion it appears that the interpretations examined, whether philosophical or artistic interpretations of literature or philosophical interpretations of art, fall into more than one category precisely because they have diverse aims. In principle and in fact, we may have interpretations that can be classified as authorial, audiencial, implicative, and relational, and within these also various other kinds. Authorial interpretations may have the aim to understand a historical author, a pseudo-historical author, a contemporary author, or even an interpretive author. Audiencial interpretations may also be classified in similar ways to authorial, with appropriate modifications, and implicative interpretations follow suit, although adding implications. Relational interpretations come in a great variety, because interpreters may seek to relate interpretanda to such different things as certain ideas, experiences, feelings, historical facts, works of other sorts, theories, and so on.

The problem with this inference is that it would appear that it allows for contradictory interpretations, both by the same interpreter and by different interpreters, insofar as they may have different aims for their interpretations and thus engage in the creation of different kinds of interpretations. Indeed, we have seen in the artistic interpretations of Borges's stories presented here that interpretations of the same stories by different artists often are not only very different, but may produce contradictory understandings. Consider, for example the two interpretations of Borges's "The Writing of the God" by Kupferminc and Franco. For Kupferminc the message of the god appears on the skin of the tiger, where it reads *"El secreto"* (The secret), and the secret may be the very tiger as a symbol of the Messiah. But in Franco's interpretation, the message of God (rather than the god) is the need for humankind to return to nature as revealed through the eyes of the jaguars. These are two very different interpretations that strongly contrast, and perhaps even contradict each other, insofar as one refers to a traditional Jewish belief and the other points to a naturalistic message.

But can we accept this result? Is it legitimate to have contradictory interpretations of the same story? We generally reject contradictory understandings. The propositions "All humans are mortal" and "Some humans are not mortal" cannot both be true or false. If one is true, the other is false. So, insofar as interpretations are understandings or cause understandings, can we tolerate that they may contradict each other? Does the fact that the same interpretandum can give rise to different and even contradictory interpretations create a chaotic situation in which interpreters are open to understand an interpretandum in any way they want and we can never reach a determination as to what interpretation is best, or even whether certain interpretations are legitimate whereas others are not? Indeed, can we judge the value and legitimacy of interpretations at all under these conditions, since there seem to be no limits beyond which interpretations cannot go?[4]

For some, the answer is affirmative, for, as adherents of the Loose-Limits View argue, there are no limits to interpretation. Interpretations of the same interpretandum can be legitimate even if they differ and contradict each other. For others, the answer is negative, and they adhere to the Strict-Limits View according to which there are rigid boundaries beyond which interpretations cannot go if they are to claim any legitimacy. No interpretations that contradict each other can be legitimate. So who is right?

Much of the contemporary literature on this issue has revolved around the question of truth, that is, whether interpretations have truth value. For some, such as Margolis, they do, but in order to make room for contradictory interpretations, the categories of truth and falsity are not regarded as mutually exclusive.[5] For others, such as Davies, the way to allow for legitimate disagreements concerning interpretations is to reject that truth and falsity apply to them.[6] We might say that, rather than following either of these paths, I believe it is more fruitful to sidestep the emphasis on truth value and use another approach.

My suggestion is to go back to the view I presented earlier as an alternative to the Strict-Limits and Loose-Limits Views, namely, the Conditional-Limits View. According to it, all interpretations have conditions, but their conditions may differ. Some conditions are *general* and apply to all interpretations; some conditions are *specific* and apply to different kinds of interpretations; and some conditions are *particular* and have to do with individual requirements and unique contexts. All conditions have to do with the aims of the interpretations in question and determine the way in which they should be considered successful or not. An authorial interpretation should not be judged by the same criteria as an audiencial, work-based, implicative, or relational interpretation. And a Freudian interpretation should not be judged by the same criteria as feminist or theological interpretations. It would be absurd to fault an interpreter who is seeking to produce an authorial interpretation for not producing an audiencial one, and to reject an interpretation that is, or causes, an understanding of an interpretandum in relational terms, because it does not produce an authorial understanding. And it would be unfair to criticize a Freudian interpretation for not achieving a work-based understanding.

The legitimacy of interpretations depends on the kind of interpretation, and the kind of interpretation depends in turn on the general, specific, and particular aims it pursues. This means that there may be contradictory interpretations, as long as they are of different kinds and pursue different aims. However, this may not apply within interpretations of the same kind. It would make no sense to say that two authorial interpretations that hold contradictory understandings of the same interpretandum are both legitimate; one of them is wrong and has to be rejected. It would not do to argue, for example, that in "The Writing of the God" Borges was trying to tell us about the Messiah and not to tell us about the Messiah. That would make no sense. But it certainly would make sense to say that the story can be understood as both being about the Messiah and not about the Messiah, depending on whether one is seeking a relational interpretation that involves Jewish culture or not. And it could also be appropriate to say that Borges himself intended to make us understand something about the Messiah and something about nature.

Another conclusion is as important as the one above, namely, that more or less strict rules about interpreting apply within particular kinds of interpretations. This is quite clear if one considers the hermeneutical traditions of some kinds of interpretations. For example, the rules that govern Protestant interpretations of the Christian Scriptures tend to follow the Lutheran view that only the Scriptures may interpret the Scriptures. But the Catholic tradition makes tradition an important factor in the interpretation of the Scriptures. Obviously, it makes no sense to compare the results in each case and judge one according to the criteria used by the other, for the result would most likely yield different and conflicting understandings.[7]

This means that the stringency of the rules about interpretation depends on the kind of interpretation in question. It also means that, although interpreters have complete freedom to choose whatever aims they want for their interpretations, once those aims are chosen, the set of rules that govern them applies. The rules may be stringent or flexible, depending on the aims in question and the source of authority on which these rules are established. The Supreme Court is the ultimate authority to resolve questions concerning the interpretation of the United States Constitution. But the Supreme Court has no authority when it comes to the determination of the legitimacy of interpretations of Borges's "The Other."

This takes care of contradictory interpretations by different interpreters, but what do we make of interpretations by the same interpreter that have different aims. What do we make of Celma's authorial and relational intent, for example? Has he produced an illegitimate interpretation because it simultaneously pursues different results?

I do not see that the answer to this question has to be affirmative. There is no reason why the understanding Celma causes in us with respect to Borges's "The Gospel According to Mark" in *El evangelio según Borges* need involve a contradiction. Indeed, suppose that we have two understandings: one is about the nature of love and another is about the way Borges thought about love. There is no reason why the understanding of what Borges thought about love has to be different from, and least still, contradict, the understanding that Celma's work produces in us. It is altogether possible, and likely, that Celma expresses in the painting what Borges had in mind in his story. Celma produced an interpretation that may create at least two understandings, one is the relation of an idea about love he has and the story Borges created, and another is an understanding that Borges had this very idea in mind for the story.

The possibility of a lack of contradiction indicates that there may be different aims for different interpreters, and even for the same author, in the interpretation of the same interpretandum. Of course, whether there is a contradiction or not in similar cases will depend on the cases, understandings, and aims in question. And this may yield different results about the legitimacy of the interpretations. Suppose that Celma had an authorial interpretation in mind and also a relational one. And suppose that the relational one results in an understanding such as the one noted, but that the authorial interpretation could be shown to be wrong insofar as we have a statement by Borges contemporaneous with the writing of the story in which he explains that he did not understand the story to be about love at all, but about the nature of religion. Of course we do not have such a statement, but if we had it, this could indicate that although the relational part of Celma's interpretation may be legitimate, the authorial part of it is not. In short, the understanding of Celma's interpretation that has to do with love is fine as long as it is not attributed to Borges. Since we do not have any evidence that Borges did not have in mind the nature of love for the understanding of his story, however, we cannot conclude that Celma's authorial interpretation is illegitimate and violates the boundaries beyond which an authorial interpretation cannot go.

A similar analysis to this could be applied, mutatis mutandis, to every one of the artistic interpretations included in this book, but this is not necessary in order to understand three key points of my analysis. One is that the matter of the legitimacy of interpretations is rather complex and requires careful consideration before any judgment can be taken seriously. Another point is that in most cases it is very difficult to issue a judgment as to the legitimacy of an interpretation, contrary to the modus operandi of many critics, who arrogantly make these judgments based on flimsy evidence and a vague understanding of the nature of interpretation. Finally, there is a need to explore further the relation between different kinds of evaluations and their dependence on different kinds of interpretations. I have said very little on the last score in this book, although some inroads have been made by others in this direction recently.[8]

Parting Thoughts

The central topic of this book is the interpretation of literature in visual art, particularly painting. The particular problem it addresses concerns the difficulty involved in providing artistic interpretations of literature when the gap between literature and visual art is so large. Indeed, the question the book poses concerns how the interpretation of literature in terms of visual art can be possible, effective, and legitimate when literature is not a visual medium in the sense that art is.

The strategy I followed began with the presentation of twenty-four interpretations of Borges's stories by seventeen visual artists, together with my interpretations of the stories and the art. However, for the sake of comparison and greater depth of understanding of interpretation, I discussed also the philosophical interpretation of literature and art. With this in mind, I turned to the theoretical part of the book, beginning with an analysis of the identity conditions of literature, visual art, and philosophy, which revealed differences and similarities between them.

The main thesis I have defend concerning philosophy, art, and literature is that the differences between art, literature, and philosophy are that works of art contain among the conditions of their identity the pictures that constitute them and also the artifacts that embody them, whereas works of literature include the texts that constitute them, and only seldom do they include the scripts that constitute those texts, let alone the artifacts through which we access them. Philosophy contrasts with both, because it does not contain the texts, the scripts, or the artifacts, in its identity conditions. This is to a great extent what creates the difficulty in the philosophical interpretation of art or literature and the artistic interpretation of literature.

Next I turned to interpretation and presented a conception of it as a kind of understanding or as an instrument to cause understanding. From this perspective, the problem posed in the book turns into the problem concerning the possibility and means of bridging the gap in the understanding of literature, visual art, and philosophy, and particularly in the instruments used to produce such understanding. But interpretations can be of many sorts that fall roughly, depending on their aim, into authorial, audiencial, work-based, implicative, and relational.

Before drawing any conclusions about the interpretations contained in this book, I examined the artistic interpretations themselves to determine how the interpreters deal with their challenge, that is, the strategies they use to provide visual instruments of understanding of the stories by Borges. This shows that the artists use many diverse techniques in the development of their interpretations, and that the instruments they created allow for a great variety of understandings of Borges's stories. I examine twelve in particular that are frequently employed: reference and title, focus, literal and metaphorical readings, transposition, elimination and addition, translation, appropriation, symbolization, and picturing.

Finally, I took up the question of the legitimacy of the interpretations the artists give. The answer is: it depends on the aims and kinds of interpretations they have created and use. And it appears that the favorite kind of interpretation is relational, because their aim, even when it includes other aims, is concentrated in the understanding of a relation between a story by Borges and something the artists emphasize. Indeed, not only in the context of the artistic interpretation of literature does this seem to be the case, but also in the philosophical interpretation of literature and art.

The claims made in this book are meant as provisional hypotheses to be tested by further investigation and analysis. However, I am certain of one thing, namely, that the thesis concerning the artistic interpretation of literature that inspires this book is in line with Borges's thinking. Indeed, for him a work of literature is meant to open rich interpretive horizons for readers, whose task is ceaselessly to explore them, something not very different from what we find in the early dialogues of Plato, where Socrates never settles on a definitive answer to a philosophical question. Accordingly, the role of reader and that of author merge in an exploratory adventure without end. As Borges tells us explicitly in the text cited at the very beginning of this book, ". . . good readers are poets as singular, and as awesome, as great authors themselves." This book, then, should be considered a beginning, rather than an end.

Notes

Chapter 14

1. Quoted by Jack Diether, in "Notes to the Program," Carnegie Hall, Tuesday Evening, November 4, 1997, 19.

2. Another view of this relation sees philosophy as sharing a method of knowledge with both literature and science. This is why, so the argument goes, it is not possible to distinguish philosophy from literature, strictly speaking. See Christiane Schildknecht, "Entre la ciencia y la literatura: Formas literarias de la filosofía," trans. José M. González García, en María Teresa López de la Vieja, ed., *Figuras del logos: Entre la filosofía y la literatura* (Mexico City: Fondo de Cultura Económica, 1994), 21–40.

3. José Luis Gómez Martínez, "Posmodernidad, discurso antrópico y ensayística latinoamericana. Entrevista," *Dissens, Revista Internacional de Pensamiento Latinoamericano* 2 (1996), 46 and 45.

4. Eduardo Mendieta, "Philosophy and Literature: The Latin American Case," *Dissens* 2 (1996), 37.

5. Gómez Martínez, art. cit., p. 45; Mendieta, art. cit., 37–40.

6. See also Foucault's "What Is an Author?" trans. Donald F. Bouchard and Sherry Simon, in Donald F. Bouchard, ed., *Language, Counter-Memory, Practice: Selected Essays and Interviews* (Ithaca, NY: Cornell University Press, 1977), 113–138; and Gregory Currie, "Work and Text," *Mind* 100 (1991), 325–339.

7. Keep in mind that in this chapter I am staying away from several other questions that are under discussion today concerning philosophy, literature, and art. For example, I do not discuss issues concerned with the morality, value, or use of literature and art, or questions that have to do with the cognitive or noncognitive nature of the knowledge we derive from literary texts or artistic visual images. These

topics have received considerable attention recently. See, for example, Martha Nussbaum, *Love's Knowledge: Essays in Philosophy and Literature* (New York: Oxford University Press, 1990), Stephen Davies, *Philosophical Perspectives on Art* (Oxford: Oxford University Press, 2007) and *The Philosophy of Art* (New York: Blackwell, 2006), and Dominic McIver Lopes, *Understanding Pictures* (Oxford: Clarendon Press, 1996).

8. I discuss these in Gracia, *Metaphysics and its Task: The Search for the Categorial Foundation of Knowledge* (Albany, NY: State University of New York Press, 1999), ch. 2.

9. For other attempts at distinguishing literary texts and works from philosophical ones, and at exploring the relations between philosophy and literature, see, for example, S. Halliwell, "Philosophy and Literature: Settling a Quarrel?" *Philosophical Investigations* 16, 1 (1993), 6–16; George Dickie, *Art and the Aesthetic: An Institutional Analysis* (Ithaca, NY: Cornell University Press, 1974); Susan L. Anderson, "Philosophy and Fiction," *Metaphilosophy* 23, 3 (1992), 207; Peter Lamarque and Stein H. Olsen, *Truth, Fiction, and Literature: A Philosophical Perspective* (Oxford: Clarendon Press, 1994), chs. 15 and 16; and Anthony Quinton, *The Divergence of the Twain: Poet's Philosophy and Philosopher's Philosophy* (Warwick: University of Warwick, 1985).

10. For my discussion of other views, see Gracia, *A Theory of Textuality: The Logic and Epistemology* (Albany, NY: State University of New York Press, 1995), 59–70.

11. Ibid., 4.

12. For a discussion of signs and their relation to texts, see ibid., 7–14.

13. For some suggestions in this direction, see ibid., 59–70.

14. Cf. Hans-Georg Gadamer, "Plato and the Poets," in *Dialogue and Dialectic: Eight Hermeneutical Studies in Plato,* trans. P. Christopher Smith (New Haven, CT: Yale University Press, 1980), 46 ff., and "Goethe and Philosophy," trans. Robert H. Paslick, in *Literature and Philosophy in Dialogue: Essays in German Literary Theory* (Albany, NY: State University of New York Press, 1994), 18–19.

15. Cf. Renford Bambrough, "Literature and Philosophy," in Renford Bambrough, ed., *Wisdom: Twelve Essays* (Oxford: Blackwell, 1974), 274–292.

16. Cf. E. D. Hirsch, Jr., "Objective Interpretation," *PMLA* 75 (1960), 463–479, and *Validity in Interpretation* (New Haven, CT: Yale University Press, 1967, 62; also Gracia, *A Theory of Textuality*, 18–19.

17. Arthur C. Danto, "Philosophy as/and/of Literature," in Anthony Cascardi, ed., *Literature and the Question of Philosophy* (Baltimore, MD: The Johns Hopkins University Press, 1987), 7. Danto goes too far, however, when he argues that literature, in contrast with philosophy, is a kind of mirror, and finds its subject only when it is read (19): first, not just literary texts require an audience, all texts do and, second, that texts require an audience does not mean that they are about the audience. For my discussion of these issues, see Gracia, *Texts: Ontological Status, Identity, Author Audience* (Albany, NY: State University of New York Press, 1996), ch. 4.

18. Indeed, some argue that it is precisely the opposition to style that distinguishes philosophy from literature. Cf. Dalia Judovitz, "Philosophy and Poetry: The Difference between Them in Plato and Descartes," in Anthony J. Cascardi, ed., *Literature and the Question of Philosophy* (Baltimore, MD: The Johns Hopkins University Press, 1987), 24–51.

19. Plato, *Phaedrus* 276–277a.

20. Some have gone so far as to argue not only that philosophy has style, but that its style and that of literature are similar. Cf. Tom Conley, "A Trace of Style," in *Displacement: Derrida and After*, ed. Mark Krupnick (Bloomington, IN: Indiana University Press, 1983), 79.

21. I am using the following edition and translation: "Pierre Menard, Autor del *Quijote*," in *Prosa completa* (Barcelona: Bruguera, 1980), vol. 1, 425–433; "Pierre Menard, Author of the *Quixote*," in *Labyrinths: Selected Stories and Other Writings*, eds. Donald Yates and James E. Irby (New York: New Directions Books, 1964), 36–44. The terms emphasized in the translation were also emphasized in the Spanish original.

22. Arthur Danto, *The Transfiguration of the Commonplace: A Philosophy of Art* (Cambridge, MA: Harvard University Press, 1981), 208.

23. Ibid., 39.

24. Margolis, "The Ontological Peculiarity of Works of Art," *Journal of Aesthetics and Art Criticism* 36, 1 (1977), 45–50.

25. I find Foucault's interpretation unconvincing for reasons I explain in Gracia, "The Presence of the Absent in Interpretation: Foucault on Velázquez, and Destéfanis and Celma on Borges," *CR: The New Centennial Review* 11, 1 (2011), and "The Philosophical Interpretation of Visual Art: Response to Mariana Ortega and John Carvalho," *APA Newsletter on Hispanic/Latino Issues* 1, 2 (2010).

26. Foucault, *The Order of Things: An Archeology of the Human Sciences* (New York: Vintage Books, 1973), 16.

27. Jacques Derrida, "Structure, Sign, and Play in the Discourse of the Human Sciences," in R. Macksay and E. Donato, eds., *The Structuralist Controversy: The Languages of Criticism and the Sciences of Man* (Baltimore, MD: Johns Hopkins University Press, 1970), 274–272; and W. V. O. Quine, "On What There Is," in *From a Logical Point of View* (Cambridge, MA: Harvard University Press, 1953), 1–19.

28. See my discussion of this text in Gracia, "Are Categories Invented or Discovered? A Response to Foucault," in M. Gorman and J. J. Sanford, eds., *Categories: Old and New* (Washington, DC: Catholic University of America Press, (2002), 268–283.

29. Foucault, *The Order of Things*, 15.

30. Ibid., 9.

31. I have discussed other aspects of Foucault's analysis in Gracia, "The Philosophical Interpretation of Visual Art."

32. Plato, *Republic* 601a–b. Some literary critics agree to the extent that they believe literature is not about ideas. Recent textualists accept this, but the position goes back to much earlier times. Danto quotes a text from Flaubert to this effect in "Philosophy as/and/of Literature,"13.

33. Note that this does not imply a disagreement with Nussbaum's view that "if the writing is well done"—and I think this applies to both literature and philosophy—"a paraphrase in every different form and style will not, in general, express the same conception." For Nussbaum see *Love's Knowledge*, 3.

34. The role of use and practice in this context is discussed by Lamarque and Olsen in *Truth, Fiction, and Literature*, particularly chs. 2, 10, and 17. See also my defense of cultural function as determining textual meaning in Gracia, *A Theory of Textuality*, ch. 4.

35. I have discussed some of these in chapter 6 of Gracia, *Hispanic/Latino Identity: A Philosophical Perspective* (Oxford: Blackwell, 2000), and chapter 8 of *Latinos in America: Philosophy and Social Identity* (Oxford: Blackwell, 2008).

Chapter 15

1. I discuss interpretation in more detail in Gracia, *A Theory of Textuality: The Logic and Epistemology* (Albany: State University of New York Press, 1995), 147–179, *How Can We Know What God Means? The Interpretation of Revelation* (New York: Palgrave, 2001), and *Images of Thought: Philosophical Interpretations of Carlos Estévez's Art* (Albany, NY: State University of New York Press, 2009), 165–168. For other conceptions and discussions of interpretation, see Paul Ricoeur, "Creativity in Language: Word, Polysemy, Metaphor," in *The Philosophy of Paul Ricoeur: An Anthology of His Work*, ed. Charles E. Reagan and David Stewart, 128 (Boston, MA: Beacon Press, 1978); J. W. Meiland, "Interpretation as a Cognitive Discipline," *Philosophy and Literature* 2 (1978), 25; Morris Weitz, *Hamlet and the Philosophy of Literary Criticism* (Chicago: University of Chicago Press, 1964), ch. 15; C. L. Stevenson, "On the Reasons That Can Be Given for the Interpretation of a Poem," in *Philosophy Looks at the Arts*, edited Joseph Margolis, 127 (New York: Scribner, 1962); Margolis and Tom Rockmore, eds., *The Philosophy of Interpretation* (Oxford: Blackwell, 2000); Stephen Davies, *Philosophical Perspectives on Art* (Oxford: Oxford University Press, 2007); and Robert Stecker, *Interpretation and Construction: Art, Speech, and the Law* (Malden, MA: Blackwell, 2003).

2. The understanding dimension of interpretation is emphasized by Stecker in *Interpretation and Construction*, ch. 1, and Davies, *The Philosophy of Art* (Oxford: Blackwell, 2006), ch. 5. See also Gracia, *A Theory of Textuality*. Not all understandings are interpretations, but there is no consensus on what sets some understandings apart as interpretive and others not. For my present purpose I do not need to present a view on this matter.

3. Apart from what I say below, the ontology of an object of interpretation can become quite complicated. I have explored the case in which it is a text in *A Theory of Textuality*, ch. 3, and *Texts: Ontological Status, Identity, Author, Audience* (Albany, NY: SUNY Press, 1996), chs. 1 and 2. What I say there about texts also applies, mutatis mutandis, to artworks.

4. I discuss this in more detail in Gracia, *Texts*, ch. 1, 18–26.

5. I give more details on meaning in Gracia, *Images of Thought: Philosophical Interpretations of Carlos Estévez's Art* (Albany, NY: State University of New York Press, 2009), 159–163, and elsewhere.

6. See Danto, *The Transfiguration of the Commonplace: A Philosophy of Art* (Cambridge, MA: Harvard University Press, 1981), 117–118.

7. I am applying here some distinctions I used concerning the authors of texts in Gracia, *Texts*, 91–140.

8. For different views about the role and identity of the author, see the various articles in William Irwin, ed., *The Death and Resurrection of the Author* (Westport, CN: Greenwood Press, 2002). For my views on this, see Gracia, *Texts*, 91–140, and the article in Irwin's collection.

9. For more on audience, see Gracia, *Texts*, 141–169.

10. See the works by Stecker, Davies, Danto, and Gracia cited above.

11. The classic statement of this position, also known as "intentionalism," was given by E. D. Hirsch, in *Validity in Interpretation* (see, for example, p. 25). See also S. Knapp and W. B. Michaels, "Against Theory," *Critical Inquiry* 8 (1982), 723–742, "Against Theory 2," *Critical Inquiry* 14 (1988), 49–68; and Nicholas Wolterstorff, "Toward an Ontology of Works of Art," *Nous* 9 (1975), 136. For more recent discussions, see William Irwin, *Intentionalist Interpretations: A Philosophical Explanation and Defense* (Westport, CT: Greenwood Press, 1999); Paisley Livingstone, *Art and Intention: A Philosophical Study* (Oxford: Clarendon Press, 2005); and Dominic McIver Lopes, who argues in particular against an intentionalist view of interpretation in art, in *Understanding Pictures*, ch. 8 (Oxford: Clarendon Press, 1996). Danto seems to come to the side of intentionalists in *The Transfiguration of the Commonplace*, 129–130.

12. Apart from these two, a derivative, third view, known as *value intentionalism*, chooses among interpretations those that maximize the value of the work. For a discussion of these varieties of intentionalism, see Davies, *Philosophical Perspectives on Art*, 167–190. See also Noël Carroll. "Interpretation and Intention: the Debate between Hypothetical and Actual Intentionalists," in Margolis and Rockmore, eds. *The Philosophy of Interpretation*, 75–95. Oxford: Blackwell, 2000.

13. See more on this in Gracia, *A Theory of Textuality*, 155–159.

14. For the emphasis on the audience in interpretation, see: Umberto Eco, *A Theory of Semiotics* (Bloomington, IN: Indiana University Press, 1976); J. Hillis Miller, "Tradition and Difference," *Diacritics* 2 (1972), 6–13; Stanley Fish, "Interpreting the *Variorum*," *Critical Inquiry* 2 (1976), 465–85, and *Is There a Text in*

This Class? The Authority of Interpretive Communities (Cambridge, MA: Harvard University Press, 1980); and Hans-Georg Gadamer, "Text and Interpretation," in Brice R. Wachterhauser, ed., *Hermeneutics and Modern Science* (Albany, NY: State University of New York Press, 1986), 377–396.

15. See more on this in Gracia, *A Theory of Textuality,* 160.

16. For more on this, see Gracia, *A Theory of Textuality,* 161.

Chapter 17

1. See Hirsch's classical statement in *Validity in Interpretation* (New Haven, CN: Yale University Press, 1967).

2. This is usually accomplished by undermining two foundations of traditional hermeneutics: the author and the signified. Foucault was instrumental in undermining the first by arguing that the author is nothing more than a construct of the interpreter. Derrida was instrumental in undermining the second by arguing that the signified is, like the author, a construct of the interpreter.

3. Other examples are the philosophical interpretations I provide of eighteen works of art by Estévez in Gracia, *Images of Thought.*

4. For a recent discussion on the problem posed by contradictory interpretations of the same interpretandum, and the various approaches adopted to deal with it, see Stephen Davies, *Philosophical Perspectives on Art,* particularly chapters 12 and 13. He reaches a conclusion similar to mine, but for different reasons, which I do not find convincing.

5. Margolis, *Historied Thought, Constructed World: A Conceptual Primer for the Turn of the Millennium* (Berkeley, CA: University of California Press, 1995.

6. Davies, *Philosophical Perspectives on Art,* chapter 12.

7. I have discussed the interpretation of texts regarded by religious communities as revealed in Gracia, *How Can We Know What God Means?*

8. See Dominic McIver Lopes, *Sense and Sensibility: Evaluating Pictures* (Oxford: Oxford University Press, 2005).

Bibliography

This bibliography does not attempt to be comprehensive; it is rather meant to provide a starting point for those who wish to explore further the topics discussed in this book. Except for sources on the artists, I have listed primarily sources, particularly books, in English. This bibliography is divided into four main parts: General, Argentinean Art, Cuban Art, and Artists. Works of philosophy in general and of aesthetics and hermeneutics in particular referred to in the text, together with a sample of sources relevant for the study of Borges, are found in the first part.

General

Adorno, Theodor W. *Aesthetic Theory*. Minneapolis, MN: University of Minnesota Press, 1997.

Aizenberg, Edna, ed. *Borges and His Successors*. Columbia, MI: University of Missouri Press, 1990.

Alazraki, Jaime. *Borges and the Kabbalah: And Other Essays on His Fiction and Poetry*. Cambridge: Cambridge University Press, 1988.

———, ed. *Jorge Luis Borges*. Madrid: Taurus, 1971.

Aldrich, Virgil. "Mirrors, Pictures, Words, Perceptions." *Philosophy* 55 (1980): 39–56.

Álvarez, Nicolás Emilio. "Borges: Autor implícito, narrador, protagonista y lector en 'Funes el memorioso.'" *Círculo* 19 (1990): 147–152.

Anderson, James, and Jeffery Dean. "Moderate Autonomism." *British Journal of Aesthetics* 38 (1998): 150–166.

Anderson, Susan L. "Philosophy and Fiction." *Metaphilosophy* 23, 3 (1992): 203–213.

Austin, J. L. *How To Do Things with Words*. Edited by J. Urmson. Cambridge, MA: Harvard University Press, 1962.

Bal, Mieke. *Reading "Rembrandt": Beyond the Word-Image Opposition*. Cambridge: Cambridge University Press, 1991.

Balderston, Daniel G. "The Fecal Dialectic: Homosexual Panic and the Origin of Writing in Borges." In Emilie L. Bergmann and Paul Julian Smith, eds. *¿Entiendes? Queer Readings, Hispanic Writings*, 29–45. Durham: Duke University Press, 1995.

———. *Out of Context: Historical Reference and the Representation of Reality in Borges*. Durham, NC: Duke University Press, 1993.

———. "Cuento (corto) y cuentas (largas) en 'La escritura del dios.'" In *Cuadernos Hispanoamericanos* 505–507 (1992): 445–455.

———, G. Gallo, and N. Helf. *Borges: una enciclopedia*. Buenos Aires: Grupo Editorial Norma, 1999.

Bambrough, Renford. "Literature and Philosophy." In Renford Bambrough, ed. *Wisdom: Twelve Essays*, 274–292. Oxford: Blackwell, 1974.

Barnes, Annette. *On Interpretation*. Oxford: Blackwell, 1988.

Barrenechea, Ana M. *La expresión de la irrealidad en la obra de Jorge Luis Borges*. Mexico City: El Colegio de México, 1957.

Beardsley, Monroe C. "Aesthetic Experience Regained." *Journal of Aesthetics and Art Criticism* 28 (1969): 3–11.

Bell-Villada, Gene H. *Borges and His Fiction: A Guide to His Mind and Art*. Chapel Hill, NC: University of North Caroline Press, 1981.

Benjamin, Walter. *The Arcades Project*. Edited by Rolf Tiedemann; translated by Howard Eiland; illustrated by Kevin McLaughlin. Cambridge, MA: Harvard University Press, 2002.

Bennett, Maurice J. "The Detective Fiction of Poe and Borges." *Comparative Literature* 35, 3 (1983): 262–275.

Bernstein, J. M. *Against Voluptuous Bodies: Late Modernism and the Meaning of Painting*. Stanford, CA: Stanford University Press, 2006.

Block de Behar, Lisa. "Disquisitions on Some Reasoned Distractions of Aesthetics." *CR: The New Centennial Review* 11, 1 (2011).

———. *Borges: The Passion of an Endless Quotation*. Translated by William Eggington. Albany, NY: State University of New York Press, 2002.

———. *Al margen de Borges*. Buenos Aires: Siglo XXI, 1987.

Bloom, Harold, ed. *Jorge Luis Borges*. New York: Chelsea Publishers, 1986.

Blunt, A. "Poussin's Notes on Painting." *Journal of the Warburg Institute* 1 (1937): 344–351.

Borges, Jorge Luis. *Obras completas*, 4 vols. Buenos Aires: Emecé Editores, 2007.

———. *Collected Fictions*. Translated by Andrew Hurley. New York: Penguin Books, 1998.

Borges Center: http://www.borges.pit.edu

Brant, Herbert J. "The Queer Use of Women in Borges' 'El muerto' and "La intrusa.'" *Hispanófila* 125 (1999): 37–50.

Bryson, Norman, et al., eds. *Visual Theory: Painting and Interpretation.* Cambridge: Polity, 1991.

Budd, Malcolm. *Values of Art: Pictures, Poetry, and Music.* London: Allen Lane, The Penguin Press, 1995.

Burgin, Richard. *Conversations with Jorge Luis Borges.* New York: Holt, Reinhart & Winston, 1969.

Cámpora, Magdalena. "'The Providential Apotheosis of His Industry': Display of Causal Systems in Borges." *CR: The New Centennial Review* 11, 1 (2011).

Camurati, Mireya. *Los "raros" de Borges.* Buenos Aires: Ediciones Corregidor, 2006.

Carlshamre, Staffan, and Anders Pettersson, eds. *Types of Interpretation in the Aesthetic Disciplines.* Montreal: McGill-Queen's University Press, 2003.

Carricaburo, Norma. "Borges/Xul Solar: Shared Readings and Divergent Productions." *CR: The New Centennial Review* 11, 1 (2011).

Carrizo, Antonio. *Borges el memorioso.* Mexico City: Fondo de Cultura Económica, 1982.

Carroll, Noël. "Interpretation and Intention: the Debate between Hypothetical and Actual Intentionalists." In J. Margolis and T. Rockmore, eds. *The Philosophy of Interpretation,* 75–95. Oxford: Blackwell, 2000.

———, ed. *Theories of Art Today.* Madison, WI: University of Wisconsin Press, 2000.

———. "Moderate Moralism." *British Journal of Aesthetics* 36 (1996): 223–237.

Carter, E. D., Jr. "Women in the Short Stories of Jorge Luis Borges." *Pacific Coast Philology* 14 (1979): 13–19.

Cascardi, Anthony J. "Mimesis and Modernism: The Case of Jorge Luis Borges." In Jorge J. E. Gracia, et al., eds. *Literary Philosophers: Borges, Calvino, Eco,* 109–128. New York: Routledge, 2002.

———, ed. *Literature and the Question of Philosophy.* Baltimore, MD: The Johns Hopkins University Press, 1987.

Cavell, Stanley. "Music Discomposed." In *Must We Mean What We Say?* Cambridge: Cambridge University Press, 1976.

Cédola, Estela. *Como el cine leyó a Borges.* Buenos Aires: Edicial, 1999.

———. "Tiempo de la imaginación y tiempo de la historia en 'El jardín de senderos que se bifurcan' de Jorge L. Borges." *Linguistica e Letteratura* 10, 1–2 (1995).

Chibka, Robert L. "The Library of Forking Paths." *Representations* 56 (1996): 106–122.

Claro, Andrés. "Borgesian Transpositions: From Ear to Eye." *CR: The New Centennial Review* 11, 1 (2011).

Conley, Tom. "A Trace of Style." In Mark Krupnick, ed. *Displacement: Derrida and After,* 74–92. Bloomington, IN: Indiana University Press, 1983.

Costa, René de. *Humor in Borges.* Detroit, MI: Wayne State University Press, 2000.

Cozarinsky, Edgardo. *Borges en/y/sobre cine.* Buenos Aires: Sur, 1974.

Currie, Gregory. "Work and Text." *Mind* 100 (1991): 325–339.

Danto, Arthur. *After the End of Art: Contemporary Art and the Pale of History.* Princeton, NJ: Princeton University Press, 1997.

———. "Philosophy as/and/of Literature." In Anthony Cascardi, ed. *Literature and the Question of Philosophy,* 1–23. Baltimore, MD: The Johns Hopkins University Press, 1987.

———. *The Transfiguration of the Common Place: A Philosophy of Art.* Cambridge, MA: Harvard University Press, 1981.

Davies, Stephen. *Philosophical Perspectives in Art.* Oxford: Oxford University Press, 2007.

———. *The Philosophy of Art.* Oxford: Blackwell, 2006.

———. *Definitions of Art.* Ithaca, NY: Cornell University Press, 1991.

de Garayalde, Giovanna. *Jorge Luis Borges: Sources and Illumination.* London: Octagon Prss, 1978.

de la Fuente, Ariel. "American and Argentine Literary Traditions in the Writing of Borges' 'El Sur.'" *Variaciones Borges* 19 (2005): 41–92.

Deleuze, Gilles. *Francis Bacon: The Logic of Sensation.* Translated by Daniel Smith. New York: Continuum, 2005.

de Olaso, Ezequiel. *Jugar en serio: Aventuras de Borges.* Mexico City: Paidós, 1999.

———. "Mínimas gotas de filosofía. 'El Otro.'" *Variaciones Borges* 7 (1999): 178–190.

de Toro, Alfonso, and Fernando de Toro, eds. *Jorge Luis Borges: Thought and Knowledge in the XXth Century.* Madrid: Iberoamericana, 1999.

Derrida, Jacques. *The Truth in Painting.* Translated by Geoff Bennington and Ian McLeod. Chicago, IL: University of Chicago Press, 1987.

———. "Structure, Sign, and Play in the Discourse of the Human Sciences." In R. Macksay and E. Donato, eds. *The Structuralist Controversy: The Languages of Criticism and the Sciences of Man,* 247–272. Baltimore, MD: Johns Hopkins University Press, 1970.

Dewey, John. *Art as Experience: An Introduction.* New York: G. P. Putnam's Sons, 1980.

Dickie, George. *Evaluating Art.* Philadelphia, PA: Temple University Press, 1988.

———. *Art and the Aesthetic: An Institutional Analysis.* Ithaca, NY: Cornell University Press, 1974.

———. *Aesthetics: An Introduction.* Indianapolis, IN: Bobbs-Merrill, 1971.

Diether, Jack. "Notes to the Program." Carnegie Hall, Tuesday Evening, November 4, 1997, 19.

Di Giovanni, Norman T. *The Lesson of the Master.* London: Continuum, 2003.

———, ed. *The Borges Tradition.* London: Constable, 1955.

Dutton, D. "Artistic Crimes." In Berkeley Dutton, ed. *The Forger's Art: Forgery and the Philosophy of Art,* 172–187. Berkeley, CA: University of California Press, 1983.

Eaton, Marcia. "Truth in Pictures." *Journal of Aesthetics and Art Criticism* 39 (1980): 15–26.

Echavarría, Arturo. *Lengua y literatura de Borges.* Barcelona: Ariel, 1983.

Eco, Umberto. *A Theory of Semiotics.* Bloomington, IN: Indiana University Press, 1976.

Eggington, William. "Three Versions of Divisibility: Borges, Kant, and the Quantum." In William Eggington and David Johnson, eds. *Thinking With Borges,* 53–72. Aurora, CO: The Davies Group, 2009.

———. "Rereading Borges's 'The Aleph': On the Name of a Place, a Word, and a Letter," *CR: The New Centennial Review* (2004).

Eliot, T. S. "Tradition and the Individual Talent." In *Selected Essays 1917–1932.* London: Faber and Faber, 1932.

Elkins, James. *What Painting Is: How To Think about Oil Painting, Using the Language of Alchemy.* New York: Routledge, 1999.

———. *The Object that Stares Back.* San Diego, CA: Harcourt Brace & Co., 1996.

Evans, Michael. "Intertextual Labyrinth: 'El Inmortal' by Borges." *Forum for Modern Language Studies* 20, 3 (1984): 275–281.

Feal, Rosemary Geisdorfer, and Carlos Feal. *Painting on the Page: Interartistic Approaches to Modern Hispanic Texts.* Albany, NY: State University of New York Press, 1995.

Feagan, Susan L. "Incompatible Interpretations of Art." *Philosophy and Literature* 6 (1982): 133–146.

Folger, Robert, "The Great Chain of Memory: Borges, Funes, de *Viris illustribus.*" *Hispanófila* 135 (2002): 125–36.

Foster, David Williams. *Jorge Luis Borges: An Annotated Primary and Secondary Bibliography.* New York: Garland, 1984.

Foucault, Michel. *Power.* Edited James D. Faubion; translated Robert Hurley, et al. New York: New Press, 2000.

———. *This Is Not a Pipe.* Berkeley, CA: University of California Press, 1983.

———. "What Is an Author?" In Donald F. Bouchard, ed., translated by Donald F. Bouchard and Sherry Simon. *Language, Counter-Memory, Practice: Selected Essays and Interviews,* 113–138. Ithaca, NY: Cornell University Press, 1977.

———. *The Order of Things: an Archeology of the Human Sciences.* New York: Pantheon, 1970.

Freud, Sigmund. *Leonardo da Vinci: A Memory of His Childhood.* London: Art Paperbacks, 1987.

Gadamer, Hans-Georg. "Goethe and Philosophy." Translated by Robert H. Paslick, in *Literature and Philosophy in Dialogue: Essays in German Literary Theory,* 1–20. Albany, NY: State University of New York Press, 1994.

———. "On the Circle of Understanding." In John M. Connolly and Thomas Keutner, eds., *Hermeneutics Versus Science? Three German Views,* 68–78. Notre Dame, IN: University of Notre Dame Press, 1988.

———. "Text and Interpretation." In Brice R. Wachterhauser, ed., *Hermeneutics and Modern Science,* 377–396. Albany, NY: State University of New York Press, 1986.

———. "Plato and the Poets." In *Dialogue and Dialectic: Eight Hermeneutical Studies in Plato.* Translated by P. Christopher Smith. New Haven, CT: Yale University Press, 1980.

García-Martín, Elena. "The Dangers of Abstraction in Borges' 'The Immortal.'" 20 (2005): 87–100.

Gaut, Berys, "The Ethical Criticism of Art." In Jerrold Levinson, ed. *Aesthetics and Ethics.* Cambridge: Cambridge University Press, 1998.

Glickman, Jack. "Creativity in the Arts." In Lars Aagaard-Morgensen, ed. *Culture in Art,* 130–146. Atlantic Highlands, NJ: Humanities Press, 1976.

Goldman, Alan H. "Interpreting Art and Literature." *Journal of Aesthetics and Art Criticism* 48 (1990): 205–214.

Gómez Martínez, José Luis. "Posmodernidad, discurso antrópico y ensayística latinoamericana. Entrevista." *Dissens, Revista Internacional de Pensamiento Latinoamericano* 2 (1996).

Goodman, Nelson. *Languages of Art: An Approach to a Theory of Symbols.* Indianapolis, IN: Hackett Publishing Co., 1976.

Gracia, Jorge J. E. "The Presence of the Absent in Interpretation: Foucault on Velázquez, and Destéfanis and Celma on Borges," *CR: The New Centennial Review* 11, 1 (2011).

————. "Painting Borges: A Pictorial Interpretation of His Fictions." In *Painting Borges/Pintando a Borges.* Exhibition Catalogue. Buenos Aires: Universidad Católica Argentina, 2010.

————. "The Philosophical Interpretation of Visual Art: Response to Mariana Ortega and John Carvalho." *APA Newsletter on Hispanic/Latino Issues* 1, 2 (2010).

————. *Images of Thought: Philosophical Interpretations of Carlos Estévez's Art.* Albany, NY: State University of New York Press, 2009.

————. *Latinos in America: Philosophy and Social Identity.* Oxford: Blackwell, 2008.

————. "From Horror to Hero: Film Interpretations of Stoker's *Dracula.*" In William Irwin and Jorge J. E. Gracia, eds. *Philosophy and the Interpretation of Pop Culture,* 187–214. Lanham, MD: Rowman & Littlefield, 2007.

————. "Meaning." In Kevin J. Vanhoozer, ed. *Dictionary for the Theological Interpretation of the Bible,* 492–499. Grand Rapids, MI: Baker Bookhouse Co., 2005.

————. *Old Wine in New Skins: The Role of Tradition in Communication, Knowledge, and Group Identity.* Marquette University 67th Aquinas Lecture. Milwaukee, WI: Marquette University Press, 2003.

————. "Are Categories Invented or Discovered? A Response to Foucault." In M. Gorman and J. J. Sanford, eds., *Categories: Old and New,* 268–283. Washington, DC: Catholic University of America Press, 2002.

————. "Borges's 'Pierre Menard': Philosophy or Literature?" In Jorge J. E. Gracia, Carolyn Korsmeyer, and Rodolphe Gasché, eds. *Literary Philosophers: Borges, Calvino, Eco.* 85–108. New York: Routledge, 2002.

————. *How Can We Know What God Means?: The Interpretation of Revelation.* New York: Palgrave, 2001.

————. *Hispanic/Latino Identity: A Philosophical Perspective.* Oxford: Blackwell, 2000.

————. *Metaphysics and its Task: The Search for the Categorial Foundation of Knowledge.* Albany, NY: State University of New York Press, 1999.

————. *Texts: Ontological Status, Identity, Author, Audience.* Albany, NY: State University of New York Press, 1996.

————. *A Theory of Textuality: The Logic and Epistemology.* Albany, NY: State University of New York Press, 1995.

————. *Philosophy and Its History: Issues in Philosophical Historiography.* Albany, NY: State University of New York Press, 1991.

————. "Notes on Ortega's Aesthetic Works in English." *The Journal of Aesthetic Education* 11 (1977): 117–125.

————. "Falsificación y valor artístico." *Revista de Ideas Estéticas* 116 (1971): 327–333.

Grice, H. P. "Meaning." *Philosophical Review* 66 (1957): 377–388.

Halliwell, S. "Philosophy and Literature: Settling a Quarrel?" *Philosophical Investigations* 16, 1 (1993): 6–16.

Harkness, James. "Translator's Introduction." In Michael Foucault, *This Is Not a Pipe*, 1–12. Berkeley, CA: University of California Press, 1983.

Heidegger, Martin. "The Origin of the Work of Art." In Julian Young, *Heidegger's Philosophy of Art*. Cambridge: Cambridge University Press, 2001.

———. *Ontology: The Hermeneutics of Facticity*. Translated by John van Buren. Indianapolis, IN: Indiana University Press, 1988.

Hernández Castellanos, Camilo. "Tzinacán prisionero en la jaula del lenguaje secreto y siginificación en 'La escritura del dios.'" *Variaciones Borges* 28 (2009): 199–216.

Hirsch, Jr., E. D. *Validity in Interpretation*. New Haven, CN: Yale University Press, 1967.

———. "Objective Interpretation." *PMLA* 75 (1960): 463–479.

Hopkins, Robert. "What Is Pictorial Representation?" In Matthew Kieran, ed. *Contemporary Debates in the Philosophy or Art*. Oxford: Blackwell, 2005.

Irwin, John T. *The Mystery to a Solution: Poe, Borges, and the Analytic Detective Story*. Baltimore, MD: Johns Hopkins University Press, 1994.

———. "The False Artaxerxes: Borges and the Dream of Chess." *New Literary History* 24, 2 (1993): 425–445.

Irwin, William, ed. *The Death and Resurrection of the Author*. Westwood, CT: Greenwood Press, 2002.

———. "Philosophy and the Philosophical, Literature and the Literary." In William Irwin and Jorge J. E. Gracia, eds. *Literary Philosophers: Borges, Eco, Calvino*, 27–46. New York: Routledge, 2001.

———. *Intentionalist Interpretations: A Philosophical Explanation and Defense*. Westport, CT: Greenwood Press, 1999.

Jacobson, Daniel. "In Praise of Immoral Art." *Philosophical Topics* 25 (1997): 155–200.

Jaén, Didier T. *Borges's Esoteric Library: Metaphysics to Metafiction*. Lanham, MD: University Press of America, 1992.

Jenckes, Kate. *Reading Borges After Benjamin: Allegory, After Life, and the Writing of History*. Albany, NY: State University of New York Press, 2008.

Johnson, David E. "Talking to Ourselves, Over Her (Dead) Body: On Heidegger, Borges, and Seeing the Other." *CR: The New Centennial Review* 11, 1 (2011).

———. "Time. For Borges." *CR: The New Centennial Review* 9, 1 (2009): 209–226.

———, and William Eggington, eds. *Thinking With Borges*. Aurora, CO: The Davies Group, 2009.

Judovitz, Dalia. "Philosophy and Poetry: The Difference between Them in Plato and Descartes." In Anthony J. Cascardi, ed. *Literature and the Question of Philosophy*, 24–51. Baltimore, MD: The Johns Hopkins University Press, 1987.

Karageorgou-Bastea, Christina. "'Funes el memorioso' o de la memoria-diálogo." *Vanderbilt e-Journal of Luso-Hispanic Studies* 3 (2006).

Kaufman, Alejandro, ed. *Jorge Luis Borges: Intervenciones sobre pensamiento y literatura*. Buenos Aires: Paidós, 2000.

Keller, Gary, and Karen S. Van Hooft. "Jorge Luis Borges's 'La Intrusa': The Awakening of Love and Consciousness/The Sacrifice of Love and Consciousness." In Lisa E. Davis and Isabel C. Tarán, eds. *The Analysis of Hispanic Texts: Current Trends in Methodology*, 300–319. Jamaica, NY: Bilingual Press, 1976.

Knapp, S., and W. B. Michaels. "Against Theory 2." *Critical Inquiry* 14 (1988): 49–68.

———. "Against Theory." *Critical Inquiry* 8 (1982): 723–742.

Koestler, Arthur. "The Aesthetics of Snobbery." *Horizon* 7 (1965): 80–83.

Laera, A. "De la periferia al Imperio: inflexiones de la relación entre ficción y dinero en 'El Zahir' y 'El otro.'" *Variaciones Borges* 23 (2007): 37–50.

Lafforgue, Martín, et al. *AntiBorges*. Buenos Aires: Vergara, 1999.

Lamarque, Peter, and Stein H. Olsen. *Truth, Fiction, and Literature: A Philosophical Perspective*. Oxford: Clarendon Press, 1994.

Lefere, Robin. "'La casa de Asterión': experiencia de la lectura vs. interpretación. Tradición y actualidad de la literatura iberoamericana." *Actas del XXX Congreso del Instituto Internacional de Literatura Iberoamericana*. Ed. Pamela Bacarisse. Pittsburgh, 1995.

Levinson, Jerrold. "Two Notions of Interpretation." In A. Haapala and O. Naukkarinen, eds. *Interpretation and Its Boundaries*, 2–21. Helsinki: Helsinki University Press, 1999.

———. "Emotion in Response to Art: A Survey of the Terrain." In Mette Hjort and Sue Laver, eds. *Emotion and the Arts*, 20–34. New York: Oxford University Press, 1997.

Livingstone, Paisley. *Art and Intention: A Philosophical Study*. Oxford: Clarendon Press, 2005.

Lopes, Dominic. *Sight and Sensibility: Evaluating Pictures*. Oxford: Oxford University Press, 2007.

———. *Understanding Pictures*. Oxford: Clarendon Press, 1996.

Magnavaca, Silvia. *Filósofos medievales en la obra de Borges*. Buenos Aires: Miño y Dávila, 2009.

Margolis, Joseph. *Historied Thought, Constructed World: A Conceptual Primer for the Turn of the Millennium*. Berkeley, CA: University of California Press, 1995.

———. "The Ontological Peculiarity of Works of Art." *Journal of Aesthetics and Art Criticism* 35 (1976): 37–46.

Margolis, Joseph and Tom Rockmore, eds. *The Philosophy of Interpretation*. Oxford: Blackwell Publishers, 2000.

Martín, J. "Borges, Funes y . . . Bergson." *Variaciones Borges* 19 (2005): 195–226.

Mateo, Fernando. *El otro Borges*. Buenos Aires: Equis, 1997.

Meiland, J. W. "Interpretation as a Cognitive Discipline." *Philosophy and Literature* 2 (1978): 23–45.

Mejía, Carlos. "'El inmortal': lectura de la flecha cretense y otras pérdidas." *Variaciones Borges* 28 (2009): 187–198.

Mendieta, Eduardo. "Philosophy and Literature: The Latin American Case." *Dissens* 2 (1996).

Merleau-Ponty, Maurice. *The Visible and the Invisible*. Translated Alphonso Lingis. Evanston, IL: Northwestern University Press, 1968.

Merrell, Floyd. *Unthinking Thinking: Jorge Luis Borges, Mathematics, and the New Physics*. West Lafayette, IN: Purdue University Press, 1991.

———. "Dogmatic Slumber or Dream? Borges' 'The Circular Ruins.'" In *A Semiotic Theory of Texts*. Berlin-New York-Amsterdam: Mouton de Gruyter, 1985.

Mesa Gancedo, Daniel. "Borges/Saura: 'El Sur.'" *Variaciones Borges* 2 (1996): 152–176.

Miller, L Hillis. "Tradition and Difference." *Diacritics* 2 (1972): 6–13.

Missana, Sergio. *La máquina de pensar de Borges*. Santiago: LOM Ediciones, 2003.

Molloy, Sylvia. *Signs of Borges*. Translated by Oscar Montero. Durham, NC: Duke University Press, 2001.

———. *Las letras y otros ensayos*. Rosario: Beatriz Viterbo Editora, 1999.

Moreiras, Alberto. *Tercer espacio: Literatura y duelo en América Latina*. Santiago: ARCIS/LOM, 1999.

Moulthrop, Stuart. "Forking Paths." In Noah Wardrip-Fruin and Nick Monfort, eds. Cambridge: MIT Press, 2003.

———. "Reading from the Map: Metonymy and Metaphor in the Fiction of 'Forking Paths." In Paul Delany and George P. Landow, eds. *Hypermedia and Literary Studies*. Cambridge, MA: MIT Press, 1991.

Mualem, Shlomy. "Borges y el lenguaje cabalístico: ontología y simbolismo en 'La rosa de Paracelso.'" *Variaciones Borges* 23 (2007): 149–171.

Nuño, Juan. *La filosofía de Borges*. Mexico City: Fondo de Cultura Económica, 1986.

Nussbaum, Martha. *Love's Knowledge: Essays in Philosophy and Literature*. New York: Oxford University Press, 1990.

Orlando, Eleonora. "Depicting Borgesian Possible Worlds." *CR: The New Centennial Review* 11, 1 (2011).

Ortega y Gasset, José. *The Dehumanization of Art, and Other Essays on Art, Culture, and Literature*. Princeton, NJ: Princeton University Press, 1968.

Oyarzún, Pablo. "The Writing of Courage." *CR: The New Centennial Review* 11, 1 (2011).

Panofsky, Ervin. *Meaning in the Visual Arts: Papers in and on Art History*. Garden City, NY: Doubleday, 1955.

Paoli, Roberto. *Borges: percorsi di significato*. Messina-Florence: Università degli Studi di Firenze, 1977

Pellicer, Rosa. "Borges y el viaje al sur." In Luz Rodríguez-Carranza and Marilene Nagle, eds. *Reescrituras*. New York: Rodopi, 2003.

Percoro, Cristina. "Opening Strategy and the Self as Illusion in Borges' 'El Otro.'" *Variaciones Borges* 6(2003): 109–120.

Pérez, Diana I. "The Ontology of Art: What Can We Learn from Borges's Menard?" *CR: The New Centennial Review* 11, 1 (2011).

Pérez, Genaro J. "The Circular Ruins." In Noelle Watson, ed. *Reference Guide to Short Fiction*. Detroit: St. James Press 1994.

Pimentel Pinto, Julio. "En busca del Sur." *Variaciones Borges* 20 (2005): 191–196.

Pineda, Victoria. "Borges y Poe, la sombra de 'The Oval Portrait' en 'El milagro secreto.'" *Variaciones Borges* 29 (2010): 127–140.

Plato. *Phaedrus*. In Edith Hamilton and Huntington Cairns, eds. *The Collected Dialogues of Plato*. New York: Pantheon Books, 1961.

————. *The Republic.* In Edith Hamilton and Huntington Cairns, eds. *The Collected Dialogues of Plato.* New York: Pantheon Books, 1961.

Podlubne, Judith. "'Sur' 1942: El 'Desagravio a Borges' o el doble juego del reconocimiento." *Variaciones Borges* 27 (2009): 43–66.

Podro, Michael. *Depiction.* New Haven, CT: Yale University Press, 1998.

Quine, W. V. O. "On What There Is." In *From a Logical Point of View,* 1–19. Cambridge, MA: Harvard University Press, 1953.

Quinton, Anthony. *The Divergence of the Twain: Poet's Philosophy and Philosopher's Philosophy.* Warwick: University of Warwick, 1985.

Ricci, Graciela. "Borges y la reiteración de lo infinito (Análisis intralingüístico de 'La casa de Asterión." In *Borges, Calvino, La literatura (El coloquio de la Isla),* II. Madrid: Espiral/Fundamentos 1996.

Ricoeur, Paul. "Creativity in Language: Word, Polysemy, Metaphor." In Charles E. Reagan and David Stewart, eds. *The Philosophy of Paul Ricoeur: An Anthology of His Work,* 109–133. Boston: Beacon Press, 1978.

Rimmon-Kenan, Shlomith. "Doubles and Counterparts: Patterns of Interchangeability in Borges' 'The Garden of Forking Paths.'" *Critical Inquiry* 6, 4 (1980): 639–647.

Rodríguez Monegal, Emir. *Borges por él mismo.* Barcelona: 1983.

Rowe, Willam, et al. *Jorge Luis Borges: Intervenciones sobre pensamiento y literatura.* Buenos Aires: Paidós, 2000.

Sarlo, Beatriz. *Jorge Luis Borges: A Writer on the Edge.* London: Verso, 1993.

Sartre, Jean-Paul. "The Paintings of Giacometti." In Jean-Paul Sartre, *Situations.* Trans. Benita Eisler. New York: Fawcett Publications, 1965.

Schildknecht, Christiane. "Entre la ciencia y la literatura: Formas literarias de la filosofía." Trans. José M. González García, in María Teresa López de la Vieja, ed., *Figuras del logos: Entre la filosofía y la literatura,* 21–40. Mexico City: Fondo de Cultura Económica, 1994.

Schreiber, Gabriel, and Roberto Umansky. "Bifurcations, Chaos, and Fractal Objects in Borges 'Garden of Forking Paths' and Other Writings." *Variaciones Borges* 11 (2001): 61–80.

Sclafani, R. J. "'Art' and Artifactuality," *Southwestern Journal of Philosophy* 1, 3 (1970): 103–110.

Searle, John. *Expression and Meaning.* Cambridge: Cambridge University Press, 1975.

Shapiro, Henry L. "Memory and Meaning: Borges and 'Funes el memorioso.'" *Revista Canadiense de Estudios Hispánicos* 2 (1985): 257–265.

Shaw, Donald L. *Borges's Narrative Strategy.* Leeds: Francis Cairns, 1992.

————. "A propósito de 'La casa de Asterión' de Borges." *Actas del IX Congreso de la Asociación Internacional de Hispanistas.* Frankfurt am Main: Vervuert Verlag, 1989.

Sorrentino, Fernando. *Seven Conversations with J. L. Borges.* Troy, NY: The Whiston Pub. Co., 1982.

Sosnowski, Saúl. "Memorias de Borges (Artificios de la historia)." *Variaciones Borges.* 10 (2000): 79–95.

Soud, Stephen E. "Borges the Golem-Maker: Intimations of 'Presence' in 'The Circular Ruins.'" *MLN* 110, 4 (1995): 739–754.

Spagnuolo, M. "Asterión y el hijo mayor de Martín Fierro." *Variaciones Borges* 19 (2005): 227–242.

Squires, Jeremy. "El olvido del ser en 'Funes el memorioso' de Jorge Luis Borges." In Fermín Sierra Martínez, ed. *Literatura y trasgresión; en homenaje al profesor Manuel Ferrer Chivite*, 295–310. Amsterdam: Rodopi, 2004.

Stavans, Ilan. *Borges and the Jews.* E-book: The International Raoul Wallenberg Foundation (www. raoulwallenberg.net/wp_content/files_flutter/6173.pdf).

———. "A Comment on Borges's Response to Hitler." *Modern Judaism* 23, 1 (2003): 1–11.

———. "El arte de la memoria." *Mester* 2 (1990): 97–108.

Stecker, Robert. *Interpretation and Construction: Art, Speech, and Law.* Malden, MA: Blackwell, 2003.

———. "The Ontology of Art Interpretation." In S. Davies and A. C. Sukla, eds. *Art and Essence,* 177–191. Westport, CT: Praeger, 2003.

———. *Aesthetics and the Philosophy of Art: An Introduction.* Lanham, MD: Rowman and Littlefield, 1992.

Stevenson, C. L. "On the Reasons That Can Be Given for the Interpretation of a Poem." In Joseph Margolis, ed. *Philosophy Looks at the Arts,* 121–139. New York: Scribner, 1962.

Stewart, Jon. "Borges's Refutation of Nominalism in 'Funes el memorioso.'" *Variaciones Borges* 2 (1996): 68–86.

———. "Borges on Immortality." *Philosophy and Literature* 17, 2 (1993): 295-301.

Stolnitz, Jerome. "On the Cognitive Triviality of Art." *British Journal of Aesthetics* 32 (1992): 191–200.

Stuart, Davis. "Rereading and Rewriting Traditions: the Case of Borges's 'La Casa de Asterión.'" *Romance Studies* 22, 2 (2004): 139–148.

Sun, Haiqing. "China of Labyrinth: a Referential Reading of 'El jardín de senderos que se bifurcan.'" *Variaciones Borges* 25 (2008): 101–114.

Thomasson, Amie L. *Fiction and Metaphysics.* Cambridge: Cambridge University Press, 1999.

Waisman, Sergio. "El secreto de 'El milagro secreto': traducción y resistencia en la obra de Jaromir Hladík." *Variaciones Borges* 26 (2008): 113–124.

Waldegaray, Marta Inés. "'La otra muerte" y 'El milagro secreto': relaciones entre literatura e historia." *Variaciones Borges* 17 (2004): 187–197.

Walton, Kendall L. *Mimesis as Make-Believe: On the Foundations of the Representational Arts.* Cambridge, MA: Harvard University Press, 1990.

———. "Style and the Products and Processes of Art." In Berel Lang, ed. *The Concept of Style,* 72–103. Ithaca, NY: Cornell University Press, 1987.

Weed, E. "A Laberynth of Symbols: Exploring 'The Garden of Forking Paths.'" *Variaciones Borges* 18 (2004): 161–189.

Weissert, Thomas. "Representation and Bifurcation: Borges's Garden of Chaos Dynamics." In Katherine Hayes, ed. *Chaos and Order: Complex Dynamics in Literature and Science,* 223–243. Chicago: The University of Chicago Press, 1991.

Weitz, Morris. *Hamlet and the Philosophy of Literary Criticism.* Chicago: University of Chicago Press, 1964.

Wheelock, Carter. *The Mythmaker: Study and Motif and Symbol in the Short Stories of Jorge Luis Borges.* Austin, TX: University of Texas Press, 1970.

Williams, Mac. "Zoroastrian and Zurvanite Symbolism in 'Las ruinas circulares.'" *Variaciones Borges* 25 (2008): 115–136.

Wilson, Jason. *Jorge Luis Borges.* London: Reaktion Books, 2006

Wollheim, Richard. "Pictorial Representation." *Journal of Aesthetics and Art Criticism* 56 (1998): 217–226.

———. *Art and Its Objects,* 2nd ed. Cambridge: Cambridge University Press, 1980.

———. *On Art and the Mind.* Cambridge, MA: Harvard University Press, 1974.

Woodall, James. *The Man in the Mirror of the Book: A Life of Jorge Luis Borges.* London: Hodder and Stoughton, 1996.

Wolterstorff, Nicholas. "Toward an Ontology of Works of Art." *Nous* 9 (1975): 115–142.

Zamora, Lois Parkinson. "Borges's Monsters: Unnatural Wholes and the Transformation of Genre." In Jorge J. E. Gracia, Carolyn Korsmeyer, and Rodolphe Gasché, eds. *Literary Philosophers: Borges, Calvino, Eco,* 47–84. *New York:* Routledge, 2002.

———. *Writing the Apocalypse: Historical Vision in Contemporary U.S. and Latin American Fiction.* Cambridge: Cambridge University Press, 1989.

Argentinean Art

Alÿs, Francis, et al. *A Story of Deception = Historia de un desengaño; Patagonia 2003–2006.* Colección Costantini. Buenos Aires: MALBA, 2006.

América, Casa de, and Daniel Maman Fine Art. *Mondongo: Cumbre en Casa de América: Del 28 de enero al 5 de marzo de 2004.* Buenos Aires, Argentina: Daniel Maman Fine Art, 2004.

Arrese, Sol, Gabriela Massuh, and Exposición. *La normalidad: Ex-Argentina; [14 de febrero–19 de marzo de 2006], [Palais de Glace, Palacio Nacional de las Artes, Buenos Aires].* Buenos Aires: Interzona Ed., 2006.

Arte argentino para el tercer milenio. Buenos Aires: Ediciones de Arte Gaglianone, 2000.

Arte, política y pensamiento crítico. Ediciones del CCC, Centro Cultural de la Cooperación Floreal Gorini, 2006.

Artundo, Patricia, and Roberto Amigo Cerisola. *El arte español en la Argentina, 1890–1960.* Buenos Aires: Fundación Espigas, 2006.

Bienal de Arte Sacro, Pontificia Universidad Católica Argentina Santa María de los Buenos Aires. Pabellón de las Bellas Artes. *X Bienal de Arte Sacro: Pintura 2006.* Buenos Aires: Pontificia Universidad Católica Argentina, 2006.

Buntinx, Gustavo. *Rasgos de identidad en la plástica argentina.* Buenos Aires: Grupo Editor Latinoameriano, 1994.

Burucúa, José E. *Nueva historia argentina: arte, sociedad y política.* Buenos Aires: Editorial Sudamericana, 1999.

Carballo, Alejandra Karina, Jean Graham-Jones, and Brenda L. Cappucio. "Raza, clase, etnia y género en la presentación de la mujer inmigrante y extranjera en Argentina (1880–1930)." 2006. http://etd.lib. fsu.edu/theses/available/etd-07102006-162009.

Cristiá, Cintia. *Xul Solar, un músico visual: la música en su vida y obra*. Buenos Aires: Gourmet Musical Ediciones, 2007.

Dávila, Miguel. *40 artistas argentinos*. Buenos Aires: Ediciones Actualidad en el Arte, 1991.

Dolinko, Silvia, and Fundación Espigas. *Arte para todos: la difusión del grabado como estrategia para la popularización del arte*. Buenos Aires: Fundación Espiga, 2003.

Dri, Rubén R., and Diego Oscar Bocconi. *Símbolos y fetiches religiosos en la construcción de la identidad popular*. Buenos Aires: Editorial Biblos, 2003.

Dubatti, Jorge, Claudio Pansera, and Araceli Arreche. *Cuando el arte da respuestas: 43 proyectos de cultura para el desarrollo social*. Buenos Aires: Ediciones Artes Escénicas, 2006.

Elliott, David, and Museum of Modern Art. *Argentina, 1920–1994: Art from Argentina*. Oxford: Museum of Modern Art, 1994.

Escombros, and Héctor Puppo. *Grupo escombros, Artistas de lo que queda: 1988–2003*. La Plata, Argentina: Grupo Escombros, 2003.

Ferraro, Diana. *La conspiración de los artistas*. Buenos Aires: Catálogos, 2000.

Fogliani, Amy. "Art as Witness: Memory of Crisis in Argentina's Dirty War." San Francisco: San Francisco State University, 2006.

García Martínez, J. A. *Arte y enseñanza artística en la Argentina*. Buenos Aires: Fundación Banco de Boston, 1985.

———. *Los primeros pintores: clima de arte en el Buenos Aires romántico*. Buenos Aires: Editorial Sofos, 1982.

Giunta, Andrea. *Vanguardia, internacionalismo y política: arte argentino en los años sesenta*. Buenos Aires: Paidós, 2001.

Glenz, Monice, et al. *El aporte del arte a la economía argentina: un primer abordaje a partir de las cuentas nacionales*. Buenos Aires: Fondo Nacional de las Artes, 2001.

Kosice, Gyula. *Del arte madí a la ciudad hidroespacial*. Córdoba, Argentina: Fundación Casa de la Cultura de Córdoba, 1983.

La Ferla, Jorge. *Historia crítica del video argentino*. Buenos Aires: MALBA-Fundación Costantini, 2008.

La Ferla, Jorge, and Mariela Cantú. *Video argentino: ensayos sobre cuatro autores: Carlos Trilnick, Arteproteico, Marcello Mercado, Iván Marino*. Buenos Aires: Nueva Librería, 2007.

Longoni, Ana, Gustavo A. Bruzzone, and R. Aguerreberry. *El siluetazo*. Buenos Aires: A. Hidalgo, 2008.

Longoni, Ana, and Mariano Mestman. *Del Di Tella a "Tucumán Arde": Vanguardia artística y política en el 68 argentino*. Buenos Aires: Eudeba, 2008.

Malosetti Costa, Laura. *Primeros modernos: arte y sociedad en Buenos Aires a fines del siglo XIX*. Buenos Aires: Fondo de Cultura Económica, 2001.

Malosetti Costa, Laura, and Julia Ariza. *Primeros modernos en Buenos Aires, 1876–1896*. Buenos Aires: Museo Nacional de Bellas Artes, 2007.

Martín, Alicia. *Folclore en las grandes ciudades: arte popular, identidad y cultura*. Buenos Aires: Libros del Zorzal, 2005.

Mena Larraín, Francisco, and Nicolás Piwonka. *Patagonia andina: la inmensidad humanizada*. Santiago, Chile: Museo Chileno de Arte Precolombino, 2007.

Moneta, R., H. Porto, and R. Rollié. *Artes plásticas y cultura nacional*. Buenos Aires: La Cebolla de Vidrio Ediciones, 1984.

Museo de Arte Hispanoamericano "Isaac Fernández Blanco. *Arte popular latinoamericano: Colección Nicolás Uriburu*. Buenos Aires: Museo de Arte Hispanoamericano "Isaac Fernández Blanco," 2008.

Nelson, Daniel Ernest. "Five Central Figures in Argentine Avant-Garde Art and Literature: Emilio Pettoruti, Xul Solar, Oliverio Girondo, Jorge Luis Borges, Norah Borges." Buenos Airtes: UMI, 1989.

Omil, Alba, and Aníbal Carrillo. *Arte y mito en las culturas andinas del noroeste argentino*. Tucumán, Argentina: Ediciones del Rectorado, Universidad Nacional de Tucumán, 2003.

Ortíz de Guinea, Guillermo. *El arte ante el derecho*. Rosario, Argentina: Instituto de Estudios Interdisciplinarios y Documentación Jurídica, Colegio de Abogados de Rosario, 1996.

Painting Borges/Pintando a Borges. Exhibition Catalogue. Buenos Aires: Universidad Católica Argentina, 2010.

Penhos, Marta. *Mirar, saber, dominar: imágenes de viajeros en la Argentina*. Buenos Aires: MNBA: Asociación Amigos del Museo Nacional de Bellas Artes, 2007.

Penhos, Marta, and Marina Baron Supervielle. *Arte y antropología en la Argentina*. Buenos Aires: Fundación Espigas, 2005.

Penhos, Marta, Diana Wechsler, and Miguel Angel Muñoz. *Tras los pasos de la norma: salones nacionales de bellas artes (1911–1989)*. Archivos del Caia, 2. Buenos Aires: Ediciones del Jilguero, 1999.

Pepe, Eduardo Gabriel. *Diseño aborigen: estudio y reelaboración de la gráfica indígena argentina*. Buenos Aires: CommTOOLS, 2003.

Peralta, Malena. *Cambio de posta: el lugar del arte en San Juan, mitos y realidades*. San Juan, Argentina: Universidad Nacional, Facultad de Filosofía, Humanidades y Artes, 2003.

Pontificia Universidad Católica Argentina Santa María de los Buenos Aires. *Arte sacro argentino*. Buenos Aires: Swiss Advisory Group, 2003.

Romero Brest, Jorge, Edgardo Giménez, and Alfredo Arias. *Jorge Romero Brest: la cultura como provocación*. Buenos Aires: Edición Edgardo Giménez, 2006.

Rueda, María de los Ángeles de. *Arte y utopía: la ciudad desde las artes visuales*. Buenos Aires: Asunto Impreso, 2003.

Sánchez, Christian, Ariel Panella, and Miguel A. Sánchez. *El otro Omar Chabán: cuando el arte ataque*. Buenos Aires: Demo Editores, 2006.

Schneider, Arnd. *Appropriation as Practice: Art and Identity in Argentina*. New York: Palgrave Macmillan, 2006.

Speranza, Graciela. *Fuera de campo: literatura y arte argentinos después de Duchamp*. Barcelona: Editorial Anagrama, 2006.

Verlichak, Victoria, and Marta Ares. *El ojo del que mira: artistas de los noventa*. Buenos Aires, Argentina: Proa Fundación, 1998.

Verlichak, Victoria, and Eduardo Medici. *En la pluma de la mano: artistas de los ochenta*. Buenos Aires: V. Verlichak, 1996.

Zubieta, Ana María. *La memoria: literatura, arte y política*. Bahía Blanca, Argentina: Editorial de la Universidad Nacional del Sur, 2008.

Cuban Art

II Salón de Arte Cubano Contemporáneo. Exhibition Catalogue. Havana: Consejo Nacional de Artes Plásticas, et al., 1998.

Alvarez, Pedro. *How Havana Stole from New York the Idea of Cuban Art*. Santa Monica, CA: Smart Art Press, 2000.

The American Experience: Contemporary Immigrant Artists. Exhibition Catalogue. Philadelphia and New York: The Balch Institute of Ethnic Studies, 1985.

Blanc, Giulio V. *Cuban Artists of the Twentieth Century*. Fort Lauderdale, FL: Fort Lauderdale Museum of Art, 1993.

———. *The Miami Generation*. Exhibition Catalogue. Miami, FL: Cuban Museum of Arts and Culture, 1984.

———. *The Post-Miami Generation*. Exhibition Catalogue. Miami, FL: Cuban Museum of Arts and Culture, 1990.

Blanc, Giulio V. et al. *Cuba/U.S.A.: The First Generation*. Exhibition Catalogue. Washington, DC: El Fondo del Sol, 1991.

Block, Holly, ed. *Art Cuba: The New Generation*. New York, NY: Abrams, 2001.

Bosch, Lynette M. F. "Layers: Collecting Cuban-American Art." In *Layers: Collecting Cuban-American Art*. Exhibition Catalogue. Buffalo, NY: University at Buffalo Art Galleries, 2006, 8–20.

———. *Cuban-American Art in Miami: Exile, Identity and the Neo-Baroque*. London, UK: Lund Humphreys Press, 2004.

———. *Past Cuba: Identity and Identification in Cuban-American Art*. Exhibition Catalogue. Fairfield, CT: Fairfield University and St. Lawrence University, 1997.

———. *Islands in the Stream: Seven Cuban-American Artists*. Exhibition Catalogue. Cortland, NY: State University of New York at Cortland, 1993.

Boswell, Thomas D., and James R. Curtis. *The Cuban-American Experience: Culture, Images and Perspectives*. Totowa, NJ: Rowman & Allanheld, 1984.

Brown, David H. *Santería Enthroned: Art, Ritual and Innovation in Afro-Cuban Religion*. Chicago, IL: University of Chicago Press, 2003.

Camnitzer, Luis. *New Art of Cuba*. Austin, TX: University of Texas Press, 2003, first published in 1994.

Caribe insular: exclusión, fragmentación y paraíso. Exhibition Catalogue. Madrid: Casa de América, 1998.

Cobas, Roberto, ed. *Museo Nacional de Bellas Artes: Colección de Arte Cubano*. Collection Catalogue. Barcelona: "Sa Nostra" Caja de Baleares, Ambit, 2001.

Cockcroft, James D., and Jane Canning. *Latino Visions: Contemporary Chicano, Puerto Rican and Cuban-American Artists*. Danbury, CN: Franklin Watts Press, 2000.

Cuba: la isla posible. Exhibition Catalogue. Barcelona: Ediciones Destino, 1995.

Cuba Siglo XX: modernidad y sincretismo. Exhibition Catalogue. Islas Canarias: Centro Atlántico de Arte Moderno, 1996.

Díaz Burgos, Juan Manuel, ed. *Cuba: 100 años de fotografía, 1898–1998*. Murcia: Mestizo A.C., 1998.

La dirección de la mirada: Neue Kunst aus Kuba, Art actuel de Cuba, Arte cubano contemporáneo. Exhibition Catalogue. Vienna and New York: Springer, 1999.

Fernández, Antonio Eligio (Tonel). "Cuban Art: The Key to the Gulf and How to Use It" and "Cuban Art: The Path of Humor." In *Memoria: Cuban Art in the 20th Century*, 31–33. Los Angeles, CA: California/ International Arts Foundation, 2001.

———. "Tree of Many Beaches: Cuban Art in Motion (1980–1990)." In *Contemporary Art from Cuba: Irony and Survival on the Utopian Island*, edited by Marilyn Zeitlin, 39–66. New York: Delano Greenidge Editions, 1998.

———. "Alternative Humour and Comic Strips: Notes on the Cuban Case." In Laurie Short, ed. *The Unknown Face of Cuban Art*. Sunderland: Northern Center for Contemporary Art, 1992.

Fuentes-Pérez, Ileana, et al. *Outside Cuba: Contemporary Cuban Visual Arts/Fuera de Cuba: artistas cubanos contemporáneos*. Exhibition Catalogue. New Brunswick, NJ: Rutgers University Press, 1987.

García, Manuel. *Historia de un viaje: artistas cubanos en Europa*. Exhibition Catalogue. Valencia: Generalitat Valenciana, 1997.

La gente en casa: Colección Contemporánea Museo Nacional. Exhibition Brochure. Havana: Museo Nacional de Bellas Artes, 2000.

Gómez-Sicre, José. *Art of Cuba in Exile*. Miami, FL: Editorial Munder, 1987.

González Mandri, Flora María. *Guarding Cultural Memory: Afro-Cuban Women in Literature and the Arts*. Charlottesville, VA: University of Virginia Press, 2006.

Gracia, Jorge J. E. "Cuban-American Identity and Art." In Isabel Alvarez Borland and Lynette M. Bosch, eds. *Negotiating Identity in Cuban-American Literature and Art*, 175–188. Albany, NY: State University of New York Press, 2008.

———. *Cuban Art Outside Cuba: Identity, Philosophy, and Art*. Web site: http://www.philosophy.buffalo.edu/ capenchair/CAOC/index.html, 2006 and continuing.

Gracia, Jorge J. E., Lynette Bosch, and Isabel Alvarez Borland, eds. *Identity, Memory, and Diaspora: Voices of Cuban-American Artists, Writers, and Philosophers*. Albany, NY: State University of New York Press, 2007.

———, Lynette Bosch, and Isabel Alvarez Borland. *Negotiating Identities in Philosophy, Art, and Literature: Cuban Americans and American Culture*. National Endowment for the Humanities Seminar, 2006. Web site: http://philosophy.buffalo.edu/contrib/events/neh06.html

Herrera, Andrea O'Reilly. " 'Defying Liminality': The Journeys of Cuban Artists in the Diaspora." In Andrea O'Reilly Herrera, ed. *Cuba: Idea of a Nation Displaced*, 301–311. Albany, NY: State University of New York Press, 2007.

Howe, Linda S. *Cuban Writers and Artists after the Revolution: Transgression and Conformity.* Madison, WI: University of Wisconsin Press, 2003.

Jaffee McCabe, Cynthia, and Daniel J. Boorstin. *The Golden Door: Artist-Immigrants of America, 1876–1976.* Exhibition Catalogue. Washington, DC: Smithsomian Institution Press, 1976.

Joselitt, David. *Loin de Cuba.* Exhibition Catalogue. Aix-en-Provence: Musèe des Tapisseries, 1999.

Juan, Adelaida de. "La mujer pintada en Cuba." *Temas* 5 (1996): 38–46.

Kuba O.K.: aktuelle kunst aus Kuba = arte actual de Cuba. Exhibition Catalogue. Düsseldorf: Städtische Kunsthalle, 1990.

Kuebler, Joanne. *Art of the Fantastic: Latin America, 1920–1987.* Indianapolis, IN: Indianapolis Museum of Art, 1987.

Kunst aus Kuba: Sammlung Ludwig/Art of Cuba: The Ludwig Collection. Brad Breisig: Palace Editions, 2002.

Layers: Collecting Cuban-American Art. Exhibition Catalogue. Coordinated by Lynette M. F. Bosch. Directed and Foreword by Jorge J. E. Gracia. Buffalo, NY: State University at Buffalo Art Galleries, 2006.

Libby, Gary R. *Cuba: A History in Art.* Daytona Beach, FL: The Museum of Arts and Sciences, 1997.

Loomis, John A. *Revolution of Forms: Cuba's Forgotten Art Schools.* Princeton, NJ: Princeton Architectural Press, 1999.

Made in Havana. Exhibition Catalogue. Sydney: Art Gallery of New South Wales, 1989.

Martínez, Juan A. "*Lo blanco-criollo* as *lo cubano* in the Symbolization of a Cuban National Identity in Modernist Painting of the 1940s." In *Cuba, The Elusive Nation: Interpretations of National Identity,* ed. Damian J. Fernández and Madeline Cámara. Gainesville, FL: University Press of Florida, 2000.

———. *Cuban Art and National Identity: The Vanguardia Painters 1927–1950.* Gainesville, FL: University Press of Florida, 1994.

Mena Chicuri, Abelardo G., et al. *Cuba AvantGarde: Contemporary Cuban Art from the Farber Collection/ Arte contempóraneo cubano de la colección Farber.* Gainesville, FL: Samuel P. Harn Museum of Art, 2007.

Montes de Oca, Dannys. *El oficio del arte.* Exhibition Catalogue. Havana: Centro de Desarrollo de las Artes Visuales, 1995.

Monzón, Lissette and Darys J. Vázques. "El mercado del arte en los márgenes de la ideología y la realidad." *Arte Cubano* 3 (2001): 8–15.

Mosquera, Gerardo. "Persistencia del uso." In *Museo Nacional de Bellas Artes.* Havana: Museo Nacional de Bellas Artes, 2003.

———. *Contemporary Art from Cuba.* New York: Arizona State University Art Museum: Delano Greenridge Editions, 1999.

———. "The Infinite Island: Introduction to New Cuban Art." In Marilyn A. Zeitlin, ed. *Contemporary Art from Cuba: Irony and Survival in the Utopian Island,* 23. Tempe, AR: Arizona State University Art Museum, 1997.

New Art from Cuba. Exhibition Catalogue. London: Whitechapel Publications, 1995.

Noceda Fernández, José Manuel, et al. *Kcho: La jungla.* Exhibition Catalogue. Turin: Hopeful Monsters, 2002.

Santana, Andrés Isaac. *Imágenes de desvío: La voz homoerótica en el arte cubano contemporáneo.* Santiago de Chile: J. C. Saez, 2004.

Santis, Jorge, ed. *Breaking Barriers: Selections from the Museum of Art's Permanent Contemporary Cuban Collection.* Exhibition Catalogue. Fort Lauderdale, FL: Fort Lauderdale Museum of Art, 1997.

Seppälä, Marketta, ed. *No Man is an Island: Young Cuban Art.* Pori: Pori Art Museum, 1990.

Short, Laurie, ed. *The Unknown Face of Cuban Art.* Sunderland: Northern Center for Contemporary Art, 1992.

Utopian Territories: New Art from Cuba. Exhibition Catalogue. Vancouver: University of British Columbia, 1997.

Veigas, José, et al. *Memoria: Cuban Art of the 20th Century.* Los Angeles, CA: California International Arts Foundation, 2003.

Viera, Ricardo. *Latin American Artist Photographers from the Lehigh University Art Galleries Collection.* Exhibition Catalogue. Bethlehem, PA: Lehigh University Art Galleries/Museum Operation, 2001.

Weiss, Rachel. "Performing Revolution." In Blake Stimson and Gregory Sholette, eds. *Collectivism after Modernism: The Art of Social Imagination after 1945,* 115–162. Minneapolis, MN: University of Minnesota Press, 2007.

While Cuba Waits: Art from the Nineties. Santa Monica: Smart Art Press, 1999.

Zeitlin, Marilyn A., ed. *Contemporary Art from Cuba: Irony and Survival in the Utopian Island,* 23. Tempe, AR: Arizona State University Art Museum, 1997.

Artists

Luis Cruz Azaceta. http://www.luiscruzazaceta.net

Alexis, Gerald. "Cuban Artists in Exile: The Case Study of Luis Cruz Azaceta." 1991. http://www.luiscruzazaceta.net/index.php

Bartlett, Thomasine. "Azaceta, Charbonnet & Chihuly." *The New Orleans Art Review,* Jan/Feb 2005.

Bookhardt, D. Eric. "Cuba Libre." *Gambit Weekly,* Dec. 11, 2007.

———. "New Orleans." *Art Papers* 29, 2 (March/April 2005): 45.

Bosch, Lynette. *Cuban-American Art in Miami: Exile, Identity and the Neo-Baroque,* 146–147. London, UK: Lund Humphreys Press, 2004.

Calas, Terrington. "Azaceta: Unkillable Desperation." *The New Orleans Art Review,* Fall/Winter 2007/2008.

———. "Notebook: Formalisms." *The New Orleans Art Review,* Jan/Feb 2002.

Clavijo, Raisa. "Luis Cruz Azaceta: Museum Plan Series." *Wynwood,* Summer 2008.

Fitzpatrick, Mary. "Yellow Wall 2 as Viewed by a Preservationist." *Preservation Resource Center of New Orleans,* Oct. 10, 2003.

Gil Fiallo, Laura. "Luis Cruz Azaceta." *Art Nexus* 4, 59 (Dec. 2005/Feb. 2006): 179–180.

Gracia, Jorge J. E., "Interview with Luis Cruz Azaceta, 2008." Oct. 17, 2009. http://www.philosophy.buffalo.edu/capenchair/CAOC/Interviews/iAzaceta.htm.

Kemp, John R. "Luis Cruz Azaceta: Arthur Roger." *ARTnews* 107, 5 (May 2008): 156–157.

Loescher, Bob. "Luis Cruz Azaceta [an Interview]." Video Data Bank, School of the Art Institute, Chicago, IL, 1990.

Maccash, Doug. "Terror Takes a Holiday." *The Times-Picayune,* Dec. 17, 2004.

McCollam, Julie. "Luis Cruz Azaceta: Painter of Exile." *Preservation Resource Center of New Orleans,* October 10, 2003.

Mennekes, Friedhelm. "An Interview with Luis Cruz Azaceta." *Readings in Latin American Modern Art,* 212–217. Ed. Patrick Frank. New Haven, CT: Yale University Press, 2004.

Moreno, Gean. "Luis Cruz Azaceta: Fredric Snitzer Gallery." *Art Nexus* 40 (May/June 2001): 144–145.

Sciortino, Natalie. "Luis Cruz Azaceta." *Artforum,* 2008.

Sciortino-Rinehart, Natalie. "Luis Cruz Azaceta—Swept Away." *Wynwood,* Nov 2008.

Torres, Andrea. "Luis Cruz Azaceta: Frederic Snitzer." *ARTnews* 104, 9 (October 2005): 178.

Turner, Grady T. "Luis Cruz Azaceta at Ramis Barquet." *Art in America* 91, 2 (February 2003): 116.

Veigas, José, et al. *Memoria: Cuban Art of the 20th Century.* Los Angeles, CA: California International Arts Foundation, 2003.

Alejandro Boim. http://www.alejandroboim.com.ar

"Boim's Masteries." *La Prensa,* June 15, 1997.

"Boim"s Well-Doing." *La Prensa,* Aug. 2002.

Boim, Alejandro. "Alejandro Boim, Painter." Aug. 27, 2009: http://www.alejandroboim.com.ar.

———. "Alejandro Boim: Alejandro Painter Argentina Blog." Aug. 27, 2009: http://alejandroboim.blogspot.com.

Boim, Alejandro, and Zurbarán. *Alejandro Boim,* Del jueves 24 de abril al miércoles 4 de junio de 2008. Buenos Aires: Zurbarán, 2008.

"Freedom and Expression in the Work of Alejandro Boim." *La Nación,* Jan.1996.

Galli, Aldo. "Facing the New Century." *La Nación,* Nov. 7, 1999.

Hansi, Didier. "Exquisite Inner Vertigo." *Artension,* 2006.

"Order Is Born out from Disorder." *Le Monde* 2, Dec. 3, 2005.

"Present and Tradition." *La Nación,* 2002.

Videla, Albino Dieguez. "Boim's Planes." *La Prensa,* Nov. 7, 1999.

Miguel Cámpora. http://www.Argentineart.com

Ricardo Celma. http://www.celma.com.ar

Alatorre, Antonio. "Heliopolis: Invitación a la lectura." *La Voz de la Esfinge,* January, 2002: 45–53.

Amodei, Romi. "Entrevista con Ricardo Celma." *La Luna y el Arte,* May 11, 2011: www.lalunayelarte. blogspot.com/2011/05/entrevista-ricardo-celma.html.

"ArtAmericas de Panamá Presents Ricardo Celma." *Art Knowledge News*: www.artknowledgenews.com/node/668.html.

Celma, R. "Ricardo Celma" 2009. Retrieved October 4, 2009, from http://www.celma.com.ar/.

"Exhibe un argentino amores y nostalgias, en Guadalajara." *Medio Mexicano,* April 21, 2002, p. F3: www.eluniversal.com.mx/cultura/22508.html.

Gracia, Jorge J. E. "The Presence of the Absent in Interpretation: Foucault on Velázquez, and Destéfanis and Celma on Borges," *CR: The New Centennial Review* 11, 1 (2011).

Juárez, Rosa Esther. "Vicios argentinos." *Medio Mexicano,* Exposición Museo del Periodismo, 2002.

"Ricardo Celma." *El Abasto,* n. 38, September, 2002: www.revistaelabasto.com.ar/38_Ricardo_Celma.htm.

"Ricardo Celma." *The Pictoral Bardon Group*: www.tpbg.com.ar/CelmaE.htm.

Romano, Carlos. "Celina Vive! Entrevista con Ricardo Celma," April 25, 2011: www.cventrevistas.blogspot.com/2011/04/entrevista-ricardo-celma.html.

"Trío Figurativo." *La Primera Perú,* March 10, 2011: www.diariolaprimeraperu.com/online/cultur/trio-figurativo_81508.html.

Laura Delgado. http://www.ldelgado.com.ar

Delgado, L. "Laura Delgado, artista plástica," (2006). Retrieved October 4, 2009, from http://www.ldelgado.com.ar/index.htm.

Héctor Destéfanis. http://hectordestefanis.com.ar

Feinsiller, Laura, and Roberto Duarte. S/T. *Héctor Destéfanis: Pinturas.* Exhibition Catalogue. Buenos Aires: Salas Nacionales de Cultura, Palais de Glace, 1998.

Gracia, Jorge J. E. "The Presence of the Absent in Interpretation: Foucault on Velásquez, and Destéfanis and Celma on Borges," *CR: The New Centennial Review* 11, 1 (2011).

Sapollnik, Julio. S/T. *Héctor Destéfanis.* Exhibition Catalogue. Buenos Aires: Centro Cultural Recoleta, 2001.

Claudio D'Leo. http://www.claudiodleo.com.ar

D'Leo, C. "Claudio D'Leo," 2009. Retrieved Oct. 4, 2009, from: http://www.claudiodleo.com.ar

Tercera Gallese, Julio C. "Claudio D'Leo: Un artista plástico argentino en el Banco Mundial," *Antiques* 3, 5 (2009): 32–36.

Carlos Estévez. http://www.carlosestevez.net

Albertini, Rosanna. "Carlos Estévez: The Theater of Life." In *Carlos Estévez: The Theater of Life.* Exhibition Catalogue. Los Angeles: Couturier Gallery, 2001.

Block, Holly, ed. *Art Cuba: The New Generation.* New York, NY: Abrams, 2001.

Carvalho, John. "What Is Interpretation? Images and Thoughts about Philosophy and Art." *American Philosophical Association Newsletter on Hispanic/Latino Issues* 1, 2 (2010).

García Gutiérrez, Enrique. "Le voyage inmobile." In *Carlos Estévez.* Exhibition Catalogue. San Juan, PR: Gómez Fine Art Galería, 2006.

Gracia, Jorge J. E. "The Philosophical Interpretation of Visual Art: Response to Mariana Ortega and John Carvalho." *American Philosophical Association Newsletter on Hispanic/Latino Issues* 1, 2 (2010).

———. *Images of Thought: Philosophical Interpretations of Carlos Estevez's Art.* Albany, NY: State University of New York Press, 2009.

———. "Carlos Estévez's Images of Thought." Nov. 5, 2009–Feb. 6, 2010. Exhibition Brochure. UB Art Gallery, The State University of New York.

———. *Cuban Art Outside Cuba: Identity, Philosophy, and Art.* Website: http://www.philosophy.buffalo.edu/capenchair/CAOC/index.html, 2006 and continuing.

Grant, Annette. "Cubans Making Lot Out of Little." In *New York Times,* June 11, 2000.

Keough, Jeffrey, and Lisa Tung. "Foreword." In *Carlos Estévez: Dreamcomber.* Exhibition Catalogue. Boston, MS: Huntington Gallery, Massachusetts College of Art, 2002.

Luis, Carlos M. "The Transparent Being." In *Carlos Estévez: The Transparent Being.* Exhibition Catalogue. Los Angeles: Couturier Gallery, 2003.

Mena Chicuri, Abelardo G., et al. *Cuba AvantGarde: Contemporary Cuban Art from the Farber Collection/Arte contempóraneo cubano de la colección Farber.* Gainesville, FL: Samuel P. Harn Museum of Art, 2007

Pinos-Santos, Carina. "Viaje al centro del hombre, una travesía de Carlos Estévez." *Revolución y Cultura* 5 (1995): 33–34.

Ortega, Mariana. "A Philosophical Hermeneutics of Visual Art: On Gracia's *Images of Thought, Philosophical Interpretations of Carlos Estévez's Art.*" *American Philosophical Association Newsletter on Hispanic/Latino Issues* 1, 2 (2010).

Schneider Enríques, Mary. "Behind the Malecón: The Unexpected Visions of Carlos Estévez." In *Carlos Estévez: Dreamcomber.* Exhibition Catalogue. Boston, MS: Huntington Gallery, Massachusetts College of Art, 2002.

Sullivan, Edward J. "The *Bestiarium* of Carlos Estévez." In *Carlos Estévez: Bestiarium.* Exhibition Catalogue. Los Angeles: Couturier Gallery, 1999.

Veigas, José, et al. *Memoria: Cuban Art of the 20th Century.* Los Angeles, CA: California International Arts Foundation, 2003.

Weinstein, Joel. "Knowingness." In *Existir en el tiempo/Existing in Time.* Exhibition Catalogue. Miami, FL: The Olga M. & Carlos Saladrigas Gallery, The Ignatian Center for the Arts, 2005.

León Ferrari. http://www.leonferrari.com.ar

Alberti, Rafael, and León Ferrari. *Escrito en el aire: 9 Poemas inéditos para 9 dibujos de León Ferrari.* Milan: All'Insegna del Pesce d'Oro, 1964.

27a Bienal de São Paulo: como vivir junto (How to Live Together). São Paulo: Fundação Bienal de São Paulo, 2006.

Ferrari, León. *Bíblia: Collages*. São Paulo: Edicões Exu,1989.

———. *Cuadro escrito*. São Paulo: Licopodio, 1984.

———. *El camisón*. São Paulo: Ed. Licopodio, 1980.

———. *"El observador": Collages*. Buenos Aires: L. Ferrari, 2001.

———. *Hombres*. São Paulo: Ediciones Licopodia, 1984.

———. *Imagens*. São Paulo: Edicões Exu., 1989.

———. *La basílica*. São Paulo: Edición del autor, 1985.

———. *La bondadosa crueldad*. Buenos Aires: Editorial Argonauta, 2000.

———. *"León Ferrari."* Nov. 30 2009. http://www.leonferrari.com.ar

———. *León Ferrari: Serie de errores & Works, 1962–2007*. New York, NY: Cecilia De Torres, Ltd., 2008.

———. *León Ferrari: Politiscripts: September 9–October 23, 2004*. New York, NY: Drawing Center, 2004.

———. *León Ferrari en La Fadu*. Buenos Aires: Ediciones FADU, 2007.

———. *Ocho años en Brasil, 1976-1984*. Buenos Aires: Arte Nuevo, 1984.

———. *Palabras ajenas: Conversaciones de Dios con algunos hombres y de algunos hombres con algunos hombres y con Dios*. Buenos Aires: Falbo, 1967.

———. *Parahereges: Collages*. São Paulo: Expressão, 1986.

———. *Poesias*. São Paulo: Ed. Licopodio, 1980.

———. *Prosa política. Arte y pensamiento*. Buenos Aires: Siglo Veintiuno Editores Argentina, 2005.

———. *Re-Reading of the Bible*. São Paulo: L. Ferrari, 1988.

Ferrari, León, Fernando García, and Andrea Giunta. *León Ferrari: "Todavía quedan muchos creyentes que convencer."* Buenos Aires: Capital Intelectual, 2008.

Ferrari, León, et al. *León Ferrari: Retrospectiva. Obras 1954–2004,* 30 de noviembre de 2004 al 27 de febrero de 2005. Centro Cultural Recoleta. Buenos Aires: Centro Cultural Recoleta, 2004.

———. *León Ferrari: Obras/Works, 1976–2008*. Mexico City and Montabaur; Germany: Instituto Nacional de Bellas Artes, Rm Verlag, 2008.

———. *León Ferrari–Henri Michaux: Un diálogo de signos*. Buenos Aires: Galería Jorge Mara-La Ruche, 2009.

Galería Latinoamericana. *León Ferrari: Planos, heliografías y fotocopias*. Havana: Galería Latinoamericana, 1983.

Giunta, Andrea. *El caso Ferrari: Arte, censura y libertad de expresión en la retrospectiva de León Ferrari en el Centro Cultural Recoleta, 2004–2005*. Buenos Aires: Ediciones Licopodio, 2008.

Lisa, Esteban, et al. *Esteban Lisa: De Arturo al Di Tella (1944–1963)*. Buenos Aires: Galería Ruth Benzacar, 2002.

Longoni, Ana, and Mariano Mestman. *Del Di Tella a "Tucumán arde": vanguardia artística y política en el 68 argentino*. Buenos Aires: Eudeba, 2008.

Pérez Oramas, Luis, et al. *León Ferrari and Mira Schendel: Tangled Alphabets*. New York and São Paulo: Museum of Modern Art, 2009.

Quiles, Daniel. "León Ferrari and Mira Schendel." *Artforum international,* 47, 10 (2009) 328.

Ramírez, Mari Carmen, Héctor Olea, and Houston Museum of Fine Arts. *Inverted Utopias: Avant-Garde Art in Latin America*. New Haven, CN: Yale University Press, 2004.

Ramírez, Mari Carmen, et al. *Cantos paralelos: La parodia plástica en el arte argentino contemporáneo/Visual Parody in Contemporary Argentinean Art*. Austin, TX and Buenos Aires: Jack S. Blanton Museum of Art, University of Texas at Austin, and Fondo Nacional de las Artes, Argentina, 1999.

Rexer, L. "Buenos Aires: The Case of Leon Ferrari." *Modern Painters* (Jun. 2005): 51–55.

Torres, Cecilia, and Modernitat Museu Valencia de Illustració. *Forma, linea, gesto, escritura: Aspectos del dibujo en America del Sur*. Valencia: Diputació de València, 2008.

José Franco. *http://tallerfrancoarte.blogspot.com*

4 artistas cubanos: Humberto Castro, Nelson Domínguez, Moisés Finalé, José Franco, 25 de junio a 9 de julio, 1987. Exhibition Catalogue. Havana. Realidade Galería de Arte.

Casanegra, Mercedes. "Contemporary Mythologies." In *José Franco: New Gods*. Exhibition Catalogue. Miami: Silvana Facchini Gallery, 2004.

Collazo, Alberto. "José Franco." *Art Nexus* 18 (Oct./Dec.1995): 106.

Franco, José. http://tallerfrancoarte.blogspot.com, Taller Franco Arte, 2009.

———. *Riing-!Grrr- De José Franco: Museo Nacional*, Castillo de la Real Fuerza, 15 de agosto-1ro. de octubre. Exhibition Catalogue. Havana: El Museo, 1990.

Gaudibert, Pierre. *Trajectoire cubaine: José Bedia, Humberto Castro, Moisés Finalé, José Franco: Centre d'art Contemporain Cac Corbeil-Essonnes*, 22 avril au 29 mai 1989, Commune D'orvieto, 3 au 30 juin 1989, Museo Civico di Gibellina, 2 juillet au 15 août 1989. Exhibition Catalogue. Corbeil-Essonnes, France: Le Centre, 1989.

Giunta, Andrea. "Mundos, José Franco." In *Mundos: pinturas, dibujos e instalaciones*. Exhibition Catalogue. Buenos Aires: Galería de Arte Laura Haber, 2004.

———. "Quince propuestas para enlazar mundos." In *José Franco: enlazador de mundos*. Exhibition Catalogue. Buenos Aires: Centro Cultural Recoleta, 2007.

Gracia, Jorge J. E. "Interview with José Franco." Cuban Art Outside Cuba: Identity, Philosophy, and Art. Website: http://www.philosophy.buffalo.edu/capenchair/CAOC/index.html, 2006 and continuing.

Hernández, Orlando. "Aló, mesié Rusó." In *José Franco: mundos: pinturas, dibujos e instalaciones*. Exhibition Catalogue. Buenos Aires: Calería de Arte Laura Haber, 2004.

———. "José Franco en busca de lo humano." In *José Franco: oficios de ojo*. Exhibition Catalogue. Havana: La Acacia, 2000.

Menéndez, Aldo. "Piel de paraíso." In *José Franco: enlazador de mundos*. Exhibition Catalogue. Buenos Aires: Centro Cultural Recoleta, 2007.

Veigas, José, et al. *Memoria: Cuban Art of the 20th Century*. Los Angeles, CA: California International Arts Foundation, 2003.

Etienne Gontard. http://www.etiennegontard.com.ar

Mirta Kupferminc. http://www.mirtakupferminc.net

Abadi, Corinne Sacca. "Algunas notas sobre la obra de Mirta Kupferminc." Asociación Argentina de Críticos de Arte, Asociación Internacional de Críticos de Arte. Oct. 22, 2009. http://www.mirtakupferminc. net/download/csacca.pdf.

Aizemberg, Edna. *Books and Bombs in Buenos Aires: Borges Gerchunoff and Argentine-Jewish Writing.* Hanover and London: Brandeis University Press/University Press of New England, 2002.

Alonso, Eva Farji-Ana, and Mirta Kupferminc. "Un camino de libertad (an interview)." Oct. 22 2009. http://www.mirtakupferminc.net/download/efarji.pdf.

Barbarito, Carlos. "Caras de Mirta Kupferminc." In *San Miguel* (June 19, 2003); rep. and trans. in *Mirta Kupferminc: Wanderings.* Exhibition Catalogue. New York: Hebrew Union College—Jewish Institute of Religion Museum, 2009.

Barbarito, Carlos, and Mirta Kupferminc. "Creadora de mundos (an interview). Oct. 22, 2009. http://www.mirtakupferminc.net/download/cbarbarito.pdf.

Fingueret, Manuela. "Honrar la vida." Oct. 22, 2009. http://www.mirtakupferminc.net/download/mfingueret.pdf.

Hirsch, Marianne, and Leo Spitzer. "Mirta Kupferminc's Rootless Routes/Las rutas sin raíces de Mirta Kupferminc." *Mirta Kupferminc: Wanderings.* Exhibition Catalogue. New York: Hebrew Union College—Jewish Institute of Religion Museum, 2009.

Kruger, Laura. "Mirta Kupferminc: Magical Realism/Realismo mágico." *Mirta Kupferminc: Wanderings.* Exhibition Catalogue. New York: Hebrew Union College—Jewish Institute of Religion Museum, 2009.

Kupferminc, Mirta. *Mirta Kupferminc: Gente del otro espejo: grabados y objetos.* Exhibition Catalogue. Buenos Aires: De Santi Galería de Arte, 2001.

———. "Mirta Kupferminc: Artista plástica," Sept. 27, 2009. http://www.mirtakupferminc.net/index.html.

———. *Mundos paralelos.* Exhibition Catalogue. Buenos Aires: Reich Espacio Giesso, 1999.

———. *Mirta Kupferminc: Obras recientes.* Buenos Aires: Centro Cultural Recoleta, 2006.

———. *Objetos y libros.* Buenos Aires: Editorial Ariel, 2003.

———. *Obra judaica: El legado.* Buenos Aires: [s.n.], 2000.

———. *Sillas.* Buenos Aires: Editorial Ariel, 2003.

———. "The Memory of the Future." In *European Review of Modern Prints, Books, and Paper Art.* Prague: Central European Gallery, 2008.

Kupferminc, Mirta, et al. *Borges y La Cábala: Senderos del verbo.* Buenos Aires: s.n., 2006.

Kupferminc, Mirta, et al. *Mirta Kupferminc: Grabados 1992.* Exhibition Catalogue. Buenos Aires: Museo de Arte Moderno: Instituto Cultural Argentino Israeli, 1992.

Kupferminc, Mirta, Abraham Lichtenbaum, and Uriel J. Sevi. *Mirta Kupferminc: Obra judaica: "El Legado."* Buenos Aires: s.n., 2000.

Kupferminc, Mirta, et al. *Iluminaciones judías.* Buenos Aires: Guenizá, 2002.

Luxner, Larry. "Art Mixed Media with Moving Message." *Americas* (2004)

Noyce, Richard. "Stitching Poetry into Art/Cosiéndole poesía al arte." In *Mirta Kupferminc: Wanderings.* Exhibition Catalogue. New York: Hebrew Union College—Jewish Institute of Religion Museum, 2009.

Plavnick, Baruj, and Mirta Kupferminc. *Hagadá De Pesaj/Hagadah Shel Pesah.* Buenos Aires: Fundación Pardés, 2006.

Rosensaft, Jean Block. "The Legacy of Loss and Longing/El legado de pérdida y añoranza." In *Mirta Kupferminc: Wanderings.* Exhibition Catalogue. New York: Hebrew Union College—Jewish Institute of Religion Museum, 2009.

Sapollnik, Julio. "Presentación." October 22, 2009. http://www.mirtakupferminc.net/download/jsapollnik.pdf.

Schwalb, Harry. "Mirta Kupferminc: International Images." *ARTnews* 101, 3 (2002): 125–126.

Sosnowski, Saul. "Mirta Kupferminc's Expanding Universe/Un universo en expansión." In *Mirta Kupferminc: Wanderings.* Exhibition Catalogue. New York: Hebrew Union College—Jewish Institute of Religion Museum, 2009.

Tala, Alexia. *Installations and Experimental Printmaking.* London: A & C Black, 2009

Toker, Eliahu. "True Person, True Artist/Persona verdadera, artista verdadera." In *Mirta Kupferminc: Wanderings.* Exhibition Catalogue. New York: Hebrew Union College—Jewish Institute of Religion Museum, 2009.

Nicolás Menza. http://www.nicolasmenza.com

Févre, Fermín. *Nicolás Menza: Reivindicación de la pintura.* Buenos Aires: La Marca Editora, 2003.

Menza, Nicolás. "Nicolas Menza." October 4 2009: http://www.nicolasmenza.com.

———. *Nicolas Menza.* Buenos Aires: N. Menza, 2000.

———. *Nicolas Menza: Pinturas 2001.* s.l.: s.n., 2001.

Menza, Nicolás, and Cabildo Córdoba. *Nicolas Menza: muestra antológica.* Exhibition Catalogue. Córdoba, Argentina: Municipalidad de Córdoba, 2003.

Sapollnik, Julio. S/T. *Nicolás Menza: Muestra antológica.* Exhibition Catalogue. Olavarría, Argentina: TGA—The Art Gallery, 2004.

Mauricio Nizzero. http://www.mauricionizzero.com

Nizzero, M. "Mauricio Nizzero" (2009) Retrieved October 4, 2009, from http://www.mauricionizzero.com/index.html.

Estela Pereda. http://www.estelapereda.com.ar

A. A. W. *Enciclopedia visual de la Argentina*. Buenos Aires: Clarín, 2002/03, fascículo 73, 1065.

———. *Arte del nuevo milenio*. Buenos Aires: Arte y Antigüedades, 1994.

———. *Argentina: El arte actual (I)*. Buenos Aires: Delfos, 1992.

———. *Documenta 88, la plástica latinoamericana hoy*. Buenos Aires: Arte al Día Internacional, 1988.

Aguinis, Marcos. "A modo de presentación." In María Elena Babino, et al. *Estela Pereda: Aquí y ahora/Here and Now*. Buenos Aires: Asunto Impreso, 2002.

———. *Estela Pereda: Terra-Caelum-Terra*. Exhibition Catalogue. Buenos Aires: Galería Van Riel, 1997.

Babino, María Elena, et al. *Estela Pereda: Aquí y ahora/Here and Now*. Buenos Aires: Asunto Impreso, 2002.

Barreda, Fabiana. *Aquí vivo. Memoria desde adentro*. Exhibition Catalogue. Buenos Aires: Museo Sívori, 2004.

———. *Arte argentino actual*. Buenos Aires: Actualidad en el Arte, 1993.

Battistozzi, Ana María. *Estela Pereda: Terra-Caelum-Terra*. Exhibition Catalogue. Buenos Aires: Galería Van Riel, 1994.

Brughetti, Romualdo. *Nueva historia de la pintura y la escultura en la Argentina: De los orígenes a nuestros días*. Buenos Aires: Ediciones de Arte Gaglianone, 3rd ed., 2000.

———. "Dos décadas de surrealismo." *La Nación*, Buenos Aires, Dec. 7, 1980.

Chatruc, Celina. "Como agua que fluye." *La Nación*, suplemento y cultura. Buenos Aires, June 20, 2009.

Chirico, Osiris. "Estela Pereda." In Jorge Taverna Irigoyen. *40 Artistas argentinos*. Buenos Aires: Ediciones Actualidad en el Arte, 1991.

———. *Estela Pereda-Ana Laplace: Tapices*. Exhibition Catalogue. Buenos Aires: Galería Arthea, 1970.

Cisneros, Florencio. "Estela Pereda en el Arch Gallery." *Noticias de Arte*, New York, 4 and 5 (May 1988).

Collazo, Alberto H. "Dibujos y objetos." *Clarín*, Buenos Aires, Oct. 15, 1983.

Curi, Marcos, and Roque Bonis. *Estela Pereda: pinturas/paintings, cajas/boxes*. Exhibition Catalogue. Buenos Aires: Galeria Marienbad; New York: Arch Gallery, 1988.

Damian, Carol. "Construyendo una realidad mítica." In *Estela Pereda: Construyendo una realidad mítica*. Exhibition Catalogue. Buenos Aires: British Art Center, 1998.

Dieguez Videla, Albino. "Estela Pereda entre cuerpos y objectos." *La Prensa*, Buenos Aires, May 19, 1985.

Drake, Shelley. "Today's Realists Use Abstraction." *Artspeak*, May 1, 1988.

Ercolano, Clarisa. "El agua que todo lo empuja." *Página/12*, suplemento Las 12, Buenos Aires, July 3, 2009.

Faccaro, Rosa. "Re-Encuentros." *Clarín*, Buenos Aires, June 5, 1993.

Fevre, Fermín. "La pintura de Estela Pereda." In *Estela Pereda*. Exhibition Catalogue. Buenos Aires: Galería del Buen Ayre, 1982.

Fernández Arbós, Elvira, and Osvaldo Seiguerman. *40 dibujantes argentinos*. Buenos Aires: Actualidad en el Arte, 1987.

Fiel, Cecilia. "Tú coserás/Thou Shalt Saw." In Estela Pereda, *Profesión: sus labores*, 27-34, 161–8. Buenos Aires: Papers Editores, 2010.

Galli, Aldo. "Estela Pereda." *La Prensa,* Buenos Aires, May 26, 1982.

Lacau, Estela Laplace de, and Estela Pereda. *Cuentos de una abuela.* Buenos Aires: Compañía General Fabril Editora, 1969.

Lebenglik, Fabian. "El péndulo de Pereda." *Página/12,* Buenos Aires, March 29, 1994.

Linares, Laura. "El torso, ese templo del corazón." *Revista La Nación,* Buenos Aires, July 27, 1986.

Linares, Salvador. *Arte argentino para el tercer milenio.* Buenos Aires: Gaglianone, 2000.

Magrini, César. *Anuario latinoamericano de artes plásticas.* Buenos Aires: Correo, 1986.

———. *Estela Pereda: pinturas serie torsos y medidas.* Exhibition Catalogue. Buenos Aires: Marienbad, 1986.

Mercado, Tununa. *4 generaciones.* Exhibition Catalogue. Mexico City: Galería Kin, 1991.

Newton, Lily S. de. *Diccionario biográfico de mujeres argentinas,* 2nd ed. Buenos Aires, 1980

Oliveras, Elena. "Los bordes de la pintura." In *Historia crítica del arte argentino.* Buenos Aires: Asociación Argentina de Críticos de Arte, 1995.

———. *Intercambio: Del uno al otro.* Exhibition Catalogue. Buenos Aires: Centro Cultural San Martín, 1985.

Perazzo, Nelly. "Invitación a la autoconfesión/Invitation to Self-Confession." In Estela Pereda, *Profesión: sus labores,* 87–91, 171–5. Buenos Aires: Papers Editores, 2010.

Pereda, Estela. *Profesión: sus labores.* Buenos Aires: Papers Editores, 2010

———. "Estela Pereda." Oct. 4, 2009. http://www.estelapereda.com.ar.

Prez, Elba. *40 dibujantes argentinos.* Buenos Aires: Actualidad en el Arte, 1987.

Quaranta, Jorge A., and Susana Inés Araujo, eds. *Argentina, el arte actual/Argentina, Its Present Art.* Buenos Aires: Editorial Delfos, 1992.

Santamarina, María. "Apuntes biográficos." In María Elena Babino, et al., *Estela Pereda: Aquí y ahora/Here and Now.* Buenos Aires: Asunto Impreso, 2002.

———. "Estela Pereda." *Intramuros* 7, 14 (2000).

Sayus, María Silva. "Pereda: Deseo de ligar cielo y tierra." *Artinf* 22, 101 (Spring 1998).

Squirru, Rafael, S/T. *Estela Pereda.* Exhibition Catalogue. Buenos Aires: Galería Lagard, 1974.

———. *Estela Pereda: Paintings/Drawings. Estela Pereda-Ana Laplace: Tapestries.* Exhibition Catalogue. Washington DC: Venerable Neslage Galleries, 1975.

Squirru, Rafael, et al. *Plástica argentina.* Buenos Aires: Pluma y Pincel, 1976.

Svanascini, Osvaldo. *Historia crítica del arte argentino.* Buenos Aires: Dirección de Relaciones Externas y Comunicaciones, TELECOM Argentina, 1995.

Taverna Irigoyen, Jorge. "Estela Pereda." *Estela Pereda: Itinerarios de aire.* Exhibition Catalogue. Córdoba: Museo Emilio A. Caraffa, 1999, and Santa Fe: Museo Rosa Galisteo de Rodríguez, 1999.

Tortosa, Alina. "Los caminos oblicuos de la memoria en Estela Pereda." *Desmemorias.* Buenos Aires: Papelera Palermo, 2006.

Vera Ocampo, R. S/T. *Estela Pereda.* Exhibition Catalogue. Buenos Aires: Vermeer Galería de Arte, 1983.

———. S/T. *Estela Pereda. Serie: Re-encuentros.* Exhibition Catalogue. Buenos Aires: Suipacha Galería de Arte, 1992.

Uribe, Basilio. *Arte religioso en Buenos Aires, siglos XVIII y XX.* Buenos Aires: Gaglianone, 1992.

———. "Tapices de Estela Pereda y Ana Laplace." *Criterio* 46, 1632 (Nov. 25, 1971).

Alberto Rey. http://www.albertorey.com

Adams, Bruce. "Gone Fishing." *Buffalo News*, Gusto, Buffalo, NY, Oct. 26

Alvarez Borland, Isabel. "The Memories of Others: Ana Menéndez and Alberto Rey." *Review: Latin American Literature and Arts* 42, 1 (2009): 11–20.

"Back to Nature: Alberto Rey's Explorations Take Him to Spiritual Places Where Art, Culture and the Environment Converge." *P/E/M Connections Magazine*, Peabody Essex Museum, Salem, MA, January/February, 2007.

Bosch, Lynette, "Alberto Rey—Cuba: Image or Reality." Exhibition Catalogue. Geneseo, NY: Bertha Lederer Art Gallery, State University of New York, 2000.

———. *Cuban-American Art in Miami: Exile, Identity and the Neo-Baroque,* 138–146. Aldershot, Hampshire, England; Burlington, VT: Lund Humphries, 2004.

———. "Crossing Borders." Exhibition Catalogue. Canton, NY: St. Lawrence University, 1997.

———. "Past Cuba: Identity and Identification in Cuban American Art." Exhibition Catalogue. Fairfield, CN: Thomas Walsh Gallery, 1997.

Brutvan, Cheryl. "In Western New York, 1991." Exhibition Catalogue. Buffalo, NY: Albright Knox Art Gallery, 1991.

Cavallero, Emanuel, "Cuban Heritage, American Upbringing Marks Artist's Work." In *The Chatauquan Daily*, Chautauqua Institution, Chautauqua, NY, July 20, 2007.

Channing, S., S. Kellner, and M. Horne. "Regional Forecast." Exhibition Catalogue. Pittsburgh, PA: Space 101; Buffalo, NY: Hallwalls; Cleveland, OH: SPACES, 1998.

Chauncey, Andrea. *Pictorial Stories from a Far Away Land.* Exhibition Catalogue. Geneseo, NY: Lamron, 2000.

"Complicit! Contemporary American Art and Mass Culture." Art Museum, University of Virginia, VA. Exhibition Catalogue essays and podcast, 2007: www.virginia.edu/artmuseum/complicit/exhibition.html.

Drucker, Johanna. "Alberto Rey: New Naturalism." Exhibition Brochure. Lawrenceville, NY: Abud Family Foundation for the Arts, 2005.

"Earth Day Programs." *P/E/M Connections Magazine*, Peabody Essex Museum, Salem, MA, March/April 2007.

Emke, Ron. *Aquaman Meets Fish of Steel.* Exhibition Catalogue. Buffalo, NY: Spree, 2006.

Gracia, Jorge J. E. "Landscapes of the Mind: Interview with Alberto Rey." In Jorge J. E. Gracia, Lynette M. F. Bosch, and Isabel Alvarez Borland, eds. *Identity, Memory, and Diaspora: Voices of Cuban-American Artists, Writers, and Philosophers*, 91–101, 113. Albany, NY: State University of New York Press, 2008.

———. "Cuban-American Identity and Art." In Isabel Alvarez Borland and Lynette M. Bosch, eds. *Negotiating Identity in Cuban-American Literature and Art*, 175–188. Albany, NY: State University of New York Press, 2008.

———. "Interview with Alberto Rey." *Cuban Art Outside Cuba: Identity, Philosophy, and Art.* Website: http://www.philosophy.buffalo.edu/capenchair/CAOC/index.html, 2006.

Gracia, Jorge J. E., and Lynette Bosch, "Negotiating Identities in Art, Literature, and Philosophy: "Cuban Americans and American Culture." NEH Summer Institute. Buffalo, NY: University of Buffalo, 2006. http://philosophy.buffalo.edu/NEH06/index.html.

Hatfield, Sarah. "One Fish, Two Fish." *Jamestown Post Journal*, Jamestown, NY, March, 2007.

Hartz, Jill, Andrea Douglas, and Alberto Rey. "Interview with Alberto Rey." In *Complicit! Contemporary American Art & Mass Culture*. Charlottesville, VA: University of Virginia Art Museum, 2009. http://www.virginia.edu/artmuseum/complicit/artists/rey_a/index.html.

Herrera, Andrea O'Reilly. *Remembering Cuba: Legacy of a Diaspora*. Austin, TX: University of Texas Press, 2001.

Huntington, Richard. "Exhibit of Regional Art Has Big Range." *Buffalo News*, Buffalo, NY, May 9, 2005.

Isaacs, Susan. *1994 Critics Residency*. Exhibition Catalogue. Buffalo, NY: Hallwalls Contemporary Arts Center, 1994.

Jacoby-Patronski, Juliana, "Alberto Rey at Mid-Stream." *Buffalo Spree*, Buffalo, NY, April, 2005.

Kellner, Sara. *The 2nd Skin*. Exhibition Brochure. Buffalo, NY: Hallwalls Contemporary Arts Center, September, 1992.

Licata, Elizabeth. "Uncharted Waters." *Buffalo Spree*, November 2004.

Markle, Greer. "Alberto Rey—Cultural Iconography." Exhibition Brochure. Ashland, OR: Schneider Museum of Art, 1995.

Maroldi, Brooke. "Two Slices: Paintings by Alberto Rey." *1990*. October 17 2009. http://www.albertorey.com/two-slices.

Merkle, Karen Rene. "Ichthyologically Accurate." *Erie Daily News*, Erie, PA, May 26, 2005.

Metz, Don, and Lynette Bosch. "Art on The Hyphen: Cuban-American Artists of Western New York State." Buffalo, NY: Burchfield—Center Art Center, 2005.

Nieves, Marysol. "Amidst the Silence: Enrique Martínez Celaya and Alberto Rey." Exhibition Brochure. Bronx, NY: Bronx Museum of Art, 1996.

Nyhuis, Philip. "Piscatorial Investigations—Best of WNY 2002—Time in Chautauqua." *Buffalo Spree*, Buffalo, NY May/June, 2002.

Ondo, Jeremy. "Cuban-American Artist Alberto Rey Brings Art to Case." *The Observer*, Cleveland, OH, November 2, 2007.

Proulx, Suzanne. "Piscatorial Investigations." *ARTSCOPE*, Erie, PA, 7, 1 (2005).

Renner, Kyle. "Artist Explores Humanity's Lost Connection With the Natural World." *The Chautauquan Daily*, Chautauqua Institution, Chautauqua, NY, July 30–31, 2005.

Rey, Alberto. "Alberto Rey." October 4 2009. http://www.albertorey.com

Santis, Jorge, ed. *Breaking Barriers*. Exhibition Catalogue. Fort Lauderdale, FL: Museum of Art, 1998.

Talley, Dan. "Silence and Darkness: Alberto Rey." Exhibition Brochure. Kutztown, PA: Kutztown University, 1997.

———. *Alberto Rey*. Exhibition Catalogue. New York, NY: INTAR, April, 1993.

———. *Wit and Wisdom: Humor in Art*. Exhibition Catalogue. Jamestown, NY: Forum Art Gallery, May 1992.

———. *Personal Territory—Artists of the Southern Tier*. Exhibition Catalogue. Olean, NY, Centre Gallery; Jamestown, NY: Forum Gallery; Buffalo, NY: Burchfield Art Center, 1991.

Veigas, José, et al. *Memoria: Cuban Art of the 20th Century*. Los Angeles, CA: California International Arts Foundation, 2003.

Paul Sierra. http://www.paulsierra.com

Acosta, Maureen, et al. *Expresiones Hispanas*. Exhibition Catalogue. The 1988/89 Coors National Hispanic Art Exhibit and Tour.

Argyropoulos, Andy. "Paul Sierra." *New Art Examiner*, May 1991.

Arnter, Alan. "At the Galleries." *Chicago Tribune*, Sept. 15, 1988.

Barker, Stan. "Artist's Market: Where and How to Sell Your Art." *The Artist's Magazine*, May 1989, 22.

Bazzano-Nelson, Florencia. "Paul Sierra and Sergio García: Naomi Silva Gallery." *Art Nexus* 2, 50 (September/November 2003): 124–125.

Beardsley, John, and Jane Livingston. *Hispanic Art in the United States: Thirty Contemporary Painters and Sculptors*. New York: Abbeville Press, 1987.

Blanc, Giulio. *Cuban Artists in the 20th Century*. Exhibition Catalogue. Ft. Lauderdale, FL: The Fort Lauderdale Museum of Art, Dec. 1993.

Bonesteel, Michael. "Paul Sierra at Halsted." *Art in America*, March 1986, 156.

———. "Sierra High on Memory Mingled with Moment." *Pioneer Press* May 11, 1989.

Bosch, Lynette. *Cuban-American Art in Miami: Exile, Identity and the Neo-Baroque*, 146–149. Aldershot, Hampshire, England/Burlington, VT: Lund Humphries, 2004.

Bravo, Armando. "Paul Sierra y la belleza de lo terrible." *El Nuevo Herald*, March 4, 2001, sec. E, 1.

Casuso, Jorge. "Cubans Haunted by Memories of Homeland." *Chicago Tribune*, Jan.1, 1989, sec.1, 1.

Colbert, P. S. "Adventures of the Mind." *Daily Herald,* Chicago, Jan. 31, 2005, sec. 5, 1.

Condon, Elizabeth. "Paul Sierra." *New Art Examiner*, Sept. 1989, 53.

Coto, Juan Carlos. "They Would Rather Die." *Miami Herald*, July 20, 1991.

Curtis, Cathy. " '¡Mira!,' Unites 29 Latinos with Taste for the Fantastic." *Los Angeles Times*, April 20, 1988.

Donato, Debora, and Antonio V. García,. *¡Adivina! Latino Chicago Expressions*. Exhibition Catalogue. Chicago: Mexican Fine Arts Center, 1988.

Gawecki, Marcia. "Paul Sierra's Call of the Wild." *La Raza*, May 2000.

Gernand, Renee. *The Cuban Americans*. The Peoples of North America Series. New York: Chelsea House Publishers, 1989.

Goldman, Shifra. "Homogenizing Hispanic Art." *New Art Examiner*, Sept. 1987, 30.

Gracia, Jorge J. E. "Interview with Paul Sierra." Cuban Art Outside Cuba: Identity, Philosophy, and Art. 2006. October 17, 2009: http://www.philosophy.buffalo.edu/capenchair/CAOC/Interviews/iSierra.htm.

Hassebrock, Ashley. "Joint Exhibit." *Sunday World-Herald*, Omaha, NE, Dec. 9, 2001.

Herguth, Bob. "Chicago Profiles." *Chicago Sun-Times*, May 16, 1988.

Hevdejs, Judy. "Looking Beyond the Myths." *Chicago Tribune*, Dec. 4, 1988, sec. 13, 20.

Holg, Garrett. *Paul Sierra: Symbols and Myths*, March 1–April 7, 2002. Exhibition Catalogue. Grayslake, IL: Robert T. Wright Community Gallery of Art, College of Lake County, 2002.

Houlihan, Mary. "Sierra Continues Artistic Love Affair with Chicago." *Chicago Sun-Times,* Sept. 14, 2001.

Huebner, Jeff. "Latino Art or Latinos' Art?" *New City*, Chicago, IL, June 7, 1989, 19.

Jarmusch, Ann. "Vision of the Americas." *Dallas Times Herald*, June 9, 1988.

Knight, Christopher. "Cocked Concept." *Los Angeles Herald Examiner*, April 8, 1988.

Krantz, Claire Wolf. "Paul Sierra." *New Art Examiner*, Jan. 1986, 53.

Laing, Mary, and Deanna Bertoncini. *Latino Expressions*. Exhibition Catalogue. Illinois Bell in cooperation with Latino Arts Coalition, 1988.

Leval, Susana Torruella, Ricardo Pau-Llosa, and Inversa López. *¡Mira!* Exhibition Catalogue. The Canadian Club Hispanic Art Tour 1988–1989.

Muchnic, Suzanne. "Visible Roots in '*Expresiones Hispanas.*'" *Los Angeles Times*, Aug.16, 1988, arts calendar, 1.

Obejas, Achy. "Sierra by Sunlight." *The Chicago Reader*, Sept. 25, 1987, sec. 1, 25.

Pau-Llosa, Ricardo. "A Convergence of Visual Cultures." *Art Internacional*, Spring 1989, 17.

———. *Paul Sierra: A Cultural Corridor,* May 9 to October 9, 1998. Exhibition Catalogue. Los Angeles: The Latino Museum of History, Art, and Culture, 1998.

Petlicki, Myrna. "Prolific Artist Paints Like a House on Fire." *Pioneer Press,* Chicago, Jan. 27, 2005, sec. B4, Art.

Porter, Dean. *Landscape of the Soul*. Exhibition Catalogue. Snite Museum, June, 1995.

Prezelus, Corinne, "Finding Our Place in the World." *Indiana Statesman*, March 17, 2000.

Rice, Nancy. "Paul Sierra." *New Art Examiner*, February 1983, 22.

Sierra, Paul. "Paul Sierra." (2009). October 4 2009: http://www.paulsierra.com.

Sierra, Paul, and Louis Newman Galleries. *Paul Sierra: Recent Work,* June 14–28, 1990. Exhibition Catalogue. Beverly Hills, CA: Louis Newman Gallery, 1990.

Sorell, Victor. "Paul Sierra." *Art Nexus Magazine* 4, 59 (2005): 161.

Southgate, Therese. "Paul Sierra." *JAMA Magazine*, Sept. 2006.

Stern, Fred. "Artists with Latin American Roots." *Mizue* (Summer 1989): 48.

Stevens, Mark. "Devotees of the Fantastic." *Newsweek*, Sept. 7, 1987, 66.

Stringer, John, Donald B. Goodall, Carla Stellweg, et al. *Aquí.* Exhibition Catalogue. Los Angeles: University of Southern California, 1984.

Thorson, Alice. "Paul Sierra." *Latin American Art Magazine* (Spring 1991).

Taylor, Sue. "Paul Sierra." *New Art Examiner*, Dec. 1982.

Turner, Elisa. "Portraying Exile as a State of Mind." *Miami Herald*, April 24, 1991.

Veigas, José, et al. *Memoria: Cuban Art of the 20th Century.* Los Angeles, CA: California International Arts Foundation, 2003.

Warren, Lynne. *Art Chicago 1945–1995.* Exhibition Catalogue. Chicago, IL: Museum of Contemporary Art, 1995.

Zuver, Marc et al. *Cuba-USA: The First Generation; In Search of Freedom.* Exhibition Catalogue: Fondo del Sol Visual Arts Center, Washington, DC, 1991.

Painting Borges

Art Interpreting Literature

Traveling Art Exhibition
Sponsored by the Samuel P. Capen Chair and UB Galleries
University at Buffalo
June 23, 2010–December 15, 2013

Exhibition Schedule

June 23 to July 31, 2010, Pabellón de las Bellas Artes (UCA), Puerto Madero, Buenos Aires
January 24 to March 15, 2012, Iris and B. Gerald Cantor Gallery, College of the Holy Cross, Worcester, MA
April 15 to July 21, 2012, Latino Arts, Milwaukee, WI
August 28 to October 21, 2012, Stark Galleries, Texas A&M University, College Station, TX
November 24, 2012 to January 24, 2013, Abud Family Foundation for the Arts, Lawrenceville, NJ
March 15 to June 15, 2013, American University Museum, Washington, DC
September 1 to December 15, 2013, UB Anderson Gallery, University at Buffalo, Buffalo, New York

Checklist

Luis Cruz Azaceta, *La casa de Asterión* (The House of Asterion), 2009, 29.5" × 29.5", markers on paper

Alejandro Boim, *El sur* (The South), 2009, 24" × 24", oil on canvas

Miguel Cámpora, *La duda* (The Doubt), 2009, 31.5" × 39.5", acrylic on canvas

Ricardo Celma, *El evangelio según Borges* (The Gospel According to Borges), 2009, 59" × 29.5", oil on canvas

Laura Delgado, *Funes, vaciadero de basura II* (Funes, The Garbage Heap II), 2009, 27.5" × 39.5", mixed media on canvas

Laura Delgado, *La otra—éramos demasiado distintos y demasiado parecidos* (The Female Other—We Were Too Different and Too Alike), 2009, 39.5" × 27.5", mixed media on canvas

Héctor Destéfanis, *La decisión de los Guthre* (The Guthres's Decision), 2009, 39.5" × 27.5", mixed media on paper

Héctor Destéfanis, *Ruinas circulares II* (Circular Ruins II), 2009, 39.5" × 27.5", mixed media on paper

Claudio D'Leo, *El inmortal* (The Immortal), 2009, 39.5" × 39.5", oil on canvas

Carlos Estévez, *Los jardines que se bifurcan* (Forking Gardens), 2009, 39.5" × 27.5", pencil and gouache on paper

Carlos Estévez, *La rosa de Paracelso* (The Rose of Paracelsus), 2009, 39.5" × 27.5", pencil and gouache on paper

Carlos Estévez, *El inmortal* (The Immortal), 2006, 46" × 46", tempera and pencil on amate paper

Carlos Estévez, *Agujero en el tiempo* (Hole in Time), 2011, 27.5" × 39.5", pencil and gouache on paper

José Franco, *El laberinto, o nadie entiende a las mujeres* (The Labyrinth, or No One Understands Women), 2010, 37.5" × 53.75", acrylic on canvas

Etienne Gontard, *La intrusa* (The Interloper), 1991, 39.5" × 39.5", acrylic on canvas

Mirta Kupferminc, *El milagro secreto* (The Secret Miracle), 4/5, 2008, 39.5" × 27.5", digital print

Mirta Kupferminc, *Con el fuego* (With the Fire) 2/5, 2008, 39.5" × 27.5", digital print

Mirta Kupferminc, *La escritura del dios* (The Writing of the God), 2/5, 2 plates, 2004, 22.5" × 27.5", etching

Nicolás Menza, *Ruinas circulares II* (Circular Ruins II), 2010, 39.5" × 27.5", pastel on paper

Nicolás Menza, *El jardín de senderos que se bifurcan* (The Garden of Forking Paths), 2000, 39.5" × 27.5", pastel on paper

Mauricio Nizzero, *El otro* (The Other), 2009, 19.75" × 31.5", ink and coffee on paper

Mauricio Nizzero, *Funes, el memorioso* (Funes, the Memorious), 2009, 19.75" × 31.5", ink and coffee on paper

Mauricio Nizzero, *La biografía de Tadeo Isidoro Cruz* (Tadeo Isidoro Cruz's Biography), 2009, 19.75" × 31.5", ink and coffee on paper

Mauricio Nizzero, *El Evangelio según Marcos* (The Gospel According to Mark), 2009, 19.75" × 31.5", ink and coffee on paper

Estela Pereda, *"Si la querés, usála"* (If You Want Her, Use Her), 1991, 39.5" × 39.5", oil on canvas

Estela Pereda, *"Si la querés, usála"* (If You Want Her, Use Her), sketch, 1991, 8.25" × 8", pencil, ink, tempera, and water color on paper

Estela Pereda, *Borges y el laberinto* (Borges and the Labyrinth), 1991, 9.5" × 7", pencil, ink, tempera, and water color on paper

Alberto Rey, *Doubting of St Thomas* (La duda de sto. Tomás), 2009, 19" × 33", oils on plaster on canvas over wood

Paul Sierra, *Asterión*, 2009, 34" × 26", oil on canvas

Index

Colombres, Ignacio, 17

Conceptualism, 16–77

Con el fuego. See Kupferminc, Mirta, works of

Conley, Tom (*A Trace of Style*), 255

Construction, 4, 28, 31, 49, 74, 256

Context, 193–194

Cristián (character), 58, 61–62, 65–66

Cuba (Cuban), xvi–xvii, 5, 9, 16, 21–22, 156, 212

Cubism, 7, 13, 17, 155

Currie, Gregory ("Work and Text"), 253

Dahlmann, Juan (character), (*El Sur*), 47–50, 55, 209, 214, 217–221, 225–227, 239, 245

Danto, Arthur: ix, 4, 157, 172–173, 177, 178, 184, 189, 190, 192, 236–245, 254–257; "Philosophy as/and/of Literature," 254, 256, 257; *Transfiguration of the Commonplace*, 255, 257

David, Juan, 16

Davies, Stephen: *Philosophical Perspectives on Art*, 254, 256, 257, 258; *Philosophy of Art*, 254, 257

Da Vinci, Leonardo: 14, 196; *Gioconda, La*, 196; *Last Supper*, 196

Death, 13, 22, 36, 43, 47–50, 55, 61–62, 66, 89–90, 93–94, 99, 104, 130, 140–141, 146, 190, 217, 220, 225–226, 246

De Chirico, Giorgio, 18

Decisión de los Guthre, La. See Destéfanis, Héctor, works of

De Kooning, Willem, 22

Delgado, Laura, 11–12, 243

Delgado, Laura, works of: *Funes, vaciadero de basura II*, xi, 12, 41, 190, 219, 222–223, 245; *Otra*, xi, 12, 27, 29, 43, 161, 206, 216, 221–225, 242–245

Depiction, 196

Derrida, Jacques: 258; "Structure, Sign, and Play," 255

Descartes, René: 79, 179, 182, 255; *Discourse on Method*, 179, 182

Description, 196

Destéfanis, Héctor, 219, 243

Destéfanis, Héctor, works of: *Decisión de los Guthre*, xiii, 143, 219, 220, 222–223, 227, 245; *Ruinas circulares II*, 292

Destiny, 6, 11, 67, 77, 79, 89, 94, 99, 119, 133

Dickie, George (*Art and the Aesthetic*), 254

Diether, Jack ("Notes to the Program"), 253

Discourse on Method (Descartes), 179, 182

D'Leo, Claudio, 6, 13, 14, 104, 199, 219, 223, 234, 243

D'Leo, Claudio, works of: *Inmortal*, xii, 101, 103, 218, 219, 222–223, 225, 234, 245

Doubting of St. Thomas. See Rey, Alberto, works of

Dream, 25–26, 31, 35, 40, 47, 50, 55, 79–80, 83–84, 87–88, 99, 120, 130, 133, 140–141, 145, 151, 172

Duarte, Roberto, 13

Duchamp, Marcel, 16

Duda, La. See Cámpora, Miguel, works of

Ecclesiastes, 79

Eco, Umberto (*A Theory of Semiotics*), 257

Eduardo (character), 58, 61, 65–66

Einstein, Albert, 129

El Greco, 12

Elimination and addition, 222–223, 224

Encyclopedia, 4, 74, 77, 176

Enemies, The, 130, 133

Entrevista, 253

Erotic, 40, 57, 62, 65, 66, 113–145, 206, 220, 245

Escritura de Dios, La: Franco, xiii, 120–121, 123–124, 169, 218, 220, 222–225, 246–247

Escritura del dios, La: Borges, ix; Kupferminc, xiii, 124–125, 218, 220, 224, 246

Espinosa, Baltasar (character), 139–142, 145–146, 149–151, 218–220, 227